A
Joyous
AWAKENING
To The One Great SPIRIT In All

LOKESH

HEMINGWAY
PUBLISHERS

Dedication

Dedicated to my Teachers

My Parents—Robert and Phyllis

Gurdjieff, Ouspensky, and M. Nicoll

Baba Muktananda and Gurumayi Chidvilasanand

Table of Contents

BOOK III Shaktipat Awakening: Phase Two

BOOK IV Teachings Of The Great Beings

Preface

I self-published this work over ten years ago. In 2020, the publishing company went belly up and would not talk to anyone or return their digital manuscripts, necessitating the reconstruction of an entirely new one! As I contemplated the effort involved to accomplish this, I knew my level of experience, understanding, and vocabulary had all evolved naturally since beginning this project a decade ago. Thus, it seemed the perfect time and opportunity for some minor editing, updates, additions, and rewrites.

I also decided to have a new Title, one that represents the essence of this account. I considered the Title, *"Getting To Know The Consciousness That You Already Have,"* which is also the essence of this story. But AWAKENING to the One Supreme Spirit in all—is our ultimate destiny, and truly—life's purpose—a sacred Experience worth sharing with all.

I also found myself asking why bother, why do I feel that this information needs to be shared, and why should someone read it? The answers to these questions will comprise this new PREFACE.

When I first started contemplating, "Why bother?" I remembered the advice of a great author and advanced soul who taught that: We should share what we value most with others. For me, there is no doubt whatsoever that what I'm sharing here is what I value the very most: a deeper understanding of myself and human consciousness itself! Another thing that came up repeatedly was: if a person discovers something of unimaginable value, truly priceless, that applies to everyone, then it is their duty, their obligation, to share it for the benefit of all.

But truthfully, I didn't actually seek it or discover it—the transcendent "state" of consciousness revealed itself to me as an act of grace! I found out later that this level of direct insight and understanding is always revealed through grace; there is no other means of access. Thus, it is truly a revelation, not a discovery. I found that many of those who receive this divine grace feel compelled to share the "good news" with whoever is ready to hear it. This is why I sincerely want to share these encounters with higher levels of human awareness, also referred to as higher states of awareness—higher states of consciousness.

Now the question is, why should someone bother to check this work out? They should do so if they are sincere seekers of truth and deeper understanding and have a burning desire "to know" more about the deepest questions of life. But even those who are simply curious and would just like to know more about their own mind won't be disappointed. Before I describe those whom I "think" are ready, let me mention a group that I "know" is ready. These are those folks who have experienced the intelligence of their heart numerous times, and who have "tasted" the mystery and miraculousness of the human spirit and want to know it more acutely. Similarly, I believe you are ready if you long for a deeper understanding of yourself and others and have been asking some of life's deeper questions, such as:

What is the purpose of life? Is there truly a purpose?

- How can I stop the ceaseless chattering of my mind?
- Why am I judgmental and hypocritical when I detest this in others?
- Why is life so troubling when it could be and should be divine?

Now, let me address those whom I think are ready. Actually, I believe you are ready:

- If you already know that external things like money, material things, new relationships, etc., will not help much with your true and deeper needs of contentment, satisfaction, and overall understanding of yourself and life itself.
- If you know that you are too busy but just can't seem to slow down, using too much screen time, can't resist or change, can't seem to do what's truly best for you.
- If you tend to worry about the future or spend too much time dwelling on past actions and efforts to reach an understanding that is inclusive and satisfying, have not been fulfilling.

Then, I invite you to come, see, and join me on this adventure to increase awareness and understanding, and its resulting contentment and deep satisfaction. Are you ready?

Introduction

I initially stated that this work was an in-depth account of a spiritual awakening to the forgotten truth of human consciousness—our divine nature, and it is written for those who feel that there must be more satisfying explanations for the purpose and meaning of life than the ones that are currently offered by science and orthodox religion. It is also written for those who believe that there must be spiritual guidance that is uplifting, sensible, and practical, and who intuitively know that life does have a deeper meaning and who sometimes wonder:

- How can I nurture, experience, and express the love that I know I have inside?
- How can I become content with myself and others?
- What happened to the magical feeling and mystery of life I experienced in my childhood and youth?

The aforementioned are certainly still the case, but now I feel that many people, even sincere seekers of truth and understanding, do not have a clear idea of what a profound and authentic spiritual awakening is, what it means or refers to, because there are so many different views and levels of experience! Presently, I feel that it is just as accurate and more helpful and meaningful to describe this "awakening" as a connection with and a knowledge of two expanded states of awareness that have been part of the human experience for millennia, but that our culture has never really recognized or understood. In other words, I could say that I experienced two higher aspects of human potential, two higher but natural states of higher consciousness that Western culture and many others have ignored and forgotten.

Before I give a brief description of these subtle and forgotten states of higher awareness, I want to make it exceedingly clear, right here in the beginning, that this sharing is not really about me personally; it is about my encounters with and understanding of the nature of human consciousness itself! Yes, it's about the one consciousness in us all, the capacities of human awareness itself—that all of us with a normal mind already possess. Thus, this is truly about everyone, because essentially, we are our consciousness and its understanding. Now, in these trying and challenging times, it is time to get back in touch with its forgotten but miraculous potential, and to get back in touch with compassion, dignity, respect, and tolerance for starters. We've been stuck in immature egos for so long that we've forgotten what we have.

I also want to state here that when I began this search for a deeper understanding in my early twenties, I was only looking for a more satisfying and practical understanding to assist me in dealing with this complex and seemingly crazy life. I was not looking for the Truth or my true self or seeking a spiritual awakening, something I was totally unfamiliar with and had no conception of! Raised in a culture that had lost touch with and was no longer open to higher states of human consciousness, I did not believe that there was a single Truth and never thought about such a thing. Again, I just wanted an understanding that was more helpful and satisfying. I did not recognize my deep longing for expanded understanding as a classic sign of spiritual yearning. But it was my good fortune, and good karma, to have a classic experience—a strong "taste" of these two rare but authentic states of higher awareness. Again, this is why I am sharing the "real good news" as best I can.

As mentioned, the first level of expanded awareness took place when I got in touch with an aspect of my own awareness that I had never known about or recognized before. Being able to see how this unnoticed aspect of our awareness naturally unfolded for me, all from my own habitual, absolutely everyday awareness, nothing mystical, mesmerizing, or chemically induced—with no need to accept a single belief or image, will make it easy for the readers to recognize this already fully present but unrecognized level of awareness… in themselves.

My first knowledgeable teacher, G.I. Gurdjieff, called this first higher level of awareness or consciousness the third state of awareness, the first two states being the states of sleep and our normal but highly conditioned waking consciousness. As my story will show, I now think of this higher state of vigilant awareness as being "consciously present" and consciously aware, which means knowing what your own mind is up to in the present moment. Now, let me give a little more feel of why a seeker of deeper understanding should get to know this capacity of their own awareness that is capable of being "consciously present" and the benefits this can bestow.

One of the first things that I noticed was that it was not easy to stay consciously present. In fact, it seemed impossible! I realized quickly that my mind had a mind of its own and would sometimes think about whatever it wanted, no matter what I wanted. This surprised me as I'd never noticed this before. Another surprising thing was being able to observe my ego and some of its pervasive cultural conditioning, at the very moment that it was happening, as if it were someone else's! I was also surprised that my mind possessed so many judgments and opinions that I did not intentionally form and that were often not called for or justified. This is expanded awareness—being consciously aware of what my mind was up to. This allowed me to begin to see some of the unnoticed conditioned habits of my mind, which, over time, helped me not to take every thought and emotion so seriously. Another shocking realization, and the most surprising, was the awareness that I was different than my thoughts!

The awareness that I could observe these culturally conditioned thoughts from this separate vantage point felt a lot more like the real me. After just a few days, it became noticeable that this newly experienced aspect of my awareness was permeated with a level of wisdom and insight that was brand new, inspiring, and refreshing. It was this subtle shift in awareness that allowed me to connect with this precious and ever-present core of human consciousness. Yes, connecting with and occupying a higher and more expansive level of your own awareness, your own consciousness, allows for emancipating new insights that naturally exist beyond one's culturally conditioned ego-centered consciousness. This new but authentic level of awareness is called the Witness, the Knower, and the Experiencer in the ancient Wisdom traditions. Getting in touch with this capacity of consciousness is an ancient, tried-and-true way that our limited understanding is transformed and expanded through our own natural powers of awareness. This is an authentic first step in the ancient quest to "Know Thyself," to leave one's limited and heavily conditioned self behind, to experience and embrace your more expanded and loving self, your true nature!

Simply by staying consciously present through this subtle shift in awareness, many of my oldest and deepest questions about life were being answered in the most surprising and practical ways. In this wonderfully expanded state, it felt like I was connected to the ever-present and miraculously intelligent core of human consciousness itself. After a short time, I realized I was indeed connected! Again, this forgotten "state of consciousness" is known as the witness consciousness or simply the pure vigilant awareness that thoughts arise into. Simply by staying consciously present in this state of pure silent awareness, without any other effort on my part and without figuring anything out, I naturally entered into what Gurdjieff and others have called the fourth state of consciousness, the transcendent state, which is the goal of the spiritual quest—the spiritual journey. Without exception, all the saints and sages of all the wisdom traditions know of this divine inner Reality. That's why they have encouraged us to pursue the spiritual journey to union with God—to seek Realization or Recognition.

A profound experience of the transcendent is referred to in the spiritual literature by many different names, a few being Nirvana, Recognition, and Realization, Union with God, the ONE, as well as the Beatific Vision, the Mystical Vision, and so many more. Aldous Huxley called it the Perennial Philosophy 1 because it keeps returning throughout the generations, for it's our essence! It is also known as the transcendent state because it transcends all concepts, images, and descriptions. It transcends—goes way beyond anything we have ever thought or could possibly imagine. This was my exact experience of this blessed State, and I immediately knew that this "State" was a gift of Grace. There is no other way of entering this totally unknown level of Awareness! I use Capital letters for the various names of this miraculous State because they refer to a direct encounter with Divinity Itself! Without exception, the saints and sages of all the great traditions knew of this Divine inner reality and thus encouraged seekers to embark on the spiritual journey to experience their own divine Nature.

I'd like to remind seekers that our ancestors felt the mystery and awe of life. Living in nature allowed them to recognize the awesome interconnectedness of things and the awareness of the great Spirit as well. The Transcendent state gives one a direct experience of these Truths, which takes place beyond our normal level of awareness. In modern times, due to many factors, we have unknowingly limited ourselves to the rational mind, forgetting all about our higher potential, which is spoken about in sacred literature over and over again! I'll say a little more about this forgotten level of human awareness shortly, but first, a little background on what G.I. Gurdjieff called the third level of awareness, which I experienced as being consciously present, because, unlike the Transcendent state, it has been barely recognized, and very little has been written about it.

A modern and much-admired spiritual teacher, Eckhart Tolle, speaks about this forgotten level of awareness, saying that it is what allows us to experience that we are not the voice in our head. *"When you notice that voice, you will also realize that you are not that voice, but the one who is aware of it."* [1] For me, this is an insightful description of and experience of the third state of expanded awareness, higher consciousness, and being "consciously present."

Becoming aware of the persistent inner voice, what we all take to be our essential self, is one aspect or level of my journey towards higher understanding. The other side, so to speak, is getting to know the one who is aware, who is capable of observing one's inner voice from a purified and detached perspective, which is the natural aspect of this more conscious awareness. This allows the one who is aware, the witness, to experience precious innate wisdom and enhanced insight, freely given on so many different levels. This was and still is the essence of my awakening, and since our consciousness is the same, it can act as a template—a foot in the door—to the awareness of your own essential nature and its innate intelligence.

The contemporary seeker is fortunate, because in this day and age, we have access to a number of teachers, both past and present, who speak about this forgotten but miraculous aspect of our nature, our consciousness. Besides Tolle, a few of the most popular Westerners of the present day are Deepak Chopra, Ken

Wilber, Jacob Needleman, and Wayne Dyer. Of course, many others are beneficial and insightful as well. Chopra and Dyer refer to this most essential and enlightening part of ourselves as the silent witness. They and others have defined it as ageless, unchanging, and nonjudgmental. Ken Wilber would add that it is ever-present, and I would add—always available!

Wilber describes this long-known but often forgotten aspect of human consciousness that matches my experience extremely well. He says, *"What is the observing self—the silent witness? And the answer given by the world's great mystics and sages is that this observing self is usually called The Self... the witness or pure presence… And this Self, a transparent witness, is a direct ray of the living divine."*[2] A direct ray of the living divine—what a beautiful, and accurate, description of this forgotten aspect of human consciousness.

Deepak Chopra portrays our condition as modern seekers in a way that particularly speaks to me. He says, *"Today, we have to look with new eyes at the mystery of existence, for as proud children of science and reason, we have made ourselves the orphans of wisdom."*[2] Yes, we have forgotten and lost touch with wisdom, with the mystery of life, with the need to know thyself, to show compassion and respect for all, and to value and apply the Golden Rule, all of these being aspects of the intelligence—wisdom—of the heart. For me, Chopra's statement explains why that which is inherent to each of us has been forgotten by so many.

I have found that even though these teachers eloquently depict this silent witness within, few speak of their own encounters with this state of consciousness. As I've read the works of others who have written about their encounters with higher states of awareness, I've often wondered how they moved from ordinary life into these rare states. How did they become interested in such things? How did they learn about them? Most do not say a word about their initial steps. Because I feel this background is helpful, this is where my account begins.

This entire offering—sharing—is in this written form we call a book. Still, in order to focus on the different stages of this journey to higher awareness and understanding, I have divided this work into four books. To complete this introduction, I will give a brief description of each of these four books. The first section, BOOK I, begins with a short account of how I became a seeker and what the initial steps of my journey were. As I've mentioned, I consider this background necessary, but even more importantly, I want the reader to see that these beginning steps are not foreign to them. My seeking, my deeper questions about life were, and are, pretty standard for many youths, especially in the 1960's! But for many of all ages as well. This seeking had nothing to do with mysticism, etc.—it was so "normal" that the reader will see that there is no real difference between us; seekers can easily relate. Therefore, many will be able to follow along comfortably and experience expanded states of awareness similar to my own. But if one wants to have these possible and natural encounters with higher awareness and the understanding that these give, one cannot be content to be just a reader of books. You have to be an active participant! This is a point that I make clear as I share what it was like coming to know the witness, the inner awareness that provides the means for inner transformation.

In BOOK II, I share my classic experiences and insights of the Transcendent, which are remarkably consistent with many others—others living in every age and reared in every culture, who have experienced this miraculous state. The higher Insights and "Truths" that all have received have been referred to as the Perennial Philosophy and the Wisdom Traditions, because they are remarkably the same over millennia, and they are exceedingly wise! Because Christianity has played an essential role in my life, I was fascinated to find that my higher experiences were in complete accord with the esoteric teachings of my first path. To see that Christianity is in extraordinary alignment with all of the Wisdom Traditions will be a boon to many.

BOOK III speaks about life after the "awakening" but is predominantly about a second, equally powerful phase of connecting with the Transcendent and how this seamlessly dovetailed with the initial phase that occurred twelve years earlier! Here I speak of meeting an authentic spiritual Master, realizing that his primary teachings, based on his own spiritual experiences, match my own almost perfectly! In this second stage or phase of "awakening," I share how I, once again, unexpectedly entered into a profound "state" of the Transcendent. Here I share my experiences and deeper understanding of the role and nature of the spiritual Master, as well as a few rare insights and experiences of the hidden inner workings of Grace. (Both of the above are exceedingly rare in Western spiritual literature, as is a detailed account of a modern-day Westerner's experience of the "transcendent state" Itself.)

BOOK IV expands on the major topics that I have introduced throughout to allow the reader to see the resonances between my transcendent experiences and the teachings of Masters of various wisdom traditions. Hopefully, it will become apparent that all of these experiences and "perennial teachings" come from the same exalted state, the ONE SPIRIT that exists in all beings. It is also my hope that from all that is presented in this work, these essential truths of the wisdom traditions are not seen as ancient beliefs, but instead seen as living truths within us all waiting to be revealed. In other words, with the assistance provided by mine and others' sharing, seekers will begin to recognize and open to these truths in a natural way, making them more accessible, meaningful, and applicable in their own lives. To look at the major topics being discussed inevitably requires repetition. Since this whole subject matter is so foreign to our culture, various ways of perceiving are helpful. In Book IV, I quote St. John telling us why he repeats himself so much. First, he says that he has misgivings about his ability to explain things and thus repeats himself because *"That which is not explicable by one kind of reasoning might be better understood by another."* I repeat things for the very same reasons. But I would rather emphasize expanded awareness, seeing the bigger overall landscape and interconnections, versus simply reasoning.

In this work, I hope to make it clear that the spiritual quest does not belong to either the worlds of the East or the West or any specific spiritual tradition per se. I may follow a particular path and be a disciple of a particular Master. Still, I neither advocate my path as the only acceptable one nor communicate it as an authorized teacher. You may find your way home by entirely different means. I'm writing about my own experiences of this rare state of awareness in the hope that it will inspire others who want vastly deeper understanding to seek these higher "states" for themselves.

There will be new terminology and new concepts. Apply those insights and teachings that resonate with your particular nature; don't worry about the others. Once you start a spiritual practice with sincere intentions, your understanding will begin to expand. It's that simple, but also requires effort, steadfastness, and patience—like everything else worthwhile.

PS: Please feel free to skip to Book IV for more information on the subjects that are not familiar to you. When in unfamiliar territory, different maps and local knowledge help greatly. Think of it as a review or as various ways of "seeing" the major topics. This is my way of helping one get more comfortable with the language and how these themes intertwine and are expressed in sacred literature. This Book can be used weeks or months after reading my story of Awakening, not only after reading it, but also after sincere participation in the practice of learning to be consciously present.

BOOK I
IN THE BEGINNING

"When a man begins to observe himself from the angle that he is not one but many, he begins to work on his being."

Maurice Nicoll

1
How I Became A Seeker

At the beginning of my junior year in high school, I fell madly in love with a classmate I'd been friends with for a couple of years. Ours was the perfect and classical first love. Jane and I spent all our free time together and loved every minute of it. Except for a short time during our senior year, the two years we spent together before heading to college were truly heavenly. Then, at the last minute, I decided to attend a different university, never thinking for a moment that this would affect our relationship. I felt our love was perfect, and we would spend our lives together just like my parents had. About two months after starting college, however, Jane let me know that things were not the same for her; she was now interested in another fellow. By Thanksgiving, our relationship was over.

This was the first real setback in my life, the first major emotional challenge I'd ever experienced. Up to this point, everything in my life had been easy. I was a top student and a natural athlete. Never having dealt with disappointment, I had naively assumed this would always be the case. So, losing my girlfriend was not only heartbreaking for me, but it was also confusing. For the first time in my life, I was forced to take a deeper look at myself. Initially, I just couldn't imagine how she could stop loving me! I'd thought love was forever. I couldn't fathom how a person could stop loving someone they had genuinely loved. Could I ever stop loving my parents or my brothers? I was shocked by the experience that such a thing could happen.

After some soul searching and some sincere self-inquiry, I began slowly to get a new perspective. I saw I had contributed to this breakup, that some of my actions had been egotistical, even hypocritical. I realized when I first started dating Jane, I would never have believed I would act in such a manner. Considering this, I now began to understand the sarcasm with which my classmates had picked the statement, *"Take good care of me, good men are rare,"* to describe me in the yearbook. That was the way I'd been carrying myself!

I want to add here that I didn't feel guilty about this new glimpse of myself that I was getting. My behavior wasn't all that bad. It was, in fact, pretty typical of a young male who has everything going for him, as they say. And I could also see that my girlfriend had behaved in some immature ways as well. So, instead of giving me a sense of guilt, this period of self-reflection brought me a new understanding. I found the experience extremely enlightening.

It was a couple of years, though, before I began to feel somewhat normal again. During this period of reflection, I resolved that with my next love, I would be careful not to let my ego take over. I would try to be sensitive to everyone's needs—mine and my girlfriend's—by staying in touch with my heart. I saw this was the only way to develop a healthy and loving relationship, and I knew it was a *must* to follow the Golden Rule, *"Do unto others as you would have them do unto you."* This would be my guiding light.

Then, to my amazement, I found that in addition to a lot of contemplation concerning the ego and the heart, I was also doing a lot of thinking about Jane. No matter how hard I tried, I couldn't keep her out of my mind. I knew it was pointless and even unhealthy to continue thinking about her, to be going over things concerning her I'd already gone over a thousand times, but this awareness was to no avail. I seemed to have little control over my own mind and emotions connected with her. So, this was something else that baffled me. Why did I have so little control over my own mind? In retrospect, I would say this was one of the main reasons I became a seeker of higher understanding.

During my junior year in college, I fell in love with another beautiful, young woman. Like my first love, we started as friends and our relationship slowly evolved into something much more. However, this relationship, which lasted three years, was not as ideal as the first one. Ustrid was one of the most popular girls on campus and received formidable amounts of attention from males of all ages, pretty much all the time. Not surprisingly, this constant attention sometimes resulted in her ego getting a bit puffed up. I could easily see how this worked, knowing I'd experienced something similar myself in high school. What I'd received, however, was nothing close to the type and level of attention Ustrid was getting.

At the beginning of our relationship, I felt she did very well at keeping in touch with her heart and not letting her ego be carried away by the waves of admiration washing over her. She was from a small town and a close-knit family, and her kind heart was one of the things that had attracted me to her. Even though she'd received a lot of attention in high school, she was still quite innocent and down-to-earth. Since we were friends before we were lovers, our relationship was centered on mutual affection. We were natural with each other; we weren't trying to impress one another with our sparkling personalities. I was still very leery of the ego-personality, both in myself and in others, feeling that it didn't represent the genuine person. Watching Ustrid's numerous would-be suitors continually reinforced my understanding, as most males couldn't refrain from making fools of themselves by falling all over her—even when she was obviously not interested. All of this, however, took its toll, and I began to see a pattern develop.

Things would go exceptionally well for a few months, and then Ustrid's social side would feel she was missing out and needed to spend more time with the campus in-crowd. I'd go along with her, but at the same time, I felt the superficiality of this more accelerated social scene. I could see how most people, myself included, felt obligated in such situations to try to be cool, as we used to say. During these times, she and at least some of her friends questioned whether I was the right "type" for her, knowing I would never be interested in having a highly active, high-quality social life. But before long, Ustrid would get bored with the falseness and superficiality of this social scene, and the two of us would return to a life centered on the heart and its natural interests. Then we'd be in bliss for three or four months until, once again, her social side was off and running, and the doubts and conflicts would come up again.

This Jekyll and Hyde dance, as I used to think of it, went on for nearly three years. Each time Ustrid recognized the superficiality of the in-crowd scene, I would think she was finally ready to leave this "cool" thing behind. In the end, she decided that this was a part of her she valued and just could not let go. Acknowledging this, along with other issues, she told me she knew she couldn't marry me and was, therefore, ending our relationship for good.

For me, there was no question that the "real" Ustrid was the one with the beautiful heart that was free of ego, but there was no denying the other side of her personality and its needs. So, I knew she was right. With my nature as it was, the two of us would be better off going our separate ways. Even though this happened somewhat unexpectedly—she had just written me an incredibly sweet love letter, saying she was ready to do anything to keep our love alive—I was surprised to find I wasn't all that upset about it. I knew I needed to follow my own inner truth, and it seemed obvious she was doing the same for herself. I felt great, knowing that there was no need to lay blame for this breakup. We had each learned a lot from the relationship, and we had experienced genuine love in it as well. I knew I'd be lonely for a while, but I also knew I'd be fine.

This powerful relationship, with its dramatic shifts between the personality, often influenced by ego, and one's pure heart, kindled in me a desire to understand these two vastly different parts of human nature. I found myself wondering, *is it possible to blend and balance these in a natural and healthy self-expression?* It seemed to me these two disparate aspects of my being had quite different likes and dislikes. I'd felt the power of the ego-personality; its complexity and how it craves things the heart isn't interested in, even some things the heart despises. I also experienced how the ego could disconnect me from my more honest and loving self—in most cases, without my even noticing at the time that this was happening. I wondered, *how does this work? Why doesn't anybody talk about this sort of thing?*

Something else that seems important to mention here is that almost every day during the last two years I was with Ustrid, I prayed to Jesus for a higher understanding of the human condition. I also prayed to Jesus to help me make this relationship work, acknowledging I wanted this girl more than almost anything else in the world. But in my prayers, I also said that if I could only have one wish, what I wanted most of all was understanding. I repeated this prayer over and over, and it never once changed. I knew it represented my heart's deepest and truest yearning.

Around this time in my senior year, encouraged by a good friend, I began to read the New Testament from start to finish. My friend thought that, since I was about to become a university graduate, I should take a fresh look at these teachings. Also, I wanted to review Jesus' teachings about lusting in your heart. Having been raised Catholic and having attended Catholic schools for seven years, I was familiar with the New Testament. However, in reading the Bible as a young adult, I was surprised to find something quite different from what I'd been taught about the Bible as a youth. As an adult, I felt the power of Jesus' great love and compassion. Missing, I noticed, was the tremendous emphasis my early religious teachers had placed on sin and our sinful nature. Stripped of that, my reading of the New Testament as a young adult left me with the distinct impression that Jesus calls on us to step up to a new way of life, asking us to live in accordance with His teachings and thereby experience the joy and love that would naturally come to a person who did that.

By this time, I'd been trying for four years to understand myself better and to live Jesus' Golden Rule: *"Do unto others as you would have them do unto you."* I found it wasn't so easy! Even though my heart was aligned with this teaching, my ego-personality seemed to have its own agenda. I had a vague notion that if people could resist the cardinal sins of pride, greed, envy, lust, and so on, they would become centered in the goodness of their hearts. But the question remained: how is this possible? Again, why doesn't anyone talk about this?

Being a typical young male, I had tons of sexual energy and felt—experienced—it was natural to have desire come up when seeing certain members of the opposite sex. I had really been struck by the Sermon on the Mount when Jesus says that looking at a woman with lust in your heart is the same as committing a sexual act with her. I'd contemplated this teaching quite a bit, but I had no idea how I could change the way I felt in these circumstances. I could appreciate that not having lustful feelings and thoughts come up would be a better way to live. I spent a lot of time and energy thinking about sex—but I didn't see how I could realistically function differently. Lust seemed to be a natural, built-in response I had no control over. What to do?

About the time Ustrid and I split up, I started talking about this issue with my local priest, a man who had studied philosophy in Rome. Besides the teachings on lust, this priest and I spoke about many of the deeper questions of life, with special emphasis on living in the ego-personality as opposed to the heart. This priest was sincere in trying to help me, but he didn't offer any satisfying answers. He did give me some books on these subjects, but these didn't help either. When I pressed him on the topic of lust, trying to gain some insight into dealing with my responses in a way that followed the Sermon on the Mount, he tried to convince me these were "ideal" teachings. He said they were meant to provide us with an ideal, to guide us toward something that we couldn't expect to achieve.

I couldn't accept this notion. I thought it was foolish. Who was I going to believe—this priest or Jesus? My faith in Jesus and His divinity was strong enough that I figured if this was what He taught, then there had to be a way to achieve it. I felt, however, that I would have to look elsewhere for guidance in reaching this goal. I had great faith that Jesus could, and would, eventually answer my desire for higher understanding. I had faith in myself, too. I knew I would just have to keep searching and be patient.

The Teaching I'd Been Waiting to Hear

Within a few months, I learned about G. I. Gurdjieff, a Russian mystic and teacher. The information came from a school bus driver on a trip with the girl's gymnastics team, which, as a new public-school teacher, I happened to be escorting. The driver and I needed to kill some time, so we went for coffee. As we talked, I mentioned to him that I had recently read the book *Sybil*, which goes into the experiences of a woman with multiple personalities. I told him I seemed to have a lot of personalities myself. I said that sometimes they seemed to take over without me knowing it.

The driver asked me if I'd heard of Gurdjieff. When I said no, he said "G" (as he is often known) had been a well-known teacher at the start of the twentieth century and had a particular appeal to students interested in the deeper questions of life. One of G's teachings is that we are all composed of many "I's," many different characters or selves that make up the totality of our identity. The driver said that since I'd already noticed this in myself, I should consider checking out G's teachings.

Intrigued, I asked the driver to tell me more about these teachings of G's, but he hesitated. He said G's teachings were so different from anything most of us are familiar with that it's almost impossible to describe them. Also, most people who hear about the teachings informally have an incorrect understanding of them. So, it would be better for me, the driver said, to be introduced to the teachings through one of the books written by G's students. He offered to lend me one if I was interested. I was interested.

I didn't get the book for a couple of months, had good intentions, but didn't get around to it until just before I was leaving to spend the summer in Montreal, which meant I only had a few days to read it before I needed to return it. Even so, that book said more to me than any I had ever read before. This was volume 1 of Maurice Nicoll's *Psychological Commentaries on the Teachings of Gurdjieff and Ouspensky.* The terminology was totally new to me and sometimes difficult to understand. Still, I pored over it because the author was addressing some of the very issues I had been contemplating for years. Since this was such a turning point in my search, I'm going to share a few of the ideas that struck me then and gave me hope that a detailed insight and an in-depth understanding were possible.

Nicoll writes that Gurdjieff's teachings are about our potential, what is possible for us, a further stage of human evolution, and a higher level of being, our natural birthright, which can be achieved by allowing one's essence to grow at the expense of one's personality. Nicoll defines *essence* as one's "real part" or one's true being. He further explains that inner growth and development can take place only by restricting your personality so your essence, your innermost sense of self, can continue to mature.

I considered this to be a good description of my own natural and intuitive struggle with my ego/personality, a battle I'd been involved in over the previous six years. In that time, I had understood *essence* to be what I called the heart, our true self or as Nicoll called it: the real part! I had also, at least partially, understood that this truer inner aspect of us could only grow and mature by restraining one's ego and its strong influence on personality. At that point, I still understood this dichotomy only vaguely, but I knew for sure that it was significant and that I had never heard or read of it before.

I knew I had experienced a fair amount of inner growth since I'd begun to perform self-inquiry, and I could also see how I had to observe and restrain my ego/personality in order to keep in touch with my heart, the truest part of myself. There was no question this effort—or "work," as G calls it—had contributed more to my own inner growth and maturity than any of my university studies. I also recognized that in a number of ways, Ustrid's and my great love and great misery and confusion were centered around this teaching, this truth about essence and personality. When we were centered in our hearts, our essences, when our sense of self was truly there, we felt the great love and bliss that comes with such alignment. When we were drawn back into our youthful ego-dominated personalities, there was no more bliss and lots of doubts and questions. Thus, we both recognized this dance between essence and personality and knew that our hearts, our loving inner beings, were the real us, but did not know how to bring these two different sides of ourselves into a balanced that worked.

Nicoll presented another related idea that had great interest for me by saying that for anyone content with the meaning of life Western culture affords, there is no point in trying to understand G's system and *"There is no point in trying to understand what Christ's teachings really mean."*[1] Nicoll further explained the Gospels. Some of its hard-to-understand teachings, such as those that are contained in the Sermon on the Mount, are not about ordinary life but are *"all to do with allowing essence to grow at the expense of personality."*[2] Nicoll refers to the teachings in the Sermon as "strange things." I certainly had never thought of them this way, but had somehow at least partially understood that they were about inner growth and development. I recognized them as clues calling us to a higher expression or way of life that would be more respectful, peaceful and joyous. But I also could not for the life of me possibly see how one could not be anxious about tomorrow or always refrain from being judgmental! It didn't seem possible. I knew I wasn't satisfied with the meaning of life given by my culture, but I was happy with my life and certainly felt fortunate to be in the land of opportunity. I just hadn't been able to get any real help with my deeper questions. What I was now reading seemed exactly what I'd been looking and hoping for. I had two university degrees, but had heard nothing about this type of knowledge and nothing that addressed the two aspects of our nature in such an insightful way! Here I was being presented with a way to better know and understand myself— my heart and my personality—and to better understand Jesus' teachings as well! Somehow, intuitively, I'd known all of this was connected. My concerns about lust and ego were more about finding a deeper understanding than they were about resolving sin and improper behavior. And I could never see how guilt could lead to deeper understanding—remorse and contemplation—yes! Thus, what Nicoll was offering in this initial look at G's teachings is what I had been hoping the local priest would be able to give me. But he couldn't. Obviously, he wasn't familiar with these other views about our potential for advanced inner growth.

Even though my understanding of these matters was still extremely limited, most assuredly much more than I'm sharing now—decades later, I had a clear recognition that this was the type of information I wanted and needed. Inner growth—a more expansive and insightful way to look—seemed to me to be the only sensible way to truly be myself and to follow Jesus' invitation to become a higher, more loving, and more joyful being.

There was one more point that struck me in this initial look at Gurdjieff's system: his teaching that man's inner life is a multiplicity and not a unity—that we are not, as most of us assume, just the same person at all times. It was my recognition of this truth that had prompted the bus driver to ask me if I'd ever heard of Gurdjieff. On this topic, Nicoll writes, *"When a man begins to observe himself from the angle that he is not one but many, he begins to work on his being."*[3] It is at that point he has begun to develop his essence, begun to work on himself, begun to know himself.

According to this aspect of G's teaching, if a person considers himself to be one entity, he cannot change. The moment a person begins to observe himself, then he becomes two: an observing side and an observed side. The observing side is not a part of personality but is an aspect of the person's deeper self, his heart or essence. This, I knew from direct experience. This observing side, the side that wanted to know more, seemed to be a more genuine part of myself, the part that naturally came forward when my soul searching first began. For me, getting in touch with my observing side was the beginning of a deeper level of honesty and integrity, which resulted in a more realistic assessment and understanding of myself. Observing my own behavior allowed me to begin to perceive my ego and a few of its major characteristics, and also to begin to recognize the intelligence of my heart, too. Both of these insights have made my personality more passive and respectful as well.

Finally, Nicoll points out that self-observation shows a person that he has practically no control over his thoughts, and he cannot stop thinking even if he tries to. This point, of course, reminded me of my experience of not being able to stop thinking about Jane even though I desperately wanted to. So, he was addressing yet another issue I had often mulled over so many times, but had never heard anyone mention anything of this nature.

In all, I had only waded through twenty-five pages of Nicoll's treatise on the subject. Still, in those few brief pages, he had touched on so many of the questions my mind had turned over and so many of the issues by which my heart had been troubled, that I knew I had, once again, become a student. Yes, the bus driver was right. I was interested in Gurdjieff's teachings.

Getting Ready to Head West

I spent the summer in Montreal working as a chef for the Canadian National Railroad, a job that I had done the previous two summers out of Halifax, Nova Scotia. I continued with my reading, but was not able to find the book by Maurice Nicoll that had caught my interest. I planned on heading out West for the winter and felt this would be the time I could learn more about Gurdjieff's teachings.

How I Became A Seeker

I spent the fall back in Maine helping my uncle with the potato harvest and preparing to spend the winter skiing somewhere in the Rocky Mountains. I left Maine in November and spent a few days in Boston, making one last attempt to get into dental school. I had been on the alternate list two years in a row and was now able to meet with the dean of the dental school through a connection I had made while teaching. This interview went well. He wanted to know what it was like to cook and travel by train, and he was also supportive of my taking the winter off to ski and read. I found out shortly afterward that I had been accepted, and with this long-awaited news, I knew that the coming winter would definitely be one of the best ever.

I was looking forward to skiing, something I hadn't done much of since high school. However, my greatest desire was to get to know myself better and to have the opportunity to see what it felt like to be in a new environment with no expectations. Teaching school in my hometown for the previous year, I had found it easy to fall into old roles, to behave in ways that friends and relatives seemed to expect of me. Some of these roles were fine, but most of them were more centered on personality than they were in the heart.

So, more than anything else, I was looking forward to being free from my youthful ego/personality. I was looking forward to getting to know myself—my real unconditioned self—better. I was hopeful G's teachings would help me do that. I was determined to be as observant and positive as I could be. I believed in the power of positive thinking and was excited at the prospect of putting it into practice in the relaxing and adventurous days to come.

Something that had stood out for me for some time now, long before my acceptance into grad school, was the awareness that my sense of self-confidence was coming from me, from within myself, and that it was not based on anything outside myself. This had been my feeling before I met Ustrid. Once I started seeing Ustrid, at least part of my self-confidence rested on being with her. There was another part that depended on getting accepted into graduate school. The deeper part of me knew this wasn't right; it wasn't true. My own sense of self-worth was what my confidence and self-esteem should be based on, nothing else. I did not doubt that by getting in touch with my heart, my truer self, I would be coming back to my true self-confidence.

So, my trip West was about much more than just skiing, much more than some well-deserved relaxation and fun. It was to be a journey toward greater inner awareness and freedom.

Before actually beginning the story of my awakening, I would like to describe another of the factors that made me a seeker of a deeper understanding of our full potential. These were two encounters with what might be called the paranormal level of experience. Gurdjieff tells us that similar encounters with the paranormal in his youth also made him a seeker of higher understanding. Sticking my hand into a pot of boiling water to select a piece of corn, while being totally drunk on my first taste of hard alcohol, without getting the least bit burnt, was my first encounter! There were over a dozen witnesses to this event, and all were shocked that I had no signs of being burnt—then or after. The second event was a vivid experience of what I would call "internal talking" or "internal speech." It came up while I was still in college. Late one Friday afternoon, after our week's classes were finished, my roommate, his girlfriend, and I were sitting and chatting, unwinding a bit from the week. In this relaxed setting, this girl and I suddenly realized we could speak to each other in our minds. We were hearing each other telepathically just as clearly and easily as we could by speaking aloud. Neither of us had ever experienced anything like this before. We could hardly believe it, but there we were, speaking to each other in our minds, without the least bit of effort!

It didn't take long for my roommate to realize something was up. Of course, most of our secret conversation was about him. He could tell we were communicating, and he assumed we were doing it with our feet by some prearranged signal. His girlfriend and I didn't tell him the truth, knowing he would never believe us. We also decided not to speak to each other internally anymore because he was getting distraught.

Shortly after I came to this decision, my ability to hear internal speech disappeared, and I have never had it come up again. However, the memory of this experience never left me. It taught me our minds have abilities we don't understand and don't talk about.

Knowing for sure that these higher states of consciousness, or altered states, are possible is another reason I had such sincere enthusiasm in my pursuit of higher truth and understanding. Part of me knew I could trust that the goal was real.

A Magical Winter in Vail

I had heard a lot about Vail, but I'd never expected it to be as spectacular as it turned out to be. The Vail Valley is gorgeous; the grandeur of the mountains is awe-inspiring. The craggy peaks shoot up on both sides of the narrow valley with silent power and magnificent presence over a town that seemed peaceful and quaint. When I arrived, the sun was shining brightly against a deep blue sky. I was beyond happy to be there, finally. Being in Vail felt visually, physically, and emotionally sublime. I was glad I had decided to make a stop there to check out the skiing before making any further plans.

How I Became A Seeker

A friend had given me the phone number of a friend of his who lived in Vail. I had made plans to stay with this guy for a few days to see whether I felt like staying in the area or traveling on to Canada for the winter. In truth, I hadn't really planned on staying in Vail. I wanted to work on my inner being. I had assumed Vail and its environs would be too superficial for me to do the hard work I intended to do. But Vail had other plans for me.

I hit it off with Doug (the friend of a friend) right from the start. He was a great host, and I soon found a decent place to stay at a price which not only seemed too good to be true, but actually was. I found the perfect job, working at a small restaurant from 4 o'clock to 9. Doug and I worked similar schedules, and we wound up spending a lot of our free time together, which meant skiing during the day and hitting the nightspots after work. Every day felt like it was one of the best of my entire life, and then I would wake up and do it all again. The soft and dry snow, warm sun, incredible vistas, and the glory of Vail Mountain gave this Easterner the feeling of skiing in heaven.

I never left for Canada. Colorado (Vail in particular) was a land of both wonder and wondering. The seeds I had gathered through my minimal experiences, study and exploration were planted in this divine setting, albeit as much by accident as by purpose and design. In hindsight, I know these seeds began to germinate right from the start of my fairy tale entrance to the ball that was Vail, ultimately making it possible for me, within a few months, to have the kind of spiritual awakening that sages speak of. Looking back, I see there were two invaluable practices or lessons that helped to precipitate my awakening. The first involves the non-expression of negative emotions, which is one of Gurdjieff's primary teachings on self-study. We will come back to that one. The second requires living in the present moment, which seemed to come naturally for me at least during that winter in Vail, where my days and nights were filled with fabulous weather, glorious skiing, great companionship, good food, and wondrous views.

Being able to ski any and every day I wanted under such great conditions, coupled with the fact I knew I would be attending graduate school in the fall, made it relatively easy for me to live just one day at a time, not thinking about the future or the past. Before I left on this winter excursion, I'd planned to read a lot, hoping this would help me in my search for a higher understanding. Unexpectedly, the experience of living in the present moment turned out to be more enlightening for me than anything I had ever read. It was wonderful to experience my mind being so clear and quiet, with no worries about the future and no concerns about the past.

A Joyous Awakening

Even though I'd been sure that taking the winter off to be a ski bum would be good for me, I was amazed to find how a simple life of skiing, working, and participating in a little of the Vail nightlife could be so beneficial to my spirit. Again, the primary reason for this was the experience of just living in the present. The feeling of being so alive and so free was just incredible. I would say it took me about a month to realize I wasn't missing TV or newspapers. And once I noticed this, I also realized I was feeling better than I had in years, and there was no reason for me to know about or worry about what was going on in the rest of the world.

After I had been in Vail for a number of weeks, it dawned on me that I had not lived solely in the present moment since the age of sixteen, since I had first fallen in love and begun to think about my future with this young woman and about which university to attend. I remembered how happy I had been as a youth and how, at that time, I had lived just one day at a time, experiencing the natural joy which, for me, seems to accompany being in nature and in the present moment. Looking at all of this, it struck me for the first time that in thinking about, worrying about, the past and the future, I was living in my mind. I hadn't even noticed this change—hadn't noticed that at some point I began to spend most of my time living in my mind as opposed to living in the real world around me.

I kept coming back to the experience of how great it felt just to be alive, to be enjoying the beauty of Mother Nature and my own human spirit. It was enormously powerful to be living in the present moment in such a stunning natural setting. Skiing in such ideal conditions, abundantly sunny, way warmer than the East, and none of its icy trails made it easy to be smiling and laughing. And it was often quiet and peaceful, which closely matched my inner state. But on powder days, the energy was high and exhilarating with skiers hooting and hollering in sheer delight, reliving the exuberance of childhood! I think any sincere seeker of Truth should experience living in the present for themselves, if they possibly can, by spending at least a couple of months living whatever is their own equivalent of a "ski bum."

A P.M.A. and the Non-Expression of Negative Emotions

The other foundational practice I actively worked on in Vail was an extension of something I had been familiar with for some time, the power of positive thinking and what a friend of mine referred to as a PMA—*a positive mental attitude*. Gurdjieff takes the practice of employing a PMA to a higher level of understanding with respect to both the source and the effect of negative energy, and this he offers as *"the non-expression of negative emotions."*

How I Became A Seeker

Since I had gotten back in touch with my own natural joy and enthusiasm, it was relatively easy for me to maintain a positive mental attitude that winter in Vail. The few times when I would forget—usually due to a change in the weather or mountain conditions—my friend Doug would remind me in a way that would immediately get me back on track. He'd say, "Just experience it," one of the popular sayings of the day, which meant: *don't get upset about it; don't be negative; stay neutral.* This advice—showing both a higher understanding of life and the effort to apply that understanding in a given situation—is close to G's teaching concerning self-study. G suggests that rather than expressing negative emotions, you can use the energy of the moment to better understand yourself by expanding your awareness of the overall situation to try to see what has initiated this reaction.

Because I know that an exercise this foreign and unfamiliar isn't easy to take in, and because I also know just how important a learning experience this was for me, and how much it taught me about myself over a short period, I want to emphasize the importance of performing this enlightening practice. There is no question that this practice of G's is an aspect of the practice of keeping a PMA. In order to maintain a PMA, you must not express negative emotions or negative energy. What I learned quickly, however, was that G's non-expression of negative emotions is not just a matter of being positive or suppressing negative energy or not standing up for oneself. His approach is all about *knowing thyself, understanding your actions, and being aware of yourself in the moment.*

First, a person who wants to practice this exercise of G's must be present in the moment to be able to recognize the negative emotion welling up and thus, be able to refrain from expressing it. This part of the non-expression of negative emotions is similar to keeping a PMA. The major difference in G's exercise is that when the occasion arises, the student of self-study uses the energy that's triggered—energy that would normally go into the expression of the negative emotion, self-defending thoughts, and so on— to examine themselves and to look at the entire situation in which this is coming up. The student then tries to get in touch with the source of this negative emotion, conditioning, unfulfilled expectations, etc., to ask themselves, *what is causing this negative energy?*

This second step is vital for the student of self-study: they must strive to find and understand the root cause of the emotion or emotions that have come up for them. Simply blaming someone else isn't acceptable, and it won't expand your awareness whatsoever. You have to see if you can identify some of the issues that set this negative energy in motion, usually before you have really thought about it!

A Joyous Awakening

From my experience with Western culture, we haven't been taught to use an adverse reaction as a signal to observe ourselves and the overall situation. For years, I had been studying and practicing the power of positive thinking, but this was mainly motivational, and it hardly resulted in my becoming more aware of myself. It was an excellent way to stay above the fray. However, I didn't learn much about my emotional habits and other cultural conditioning from this practice. So, I didn't know anything about these habits or this conditioning when I first tried to participate in this new exercise, the non-expression of negative emotions.

As I mentioned, I'd recognized something special in G's teachings when I first read about them, even though I wasn't quite sure exactly what it all was. What I did know is that G's approach seemed to speak to the real "me" inside in a way nothing else had. At this point, during this winter of 1974–1975, while living in Vail, the only aspect of G's teachings I understood well enough even to attempt to practice was Maurice Nicoll's invitation not to express negative emotions and, instead, to use the energy generated by that emotion to explore the overall setting, internal and external, that is generating it. This seemed like a perfect way to begin fulfilling what was the primary purpose of my winter adventure, to know myself more deeply.

When I was younger, I'd had a quick temper, but as I got older, I began to appreciate the benefits that came to me from keeping my temper under control. Working with the power of positive thinking, I appreciated the instruction not to let yourself get negative because, as we used to say, *"It will only bring you down."* From the very first time I read Nicoll's statement that we have *"a right not to be negative,"* I knew G's practice was not the same as having a positive mental attitude. This practice of being positive did not, at least for me, naturally carry with it the invitation to understand the underlying cause of the negative energy I was experiencing. The negative energy seemed to come up automatically. Since for years I had been looking for a better way to understand my mind, I was eager to try this new practice, the non-expression of negative emotions.

Being in Vail, as I have said, was so sweet that days would go by without any opportunity to participate in this new practice. The first time I recall putting G's teaching into practice was in my workplace at the restaurant. Inevitably, something would be wrong with an order, and a waitress would bring the food back and let the cook know about the customer's complaint. It seemed that it was a natural reaction for a chef to give free expression to his negative reaction concerning this complaint, blaming either the waitress or the customer. I had worked with various chefs during summer vacations from college, and I couldn't recall ever seeing one of them acknowledge any wrongdoing on their own part; they always seemed to blame the problem on someone else.

How I Became A Seeker

I knew I had the same tendency, but when a potential situation came up, and I was able to catch myself before I said anything negative, I realized that I was being given an opportunity to practice G's exercise. So, instead of blaming anyone or complaining, I told the waitress, in a very polite way, that I would be happy to rectify the situation and that it wouldn't take me long to do it.

I wasn't sure what G meant about going to the source of the negative emotions, so in the moment, I had no idea of how to take the next step. But that first step worked exceptionally well. It was nice to see how surprised the waitress was, and I could see there was no real reason for me to get upset about this. The restaurant hadn't been that busy—we never were—and it was easy to take care of the situation. Besides, why should I allow myself to get upset over anything so trivial?

Of course, customer complaints come up all the time in a restaurant, so I knew I would have lots of opportunities to learn more about G's practice. And I also knew that negative reactions take place in many aspects of life, practically daily. Thus, there would be no shortage of opportunities to practice in many different settings.

After skiing all day, it was easy to be in an upbeat but mellow mood and thus, easy to handle these potentially negative situations with a light touch. Before very long, I could see—and by that, I mean I truly experienced—that this seemingly natural tendency to defend myself by blaming others is just a learned response, a conditioned reaction. One that I probably learned from the chefs on the train, and many others, too. Over time, it became obvious to me just how this response worked. The waitress would tell me about a problem and, whether or not she blamed me, a defensive—and definitely negative—energy would come up inside me. Whether it was instinctive or conditioned, it felt like a natural response. I decided the response was most likely learned or culturally conditioned. But what was most interesting for me was that after I had done this repeatedly, observing my response, the same energy would still be set off inside every time a situation came up, even though the negative energy would quickly subside once I acknowledged its presence.

I'd expected that once I saw how this pattern works, it would stop happening—the negative reaction wouldn't be set off in the first place. The fact that it continued demonstrated to me how deeply ingrained some of these habitual reactions can be. It also underlined for me that I had to remain alert in order to stop these negative emotions from interfering with or ruining my mental state and that of many others around me.

A Joyous Awakening

After a few months, I could appreciate just how precious this exercise is, so enlightening and so emancipating. Also, before long, I could see what I was doing in practicing this exercise—attempting to perceive the situation at hand—was actually quite scientific in a way. I had a Bachelor of Science degree in analytical chemistry, and so I had some training in the scientific approach. I could see the vast difference between taking steps to overlook a negative reaction (which was often the case in trying to maintain a PMA) versus trying to understand the pattern that set off the negative reaction in the first place, in the very moment that it was happening.

I decided G's direction to use the energy set off in a negative situation to become more observant of that situation is more than scientific; it is absolutely brilliant! By the time the ski season was coming to a close, I was convinced that many of my negative emotions were learned responses, negative reactions that would take place automatically if I didn't really pay attention—if I weren't truly present in my awareness. I was convinced this practice of G's was an extremely useful tool to help me understand myself, or, said another way, to appreciate my programming. His method was far superior to all my previous attempts at self-study—trying to be positive, putting myself in another's shoes, and so on, because it was me observing myself as the situation was unfolding. I was both the observer and the observed, in the very moment it was taking place!

So, thanks to my good fortune and my own self-effort, I left Vail in the spring, knowing I could keep my natural joy at the fore if I lived in the present and kept my negative tendencies from interfering with my inner state. I had seen firsthand that it is the defensive habits of our minds—tendencies that grow from our expectations, worries, regrets, and so on—that set off our negative emotions. With this new and oh-so-precious understanding of myself, plus the experience of so many great days of skiing and some dear new friends, I left Vail in the highest of spirits.

I was determined not to lose this wonderful new perspective when I got back East. This would require that I not fall back into my old patterns of personality, patterns that most everyone expected from me. Nicoll said some people did not want to give up their negative emotions because they liked to complain, and this gave them their identity. I certainly knew people like this in Maine, and I also knew I was sometimes one of them. I loved to complain about the weather, the educational system, the unfairness of the justice system, etcetera. It was easy to find something to complain about, but I now realized I would be much happier if I practiced the non-expression of negative emotions. Then I would be learning about myself instead of showing off my intellect with my in-depth complaints! Rather than falling into the old patterns and wasting my energy, I was committed to using energy to observe myself. I knew it was through being conscious of myself that I would have a better chance of holding on to my great state of mind.

A Few Surprising Side Effects

Luckily, in northern Maine, I was treated to almost perfect weather for the month of May. This, along with the pleasure of spending time with family and friends, made it easy to hold onto the great energy I had taken home with me from Vail. I did some substitute teaching and played a fair amount of golf before getting ready to head to Vancouver, British Columbia, to work for the summer. I left Maine in early June, giving myself time to be in Vail again before heading north to British Columbia. I'd had so much fun there and had met so many nice people; I looked forward to seeing them again and discovering what Vail was like in the summer.

Before I left, I took my old car, which was starting to give me quite a lot of trouble, to the best mechanic in the area. Looking it over, the mechanic said he would never attempt to drive it to Canada's West Coast. It was too old, he said; it had too many miles on it, and taking it on a trip like that wasn't a smart thing to do. I respected his advice, but I couldn't heed it. I wanted to have a car to use while I was in British Columbia, and I couldn't afford to buy another. My car was going to have to make the journey or die trying. I felt I had had such a positive attitude for so long; no matter what happened with the car, I wouldn't allow it to get me down. With this staunch attitude, along with the knowledge that the "going" may not be easy all the time, I started driving west, determined that we (both my car and I) would make it.

Sure enough, my positive attitude was tested all too soon. I hadn't gotten any further than Pennsylvania before my old Plymouth Cricket began sputtering, coughing, hiccupping and then groaning into a deathly silence. I coasted over to the side of the interstate before coming to a complete stop. Fortune was with me: I was only a short distance from an exit and a service station. A mechanic there was willing to take a look. Less than half an hour after I was sure my car had given up completely, this Pennsylvanian mechanical savant was poking around my car's ragtag engine. He replaced a couple of fuses, charged me $5, and told me I was good to go.

Even though I had been working hard on keeping up my non-expression of negative emotion, I still laughed, of course, and asked, *"Are you kidding?"* *"No,"* he informed me. *"One of your fuses went and caused the fuel pump to stop pumping."*

A Joyous Awakening

Then, in Nebraska, my car started the same sputtering and coughing. My initial reaction was that it didn't matter because I was close to Vail by that point, comparatively, and, therefore, I was sure everything would be fine. I pulled off the highway into a ranch because there wasn't much else around. I was kind of out in the middle of nowhere. The ranch looked a bit shabby and run-down, but the proprietor turned out to be a great fellow. He dropped what he was doing to take a look at my car. He was handy with engines, which was my good fortune. A few adjustments with his screwdriver, and that was it! He told me the carburetor needed a slight adjustment due to the change in altitude. He thought that's all I would need. So, once again, at almost no cost in money or time, I was back on the road and driving. Then everything was smooth sailing. Little did I know that I was being prepped for a classic spiritual awakening!

2
The Awakening Begins

On the drive to Vail, I was pretty much on cloud nine. The trip had turned out to be so much easier than I had anticipated. I stopped at a scenic lookout for the breathtaking view down into the Vail valley. From there, as the road winds through the valley, the mountains shoot up on both sides of the highway, and the fresh air from the high altitude has a feel and look all its own. For me, the feeling of simply being alive was incredible. I could see I hadn't lost any of the beautiful state of being that had been building in me for months now, rather than fading as I had feared.

Throughout my drive across the country, however, I'd been very much aware that I hadn't really gained any insight into life's deeper questions, the questions that had lived with me for years. The day I had left Maine, a very deep part of me was optimistic, even excited, by the notion I was on the precipice, somehow, of discovering more about and a better understanding of the real purpose of life. I had been thinking about this, searching for it, for seven years. I had no idea how the answer would come, but I knew I should remain positive and vigilant.

Even though I had been on this search for years and had only three months left before grad school, I had the feeling there was still plenty of time, along with the sense that I was on the verge of a significant breakthrough. I remember thinking that it was interesting to experience this sort of intuitive insight just as I was beginning my last big excursion, just before becoming immersed in graduate school. Another part of me was a bit doubtful about all this, knowing life-altering breakthroughs are not expected. However, my practices of living in the moment and not buying into negative energy allowed me to mainly ignore those doubts, to be content in doing what I was doing, and to keep my mind open. Many great and unexpected things had already happened to me in the last year, so how could I have any idea what was in store for me in the Northwest!

Once in Vail, I went to Doug's house and found that he had just finished the first weekend of Est, the Erhard Seminars Training. Over the winter, I had spoken about Est with a friend of Doug's, so I had a vague idea of what the training was about. Of course, Doug, fresh from this experience, was happy to fill me in on more than a few things I couldn't have learned in my brief introduction to it. I was amazed at how high he seemed to be—definitely a few notches up from where I had seen him this past winter—even though, as I've said, he was one of those people who was almost always in a good mood. I could see in his face and his eyes that he was on a natural high. He was radiating joy and could hardly stop smiling. There was absolutely no doubt he had had a great time at this seminar. Not only had it lifted his spirits, but he also seemed to be experiencing a heightened sense of inner freedom and natural joy.

The next day proved to be remarkably interesting when one of our friends, having heard I was back in town, came over to visit. This particular fellow was well-known for his acute negativity. He always seemed to be upset about something. His entire personality was built around being negative. He was a perfect example of Nicoll's description of a person whose identity is connected to his negative outlook. True to form, while visiting with us, this fellow started to indulge in these same old negative patterns. For me, this habit of his now took on a whole new perspective because of my experience with the non-expression of negative emotions. Doug seemed to have a new reaction as well.

Doug was getting annoyed with this guy for being so negative, even though he was no different now than he'd ever been. Before long, I could see that Doug had lost the special glow he had when I'd arrived. He and this fellow had been good friends for years, but they often nipped at each other, and sometimes Doug would get upset with him. Because of his uplifted state and new outlook from the seminar, I had expected Doug wouldn't be as influenced by this fellow as he sometimes was. But, if anything, Doug was more affected than before. This seemed to be because the fellow wasn't going along with the newfound perspective Doug had gotten in his seminar.

After the fellow left, Doug settled down nicely, and we joked about how foolish and wasteful negativity is. But over the next couple of days, I noticed that Doug was not able to recapture his natural high. That one incident had, so to speak, burst his bubble. I found it fascinating. I didn't understand why this other guy's behavior could have had so strong an effect, but it indeed appeared to.

Doug asked me to accompany him to what he called his midweek pep rally. Between the two weekends of the Est training, there was a meeting on Wednesday night to reemphasize some of the concepts learned in the first weekend and reenergize everyone for the second weekend. This pep rally, like the seminar itself, was in Aspen.

I was going to be leaving the next day, heading up to Idaho to visit my uncle, so I decided to go along for the ride. Even though I wouldn't be able to attend the meeting, it would still be fun to go to Aspen. The scenery between Vail and Aspen is lovely. Glenwood Canyon is a spectacular place formed in part by the mighty Colorado River running through it, and though much smaller than the Grand Canyon, it is still breathtaking. And I did appreciate that it might be a long time before I could return to this exquisite part of the country.

I had just started reading *In Search of the Miraculous* by P. D. Ouspensky, another of Gurdjieff's main teachers. When I was in Maine, I had run into my favorite bus driver—now a friend—who had turned me onto Gurdjieff. Our conversations about Gurdjieff's teachings had rekindled my excitement, and he had highly recommended this book by Ouspensky. Even though I had been practicing not expressing negative emotions and had been drawn by the idea of self-study, I really didn't know much about Gurdjieff's teachings. By the time I arrived in Vail, I had read and enjoyed several chapters of *In Search of the Miraculous*. Up to that point, the book had mainly seemed autobiographical: Ouspensky talked about how he had met Gurdjieff and some of the things which had taken place in the "early days" they had spent together. They had traveled through Russia and some parts of the Far East. It was interesting, but as far as I could tell, he was just telling a story and hadn't yet gotten around to discussing the exciting philosophical concepts I was waiting for. The truth is, he had. I had missed them.

The Ancient Practice of Self-Remembering

While Doug was at his Est session, I started reading Chapter 7 of Ouspensky's *In Search of the Miraculous*. Ouspensky was talking about G's concept of self-remembering. I had come across *self-remembering* the past winter in Kenneth Walker's *A Study of Gurdjieff's Teachings*, but didn't really know what Walker meant by the term. So, I was excited to see it show up in Ouspensky's book. I thought, I hope I am finally going to find out what this practice of *self-remembering* is about. I had often thought about it, but I could never make any sense of it.

Ouspensky connects self-remembering with self-observation and indicates that through these exercises, you can drastically increase your awareness and understanding of yourself. Finally, I was seeing something about self-remembering that resonated with me. I recalled that in the preceding chapter, Ouspensky talked about the necessity of self-observation and how this is a starting point for a deeper understanding of yourself. As mentioned, I had done a lot of self-observation during the last few years. During that time, I had often tried to see myself from multiple points of view so I would be more informed and thus more aware of how I tend to act or react in different settings.

I flipped back to Chapter 6 to refresh my memory on what Ouspensky had said about self-observation. I found I had underlined, *"The chief method of self-study is self-observation."* 4 This struck me when I first read it because I had done some version of this automatically after my first relationship ended in order to understand how things could have fizzled so easily and quickly. Again, I had been experiencing the truth of it for myself in the past several months. And yet I had never heard of—self-study—until I was exposed to Gurdjieff.

A Joyous Awakening

In the same section of Chapter 6, I noticed something else I had missed the first time—Ouspensky's talking about G's teaching on inner slavery. Basically, he says that when people don't have self-knowledge and are unaware of their mechanical and conditioned nature, then those people are at the mercy of the forces acting upon them, both inner and outer. This was something that I had experienced often and thus could attest to! Ouspensky continues: *"This is why in all ancient teachings, the first demand at the beginning of the way to liberation is to know thyself."* 5

Several aspects of this aroused Ouspensky's interest. The first is the possibility of self-change. On this, Ouspensky writes, *"By beginning to observe himself in the right way, a man immediately begins to change himself."*6 I experienced this during my freshman year of college, during my relationship with Ustrid, and again this past winter through my non-expression of negative emotions. This change was observed in my understanding and actions as well. Secondly, Ouspensky writes about the significance of negative emotions, saying, *"Besides being a very good method of self-observation, the struggle against expressing unpleasant emotions has at the same time another significance. It is one of the few directions in which a man can change himself or his habits without creating other undesirable habits."*7 I had been experiencing the truth of this— dramatically so—for the past five months. So, I didn't have to believe Ouspensky; I knew the validity of these particular teachings already.

Returning to Chapter 7 and Ouspensky's discussion about self-remembering and self-observation, I felt a distinct sense of excitement. I knew I might be on the verge of discovery! What I had been searching for over the years seemed as if it could be just around the corner or, in this case, the next page or two. As I flipped the page, the first thing I read was this: *"Not one of you has noticed the most important thing that I have pointed out to you; that is to say, not one of you has noticed that you do not remember yourselves. In order to really observe oneself, one must first of all remember oneself. You are not conscious of yourselves. Only those results that are accompanied by self-remembering have any value; otherwise, you yourselves do not exist in your observations."*8

I had no idea what he meant by *self-remembering*, but I hoped I was about to find out. Ouspensky says that his own first impression of self-remembering reminded him of his earlier attempts at stopping thoughts, a technique he learned in connection with yogic practice. However, he notes in the practice of self-remembering, one has to direct part of one's attention back onto oneself. This means that in addition to having your attention on the things around you or your thinking, you also have to have awareness of your own self, of what your mind is up to, in addition to your everyday awareness. This is the way to be present in your own observations. Ouspensky demonstrates how our awareness operates with and without self-remembering through some simple diagrams, which helped me grasp the gist of his meaning, because it certainly wasn't obvious. I had never heard anything like it. He explains that when people are in their normal waking consciousness, their attention is in one direction only. It's directed toward or focused on what they observe, or what they are thinking about, which he represents with a line with one arrowhead:

I ⟶ The observed phenomenon

To have true self-observation, to be in the state which G calls self-remembering, Ouspensky says, a person needs to have their awareness directed toward the object perceived, inner or outer, in the way they always have. Then, have another aspect or line of awareness that they never knew about, never realized they were capable of—come back upon themselves. This he represents with a line with arrows pointing in two directions:

I ⟷ The observed phenomenon [9]

Seeing this, I knew that my own attention had always been focused in one direction only—either within me or outside of myself. I had been hoping this book would give me a better understanding of G's self-remembering, and I was not disappointed. This idea that one could learn to divide one's attention, one's total awareness, really struck me, as I had never heard anything like it in my formal education. Of course, I had experienced dividing my attention; I had often read entire pages while my mind was thinking about something else. I had also experienced, more than once, driving along lost in thought and then suddenly realizing that I hadn't been consciously aware of driving in the least! However, I had never deliberately divided my attention for the purpose of becoming more familiar with my thoughts and actions, for the purpose of knowing myself better.

The other part of Ouspensky's description of self-remembering—the experiments in stopping thought—was also totally new to me. I had never read anything about anyone trying to stop their mind from thinking, and I had certainly never heard anyone I knew speak about such a thing. I read on eagerly.

Ouspensky writes that his first attempt at self-remembering—or, more accurately, self-observation accompanied by self-remembering—showed him this was not the same as self-analysis but, instead, a new and much more interesting and exciting state, a much more alert and focused state. I could instantly see what I had considered to be self-observation—G's self-study—was in truth closer to self-analysis than it was to being real self-observation, with no analysis. I could also see that what I had been calling self-inquiry— observations and contemplations of my behavior—had taken place in hindsight, always after the fact. I was always thinking about situations that had already occurred and asking myself if I could or should have handled them differently. From this perspective, I could see that these were examples of self-analysis rather than the self-observation that had to be done in the present moment, for instance, when practicing the non-expression of negative emotions. By definition, G's practice of self-observation has to take place in the present, not in hindsight.

At the time, I wasn't at all sure how my experiences of these past months, in connection with negative emotions and living in the present, especially while skiing, related to G's self-remembering, if they did at all. Yet, I sensed an inner excitement rising as I realized just how much I had already learned about myself from G's first lesson concerning deeper awareness of a few of my chronic negative emotions.

Ouspensky further describes his initial understanding of self-remembering by saying that, *"He realized moments of self-remembering, of heightened self-awareness, do occur naturally in life, although only very rarely. Such moments can happen when you're experiencing new and unfamiliar surroundings and situations—while traveling, for instance, when suddenly you look around and think—how strange it is… I, and in this place, or when you're experiencing danger, or when you hear your own voice.*[10]

My first thought upon hearing this somewhat strange response of Ouspensky's was that I, too, had the experience of hearing my own voice and also of thinking, I, and in this place! This had happened on my first sight of the Grand Canyon. I had seen this natural wonder on TV several times and seen countless pictures of it in magazines. Still, when I found myself standing on the edge of that astonishing marvel, seeing for myself the gash torn in the earth by the elements of millennia, I became hyper-aware not only of my surroundings but my place in those surroundings. It sounds strange to say it aloud, but I felt as if I was looking at myself looking at the canyon! I would venture to say that this feeling I sensed there in Arizona has been shared by many others and in many other places.

Armed with what I had learned from Ouspensky and G, I could look back and see my memories of the experience contained more awareness of my own feelings of self than what I actually saw of the canyon. The same was true the first time I went to San Francisco. For many years, I had wondered what it would be like to see California, and especially to see San Francisco. When I finally traveled there, I was more aware of my own reaction than I was of the scene in front of me that I was presumably observing. It was as if a part of me found it hard to believe I was truly there in that place. I assumed that it was this type of hyper-awareness or split awareness that Ouspensky meant in his description of his first experience of self-remembering and the expression I, and in this place!

The Awakening Begins

This relates to another point Ouspensky makes in connection with self-remembering. He emphasizes that all our truly vivid memories, like they happened yesterday, are valid examples of self-remembering. This is the case because these memories encompass not only the event but also what was going on at the time in our emotional and intellectual selves. In other words, using Ouspensky's definition, we sometimes did have a line of awareness back upon ourselves! Most of our other memories are only about the outer events; in these, we don't have a strong memory of our being right there or of how we actually felt at the time.

Just in reading this, and finally getting some feel for what G's term means, I could feel a change in my own being, a change in my understanding of myself. Sitting there waiting for Doug, I started reflecting on my own life and saw that certain of my memories were vivid remembrances of various situations I had experienced. It was easy to vividly feel many things about those particular incidents, especially to remember my emotions and thoughts at the time the incidents had taken place. As Ouspensky observes, almost everything else I remembered about my childhood—or even, for that matter, about the last few years—concerned events I knew had taken place but could not really remember with clarity. These memories were nothing compared to the more vivid self-remembrances, which were rooted in a much deeper level of awareness or a more consciously present state of awareness.

Now, I have a much better understanding of what G means when he says you yourselves do not exist in your observations. Clearly, in these very vivid memories, I had existed in my observations at the time. I wasn't just looking at the Grand Canyon; I was also vividly aware of my own self—my "feeling of self" is the way Ouspensky puts it—as I was looking at the canyon. Again, even though I still wasn't sure about how precisely to practice this self-observation accompanied by self-remembering, I was excited about trying it out, about trying to keep part of my awareness focused back on myself. Intuitively, and experientially as well, from my previous work with the non-expression of negative emotions, I knew this practice would be insightful and potentially bring great rewards. My upcoming drive to Canada, being alone in my car, would provide the ideal atmosphere for this tantalizing new practice of self-study.

Once again, I had an incredible feeling of adventure as if I were setting off to explore something totally new about myself. I understood this was what I had been looking for, the means by which I could better understand myself. My sense of anticipation was keen.

About the time all these thoughts and impressions were going through my mind, Doug came out of his mid-week session. It was obvious he had returned to the high emotional state he had been in a few days earlier. Now we were both experiencing high spirits, and this made for a very enjoyable trip back to Vail. I shared with him what I had just gleaned and asked him if he was familiar with any of those ideas. He responded by volunteering that this practice was basically what he had been hearing about in the Est sessions.

The next morning, Doug and I got together with another good friend, who was also an EST graduate, for a send-off breakfast before my departure for the Northwest. Still highly excited about what I had learned the previous evening in Aspen, I decided to read Ouspensky's first experiences of self-remembering. They both agreed that the diagram showing how part of your awareness is focused back on yourself is key and that it could truly help a person get free from some of their conditioning—or, as we used to say, from some of their own stuff!

My Mind Can't Stay Present or Still

Feeling the excitement of being on the brink of genuinely new adventures--both an inner and an outer one—I left Vail in good spirits and with one goal in mind: I was intent on practicing self-remembering. This idea of keeping a part of your awareness on yourself, in addition to your normal awareness, struck me as unique and potentially quite fruitful. It was an idea I would never have thought of on my own.

I was only a few miles out of Vail when I began to see how difficult a task this was. After ten minutes, I realized I was going to have to turn off the radio; it wasn't helping me at all in my task of remembering myself. I found myself unconsciously singing along or thinking about something the announcer had said. But even without the radio, I saw that it was still incredibly difficult to keep a part of my awareness on myself. I would tell myself I could do this, that I was resolved to do this practice of self-remembering. I would sit up straight in my seat, determined to keep an eye on myself—which is how I first experienced this practice—but even with this clear intent, I couldn't hold this split awareness for even fifteen seconds. At some point later, I would realize my mind had wandered back to its old meandering pathways of thought. I will admit I was surprised my mind had such a mind of its own—and even more surprising, I had never even noticed this before!

I recalled that Ouspensky had said this practice of self-remembering reminded him of his attempts at trying to stop his thoughts, which is another practice I had never thought of doing before. After I had tried self-remembering for about an hour, I realized it simply could not be done with my mind full of thoughts. With each traitorous thought clamoring to carry my attention away, it seemed impossible to keep an aspect of my awareness back on myself as required for self-remembering.

Before long, I came back to what I had learned in the past winter about the importance of being in the present and remaining alert. I could see I had to be present and alert in order to have a chance at practicing self-remembering. But even with this insight, I would hold my dual focus for maybe a minute or less—mostly less—before my habitual mindset would kick in and I would start thinking about some random thought. Whatever that errant thought was, off my mind would run, following it down a rabbit hole. At some point, I would recall my mission and realize: *"I am just doing the same old thing here. I am not participating at all in this practice of self-remembering. I can't keep enough awareness of myself to remember my goal, let alone stay in the present."[11]*

I knew it was a waste of time to continue to go over old thoughts that I had already gone over a thousand times, but I seemed to have no control over the matter. So once again, I tried to start anew: sitting up straight in the car, ensuring I was physically comfortable, and renewing my desire to really participate. If I was lucky, I was able to scratch out a few seconds or even a minute or two of being aware of myself in the car, my body posture, and the sense of wonder I felt looking around at the rugged mountain scenery through which I was driving.

In this beginning stage of trying to practice self-remembrance, one of the things that became noticeable was that, when I was able to do it for more than a few seconds, I was always aware of my own breathing. Never before had I been especially conscious of breathing. In my whole life, the only time I had ever been aware of my breath was when I was out of breath from running or doing some other strenuous exercise. Now, during the few moments when my mind was quiet, I could hear my breath going in and out. It was odd because just that new experience of hearing my breath was enough to make me—allow me—to lose my concentration. I realized that if I wasn't so aware of my breath, I might be able to be a bit more focused on my mind. That awareness never lasted too long because I would again forget about my intention to stay focused on the present moment and end up talking to myself about this or that. I would just fall back into my ingrained habit of thinking about whatever topic my mind had latched on to at the given moment and go along for the ride.

So, at this early stage, self-remembering seemed almost impossible for me to do. Pondering this, I remembered reading Ouspensky's description of this very phenomenon. Ouspensky says he first tried to practice self-remembering while walking down the streets of St. Petersburg. He tried to keep his attention on his surroundings—especially the houses on quiet streets—while at the same time, he was trying to keep part of his attention focused on himself. He wanted to exist and be consciously present in his observations. He did not want to be lost in thought while strolling about the city. And like me, he found that it was not easy to keep his attention on self-remembering. He writes that he began to feel a *"Kind of ridiculous irritation' with himself for being so inept, and he made a firm resolve to keep his attention on the fact that he wanted to remember himself. For a few blocks, he did quite well, but then he had the urge to have a cigarette, and, with that, he forgot to practice self-remembering. He was lost in his thoughts, and about two hours later it was, he writes, almost as if he 'woke up'— when he remembered he wasn't remembering himself!" 12*

Now, I could really appreciate his observation, *"and suddenly I remembered that I had forgotten to remember myself."* When I first read this weeks ago, without having tried to practice self-remembering on my own, Ouspensky's experience didn't really resonate with me. After having tried, I recognized that this was exactly what I was going through myself. I couldn't remember to stay focused for more than a few minutes at best. Like Ouspensky, I felt some irritation with myself and disbelief that I couldn't keep myself in my awareness—I could not stay in the present. Since I had thought I could do anything if I sincerely applied myself, I was amazed that I could not seem to do this practice of self-remembering. I had never realized that my mind was so undisciplined and unruly. I had always been good at athletics and schoolwork. I just assumed I had well-developed powers of focus and concentration. Yet, I had to admit when it came to self-remembering, I had the attention span of a two-year-old!

As much as it frustrated me, this acknowledgment amused me. I would never have believed I had so little control over my attention! Wondering what I could do to improve, I recalled Ouspensky mentioning that it helped him greatly to notice fine details about the neighborhoods he was walking through while he was practicing self-remembering. Taking note of the varied architecture of the homes, the age of the trees or the size and types of gardens seemed to satisfy the part of his mind that always wanted to be busy and allowed the other part of his mind to focus back more easily on himself.

I decided to try the same thing with the spectacularly beautiful scenery through which I was driving in Western Colorado and then Utah. I had never before traveled through this part of the country, and the vistas were new to me. I focused intently on the views, looking at all the angles of the mountains, the lay of the shadows, and the hue and tone of the colors, and I found this was better for keeping my attention focused than looking around in a general way. With this new understanding, I started focusing on the scenery in a much more detailed and conscious way than I normally would have. It really helped. Keeping my mind active and focused not only gave me something outward to latch onto, but it also kept my mind clear of other intruding thoughts and allowed me to go a bit longer with my self-remembering than I had previously been able to manage.

Still, before very long, I would get caught in an errant thought, follow it along to think about many other things and all the associated ideas that went with them—and forget entirely my intention to be more aware of the scenery and of myself. I would find myself driving along, and I would realize that for the last so many minutes, I had been thinking about this and that, neither looking at the view nor being aware that I was thinking about a million other things. It struck me yet again that I had done this all my life and had never even noticed it. I wondered how many people had ever noticed it. I knew that essentially everyone's mind does this a lot of the time, and very few notice. Modern culture doesn't understand this state of at least trying to be consciously present.

Realizing how ingrained this habit was—just renewed my vigor to master it. I got into a stubborn stance where I thought: *I'm going to conquer this thing!* I had always thought of myself as a capable person, and I was determined that this tendency was not going to get the better of me. I felt somewhat embarrassed that I was such a klutz when it came to remembering to remember myself. The only other pursuit I had been terrible at when I first tried it was golf. I kept right on playing golf until I could do it reasonably well. Since, with most other skills, I was a natural right from the beginning, I wasn't accustomed to failure.

So again, I would sit up straight in my car and look intently around me. I also slowed my speed so that driving took less of my concentration. I could see that this detailed and heightened focus was extremely helpful in the act of self-remembrance. The more intently I looked at the landscape, the more engaged it kept part of my mind, and the easier it was for the other part of my awareness to focus on myself. Sometimes I caught myself slouching in the car seat, and at times I began to feel tensions in my body I had never noticed while driving. Becoming aware of those things, it was easy to adjust and let the tension go.

As I mentioned previously, when I was in a focused state, with my mind clear and alert, I was a little bothered by the sound of my own breath. This began to amuse me because it was also evident that this sound had always been there in the background. It was just that my mind was always busy thinking about this and that, scheming about this and that, and worrying about who knows what! With all that mental activity going on, I had never noticed there was this *sound* associated with my breathing.

I didn't even know whether I was breathing in my normal pattern. All I knew for sure was that with no internal talking going on, the breath sounded noisy and felt unnatural. I assumed it was natural and normal for people to experience this sensation when their minds were focused and quiet. I wasn't having difficulty breathing; it just felt weird to be so conscious of the process. I was not the least bit worried about it. I was just amazed at how noticeable it was. I thought: *being aware of the breath was just part of becoming more aware of myself. And that's the whole purpose of self-remembering: to become more aware of myself in the moment.*

Each time I caught myself being lost in thought, I would be a bit disappointed. At the same time, however, at this stage, it was humorous because I kept being amazed at how I had never before noticed how little control I had over what I was thinking about, and how my mind would jump from one thought to another without really noticing! It also struck me that since I had nothing else to do on this drive, I might as well continue to try to bring my mind under rein instead of just allowing it to wander off and think about everything under the sun. I thought: *I am already great at that, and now that I'm aware of how unconscious I am, I must do something about it!*

With that thought, I made another firm resolution. I planned to continue with this technique, not just for a short time. I decided to keep practicing self-remembering today, tomorrow, and the next day. I decided I was going to keep doing this practice until I got it—until I could stay "awake!" as G would say. It struck me that this focus was probably like what someone would have to do if they were what's called the *point man* in a war. As a point man, a soldier must have his mind extremely alert to all the various things going on around him. If his mind gets caught up in daydreaming, in thinking about his girlfriend back home, wishing he were with the other guys, or thinking about whatever, he won't last for long. With that type of non-attention, it would be relatively easy for the enemy to pick him off. Only by being completely aware of his surroundings could a person hope to survive in a situation like that. A point man needs a focused, quiet, and alert mind that's capable of remembering itself and its predicament, all of the time.

A couple of fellows I went to high school with were killed in Vietnam, and both had been acting as point men when it happened. I found myself wondering if their minds had been thinking about home when they were killed and if that was part of the reason they hadn't survived. I wondered, too, if the armed services teach a technique like self-remembering so that these fighting men are prepared.

By the time evening was starting to set in, I felt I was making some gains, however small. My irritation and disappointment with myself had diminished by leaps and bounds. I was getting used to the idea that this practice just wasn't as simple as I first thought it would be. I remained determined, but I was also resigned to the idea that this was going to be a long-term project and success was not going to happen any time soon.

That evening's sunset was exquisite: all the colors of the mountains banded against the palette of the western sky in a stark and striking array. I had pulled off the road so I could focus on the wondrous display and enjoy the feeling of awe that watching a sunset can bring forth. As the spectacle faded, I had the thought that enjoying the sunset is somewhat similar to G's technique of self-remembering in that while watching sunsets, my mind is often quiet with no internal talking or thinking going on. It occurred to me that perhaps this is why people like sunsets so much.

For many people, it is probably one of the few times they are in a relaxed, focused, and in the present state. What can also happen, of course, is that instead of just enjoying the sunset, they can get lost in thought and focus on the beautiful sky for only a few seconds before their minds are once again lost in thought. When this is the case, they don't experience the joy that sunsets can evoke. I found myself wondering why I had never heard anyone speak of such things.

I continued to drive for a while after darkness had set in. I was feeling so good that I just wanted to continue driving and practicing self-remembering. It wasn't long before I realized I had missed the turn-off, which was to take me north. This amused me because here I was, trying to become more present and more conscious of myself and in so doing, I had forgotten to follow my planned route. I laughed at myself, thinking: *Well, this is about par for the course.* All day long, I had been proving to myself that I was not in control of my attention. Here is one more item of evidence. Acknowledging this, I decided to continue down the road I was on and not turn back. I would find another road north. I didn't want to turn back. It was mainly a symbolic choice; I didn't want to return to my former undirected and undisciplined consciousness. I vowed to follow this adventure wherever it led. On the practical side, I knew that if I just kept heading north, I would get to where I wanted to go.

I'm Amazed That My Mind Is So Conditioned

As the end of the first day of practicing this new technique was nearing, I was impressed with what I had learned about myself in just one day. I had an appreciation of why G says you are "awake" only when you are in a state of self-remembering; otherwise, you are in a state of waking sleep—a heavily conditioned state. The way my attention was jumping from one thing to another, often without finishing the first line of thought, was certainly akin to my experience of the dream state. Remembering G's statement: *"Try to remember yourselves when you observe yourselves."[13]* Only those results will have any value that are accompanied by self-remembering. Otherwise, you yourself do not exist in your observations." This statement, this truth, now had so much more meaning for me. Now I understand what it means to exist, to be present in your observations! By not expressing negative emotions, I learned quite a bit about myself the past winter in Vail. I had seen, for instance, that in the past, many of my responses were conditioned reactions to particular situations or accusations. But now I had a new perspective on my conditioned state. I could see that not only were certain of my responses conditioned, but, in a sense, my entire mind was also conditioned! In just one day, I had learned more about myself than I would ever have believed possible!

I had decided I would sleep in my car that night, so I could pull off the road whenever I was ready to stop. As I was preparing to fall asleep, I was amazed to see how much natural excitement and enthusiasm I was experiencing. I resolved to begin practicing this new and powerful exercise from the moment I woke up.

Just before sunrise, I opened my eyes and was instantly wide-awake. Even though the sleeping conditions in my car were not exactly ideal, I felt great. My mind was clear, quiet, and truly alive in the present moment. That lasted for less than a minute. It wasn't long before I started thinking about a bug crawling on my windshield. After a couple of minutes of speculation over the bug, I remembered I had promised to begin remembering myself right from the very start of the day. I was not really surprised. My mind was up to its old tricks practically from the moment I woke up.

With this awareness of my mind's tendencies, I decided: *Okay, let me sit here for a few minutes, observe my surroundings, and allow myself to become focused in the present.* I sat there in the car, just as I had done the day before, slowly and diligently focusing on the scenery around me. But at the same time, I was vigilant in keeping this other aspect of my awareness focused on myself, to make sure my mind didn't start wandering off into some other land of thought. Once I felt pretty focused and alert, I reaffirmed my commitment to stay "awake." Then, map in hand, I developed a new route to get to Idaho in time to meet my uncle, who was expecting me by 5:00 p.m.

With the sun just starting to rise in the east, I promised myself I would take a little time and get focused in this more alert state of self-remembering at the beginning of each day. This would be far superior to simply letting my mind roam around at will without my having any awareness of what it was doing. This was to be my number one responsibility for this summer of exploration.

My experience that morning was very similar to the day before, even though I was decidedly a tad smarter about the process. Keeping my attention focused on the scenery, as I described, continued to help a great deal, and so I was able to stay in the state of self-remembering for longer stretches. But at the same time, my mind was still continually reverting to its habit of *thinking-thinking-thinking—*

a state in which there was no sense of self or the present moment. I could appreciate that I was improving, but I realized it was only in a matter of slight degrees. It was slow going.

I had plenty of time, so I stopped along the way whenever I saw a beautiful spot where it was easy to pull off the road. Then I would find some place comfortable to sit, and I would try to become absorbed in the view, which was much easier to do when the car wasn't moving. All the while, I would be practicing self-remembering. These little exercise breaks helped, but after a short time I would discover myself immersed in unintentional and unwanted thinking.

As I was nearing my uncle's place, my first reaction was to think: *Oh, no, I wonder what it's going to do to my newfound awareness to be around someone else. Will interacting with my uncle make me lose what little wakefulness I have attained?*

Interestingly, the part of my awareness that was watching me heard this thought and laughed. I could hear this other part of my mind, the watchful part, respond. It told me: *It doesn't have to be that way. You can maintain this state just as well in the presence of other people as you have been doing alone. The key to your success is your will and intent; it's not where you are. Just stay focused and keep an eye on yourself, and things will be fine.*

I knew this deeper part of myself was absolutely right.

This experience of self-observation, accompanied by self-remembering, reminded me of when I was younger, and my two older brothers and I would go out to mow lawns or shovel walks to earn spending money. My brothers were a little shy and always wanted me to knock on the door and ask for work. I remember distinctly feeling I didn't want to do this either. I didn't have any seniority—and I didn't want my brothers to tell me to get lost—so, I would dutifully go knock on doors and earnestly ask for work. The process of doing that, repeatedly, made me realize it wasn't such a terrible thing, and almost everyone was nice. I learned I didn't always need to listen to that part of me that was afraid and hesitant. This new technique of G's was helping me to reconnect with this other part of myself, which observed and learned, a part I had been wanting to recapture for the last number of years.

Later in the day, while waiting for my uncle at a local truck stop, I was again amazed and amused to hear my mind, wondering if this was the right place and time for us to meet. I could hardly believe what I was hearing. Obviously, it was where he had asked me to meet him. I wouldn't have been able to find the place if he hadn't given me directions to it. I wondered: *how can my mind do this when it's clearly the right place?*

I could now understand other people's formerly unbelievable statements and fears. I remembered Ustrid wondering if she looked all right when she always looked gorgeous. I had always understood it when other people felt that way, but not beautiful Ustrid! Considering my own experiences of late, I could understand her doubts and fears. Sort of. Anyway, I saw this is what the mind does, even though I still didn't see why it would do it, continually, and especially in unfamiliar surroundings.

Trying to Stay "Awake" Amongst Wine, Women, and Song

My uncle showed up a few minutes later. After the initial greetings, some coffee and catching up on family news—I hadn't seen him for a couple of years— he suggested we go to the area's favorite cowboy bar for some supper and a little local entertainment. Even though the setting was a little loud, it still provided an atmosphere conducive to pleasant conversation. I didn't feel any need to tell him about my practice of this technique of focusing my mind in a new way. My only desire was to do it: to remember to remember myself. This cowboy bar atmosphere was great in that I had never been in a place quite like it. As the ambiance was totally new to me, it had a similar effect on me as being in the midst of a spectacular landscape: it gave me something easy to focus on.

In fact, I found this new atmosphere and companionship helpful to my cause. I had noticed a tendency, earlier in the afternoon, to start analyzing some of the new insights and feelings I was experiencing from the practice of self-remembering. While doing this, I realized I wasn't actively practicing self-remembering. So, this new environment made it easier to simply practice the technique of being aware of what was happening around me and in my own mind. My goal for the weekend was not to analyze anything, but to put all my energy into trying to, as Gurdjieff put it, stay "awake." The cowboy bar and my uncle's company in Idaho were an excellent place to start!

As the evening wore on, it became a little difficult to continue with my self-remembering. My cousin showed up, and I found that, when I was sharing stories about myself and the family back home, it was all too easy for me to get caught up in those stories and forget all about keeping myself present in my observations. It was easy to revert to the feelings I had at the time of the incident I was describing and forget all about self-remembering. After the storytelling was over, I settled back into this new energy pattern of mine and found that my ability to practice this double focus started getting stronger. The state of self-remembering began to return, even though the majority of the time, my mind would keep losing its focus and start thinking about old times back East.

Throughout the evening, my uncle had been asking me to ask this particular young woman to dance. Even though she was quite attractive, I told him I was fine just where I was. As the night progressed, he kept saying, *"Go ask her to dance."* Finally, I was ready.

The Awakening Begins

We started dancing, and initially everything seemed fine: I was able to stay in the practice of self-remembering. After a few more steps, I began to feel that old habitual sexual attraction rising. Thinking about sex destroyed my focus in terms of self-remembering. As my mind wandered, it hit upon the idea that the urge to have sex with this virtual stranger seemed to come from the same place inside of me where the inexplicable anxiety had come from earlier about whether I was at the right truck stop for the meet-up with my uncle. These feelings just felt like conditioned responses driven by circumstances. Often when dancing with an attractive woman, I would have thoughts about sex. It seemed a natural response, but was it? Or was it a conditioned response? It certainly seemed similar to the conditioned negative responses I had been working with when I was practicing the non-expressive negative emotions. I assumed they both were conditioned responses; the only difference is that one was sexual in nature, driven by hormones, while the other was probably a result of cultural conditioning. With that understanding, I did my best to stay in a state of self-remembering, and we ended up dancing for quite a while and having a good time.

My uncle and some of his friends were leaving to carry on the festivities at one of my uncle's 'friends' houses. I invited this young woman to join us, and she said, *"I don't know if I should."*

With all the new insight I was experiencing into the workings of my own mind, I said, *"Is that the way you really feel, or are you more concerned with what other people will think? You should be aware of and follow your own inner feelings. If you really want to do something and feel okay about doing it, don't worry about what someone might think."*

She said that, on second thought, she would like to spend some more time together, even while acknowledging that part of her didn't think it would look quite right. During this party, I continued speaking to this young woman about the mind in an effortless way. One of the main things I learned recently, particularly over the last two days, was how conditioned our minds are. Another was how my mind, at times, worries more about what others might think than it does about my own feelings. This, too, was not just a tendency of my mind but of the human mind in general. Seeing how this young woman was concerned about what others thought, I talked to her about the importance of paying attention to yourself and not being afraid to get in touch with your own feelings and respect them. (Remember, this was the mid-1970s, when people were very much concerned about getting in touch with their feelings!)

She asked about my experience of Vail, and I told her my experiences of realizing how important it is to live in the present moment and my realization that many of my negative emotional reactions were conditioned responses rather than conscious choices. I related this to living your own life versus being controlled by others' expectations. It's lovely to be aware of the overall situation—aware of others' needs and concerns—but you always need to listen to the deeper part of your own self.

A Joyous Awakening

Throughout our conversation, I was doing quite well at staying awake—in G's sense of the word—but I also continued to experience feelings of sexual attraction. Part of me realized that even though I was relating to her honestly about what I had been learning recently, there was definitely a part of me trying to maneuver myself into a position to have sex with her. I couldn't deny that some elements of our conversation about the mind, like my emphasis on choosing to do what we wanted to do over curtailing our behavior because of what others may think, was an attempt to get this young woman to admit to herself that she was feeling some of the same sexual urges I was experiencing, and to acknowledge she would like to express them as much as I would.

A part of me wanted to experience intimate romance in this newfound state of mind. I wondered if having sex in this new state of awareness would be a bit like having sex for the very first time. As fate would have it, she was feeling about the same as I was and decided she wanted to take me home with her, even though she still had qualms, knowing everyone at the party would know what was happening and would form an opinion. The intimacy of our evening's interactions set us up perfectly for a more natural progression of our relationship, alone in the early morning hours. My level of energy was still high from the last few days of further self-discovery. Still, the added anticipation about making love to this attractive young woman, interestingly, helped me regain an even better sense of focus. I really wanted to be "awake" for the upcoming events.

During our lovemaking, I realized that I did not feel any different than I normally did. In fact, I was surprised to see that my focus during sex was very similar to G's self-remembering! This came as a total surprise. I had not seen or intuited any connections beforehand. I could now see that when making love, I had naturally split my focus in a way that was similar to self-remembering: one part was riveted on my lover and the other part on myself. What was different now was that this was the first time that I was aware of the way my mind was focused during sex. I also realized that my mind never tends to think or participate in internal talking while having sex. Thus, for me, lovemaking was a little like self-remembering: my mind was focused, quiet, and as present as it could be. I thought, No wonder lovemaking is such a cherished experience.

I departed with the rising sun, rejuvenated from the early morning activities and some unexpected insights. As I was walking back to my cousin's place, I was trying to keep present in the state of self-remembering. Once again, I used the new surroundings to help keep my mind in the present so that I could keep my attention on myself instead of reliving the memories of the recent past. I tried to imitate Ouspensky, who first practiced self-remembering by looking intently at the houses while walking the streets of St. Petersburg. Soon, I became aware of the thought: *"Boy, am I going to be tired today, I didn't get any sleep at all last night!"*

Noticing this thought, the observing part of my mind felt, *"That does not necessarily have to be the case. Let's just try to stay focused in the state of self-remembering and see how things go. Right now, so many wonderful vibrations are coursing through me, and these last few days have been so incredible. Let's just see how it goes. It will be interesting to 'watch' how I will feel versus getting caught up in my thoughts."*

Shortly after I got to my cousin's place, my uncle showed up and, with a big smile, asked me how I was enjoying Idaho. I returned the grin and said, "So far it's been great." I realized that he was most likely referring to the sex with this acquaintance of his, but I was actually speaking about the whole experience that I was having with self-remembering since I arrived. The time spent with this young woman was great, but it was not comparable to the experience, insights, and energy I was gaining from this new practice of self-remembering.

My Mind Is a Real Idiot

On our way to the mountains for some sightseeing and fishing, we stopped at a village that consisted solely of a general store with a porch that was pretty much rotted away and a place to fix tires out back. While my uncle was getting a tire fixed, I sat on the porch enjoying the sunshine and the scenery and intently trying to stay in a state of self-awareness. A couple of young fellows pulled up in an old truck, and as they were heading into the store, I heard myself say: "These guys are a couple of real hicks." They were both wearing fancy cowboy outfits with boots to match. Being from the Northeast, I wasn't used to seeing anyone even remotely dressed like this.

The part of my awareness that I am calling the watcher of my mind immediately "knew" that my reaction to seeing their outfits was conditioned and prejudiced, too! I also immediately realized that my mind was the real idiot, not the guys in the truck. I had experienced it's foolishness so many times over these last few days that it wasn't really that surprising or shocking. And I could see that it was similar to my experience with negative emotions in that the thoughts were triggered by their clothing, again, more of a reaction than a conscious choice! This, once again, essentially confirmed G's teaching that we are at the mercy of outside influences. Since I had been observing myself for a few years, I'd been aware that my mind had made its share of faulty judgments, but generally had not noticed this until later. With today's unsought outburst, I realized this the very moment it was happening, thanks to G and his students. Self-remembering was expanding my awareness and understanding at the very same time—remarkable!

That weekend with my uncle, I realized that it wasn't any more difficult to stay in a state of self-remembering in the company of other people than it was to do it while alone. Of course, it wasn't any easier either. We had a great time, and both wished that we had more time together. I felt that my uncle had picked up on my inner state of high, wonderful, and easy-going energy, even though I had not said anything to him about what I was practicing or experiencing. I wanted to tell him about it, but somehow, I knew there was no way to just tell someone about this unheard-of practice. One truly had to be a seeker of higher understanding to be ready for something like this, and actually try something this foreign.

After a wonder-filled weekend, I looked forward to traveling through more new and unexplored country, the states of Oregon and Washington, trying to stay consciously present in the enlightening state of self-remembering.

The Sermon on the Mount and Self-Remembering

One of the first things I did after leaving my uncle's place was to buy a copy of the New Testament. I'd thought about this before arriving at my uncle's, but decided to wait until after the visit so it would not interfere with being fully present with him. My main purpose in obtaining the Bible14 was to be able to see exactly what Jesus had to say in the Sermon on the Mount. As I've mentioned, I had often wondered about this part of Jesus' teaching, intuitively feeling that it was an important key to understanding and following His teachings. As a young male, I would wonder how it was possible to live without desire or being anxious about tomorrow? Both of these things seemed so natural and so normal. How can such things be sinful or avoided? Again, I had thought about these teachings and asked questions about them, but had never seen anything the least bit helpful. I was able to somewhat see that if one could live by these, life would be a lot easier and more enjoyable, but the "how to do this" seemed impossible! Now, however, with just a few days of practicing self-observation accompanied by self-remembering, I could finally see how this seemingly impossible task might be possible!

During the last couple of days, I'd begun to see how my mind was highly but stealthily conditioned and much more judgmental than I would have ever believed. As G pointed out, I acted much more mechanically than I did consciously. I also experienced how the part of myself that was capable of observing my mind and its habits did not seem to be conditioned—worried, lustful, judgmental, etc. In fact, my experience was that this part of my mind or better yet, my awareness, was very calm, detached, and oh so sharp, so vigilant. There was no question that this more aware aspect felt like the real ME. The Me that was not so socially conditioned, so ego-centered. It was closer to my heart's awareness and the ME that is able to remember myself and see what my habitual mind is up to! In other words, I could see that this part of myself was not under the same influences as my habitual self, my so-called "normal" self. And I could also see that it was this observing part of myself that had the potential and ability to follow Jesus' teachings in the Sermon. At the same time, it was watching all of my mostly conditioned thoughts! The key being that my sense of self, the real ME, was not in my habitual thoughts and feelings as it had always been. This was not a rational solution as I'd been hoping and looking for, had been assuming was the only possible way. No, just a shift in perspective that you could experience for yourself, by yourself—no beliefs required.

After I got the New Testament, I drove for a while enjoying the scenery, which was exquisite, and as I'd done for the last number of days, I made a concerted effort to be in the relaxed and vigilant state of self-remembering.

When I got to a particularly beautiful spot, I pulled off the road, sat on the hood of my car and started reading the Sermon, something I hadn't done in years. After a little while, I saw another vehicle driving up towards where I was parked. Upon seeing this, my habitual mind immediately started thinking: "*This must be the owner coming to tell me that I have to leave, that this is his property, and he doesn't want people using it. What a shame I'm not bothering anybody and will be leaving shortly.*"

Fortunately, I was well centered in self-remembering, and thus heard this conditioned part of my habitual mind doing its thing! As the watcher, I laughed at this part of myself, beginning to realize that it just can't help itself. It turned out that it was right about the man being the owner, but he was friendly and sweet and was not the least bit concerned that I was using his property for a short time.

He saw that I was reading the Bible and started talking about the Lord. I told him that I'd recently had some new and startling insights into the teachings of Christianity, and I'd wanted to reread the Sermon just to make sure I was remembering them correctly. I also told him that I was supposed to start dental school in the fall, but was now feeling that maybe I should put all of my efforts into knowing God better and sharing my insights with others instead of going to grad school. He calmly proceeded to tell me that he had just gotten out of the hospital, where he had officially died but had been miraculously brought back, and now, he felt sure that that had happened just so he could meet me. Then he looked me right in the eye and told me that I should follow through on my plans to become a dentist and also continue my newfound relationship with God. I could and should do both. His presence was so powerful that from that moment on, the thought never came up again.

As I read the Sermon on this, let's say, interesting morning, I kept in the foreground of my mind what I'd been learning and experiencing about the part of my awareness that made it possible for me to remember myself. (And let me say here that I was sure that this part was available to everyone; there was nothing special about me.) My experience of this aspect of my awareness made it clear that it was indeed one authentic way to follow the seemingly impossible teachings in the Sermon. Was there any other way?

There were two other parts of the Sermon that I had forgotten were in it, which had a lot of meaning for me on that special day. The first teaches, "*Ask and you shall receive, Seek and you shall find, and Knock and the door shall be opened.*"(Matt 7:7–8) I knew deep in my being that this was true. I had been experiencing it most profoundly these last few days, but truly for months and for years as well. If you don't seek, don't ask, how will you ever find new understanding? Effort is required for advancement and for looking outside your conditioned culture for some fresh insights, which now seem obvious and sensible.

The second teaching is contained in two similes: Jesus says that one who hears his words and acts upon them is like a man who builds his house on stone, and then he compares this wise person to one who does not act on his words and is like a foolish man who builds his house on sand. (Matt 8:24–27) I could see that I had acted on his words in the Sermon by contemplating them, more than once, and by seeking more satisfying answers, wherever I could find them. Again, based on my own enlightening experiences of these past few days, I knew that a much more conscious state of self-remembering was tantamount to building your house, your understanding on solid ground, because its insights were so profound and practical too! And they did not contain a single belief! The one who does not act on his words in the Sermon, does not contemplate them, and does not seek beyond his culturally conditioned *beliefs*, is building his house, his understanding on the shifting sands of belief, which, all too often, tend to keep one from seeking and asking pertinent questions and, as I realized later, from maturing.

These insights made it clear to me that I had finally found what I had been seeking and asking for for almost seven years now. This was the key to the breakthrough I'd sensed was possible just weeks ago. And it showed me that my intuition that the Sermon was an important Key to understanding Jesus' teaching and his promise that such will make one's life happy and fulfilled was correct. Feeling unimaginably uplifted, I pulled back onto the highway, experiencing excitement, hope, and trust that I'd never known before, and never truly expected!

Later that afternoon, as I was cruising through Oregon, the beautiful sunny day had turned into a rainy, foggy one. The thoughts and emotions that came into my mind seemed to follow suit, even though I didn't notice this, having lost touch with self-remembering. One of the thought patterns that kept recurring concerned the young lady with whom I had spent Friday night. I remembered that my uncle had said that he thought that she was divorced, and it struck me that I had not clarified that with her. Thus, I didn't know if she was divorced or just separated.

A part of me was feeling guilty about this lack of clarity. I felt that I should definitely have asked about this. My religious upbringing had taught me that it is wrong to have intimate relations with a married woman. I also thought that maybe I hadn't taken the time to ask her about her marital status because I didn't really want to know; it could just be trouble and interfere with the natural flow. But honestly, as far as I could remember, once we were together, I had totally forgotten about this subject.

Since I had read the Sermon, different thoughts had been coming up all on their own, and now I was remembering that Jesus taught that one should not have relations with a married woman and also a man who marries a married woman commits adultery! I started to feel remorseful and guilty about being with her. Thoughts about premarital sex and religion played in my mind for quite a while. Then I rediscovered another thought: *"If two adults want to participate" in sex, it's fine to do so as long as they are responsible and honest about their feelings.* When I saw this, a thought came up through my mental fog. I was surprised that I had completely forgotten about this long-held thought—belief.

After mulling over all of this for some time and trying to discern what is truly right, especially the part concerning a divorced woman, I finally became "AWAKE" again! I realized that I had gotten carried away with old religious beliefs and guilt about sex, another religious belief—deep cultural conditioning. In other words, I, my sense of self, had become completely identified with my habitual thoughts. I had totally forgotten to remember myself, to be consciously present, to be the awareness that these were arising into. I had to laugh at myself because it was not more than a couple of hours ago that I had felt so good about seeing a more expansive perspective about sex and lust, i.e., the inner part of my awareness that can remember myself, the inner vigilant PRESENCE, can follow the Sermon, but my habitual mind cannot. With that, I just let all of those thoughts and emotions go and focused on getting back into self-remembering; just watch my mind instead of running off with its thoughts!

The Oregon landscape was wonderfully eerie with fog rising along the river and hanging in the mountains. Even with this beautiful and unusual scenery, I wasn't able to stay focused in the way I had been the last couple of days. There were so many emotions being stirred up that I found it hard to keep from getting pulled into these thoughts. But, by now, I was well aware of the difficulty of not identifying with one's thoughts; I'd been doing it all of my life!

I remembered the great love I'd had for Jesus when I was a child. Like many children, I was touched by His kindness, compassion, and love for all, which opened my own heart and allowed me to feel great love inside myself. As I grew older, it was quite disappointing to realize that very few people seemed to truly attempt to live as Jesus taught: treat others as you would have them treat you, and refrain from the self-love and self-righteousness of the Pharisee. By the time I reached my early twenties, I realized that it wasn't so easy to follow these teachings that I'd felt the truth of when I was young. I knew that part of me really wanted to follow Jesus' teachings and even thought that I did live by them reasonably well.

But, as I've said, when I looked a little closer, I had to admit that I was as guilty as the people I saw as hypocrites. In my relationships with my girlfriends, for instance, I had done things that would have disappointed or even bewildered me if they had done the same to me! Most of this behavior had to do with sex, but some of it was just plain old lack of self-respect and common decency toward others. Over these last few days, it was refreshing and enlightening for me to see the nature of my mind through the vastly higher awareness of self-remembering. It helped me make some sense, finally, of some of the actions I'd taken toward Ustrid—and she toward me—that had been the source of considerable concern for me these last couple of years. I'd realized that most of us participate in hypocritical behavior unwillingly, and, for the most part, unknowingly.

As I was having these sorts of thoughts and insights, I found myself feeling overwhelming gratitude and love for Jesus that I had not experienced in many years. There was no question in my mind that it was His behavior and teachings that had made me a seeker of higher understanding, which had finally connected me to G and his teachings. My long-time hopes and prayers were being answered. These feelings were precious and greatly appreciated, but I was also vaguely aware that being so emotional did not allow me to practice self-remembering the way I understood it—I was too connected to the thoughts and emotions rather than being the observer of them!

A Couple of Interesting Insights

By evening, I felt that I was decently connected to the state of self-remembering the way I'd been over the weekend. Feeling relaxed and focused, an image relating to the various thoughts and emotions of this day arose spontaneously. It seemed that this exercise or practice of trying to be more present, being aware of what my mind is up to, versus being totally identified with every thought and emotion, was like removing a pressurized cap from my mind. The pressurized cap was a result of the mind's unnoticed conditioning and attachment, and its unnoticed, unceasing and undisciplined activity. It occurred to me that once my mind became more calm and more focused via the effort to observe my mind, then it seemed natural that the thoughts and emotions under the most pressure, under the deepest conditioning, would be the first to come out. This insight helped me to better understand the intense emotional activity that had taken place in my mind earlier.

As I pondered my experiences gained via G's insights, I could appreciate how much cultural and religious conditioning I had accumulated and how this was directly related to my beliefs. I'd had some vague awareness of this in a general way, but now, thanks to G, I was aware of the limiting and pervasive nature of this conditioning at a much deeper level. It felt like a major cleansing, a lightening of my load, had taken place, and once again, I felt great.

The next morning, awakening in my little car, I was excited to be arriving in Vancouver, British Columbia and was committed more than ever to making a super effort, as G put it, toward being in a state of self-remembering. Similar to the previous day, the morning went well. The day was sunny, and the scenery was captivating, helping me stay present and not run off on different trains of thought. I had lots of time to stop and just consciously take in the views of this state that I was seeing for the first time. The sunlight and the more expansive horizon seemed to contribute to my being quieter and more focused internally.

As I drove northward, another surprising insight popped up. I saw that having myself in my awareness at the same time that I'm participating in other normal activities is like applying the scientific method back onto myself! The detached part of myself that can observe myself fits the scientific definition of an objective observer to a T. For an investigation to be considered scientific, the data must be obtained through objective observation. The operative term here is *Objective*, which is devoid of opinions and beliefs. This is the only way to collect reliable data and trustworthy facts that, in time and often with the help of mathematics, can reveal their hidden insights and pave the way for deeper understanding. This method has been proven beyond doubt and belief.

When this insight came up, I was a little surprised to see that G's self-remembering—the practice that I was using that was dramatically increasing my understanding—was so similar to the scientific method, the way science has always increased its understanding! Right away, I knew this comparison was valid.

In the preceding five days, through this effort to remain consciously present, I had directly experienced that this part of my awareness that is capable of observing, of watching my habitual mind, is indeed an objective and detached observer. And, as I've said, I also experienced that my habitual mind is not really objective when it comes to looking at my culturally conditioned beliefs. Especially knowing that I never really considered them to be conditioned the way I did now. Again, through G's practices, I'd seen that basically all of my negative reactions and many of my culturally conditioned thoughts, such as *"What will people think? Is this the right thing to do?"* and so on, are all culturally conditioned. Already I was starting to see that many of my mind's habitual ramblings and reactions were much more expressions of my conditioning than they were of ME. What felt like the real me was this deeper, more objective part of myself that I was just beginning to become familiar with.

After these thoughts and insights, I began wondering why I had never thought to apply the scientific method to my attempts at self-observation and analysis. But almost immediately, I realized that this would be pretty much impossible for someone who had not been taught about their capacity to connect with this deeper and more objective part of their mind, just awareness itself! It was obvious that to learn about self-remembering, you have to have a teacher.

Reflecting further on my experiences of this more conscious part of myself, I saw that it seemed to be naturally free of judgments, conditioned beliefs, etc. It also seemed to be devoid of thoughts and negative feelings altogether. It was simply pure awareness, which is probably why it appeared to be so objective, and at the same time, so much the real me. This is exactly what I'd been hoping and looking for!

A Christian Is Not One Who Simply Calls Himself A Christian

As I was approaching the Canadian border, I decided to do one last bit of sightseeing in Washington State. Having grown up in Maine close to the border of Canada, I was curious to see another border town, pretty much on the exact opposite side of the country. I found that in a lot of ways, it was similar to the town I grew up in. After a short look around, I decided to just relax for a while, since I was in no rush, and treat myself to some more of Ouspensky's book. As I picked up his book—"In Search of the Miraculous, which struck me again as an incredibly appropriate title, the book happened to fall open to chapter 6, where G is discussing Christianity with his students.

I had read this same chapter earlier and had completely forgotten that he had spoken about Christianity. With yesterday's explosion of religious thoughts and emotions, I felt that this was a nudge from fate and that I had better read this chapter again. Once I got into the chapter, it seemed that I had never read it before. There were a number of G's statements that now had great meaning for me, statements that hadn't struck me at all just a few weeks earlier. I could see that by sincerely participating in self-remembering, I'd gained a whole new perspective on myself, on the nature of the mind in general and on the value of G's precious teachings.

Asked by one of his students, *"How can we become a Christian?"*

G responds: *"First of all, it is necessary to understand that a Christian is not a man who calls himself a Christian or whom others call a Christian. A Christian is one who lives in accordance with Christ's precepts: such as we are, we cannot be Christians."[15]* My immediate response was that this is most certainly the case. It was apparent that this definition was a lot stricter than our culture was used to, but it seemed to go well with the Sermon on the Mount, which many claimed to be the essence of Jesus' teachings. These teachings require a person to be responsible for thoughts as well as actions. If we take to heart what Jesus says about lusting and not being anxious about tomorrow or judging, let alone seeking and knocking, then it is obvious that most of the people who think of themselves as Christians are not even trying to follow Christ's precepts and are not, therefore, truly Christians!

G goes on to say, *"With us, everything just happens… Christ says love your enemies, but how can we love our enemies when we cannot even love our friends? Sometimes, 'it loves' and sometimes 'it does not love.'"[16]*

I laughed when I read that because I, too, had used the word 'it' to represent the conditioned and mechanical aspect of myself. When I'd seen those two fellows a few days previously in Idaho, it (my conditioned response) didn't love them; it thought of them as a couple of hicks. If, instead, I had encountered a couple of attractive young women dressed up as cowgirls, it might have been quite favorable toward them, or even more.

G points out that, "such as we are," in our regular or habitual state of mind, where we have no awareness of our conditioning or of our deeper self, the awareness that I thought of as—the watcher of my mind—"We have no choice!" Just mechanical responses. We often respond according to our culturally conditioned reactions to outside circumstances and stimuli, not according to our own true priorities. How can we follow Christ's teachings when we are not sufficiently aware of ourselves and not in control of a lot of our thoughts and actions? Most of the time, we are not capable of truly conscious choices, but too often only knee-jerk reactions.

G's observations reminded me that this was my experience, my take when pondering, How can it be possible not to experience some desire when in the presence of a woman that I am strongly attracted to? I also remembered my talks about this seemingly unsolvable problem with the priest who had studied philosophy, and how all he could come up with was that Jesus was presenting an ideal and not something we could ever hope to achieve. As I mentioned, I had thought, *"Who am I supposed to believe, this priest or Jesus?"* It seemed obvious to me that if I'm going to believe at all, I might as well believe in Jesus. Now I was glad I did and also glad that I followed His advice to *seek,* because it now looked like I had found!

When I read the New Testament in college, the understanding I came away with was that Jesus was encouraging us to follow Him; to rise up to His example and teachings. If we could do that, we would experience the truth of His teachings for ourselves. Again, I had some vague feeling that if a person could follow Jesus' example and teachings, then that person would experience a higher part of themselves and experience all the goodness that went with it. Now, with G's help, I was starting to feel it and just barely beginning to understand it.

In the same section, G also said in order to be a Christian, you must be the master of yourself, and to do that, you must be responsible, and I thought: and to do that, you must be self-aware. G also reiterated that, as we are now, with essentially no awareness of our habitual and conditioned nature, we are enslaved to outer influences and inner emotions. (I repeat this in this updated version because we see the truth of this every day in the media and in the life around us.) G reminds us that since a slave has no choice in his actions, he can't be responsible for them. This struck me as extremely insightful as well as true and was another vivid way to remind his students that they were not as in control of their thoughts and actions as they thought they were. Another of G's teachings is that, "*We have no real self-attention—we just think we do—we just assume we do.*"[17] Based on my own experiences, I knew that I did not possess much self-awareness, the way I'd always believed. If anyone follows G's teaching on self-remembering, they will see the truth of these little-understood teachings.

G goes on to say that if one does not know himself, is not aware of how he really is, is not aware of his ignorance, and of his deeper nature and ability to be the watcher of his mind, he cannot become free. As stated, I knew that my mind's uncalled-for reactions were not free and conscious choices. I knew that most of us would never believe how little freedom we have without experiencing this for ourselves. And what other way was there to gain direct experience than through the little-known but ingenious and highly efficient practice of self-remembering?

Here I was with two college degrees, born in "the land of the free," and I was just beginning to have an inkling of what real freedom was truly about. The key, I was finding, was to truly "*knowing thyself*" versus assuming I already know myself. The final irony was that I was learning all of this from G, who was an Armenian-Russian, someone from a country that was not associated with personal freedom!

I was also pleasantly surprised, actually shocked, to see that the essence of Christianity and freedom are dynamically interconnected, something I found amusing because I'd always equated religion, not with freedom, but instead with rules and restrictions.

G tells his students that the command to "know thyself" is generally ascribed to Socrates, but actually is the basis of schools far more ancient than the Greeks.18 I was vaguely familiar with the teaching to *know thyself,* and, as stated, had been trying to do so on my own and had learned a lot. But I certainly could not say that I got any help from my education or religion. Now, thanks to G and his students— P.D. Ouspensky and M. Nicoll, I was beginning to appreciate the immense importance of following this ancient teaching. I was also starting to realize that modern culture had no understanding of this profound and practical Teaching, which could dramatically enhance one's understanding of themselves and others, in less than a week! And, absolutely no beliefs required!

This call for humanity to "know thyself" and its connection to ancient schools, true freedom and the essence of Christianity set off so many related insights that I could not get them all written down. Writing as fast as I could and feeling a touch of frustration, I, the watcher of my mind, heard myself say: "*What a shame that I'm not able to record all of these great insights.*" At that precise moment, a rock hit my parked car, deflected from a passing car. The unexpected and sheer force and sound of the rock underscored this re-awakening to the state of self-remembering, to getting back in touch with the deeper awareness that is free, that is just present and "so Awake," as G referred to it.

Since my real desire and commitment of these last days was to just keep centered on the witness, and keep reconnecting as needed, I knew that I didn't need to "worry" about recording all of the insights that were arising. I also knew that my intense practice of self-remembering was the key to the many insights that I'd had over these last few days. I felt sure that as long as I just continued to persevere as I had been, insights would continue to come forth, and my understanding would continue to evolve. With that in mind, I headed back to the highway, anxious to see Vancouver, British Columbia, a city I'd heard much about.

The Beauty and Magic of British Columbia

As I was approaching Vancouver, I felt so excited to be able to live in a new city that was right on the coast with huge mountains to admire and hopefully, venture into soon. It was similar to the special feeling I had arriving in the Vail valley, just hard to believe that it was finally happening. But since then, my level of awareness and understanding had advanced and expanded so greatly and so miraculously that I was now on a venture that was totally new, and with—oh so much fun and satisfaction. I couldn't help but wonder: "*What will this summer of exploration bring?*"

A Joyous Awakening

I decided to go to the beach right away, as this was one of the best assets of Vancouver that had been mentioned time and again. And I was not the least bit disappointed. The beach had lots of beautiful sand and was obviously very well taken care of. There were mountains all around, unlike the mountains in Bar Harbor, Maine—these mountains, the Canadian Rockies, were huge! There was a trace of fog or light clouds in the sky, and this gave the effect that the snow-covered peaks were suspended in midair. I had never seen anything quite like it. Wow, what a way to begin my stay in the Northwest. The combination of the sand, sun, the mountains, and the energy I was feeling made the moment indescribable and unforgettable! I could say that I never felt more alive or more energized.

I waded into the water, which was much warmer than I expected. The Pacific Ocean in San Jose, California, was freezing all summer. After swimming around for a short time, it struck me that this ocean hardly seemed salty. I wondered if I wasn't noticing the salt because of the uplifted state I was in, but immediately recognized that, as one more of my "minds" reactionary statements. After a couple more minutes, I took some water into my mouth purposely, just to taste it, and sure enough, it was not that salty. It was almost similar to swimming in a Maine lake, which I always preferred to the ocean because of the salt on my lips and skin. Again, another unexpected treat to this already unique and special day. Finally, I asked one of the locals how this was possible. He told me that it was due to a huge river emptying into the ocean just around the bend. Knowing the cause didn't dispel the sense of magic, inner and outer, which lasted not just for the rest of the day but for the rest of the summer!

I spent the rest of this first day on the beach, jogging and exploring its many sandbars. After a long road trip, it was wonderful to experience this sort of needed exercise and feeling of freedom to move. It was also fantastic to sit in the warm sand with the sun on my back and let my senses take in all the new and stimulating sensations while I, the watcher of my mind, enjoyed the wonder of it all. This heavenly setting made it easy for me to remain focused and quiet within. It felt so good to be in this setting that I stayed there all night, in the back seat of my little car.

The next day, I went by the Canadian National Railroad headquarters to let them know that I was in town and to see when they thought I could start work. They told me that everything was set, but that the way the schedule looked, it would be about a week before they would need me. I said that would be fine, as I had not gotten a place to stay yet or explored any of this beautiful area. I went by a local college to see if there were any notices for a roommate. I was lucky to find a room in a nice section of town fairly close to one of its many beaches. It was with a few college students who needed someone just for the summer, which was just perfect for me. I had my own room. They had some winter quilts that I used as a bed, and I could use their phone, too. So, everything quickly fell into place with hardly any effort, and I knew that this was just another manifestation of the magic I had been experiencing for months. But my inner state was absolutely the best part and the most impressive and satisfying, way beyond anything I could have imagined or wished for.

From the moment I arrived in Vancouver, I had a natural inclination to jog on its lovely beaches. Up to this point in my life, I had never enjoyed running. But suddenly running was a very rich experience for me. As I ran, I was able to get in touch with my body and mind in a way that was new and exhilarating. I couldn't say for sure, but I knew that this was most likely due to my elevated state of awareness. The scenery was exquisite, and being able to jog in my bare feet was wonderful as well. It was a nice added dimension to do something physical, jogging and swimming, while trying to stay present in the state of self-remembering. This, combined with my exploration and reading, made for a wonderful start in the Northwest.

3
G's Teachings on the Quest to Know Thyself

To carry on with G's teachings, I naturally returned to chapter 6 concerning "know thyself." It was so clear to me that this is what I'd been yearning for, for years. G's view was that practically everyone, in their present state of awareness, was a long way from self-knowledge, even an incipient level of genuine self-awareness. His key to self-study—today we would say self-inquiry—is intense self-observation, trying to become aware of what you are really like. As I've said, this is what I naturally did upon my first love leaving me. If you want a more comprehensive understanding of yourself, you have to step back and look at the bigger picture. You might say that you have to separate from your habitual mindset and try to look at yourself with more objective and scrutinizing eyes. Again, very similar to the scientific approach. G said that people must look at themselves as if they are looking at someone else entirely. He said you have to get to know how you really are, not how you think you are or imagine yourself to be. I had to admit that I had never, even remotely, done this until I participated in self-observation accompanied by self-remembering. Like many others, I had tried to look through another's eyes, which is helpful but still contains a lot of conditioned beliefs, etc. And I now knew that such would never allow one to see, to experience, what I had in these last few days!

Another related question posed by G's students was, *"Why was this knowledge about 'know thyself' so secretive and hidden?"*[19] G's answer was that this knowledge is not hidden. It's that people do not seek it out. His point was that, basically, people are happy as they are and that, as they are, they are not interested in this knowledge that he's talking about. He pointed out that this type of knowledge is not necessary in everyday life. It is only for those who truly want a deeper understanding of life. He also said that those who really want it will find it. This certainly reminded me of Jesus' teaching of: *"Seek and you shall find"* and *"Ask, and you shall receive."* And I was also aware that most did not have a true desire for a much deeper understanding of this hard-to-understand life. Most thought this endeavor a waste of time and that there weren't any answers anyway, just a fool's errand.

A Burning Desire For Deeper Understanding Is Needed

This burning desire "to know" and "to seek" was what led me to G's teaching. I've mentioned that while talking to a bus driver, waiting for the girl's gymnastics team that I was chaperoning, he asked me if I had ever heard of Gurdjieff because I was mentioning that while reading the book Sybil, I could see that I too had a number of personalities, depending on the circumstances. He said that since this was one of G's main teachings, seeing one's many aspects of personality, thus, I might want to check him out. As I'm sharing, I did, and it was the breakthrough I was hoping for. This is a great example of simple self-observation and a genuine desire to expand your understanding of yourself and how doing so can lead to things that you could never have expected.

Another point that G made to his students was to just stick with observation, keen and vigilant observation, but no analysis. He said that analysis results in a seeker getting caught up in questions and forgetting about simply observing himself. Yes, I'd already experienced the truth of that a number of times and could appreciate how it can't be otherwise! Through my study of chemistry, I have realized that if you jump to conclusions or theories based on a small amount of data, it is generally a rookie's mistake. Again, whether self-study or science, analysis takes your focus from objective observation, especially in the beginning. In both cases, by remaining fully focused on the data, the insights will begin to emerge on their own. I had already seen the truth of this, even though I had barely begun these practices.

How Do We Become So Conditioned?

Earlier, G had spoken about how we have become so mechanical. Today, we would say: How do we become so programmed, so culturally conditioned? G taught that this was due to our propensity to mimic, our desires, our need for love and acceptance, our need to avoid non-acceptance, insult, etc., and finally, our knowing nothing of authentic self-study or authentic self-awareness. I certainly knew the truth of all of these insights and was beginning to appreciate how conditioned my thoughts and emotions are. And also, beginning to have an idea of what authentic self-awareness really means. This was quite humbling, as I've shared, but I knew that what I—the watcher of my mind—was "seeing" was valid and oh so enlightening and practical.

Another aspect of self-observation is the need to become aware of habitual daydreaming, imagining, fantasizing, and what M. Nicoll[20] called making accounts against others, i.e., what they owe me, how they don't appreciate me, etc. G was not against creative thinking; I might call it conscious or intentional brainstorming. He was against having your mind on what he called "auto-pilot", just wandering around with no conscious intent or awareness. Again, I'd already experienced this many times, and there was never any intent, just unconscious habits and certainly no true self-observation involved. And I had begun to see not only how mechanical they were but how repetitive they were, and how I'd never truly observed this. Again, the practice of being more aware of what my mind's habits actually were—showed me, in real time, how often my mind engaged in these fruitless activities.

Honest self-observation would show one that, as G taught, they were at the mercy of outside influences and massive cultural conditioning, and most would not believe this until they observed it for themselves. I knew the truth of this when being criticized or when someone flipped me the "bird!" G's point was that one has to truly see how this works, how our mechanical responses, I'd say conditioned reactions, are not truly free choices. Then you are beginning to practice self-study, beginning to know yourself. Another of G's major teachings concerning self-study was the non-expression of negative emotions. Having already spoken about this practice, I'll just remind the reader how much this exercise taught me about myself, and how much it expanded my awareness.

The Necessity of Seeing One's Predicament

"The last point that I'll make about G's teachings about getting to know thyself is about the need to see our 'predicament.'" [21] One had to accomplish this before they could begin to participate in "real psychology" the term G used for the study of our true potential—the different levels of awareness available to the consciousness that *we already have!* This teaching about knowing and acknowledging our "predicament" is one of the best I've seen in my studies about expanded self-awareness. As my story shows, I had seen my predicament in that I had directly experienced how I could not stay present, could not keep my mind from endless and uncalled-for chatter, and how it was often at the mercy of outside influences. And, how much unnoticed cultural conditioning my thoughts and emotions contained. How these influences influenced the way I saw myself and the world around me. Also, the direct experience that is part of my awareness, that can independently observe my thoughts and emotions, is much more the real me than those thoughts that I always believed myself to be. Once I had experienced this level of my awareness, I knew that I could not just go back to being my old mechanical self, as G might say.

To understand our "predicament," we must realize that we are not as free and in control as we think. His way of illustrating this was by saying that if a person does not know he's in jail, he won't try to escape! And it isn't enough to just be told about this because we believe that we are in control and already free. I could see that I would not have believed G, for sure, as we used to say, if I had not already pursued his recommended practices intently. Yes, as he said, don't believe him—do the practices and see for yourself.

A Teaching Story of G's

To illustrate how we are all at the mercy of outside influences, which is blatantly obvious today, G tells a great story: In the story, a man is having breakfast at a fine restaurant. As he is being seated, he notices a couple of women about his own age, sitting at a table close by. While he's reading the morning paper and eating his meal, he overhears these women talking about him. One is saying how it was so nice to see a man so well dressed and groomed, and how things would be so much better if more men would do the same. The other women are commenting on his posture, his rugged lower jaw and how these made him so manly and attractive. These women continue to discuss their likes and dislikes in men in general. As he is taking this all in, the man is, naturally, very flattered and starts feeling good about himself and about these women who have such excellent taste and judgement. During the remainder of his breakfast, he continues to think of himself in a positive way and to dwell on memories to support this image. He leaves to begin his work day, smiling at the women and bidding them a good day. He shows up at work in the best of moods, and his secretary asks him why he is in such great spirits so early in the day. He responds that there is nothing in particular; he just happens to feel fresh and ready to go! G then describes the same fellow in the same setting, but now there are different women sitting next to him. While eating breakfast and reading the morning paper, he overhears them asking how any man could wear such a combination of clothes he has on today. His tie doesn't go with the suit, and the suit isn't made for his type of build. They don't like the way he wears his hair or that he has a mustache. The women carry on about how men need to take better care of themselves and pay more attention to themselves, and so on.

Now, this same fellow is beginning to feel resentment and anger towards these two insensitive witches. He wonders how they can be so judgmental when they don't know the first thing about him. If women would just mind their own business and quit gossiping so much, the world would be so much better off. His mind continues to bring forth other instances when other women were critical of him and others, even when they had no good reason to be. He leaves in a huff while giving these old biddies a disgusted look! Once the man arrives at work, his secretary recognizes his foul mood and knows she needs to lay low!

Anyone who possesses even a tiny bit of self-awareness and honesty will admit that they have played out these scenes and roles many times. We all have! The problem is that since this type of thing is rarely talked about in our culture, we tend to think that it is normal and inevitable, if we even notice it at all. This is a great example of assuming that we have real self-attention and freedom of choice as well. We are satisfied with the excuse that everybody does it, and we don't learn a thing—we don't expand our awareness one little bit. If we practice self-remembering, keeping ourselves in our awareness, we will truly begin to *know thyself.*"

Yes, do the practices every day as you move through the day, and you will soon become aware of your and everyone else's "*predicament*"! Remember, this is a big step forward on the evolutionary journey, something to be grateful for—certainly not a negative. This level of heightened awareness expanded awareness lets you know that you are ready for the quest to "know thyself."

What's the Most Important thing?

After spending some delightful time at the beach, I decided that I would look at the beginning of chapter 7 of Ouspensky's "In Search of the Miraculous", because it really was miraculous what it was helping me to discover for myself—about myself. At the beginning of chapter 7, G asks his students, *"What is the most important thing that we notice during self-observation?"* After a number of replies, which G was unsatisfied with, he tells them that none of them has noticed the most important thing, *"Not one of you has noticed that you do not remember yourselves... In order to really observe oneself, one must first of all remember oneself... Only these results will have any value that are accompanied by self-remembering. Otherwise, you yourselves do not exist in your observations."* [22]

G's words sent a wonderful ripple of energy throughout my body. Such was a beautiful reiteration of what I—the witness—knew to be the exact truth. It struck me too that when I had first read this in Aspen—this takes place just before Ouspensky's description of self-remembering—none of it had meant anything to me. Without the experience, these words had been meaningless. Boy, had I come a long way in a week! I had learned more about myself in this last week than I had in my whole life!

I also had to chuckle because G had also been quoted as saying to his students that they were not conscious of themselves—with you "it" observes, "it" thinks, "it" laughs, etc. Again, I, too, had just naturally referred to this unconscious aspect of myself—my uncontrollable mind—as "it." The word I, now only referred to the part of myself that was the watcher or witness, as this felt like the real me. The habitual, unasked-for and uncontrollable part of my mind was something other than myself. Thus, the word "it" seemed appropriate.

I had returned to the part of Ouspensky's book that had initiated my awakening by giving me the clue I needed to begin the practice of self-remembering. In my original account of this journey, I presented some other things from Ouspensky's book that I thought would help the reader better appreciate what I knew to be the essence of G's teachings, before attempting to share my experience of the Transcendent state. And I knew that it was time to move on from the moment-to-moment sharing and to begin speaking about my adventure in a more general way. Back in 1975 and now again in 2024, I want to remind everyone that this story I'm sharing is not really about me personally; it's much more about getting to know the consciousness that "You" already have, but don't know how to fully utilize! Now, decades later, it makes more sense to speak about these remarkable and enlightening teachings of G's by showing that they are simply his version of the many and varied spiritual teachings on this planet that are trying to help a seeker get in touch with their capacity for inner growth and how to start employing it and enjoying it! For me, it will make more sense and be more helpful for the reader to see how expansive these teachings are that ask us to "know thyself." And how inclusive they are in that they always refer to everybody! In other words, I want to introduce a larger and ancient group of teachings that emphasize the need and value of turning within to their own innate wisdom that already exists in their miraculous awareness.

After speaking about these ancient teachings, I will present one more of G's gems to help us appreciate the immense practical value of these poorly understood spiritual teachings that have been ignored and forgotten. I have chosen to call them the elementary or essential esoteric teachings, the EETs.

4
The Essential Esoteric Teachings

When I first discovered G's teachings, as I'm describing, I had no clue that these teachings were his version of what Huxley called the "Perennial Philosophy" and others now refer to as the "Wisdom Traditions." So now in this update, I'm still going to speak about another of G's teachings, but first introduce the reader to what I'm calling the Essential Esoteric Teachings. G told one of his students that you could call his teaching esoteric Christianity. Esoteric means "inner," which refers to our inner awareness or simply our conscious awareness and its capacity and destiny for inner growth and development. This is a very different expression and understanding compared to the orthodox Christianity that many of us grew up with, and is still essentially the only form of Christianity that we are aware of, which asks and expects us to have the same understanding, actually the same "beliefs" at 88 as we had at 18! I have experienced for myself that esoteric Christianity has the same message as all the other Wisdom Traditions, as you will explicitly see in the next chapter on the Transcendent state and also in the last Book of this work. By looking at a few of the basic teachings underlying all of these traditions, verse G's particular rendition will educate and benefit the reader in a number of ways. The first and most important is to be open to the fact, yes fact, that all of our most ancient and beloved traditions—Hinduism, Taoism, Buddhism, the Sikhs and Sufis as well as the mystical traditions of many others, mainly Greek and Egyptian, have the same message, the same Truth.

Another is to show the relevance of these teachings in the present day to help one understand this crazy world that we're facing and to prepare the reader, seeker, to better follow and appreciate my unsuspecting preparation for, and my experience of the transcendent state of awareness, something our culture has mostly forgotten about. This has resulted in most of us being totally ignorant of these teachings and their ability to expand our understanding in a very practical way.

I've chosen to use the title—Essential Esoteric Teachings because, for me, it's more accurate and descriptive compared to the term spiritual teachings. The word essential is defined as: absolutely necessary and extremely important, and that is my goal, to only mention the most basic and most important teachings to keep this simple. Again, esoteric means inner and refers to teachings that help us understand our inner or psychological life, and its potential for increased understanding and maturity. I mentioned the term perennial because it is helpful in reminding us that these same Teachings always keep returning, and the term wisdom is certainly descriptive of them, but neither emphasizes "inner!" G's practices of not expressing negative emotions and self-observation accompanied by self-remembering are genuine esoteric teachings, because they are totally about getting in touch with what we are really like, our inner life, and its "predicament." Thus, all of these teachings are specifically designed to help us "know thyself," or as a Japanese sage put it: *"To get to know the consciousness we already have."*

Here is my short and simple list of these ancient teachings:

A. You should never take any religion, philosophy, etc., on blind faith. G and all of the great saints and sages of these Essential Esoteric Teachings—EETs—specifically say, don't believe me, just do the practices, and see for yourselves what your experience is.

B. What matters most is not what you believe, but how you behave! Yes, all of the sages of these traditions strongly promoted benevolent, well-meaning, and kindly behavior. Hopefully, it is evident that this is the exact opposite of how the majority of people, and so-called religious people too, function in this present age.

C. All of the esoteric teachings are about exposing and uncovering the falsity of our egos. In these ancient traditions, ego is defined as our individual sense of self, with all of its likes, dislikes, beliefs, cultural conditioning, etc. (Here, the sense of self that we experience when we are in our habitual thoughts and emotions is ego, but when our sense of self is in the witness, we have transcended this limited sense of ego, sense of self. This is a very different view and *experience* from how we define ego in the present, which contains no awareness of our capacity for inner growth.) These traditions tell us that there is a higher Reality that transcends our mind and senses, and that's one reason it is called the Transcendent. In other words, in order to experience the transcendent state, you have to go beyond your individual ego and your individual sense of self. This is when you experience your true nature and its divine origin. In Christianity, this is referred to as union with God. The word religion, I'm told, comes from the Latin word "religio," which means to bring together, as in ligating an artery. Thus, it refers to a union! In India, it is called Realization, Enlightenment, and Nirvana. In a generic sense, the Transcendent experience is described as the oneness with all things and as our true essence and Nature.

D. To aspire to this state, or towards this level of awareness, is known as the Path or the Way, and the spiritual journey. It's always about compassion, kindness, and forgiveness. Again, it's about behavior, not beliefs! These and similar qualities form the spirituality of the Wisdom Traditions—the EETs—they were, and still are, the way to be, the way to go forward and develop inner growth and transformation—as designed! Yes, we are designed for this. Karen Armstrong, one of my favorite modern authors, tells us that all of the sages, after they experienced the depths of the Transcendent, knowing that they could not hope to describe it, advised people to follow the Golden Rule and knew this would take them in the right direction, back to their deeper and essential awareness—their true Nature that is already within them. And she also tells us that none of these sages were interested in establishing an organized religion. Individuals had to have faith in their Teacher and make sincere efforts to follow the golden rule, staying focused within and seeing themselves in the other.

E. The final teaching that I'll mention here is that all of these EETs came from the Transcendent state and were experienced by the sages in the profound depths of this blessed State of awareness. I can vouch for this teaching, having experienced the truth of it before ever hearing about it. (This is one of the main reasons and the energy behind this book, as will be seen throughout the rest of this presentation.) Again, Esoteric Teachings have absolutely nothing to do with beliefs, or assumptions and conclusions, as Plato told us. My experience was that these Truths were revealed to me, as I'll share in the next chapter. That this can happen and has happened to many is one of the forgotten truths of human consciousness!

A Few Thoughts on the Golden Rule

Now I'm going to present a few thoughts on the Golden Rule as a way of emphasizing the importance of this primary esoteric teaching that most people know of and feel the truth of. Still, at the same time, don't actually pay attention to all that much, especially when emotions are running strong or deep conditioning is involved. For one to truly follow this Sage advice, you have to employ compassion, have to see the humanity—the Spirit—in the other, and to actually do this, you have to be consciously present. The struggle to become consciously present is about inner awareness and commitment to the Golden Rule, about uncovering culturally conditioned beliefs and emotionally conditioned reactions. Each time we *consciously participate* in following the Golden Rule—*consciously participate in life*—we are going beyond our ego and its pervasive cultural conditioning, transcending our limited and small sense of self. This conscious effort is also known as getting in touch with the *"intelligence of our heart,"* the one Spirit within all of us. Again, this is a universal way to uncover and expose your own individual ego and begin to move and mature beyond it. The Golden Rule is the primary esoteric teaching because we do know its truth, and it does give us the direct experience of "transcendence" when we actually consciously follow it! This is why all of the genuine sages advised it, knowing it would result in inner transformation if sincerely attempted. This acts as a purifying process by making us aware of our petty and immature egos. At the same time, our more expansive awareness is naturally compassionate. The deeper understanding of ourselves that continues to evolve is the Path, which is "the Way" to fulfilling our potential, as we are designed and destined to do.

Beauty and the Beast

These universal and ancient EETs have a number of expressions that people are familiar with, but have no idea of their inner meaning, which is the transcendent. Many of us are familiar with the story of Beauty and the Beast, but don't recognize it as a story containing the EETs! Many other fairy tales, allegories, and epic tales do the same. Still, I'm only going to give my take on Beauty and the Beast, again, as another expression of esoteric teachings.

This story tells us that an older woman asks the prince of the castle for food and shelter, and the haughty prince refuses her. Seeing that she is old and, in his mind, decrepit, he refuses to help her. Because he has no compassion, she puts the curse of becoming a beast upon him. The prince we are told is young and immature, and thus full of himself and not capable of genuine compassion, the most important quality of esoteric-spiritual teachings. When we don't possess this most human of qualities, we are stuck in our lower and "beastly" nature. The terms beast and dragon are a couple of names for the underdeveloped ego in these ancient stories. The story tells us that only true love, the genuine compassion of a pure heart, can break the spell—the illusion that we are our ego. Yes, to break free from our small and petty ego, we must connect with the intelligence of our loving heart. Again, this means that we must experience our sense of self, our authentic self, as one with our purest and naturally compassionate nature. How do we accomplish this, as our ego does a superb job of posing as our true self? A pure case of identity theft! We need a role model that is already established in this state of pure love, which is naturally compassionate and kind. Enter Belle, who embodies this perfectly and is willing to live with the beast and try to help him experience true love, even though this is almost entirely foreign to his beastly nature. Belle represents a being that has become established in her highest nature, her divine Nature, the goal of esoteric teachings. So, in time, her love and radiance weaken and finally break the spell, and the beast returns to his human form. Yes, to truly be "human," we must transcend our immature and underdeveloped ego, one of the primary teachings of all the authentic esoteric traditions. Lastly, he not only returned to his human form but his princely position, too! This position of royalty represents our highest nature, our divine Nature, our true Essence. Yes, this is another primary teaching of all of these Traditions, and this Teaching has nothing to do with belief or faith. It is based on direct experience when you are immersed deeply and profoundly in the Transcendent State, complements of Grace!

The Ugly Duckling is another even better fairy tale speaking about our true and highest Nature. The immature duckling is physically awkward and psychologically distraught, just like many teens in the ugly-duckling stage of growth. But when the duckling becomes fully mature, it is a beautiful and contented swan.

The swan in the ancient Vedic texts is a profound symbol of spiritual mastery and the nature of the soul. In other words, the symbol of the fully mature swan represents our divine Spirit.

This story is about us—about our full potential as human beings. And, we already have all we need to experience this destiny, this divine State, already built in. We just need the operating instructions! These are present in all the Wisdom traditions. You also need a guide, a teacher who has already tread this path to the One Self in all.

The Teaching About Knowledge and Being [23]

Now I'm going to return to the last of G's teachings that I'm sharing, and, like his other main teachings that I've shared, his teaching about "Knowledge and Being" was and still is a gem that has helped deepen my understanding of myself, others, and the craziness in our society and our world. This will demonstrate the practical value of these teachings, in addition to those I've mentioned and reiterate the need for sincere participation in authentic esoteric— inner practices. Before I can speak clearly about this teaching, and this is a teaching, a way to expand one's understanding—a contemplation—instead of a practice, I need to speak briefly about negative energy. G taught that instead of love making the world go around, so to speak, it was negative energy that does so! This view, actually an observation, was expressed about a hundred years ago, and as most of us know firsthand, negativity is many times worse today. And I would certainly hope that many can easily see that inflated egos, immature and highly culturally conditioned egos, and their lack of respect, let alone compassion, have a lot to do with this sorry situation. It may be harder to see how the intolerance and haughty self-righteousness of so many who believe in the superiority of their orthodox religion, which, for me, is more politics than religion because it's all about immature ego, not only contribute to this negativity but, in many respects drives it and fan its flames.

Now, let me remind us of how negative energy is expressed in a few other ways in many societies, but definitely and pervasively in our own:

It's the root cause of high anxiety and stress in so many, but especially in our young and in too many of our seniors as well.

How it underlies and results in anger, frustration, domestic violence, weaponized gossip, judgments, lies, distortions and on and on.

This results in feeling sorry for oneself, that nobody cares or appreciates me, which keeps us from growing and maturing.

Results in no respect or tolerance, no kindness or forgiveness (all aspects of esoteric teachings), and more and more, it's all about my grievances and my rights.

And way too often, it is the cause of trouble and the ruin of all manner of relationships and the joy and growth that should be gained from them.

These reminders are just to emphasize G's insight into how much trouble negative energy truly causes, and shortly we'll see how this is better understood and dealt with via G's wisdom expressed in his teaching about the relationship of "knowledge and being," which refer to two different sides or aspects of ourselves. Often referred to as our rational and spiritual sides.

This teaching says that for hundreds of years we have emphasized knowledge, taught and nurtured knowledge, but our being or essence—our inner sense of self—has not been assisted or nurtured in like amounts. Due to this fact, we are way out of balance, and this results in our obvious dis-ease and all manner of dysfunction. Yes, so much knowledge, so many facts and fictions of history, knowledge of the sciences and of ours and other cultures and knowledge of how to accomplish so many practical necessities. All good, all necessary to help us grow and prepare for adulthood and its responsibilities. But when our being, our essence—our inner sense of self—is ignored, is not addressed, and not nurtured in like amounts as compared to factual knowledge, then we end up with imbalance, frustration, and an inability to mature inwardly—emotionally—as we should. In this modern day, many of us feel that we are genuinely overrun with all manner of knowledge that's become way too much, more like pollution or over-eating, more confusing and unsettling versus inspiring and enlightening. And even though the word "being" is not a term we easily understand, many relate to and personally understand that their essence, their inner sense of self, is struggling and is in dire need of nourishment, deeper understanding, and practical advice that's readily felt! And really useful! It knows that it has been ignored and left on its own—to deal with all that keeps coming at us relentlessly! And many now know that more and more information is not going to help with our dis-ease or our need for more satisfying and practical understanding, so how can we escape this "predicament", this catch-22? We need to know more, but...

Since we definitely and easily relate to the knowledge side of G's teaching, which I've been emphasizing, let me speak about "being" to help us, to help anyone escape their many levels of dis-ease and begin to understand others' dis-ease better, too. And understand our present society that seems to be more angry and dysfunctional as the years go by. I'd say that we don't have a good feel for "being" because, as G said, it is not spoken of or hardly acknowledged in our culture. We can agree that the being of a saint is very different than that of a great sinner, or the being of a person that's completely honest is much greater than that of a con-man, or a scoundrel. A saint and an honest person are examples of knowledge and being, in proper balance and healthier development. But this knowledge still doesn't address the almost complete lack of acknowledgment and nourishment of our inner life in our education, be it secular or religious. This brings us back to G's and the essential esoteric teachings concerning self-knowledge and *exposing* our ego and all of its "stuff," especially its immaturity and heavy conditioning. Since we've looked at the "knowledge" part of G's Knowledge and Being via my sharing and G's teachings on self-study, I'm going to now focus on being. This requires some repeat of esoteric teaching about ego and inner growth, but since this is the crux of the problem, and has been the case for thousands of years, and is still the case, a little repeat and a more thorough look seems appropriate.

Being—Our Inner Most Sense of Self—Is Capable of Growth

Let's start with the reminder that ego in these ancient esoteric teachings refers to our individual sense of self, our I and **me,** which is our absolute most essential feeling of self, feeling of—Me. Thus, everyone has an ego, and this cannot be otherwise. Therefore, ego is not about bad or good, right or wrong; it's about knowing and acknowledging ourselves as we truly are so that we, our sense of self, our awareness of our deepest essence, can begin to grow and mature. In other words, our "being" is the same as our essence or ego, and it is capable of inner growth and transformation if properly educated and nurtured. Our culture doesn't actually talk much about ego or about our inner sense of self, and how so many are struggling with this, or how we can tackle this tragedy. Getting back in touch with esoteric teachings and their practices that show us how to initiate the inner growth that is natural to us can and will begin the change and transformation that's so obviously needed.

I hope that the reader can easily see how much inner growth and practical understanding I experienced simply by following G's teachings that I'd read in a book! My inner being, my sense of self, was transformed quickly and permanently in just a few days! This growth and the understanding that automatically accompanied it were beyond my wildest expectations because these expectations were limited to my previous experiences and my limited world view. Getting to experience the deeper awareness that I first called "the watcher" of my undisciplined mind was the game-changer, as we say today. Again, beginning to become familiar with this capacity of my and everyone's consciousness increased my understanding exponentially and in a way I'd never experienced or expected. It was able to expose my ego as I've stated, because the witness is separate from it—truly separate and objective, which is exactly what's needed to discover deeper understanding. Since our culture, and pretty much every culture, seems to have missed this most important capacity of a human being, of human awareness that we all already have, let me say a few more things concerning my ongoing experience of this miraculous level of awareness.

Again, it showed me that I completely and unknowingly "identified" with all of my thoughts and emotions without ever thinking a thing about it. They're my thoughts, so they must be me. In other words, it showed me and let me experience for myself that I was not these thoughts and emotions that I always assumed I was. This is why the ego has been dubbed the "impostor." When this is the case, which it is for essentially everyone on the planet, our ego, our sense of self, cannot expand and begin growing. The proof of this is in world history and our present levels of dysfunction that are obvious to many! Hearing words such as: arrogant, selfish, stubborn, or being very defensive and easily insulted, which we all know well, refer to an underdeveloped ego. We all know the feeling because, as the saying goes, "Been there, done that!" For me, the cause and nature of these familiar human emotions is immaturity. Without proper education, it is very difficult to mature as designed. Can you sense the truth of this and acknowledge how hard it is to change? The point is that it's difficult to move beyond this aspect of ego, of our sense and level of self, without getting in touch with the "pure vigilant awareness of the witness" that truly is an aspect of our essential self. Over the years, I have naturally referred to this forgotten capacity as the "pure vigilant awareness of the witness." This natural capacity of our awareness, which is built in and ready for use, is custom-made, you might say, for unmasking our very own ego and its pervasive cultural conditioning and its all too often immaturity!

Why do I and many others call this unknown aspect "pure"? It has also been called the "knower, the experiencer, and the noticer", but all call it pure because it is completely free of the thoughts and emotions associated with our habitual mind, and with our limited and heavily conditioned sense of self. This level of objectivity, of awareness, has to be experienced directly because it is unique and unfamiliar. It is not attached to any thoughts or emotions and therefore is free of all that comes with those feelings, conditioned or not. Again, you have to experience this ability, this capacity for yourself, to begin to understand what it is like to be free of attachment. The perspective from this level is freeing, purifying, and enlightening all at the same time. But this part of our inner sense of self, the pure vigilant awareness of the witness, also easily recognizes the thoughts and emotions of the Heart, the genuine intelligence of the Heart, a symbol of the spirit within. Yes, this deeper and purer awareness that is the witness is well connected to the Heart. I see it as interfaced with the spirit, and that's one reason that its insights and intuitions are so insightful, so different and amazing. And that is why it also easily recognizes the thoughts and emotions of a bleeding heart!

A Natural Feedback System

Before moving on, I want to share a couple of more gems about the pure vigilant awareness of the witness that needs to be included here. I spoke about how when we truly follow the Golden Rule. It helps us go beyond and thus transcend our small and conditioned ego, our conditioned sense of self. The pure witness does the same thing but even on a higher level because it does so without any hesitation, struggle, or conditioning. Again, being connected with the level of awareness that is the witness is the natural way to transcend our limiting, immature, and heavily conditioned awareness that keeps us from evolving as we can and should. While intently trying to hold onto this ever-so-precious "state" in 1975, I realized that it was acting like a built-in feedback systems that keep us in balance, in a state referred to as "homeostasis." These systems automatically regulate blood pressure, respiration, hormones, and many other things that we need to stay balanced and healthy. Our bodies do this work without us having to be consciously involved. But there is no such system to keep our minds and emotions in a steady state of balance and health. The pure vigilant awareness that is the witness can and does accomplish this by knowing what our minds are up to and by not being "identified" with its thoughts and associated emotions. Thus, there is a means, a way to know what our mind is up to, similar to our body knowing what our blood pressure is, but it is not automatic and unconscious. Instead, it requires and demands conscious effort. I have to assume we were designed this way so that we would, at some point, at some level of suffering, as the Buddha might say, seek higher understanding.

Let me share one more thing on the witness that has struck me recently while preparing a podcast. I had the insight that being in this pure vigilant "state" is tantamount to being in the "catbird" seat, the absolute best place to be! In this position, I am completely aware of and consciously in touch with both aspects of my awareness at the same time. And this is in real-time, the present moment, and is available during my routine, versus requiring a special time for practice. Having my sense of self in this juncture point of conscious awareness and my habitual awareness provides me with a vastly expanded awareness that is not attached or identified with the contents of my habitual awareness, which is exactly what is needed to have a clear perception and authentic, free choice. For me, this is what G meant when he asked his students to be "awake." I haven't seen another spiritual practice that can compare with this teaching about our ability to become consciously present in the moment. Being "Awake," being consciously present, is the ultimate meaning and experience of: Be Here Now. As another saying goes, *"This is the real thing—go for it."*

Another way to recognize and appreciate this teaching about our being, our sense of self, and its ability to grow and flourish is to remember and consciously realize that we are our Consciousness, our deepest understanding, and all that it contains or does not contain. Let me share a few esoteric teachings on this poorly appreciated but undeniably accurate insight that I was never asked to contemplate in my formal education. Maurice Nicoll, another of G's students, whom I will talk a lot about in the next chapter, said, *"We are our understanding,"*[24] and also made the point that our level of understanding cannot rise above our level of being, our inner sense of self, and all it contains. This has been and still is my experience exactly, but this has not been understood by our culture, which still believes that the way to higher understanding is more and more facts. Our level of being, our level of inner development, is not really considered, often, not even mentioned, even though this truth is evident everywhere you look. A modern version of this that I believe comes from the "motivation" industry is: You can't rise above your own self-image. Again, our self-image is based on our level of being, level of understanding, and sense of worth, and this has to evolve and mature before our overall understanding can expand and mature.

A similar esoteric teaching that comes from Yoga is: The world is as you see it. The evidence of these truths is so overwhelming. So obvious in the extreme politics of the left and right, and in the no compromise, no growth, or compassion of fundamentalists, worldwide. And it certainly applies to the millions embroiled in negative energy expressed and defined above, and to so many stuck in depression and other forms of mental despair. If any of these groups understood the above truths about their conscious awareness and their ability to radically change their level of awareness and understanding, their sense of self, all by themselves, via all that I've spoken about, they could have hope as well as life-altering experiences and the joy that accompanies them. Life is a mystery, and esoteric teachings appreciate this fact and the fact that we truly are our awareness and that this Consciousness is meant to and capable of miraculous expansion and transformation. This is why the Sages focus on our built-in ability for inner growth and transformation and not on beliefs that feed our immature egos and the self-righteousness that such egos are prone to!

A Joyous Awakening

Now that we have looked at this concept of "knowledge and being" via esoteric teachings, hopefully, it is easy to see why getting to know the Consciousness that you already have is your easiest path to finally understanding yourself, the world you live in, and some of the teachings that you've heard but never really understood. It can provide answers to many of our why, why, and whys. Hopefully, it is also clear that anyone can begin to evolve and mature as designed. You don't have to be really smart or rich. You just have to be open-minded and willing to participate as instructed. You just have to do the "work," as G expressed it. Again, remember that your own Consciousness is a miraculous gift and that it already contains everything that you need! Nothing to figure out; just do the best you can every day, and you will see results that you easily recognize—just like I did.

A Few More Esoteric Teachings

Let us now look at a few more esoteric teachings to finish this brief overview. Hopefully, a couple will be more familiar and will remind us of their importance and assistance in living a more conscious, more meaningful, and thus happier life. The command to "Arise and Awake" is one of the oldest and most repeated teachings, but now has little meaning beyond petty politics. Arise means to get up and do something, get involved, don't just stay put! Awake is what I have been talking about in various ways. Another teaching that is a part of many traditions is: Use Death as your Advisor; live your life as if you only have a short time to live, because such will keep you focused on the most important things, things of the Heart. Another teaching that is complementary is: Your **understanding** is the only thing that you get to take with you when you depart your body. Think about it!

All this being the case, how can you not make the effort to participate in and take advantage of this greatest of challenges and opportunities? If there is even the slightest remnant of the desire "to know" a deeper and more satisfying truth, don't let your habitual thoughts keep you from following your heart, your inner spirit's desire to know and experience a higher truth. Again, arise and awake and don't pass up this most precious of opportunities.

Another teaching that many people have heard of but don't know what to think of is: Reincarnation! All I'll say here is that it is difficult for most folks to look honestly at themselves, so they don't make much inner progress in a lifetime. Thus, they need many more chances for inner growth. They need more lifetimes to evolve. Another of these teachings is that all souls will eventually merge back into the divine Spirit they came from and truly are. This view is consistent with

67

an All-loving and All-merciful God, whereas without reincarnation, such is NOT the case.

An esoteric teaching that some are familiar with but have little to no understanding of is: Leave self behind in order to find your true self. Hopefully, you now have a much better appreciation of this esoteric truth and even know how to begin following its message.

I'll end this section by stating the primary teaching of all the esoteric traditions, which comes from and is based on direct experience: Everyone's essence, our true Nature, is Divine. This reiterates one of the primary teachings that tells us that there is a higher Reality that transcends our normal mind and senses, transcends all and every concept and is therefore called the Transcendent.

As individuals, we can't expect to change society, but with proper knowledge and effort, we can change the level of our being, the experience and understanding of our deepest sense of self. You just have to keep at it, like a child learning to walk, nothing to fret or worry about, no negatives, just detached practice, just get up and keep trying. If you do, you will improve, you will expand your awareness. And remember that you are the only one who can do it, and it will always take place in the privacy of your awareness. It is necessary that we uncover our ego, the immature ego that we see in others and how they would be better off without it. Again, the very best way to truly see our ego is via the witness because it happens in real time, at the moment our ego is playing one of its many roles! Knowledge of the witness state and its connection with the intelligence that is innate within us all has been abandoned and lost for eons, but not anymore. As the saying goes, "It's there for the taking." Again, don't let your lazy and fearful mind talk you out of taking up the ancient call to Know Thyself. It's the opportunity of your lifetime and your birthright as well!

Finally, we have reached the end of this section on esoteric teachings and also the end of Book I, and as the saying goes, *"I've saved the best for last."* The last esoteric teaching I'll mention for now is "Rebirth"! Many, including myself as a youth, heard this teaching and had no clue what it was about. Based on my own expanded awareness of my inner experiences, I'm going to tell you what rebirth means to me, and we'll see in the following chapters that this is consistent with the ancient esoteric teachings.

As I've expressed in detail, once I became well connected with the pure vigilant awareness of the witness, I was positive that this awareness was the real me, not the thoughts of my habitual and conditioned "mind." I knew that I had left my personal sense of self behind and acquired a more expansive and freer sense of self. In a way, I had a new identity; according to esoteric literature, I had experienced a rebirth! This was tremendously emancipating, because I was not identified with all of my old thoughts and emotions in this new experience of myself. Even though I did not see it this way at the very beginning of this adventure, this new sense of self and all-encompassing new understanding is most definitely a rebirth. The only way to truly understand this is to experience it for yourself. After I experienced the profound depths of the Transcendent State, I and all who have experienced this blessed State automatically and effortlessly acquired a new Identity. This is the Rebirth that is spoken of in the Gospels, the rebirth that is required to enter the Kingdom of Heaven, the place where God lives! I saved this for last because it only happens in the Transcendent State, the State that is the goal of all the esoteric teachings. Now, you are ready to hear about my experience of that level of supreme awareness. I asked you at the end of the Preface if you were ready. If you have gotten this far, you are now ready.

Before we turn the page, I must remind you that all of the great ones throughout history who have had profound experiences of the Transcendent have unequivocally agreed that this divine Experience cannot be described! And I agree completely. So, think of these next chapters concerning the Transcendent, not as a description of it, but my story of the things that took place while it was happening. Also, think of it as my interpretation of what I was experiencing. Such is quite different from a perfect description. It's a little, and I want to emphasize little, like being deeply in love and trying to describe what that is like to one who has never even remotely experienced that feeling. To know it, you have to experience it for yourself. There is no other way. Again, my writing is to share my experiences and insights to encourage others to seek this miraculous State of the Transcendent for themselves. It's a rare occurrence, but my own experience of the Transcendent shows that it is possible, and the insights and intuitions that come as you journey towards higher levels of awareness are too precious to be passed up. As my story demonstrates, just stay connected with the pure vigilant awareness of your own consciousness, and it will do all that's necessary; there is nothing to figure out. As the Buddha is quoted as saying: "Come see"—What's there to lose?

BOOK II

" Yoga is the stilling of the modifications of
the mind
Then the Self is revealed."

Patanjali Maharishi

5
The Transcendent State

On the afternoon of June 20, while sitting on the beach intently looking at the majestic mountains and intently practicing "self-remembering," as I had been for the previous eight days, I naturally and ever so gently entered into the transcendent state of consciousness. This was totally unexpected as I didn't know that this was a possibility. I literally had no information or images of it at all. My "mind," as I was calling it, had become totally quiet. Essentially all of my questions had been answered beyond my wildest hopes, and I was just thoroughly enjoying the peace, stillness, quiet and profound contentment of being immersed in the silence and crystal-clear awareness of the witness. I had never been happier or more pleased, more thankful, or more excited to be alive. I had no desires, no needs, no concerns whatsoever and was just totally satisfied to be able to be so "awake" and so enjoying myself and the beautiful surroundings. Life was truly perfect, much more than I could have ever hoped for. It felt like I could have remained in this state of complete satisfaction and contentment forever. It was in this state of wanting for nothing that I received everything!

With my awareness wonderfully immersed in the witness, the deeper and pure awareness that I had naturally come to know as the real me, yes, the conscious awareness that had already revealed so much, so much intelligence and trustworthiness—was now ever so gently and smoothly beginning to unveil an unimaginably vaster, more expansive, and completely unknown level of, or manifestation of awareness. It could also be described as an infusion, a permeation or in-flowing into my presence; it's just so hard to describe something so ethereal. But being so immersed and so consciously present in the witness, I was not the least bit concerned, disturbed, or unsettled by its appearance. It could also be described as slowly bubbling up into my awareness, as it was obvious that it was coming from inside, not outside! Again, it was no different than my witnessing-awareness, just an expansion of it that was beyond previous experience.

Now this wondrous and exquisite level of self-remembering was making it clear that something exceedingly subtle, but at the same time obviously very powerful and completely new, completely different from anything I'd ever known, was beginning to make itself known. But again, I was not the least bit stressed by its appearance, as it was so peaceful, gentle, pure, and flowed in like a divine fragrance. It was in this harmonious and, without doubt, curious and excited state that this unknown part of myself began exposing me to an aspect of myself that was unimaginably and undeniably sacred and divine. Even at the very earliest moments of this unexpected Presence (capitals for divinity), it was blatantly obvious that this awareness was permeated with never-experienced feelings of recognition of profound sacredness and divinity!

Now, the pure vigilant awareness of the witness, that I knew to be not only myself but everyone's truer self, instead of watching my "mind," was now calmly watching this unimaginably blessed and pure Energy reveal itself. Yes, in its barely perceivable appearance It was without question sacred and Divine. Can't say how I knew that, just did, actually. I felt this in every fiber of my being; no thoughts were present—just vibrant awareness. Or maybe it's more accurate to say that the pure awareness of the witness "knew" it in every fiber of its being!

As I've said, through the pure perception of the witness, I was familiar with the awesome intelligence and wisdom of the silent inner conscious awareness, but could never have imagined It or expected It to possess such an overwhelming expression—quality of Divinity. I felt that this emerging intelligence, spirit—not sure what to call It—had to be connected with, and an expression of the deepest aspects of Consciousness Itself. So now my vigilance and focus were totally trained on this blessed emergence. Instantly, I knew that, like the rest of my "awakening," all I had to do was watch and be present and let IT show me and teach me what It wanted. Again, I cannot stress enough the inconceivable expansion that my awareness was feeling, no limits, no boundaries and no previous experience or knowledge of any kind with this level of Awareness. But this new magnificent and truly miraculous energy that was revealing Itself ever so gently was so completely fused in, soaked in, and permeated with sacredness and divinity that I could only watch in awe and with a level of respect that I had never felt before. Years later, I read that Ralph W. Emerson described this Presence as making one want to bend a knee; for me, it was similar but included the feeling and need to bow and pranam!

I want to reiterate that my own state as the witness experienced no change in its own awareness, but I was most definitely wonder-struck and in awe of this holy awareness unveiling itself; this could not possibly be missed or ignored! All this was taking place without words, just knowledge and awareness arising, being revealed to me in a manner that was totally new to me. This has been referred to as direct knowledge, which I'll look at shortly. I also want to reiterate that there was no question that this unheard-of level of consciousness was still an expression or manifestation of the same pure silent awareness that I had come to know through my practice of self-remembering, but now that awareness included a power and feeling of universality and authority beyond description! So just as I knew with certainty that the witness and its awesome intelligence was my true essence, now I was being shown, somehow, that my essence is intertwined with universal sacredness and Divinity!

I want to be very clear that this entirely new and wondrous "State" was not in any way connected to, or a result of, any previous insights or anything to do with Gurdjieff's teachings already discussed. It transcended every single thought and concept that I had ever been exposed to or imagined. This is one of the main reasons it is known as the Transcendent! I would also like to state that this happened with my eyes wide open, while enjoying the gorgeous scenery, and this change in my inner state was wholly inner and did not involve any change or alteration in vision or bodily awareness. In other words, the entire change—shift—took place within my awareness and understanding.

Acknowledging the unfamiliarity and difficulty of expression concerning the transcendent state, I'm going to draw from some of the sources I've come across in the years since my awakening in order to help me describe this state that is beyond description! This will give me the opportunity to share the views and experiences of Masters who speak eloquently and accurately, based on my own experience, about the transcendent state and the spiritual journey. Without the help of beings such as them, I wouldn't be able to speak of my experiences with this rarely experienced aspect of human consciousness with as much clarity.

A Couple of Ununderstood Capacities

There were a couple of very distinct qualities or characteristics that are intimately associated with this "State." The difficulty in describing this level of consciousness, combined with the fact that most are unaware of it, tells me that some more information is needed to provide background education and a starting point. The *first* of these refers to the necessity of a quiet or still mind to be in a position to "receive." This is almost completely unknown in our modern culture. The *second* is about the nature of the knowledge that is received from pure Spirit, which is often referred to as direct knowledge for reasons we'll look at shortly, which is another unknown truth in modern times. But first, let me speak about the need for a quiet mind that is spoken of by essentially all of the esoteric traditions.

"Be Still and Know That I Am God" Psalm 46 vs 10

This Psalm is one of the best known but poorly understood statements speaking about this need for a still mind, and the result as well! As the introduction to Book II, I quoted the ancient sage Patanjali's Yoga sutra which again tells us that if we attain a still mind, the Self, the Supreme Spirit, will reveal itself to you. As we will see, Patanjali's revelation is the same Knowledge and Experience that the Psalm speaks of!

The Transcendent State

When I first read Patanjali's sutra years after my awakening to the Transcendent, I immediately knew that this sutra, this experiential truth, described my experience perfectly. As indicated above, it was easy to see that a busy mind would not be able to notice such subtle Presence, and if one still takes every thought and emotion as their self, they are just not ready to receive, not ready to know. Very early on, as this new level of awareness was arising and unfolding, I thought of G's statement that the most important thing was to remember yourself and realized that he knew that being consciously present in the silent witness would put one in a position to be able to receive this level of revelation—this level of Recognition!

G said that his way was the way of the sly man, the way to what he called Objective Consciousness, what others call Realization, Recognition, or union with God. What I think he meant by *the way of the sly man* was that by learning to become consciously present, as I've described, by putting your focus and effort into aligning with the witness, versus trying to stop thoughts, you automatically quit "identifying" with them. As I experienced for myself, my "identity" naturally shifted to the more expansive and conscious awareness of the witness, making it easy not to worry about thoughts and not to have my sense of self in them as I always had. This naturally allowed my mind to be still without trying to suppress it, which is immensely difficult. G's point was that monks, nuns, and meditating yogis tried for years to still their minds to have an experience or glimpse of God, of Union, and very few succeeded over the centuries! Based on my reading and experience, I have to agree with G's brilliant observation. Another aspect of this, of self-remembering that needs to be acknowledged, is that the way of the monk and yogi necessitates leaving the normal world, which isn't realistic for most, but even more importantly, self-remembering is meant to be practiced during one's normal daily routine in real time, at the moment life is happening! This is how you get to truly "see" what I have described in detail, that you are not your thoughts! You are their observer! This is how natural inner growth and transformation begin. Suppressing your thoughts, feeling guilt and frustration with not being able to do so, for decades, is the slow way to tread the path. Thus, the sly man or woman is the clever one who can reach their goal faster, with greater ease and accumulate a much higher level of understanding on different levels, all at the same time. G also claimed that the esoteric meaning of the cross referred to this faster and more natural way to Objective Consciousness. The vertical line of the cross referred to this sly way of shifting your sense of self to the witness as a path, and the horizontal line represented the way of the monk and yogi, the long and arduous way to the goal. I have never seen anyone else say anything like this; it matches and explains my experience very well.

A Joyous Awakening

It's important to mention that years later, I was introduced to a little-known esoteric teaching referred to as Kashmir Shaivism that was popular in the nine and tenth centuries in northern India. Most of the sages of this tradition were regular folks with family and corresponding responsibilities, and as far as I know, their teachings were open to all. Like so many others, they too taught that the stopping of thought was the best means and fastest way of experiencing the Transcendent. But they also stressed, for those who were ready, that when a seeker keeps his mind in universal consciousness, the witness, via intention and effort, he becomes used to regarding the witness as his real self. The Kashmir sage continues by saying that one who follows this practice will, in a short time, attain absorption in the Self! The Transcendent. Again, my experience exactly! This sutra, this teaching comes from the book titled: *The Splendor of Recognition,* again, this title describes my experience exactly!

I would like to emphasize **"short time"** because with the way of the monk and yogi, it can take decades, and odds are that there is no absorption into the Transcendent period. Such a **short time** is essentially unheard of, and most likely not believed by many who have tread the Path for years. The other thing I want to point out is the expression "universal consciousness" representing the witness. As I experienced, the deeper sense of self that is always consciously present, which I'm calling the witness, is the same for all. Everyone already has it as part of normal consciousness, and therefore it's universal and normal! Thus, this practice of the sly man is not G's alone, as it was being openly taught and practiced over a thousand years before G was born. A seeker should know that having an experience of the Transcendent is not impossible. It is available to one who is willing to work and sincerely wants *to know.* It's time for seekers throughout the world to know that meaningful and practical transformation is readily available through self-remembering—their own awareness. How else are we going to get people who are truly desirous of deeper understanding—to participate in inner growth and a maturing of the potential they already have— built in?

The Forgotten Capacity—Direct Knowledge

Now to another unfamiliar topic before returning to 1975 and my journey of entering deeper into the Transcendent. This has to do with how one receives and experiences what is known as "direct knowledge" and has also been referred to as unmediated knowledge, which simply means that it does not come through the senses or the mind, like every single bit of other knowledge we have! Yes, knowledge that our culture never speaks of because it has no understanding or awareness of it. That's why a little more preparation is appropriate.

The Transcendent State

In the sacred esoteric scriptures of India, this knowledge is referred to as knowledge of the Self, Knowledge that comes directly from the Supreme Spirit Itself and cannot be obtained in any other way. In other words, one has to receive It or have It revealed while in the Transcendent State—this is my experience and understanding. With this as an intro, I'm now going to make a number of statements that represent my first encounter with this miraculous "Knowledge" and provide some context as well.

As I've said, the energy or essence accompanying this awareness, even before it solidifies into knowledge, is one of an unknown Authority and Presence. Similarly, everything about this Intelligence that was revealing Itself told me that this has to be Grace, as It was beyond anything I'd known. Instantly, I knew that Grace was real! Again, I "knew" this because, as the definition says, the Transcendent is totally beyond the normal mind and senses. This Knowledge arose, was freely given, without any desire, deliberation, or asking; it was simply arising in my awareness. The most unique thing about this Knowledge, for me, was that the Knowledge and its understanding were one thing—one entity. In other words, this Knowledge contained its own understanding, like two sides of a coin that can't be separated.

Essentially, all of the knowledge we encounter and accumulate requires a *learning curve*, as the expression goes. Learning to walk is an accumulation of knowledge and experience, and finally results in the understanding of how to walk. Learning chemistry and dentistry took a lot of contemplation of the knowledge presented before true understanding arose! Another way I experienced this direct knowledge was that it was knowledge and its understanding fused into an inseparable whole because it is one Intelligence— one Divine Consciousness!

Another thing about direct Knowledge is that It becomes part of yourself, part of your identity, your deepest sense of self. Very similar to the feeling that the witness was my deeper self, but now being aligned with this direct Knowledge of the Self, that identity was now saturated with Divinity Itself!

This revelation of the Divine Spirit, for the one who receives it, cannot be questioned, and you *know* that it is absolutely a Revelation coming directly from the Divine. This revelation has nothing to do with the future. It's all about the present, and it's all about communion and the "experience" of Union with the one SPIRIT in all. As we'll see in Book III, St. John of the Cross, a Spanish mystic, tells us that when in Union with God, our own understanding becomes one with the Divine. The only other American I know who has written about a similar "Awakening to the Transcendent," Franklin Merrell-Wolff, expressed what I'm calling direct Knowledge as "Knowledge through Identity," an awareness of

A Joyous Awakening

Divine Spirit by being One with it. He says, *"God is either Known directly through Identity or not known at all."*[1] For me, this is the same as saying that you can only know God—experience your Self—by His Grace alone.

Franklin Merril-Wolff is one of the very few scientifically educated Americans who has written extensively of his own experience of the Transcendent, which took place in the 1930's, in his book *Pathways Through to Space.* His sharing of his experiences and understanding of *Knowledge in Identity* echoes St. John's description of Union with the Divine. In a modern image, it is like two smartphones exchanging information just by coming together; no effort required; it happens automatically.

Now I'm going to let Rumi, probably the most famous and prolific of the mystical poets, tell us about his experience of the Transcendent and Its direct Knowledge, the Knowledge through Identity—through Union.

"It's an immediate intuitive apprehension of Truth—that leaves no room for interpretation."

To round out this section, I will now offer some related statements and knowledge that will help one develop a little better feel for this never talked about Knowledge and, also, provide some needed context. This direct Knowledge of the Self is the genuine "rebirth" that's necessary to enter the "Kingdom of Heaven", the new Identity. Likewise, it is the authentic Baptism of Spirit, the initiation that reveals your true Nature. Another is the Yogic teaching: "There is no purifier equal to Knowledge of the Self." Because it rids you of all the old "identifications" with your individual and personal history, posing as your true self. For me, it's also the highest meaning of: *"Leave yourself behind in order to find your true Self."* When you leave this old self behind, you leave behind all the worries and confusion that go with that level of misunderstanding. Your new identity no longer identifies with that limited knowledge. Direct Knowledge is neither conceptual nor perceptual; again, it's beyond the mind and senses, and has nothing to do with accumulations of knowledge. This is the meaning of the esoteric teaching: The mind and senses cannot know the Self!

Lastly, direct Knowledge of the Self allows you to see, to be consciously aware, of the same Self in others, and this, for me, is the source of genuine compassion, a compassion of Recognition, not pity or guilt.

Before returning to the continuation of my account of the *"Self-Revealing Itself,"* I want to reiterate that this level of knowledge and experience is totally removed from our everyday experience of knowledge and wakefulness. In other words, the Truths revealed are essentially different facets of divine Spirit, meaning they are all different aspects of One truth. In order to speak of them, I have to speak of them in an order, one at a time and try to pass on this experience that is indescribable! I think it will be helpful to think of the information being revealed as being similar to a picture slowly coming into focus. First, you see different parts of the picture, roughly outlined, we'll say, that seem to be different, but after the whole picture comes into focus, these seemingly different parts are necessary aspects of the whole picture. Also, remember that analogies and metaphors are not meant to be perfectly accurate, just helpers to understand something as yet unknown.

The Self Continues to Reveal Itself

Let me first bring you back to the scene. I am sitting on the beach in mid-afternoon, pretty much at the summer solstice. Thus, the sun is high above, and the mountains still look like they are floating high in the sky. I'm in absolute awe of what's being revealed to me, and I'm securely centered in the witness and know that all I have to do is stay consciously present and allow It to reveal what It chooses, just as It has done these past many days.

To start, I have to remind everyone of the distinct Presence of Divinity and Grace, something that I was never sure was real. One of the initial revelations that accompanied this unimaginably new awareness was the perfectly clear knowing and *direct experience* that I was not different from the Self, from divine Spirit. To say the least, this direct Knowledge was shocking to what I'd always been taught, but, as I've said, this Knowledge and its understanding come as one unit and cannot be questioned, as this level of Consciousness is beyond the relativity and duality of our everyday awareness. As Rumi put it, *"There is no room for interpretation!"* The second "given," second truth, entwined with the first one, is, This is the case for everyone; as everyone's true Nature is Divine,"—it was not particular to me. Again, it is true for all and everyone—no exceptions!

Another similar but slightly different version of this Knowledge of the Self-revealed to me that this Self, the One and only Spirit, had always been there, always been within me and within everyone. Due to our busy and unrelenting minds, we are just not able to connect with It. (I find it interesting that the most common and descriptive words used to inform us about the undiscovered Self are "revealed", "remembered", "recognition", and "realization"—all begin with R. Maybe it's because the Self is what we "Are!") From this new State of Awareness, it was easy to see why a mind full of thoughts and emotions could never be subtle, still, or vigilant enough for the Self to reveal Itself! Another way of understanding this is remembering that this level of consciousness is light-years beyond our normal awareness and its propensity for thinking, and our propensity for identifying with all of our thinking. The EETs tell us that the Self is the source and essence of our mind and intellect, and this is why and how it surpasses these so profoundly. And Ken Wilber correctly reminds us that transcending the normal intellect does not mean discarding it, transcending means going beyond but including—not abandoning! This has always been my own experience as well.

Ultimate Truth Only Comes from Within

The next aspect of the Self that was unveiled let me know that the Self and Its revelations were—ARE—the highest Truth and Reality, period! Without being able to say how, there was no doubt that this level of expanded Awareness, or should I say the subtlest level, was—IS—the pinnacle of Knowledge and Understanding. There is nothing higher, which was another totally unexpected "given." Along with this direct Knowing was the subtle but strong intuition that the Self, this mystical and limitless divine Consciousness contains all knowledge and understanding. I had inklings of this during a few of my deeper connections with the witness, but not at this level of profundity. I also remembered that this is essentially what we were taught, as young Catholics, about the Absolute Being, but never told that we could come to know some aspect of this Truth for ourselves. In my initial seeking, I wanted truth and understanding that would help me make better sense of myself and this crazy world. In all the years I'd sought deeper understanding, what I hoped for was a rationally based perspective on life and a practical means for implementing it. I hoped that I would get exactly what I had been getting these last eight days, and even this was way more than I ever expected. I never expected, never imagined anything like my experience of the Self, never dreamed that this level of Truth could be Known, again, without Grace, it's impossible. When I say known, I'm referring to what was revealed as I'm describing, *not known in its entirety*, only what is given!

I want to remind the reader that these Truths were revealed over about four hours, meaning it was slow and subtle, not one right after another. Therefore, most of this time was spent in pure vigilant silence as I was moving around the beach, in typical beach fashion, as well as sitting cross-legged in the sand. I also want to remind you of what I've said about communion, Union, and Knowledge in Identity to provide a way to begin to relate to the fact that during this entire period the Self, the One—Spirit in all, was consciously Present, not as another, as separate but as my underlying Identity, just pleasantly noticeable, but absolutely there! I reiterate this, along with the realization that Self Knowledge is the Ultimate and, at the same time, the perfect cleanser and purifier of what's called Maya, the illusion that we are the body and our habitual mind and all of its "stuff."

At this highest level of awareness and Identity, this lower identification is wholly removed, like waking from a dream; once you are awake, you can no longer identify with the dreamer and easily and instantly identify with your waking self. As I've said, after practicing self-remembering for just a few days—all day long! My identity shifted to the witness, the watcher. However, this identity still included the body and much of my personal history. This new level of Identity was on such a different scale of freedom, perception, and inner Authority, and it had a pervasive "Universal" aspect or quality to it. To say that this State of Knowledge in Identity is way beyond the mind, is astonishing, astounding, uprooting or mind-boggling—it still does not even give an inkling of what it is like to experience this blessed state.

The tales of the prince and princess who have forgotten their true identities and think that they are commoners flashed into my awareness. I "knew" that this was a story about all of us forgetting our royal Identity but one day regaining the Truth of our high State. Another insight that arrived with the above was the high place allotted to "man" in the ancient teachings, being above the angels. And being made in the image and likeness of God, yes, and even more so!

Sometime after all of the above, the Self allowed me to feel the supreme Truth of I AM THAT—one of the most profound statements in the ancient sacred teachings of India and one that I was totally unfamiliar with. But once again, understanding was interwoven in this direct Knowledge and provided me with a deeper and fuller realization of Identity with the Self. In Its initial revelation, this divinely intelligent Self gently informed me that I was not different from It—not to overwhelm me, who knew nothing of this possibility or built-in capacity. And now that my awareness has expanded, It is able to show me a higher level of Identity than—not different. Now I knew with certainty that my deepest sense of self, my purest "Essence" was indeed a child of God, actually a manifestation of the divine Spirit! Yes, and this being the case, I, as divine Spirit, am immortal! Again, this Knowledge and Understanding permeated every aspect and fiber of my being, having nothing to do with conclusions or beliefs, another profound "given" that was beyond doubt. Immediately after absorbing the full force of this unexpected "good news," I remembered waking up in the dead of sleep a number of times last summer while working on the train and being absolutely aware of the fact that one day I would die. I would no longer exist! I somehow couldn't believe this, as life seemed so natural that it just didn't seem possible that I would cease to exist. It also seemed weird and unexplained that I would continue waking out of deep sleep with this evident knowledge of certain death being so real and mystifying, when I never ever thought of it otherwise. Now I wondered if this was connected with this Spirit that was revealing Itself to me? Almost a half-century later, I know it was!

Another offshoot, or better yet, interwoven Truth and Knowledge of the Self, is that it is the Source and Essence of myself and all sentient beings, with no exceptions. And, the entire universe and everything in it as well! Again, this understanding has nothing to do with conclusions or beliefs. In the days following these Revelations, it was easy to see the Self as the underlying consciousness in human beings, in nature, and in friendly dogs, too!

Indescribable and Undefinable Bliss

A completely different aspect and experience of my Self was the joy and the never-experienced Bliss that went with and was a part of this Knowledge. The Bliss, again, a capital letter to represent Divinity that accompanied this State of the Transcendent, was enormous but again not describable. Another thing about it was that it was obvious that it was strictly coming from inside of myself, and had nothing to do with my ego, thinking that I'm special or anything to do with my senses, which I knew had previously been the source of my greatest joys and bliss. It would be accurate to say that before my Self revealed itself, I was in bliss, as I said, I was perfectly content, satisfied and as happy as I'd ever been or could have imagined I ever could be. But this experience of Bliss of the Self is at a level so far beyond anything previously experienced that we should have a different word for it. As with the direct Knowledge I've been speaking of, this Bliss was felt in every part of my being, not just my body!

Baba Muktananda, my first living Master, expressed the divine joy associated with this State and the Knowledge that emanates from it very accurately:

"True knowledge is not dry; it releases bliss.
If it does not release bliss, it is not knowledge" [2]

Yes, the highest Knowledge—direct Knowledge—only comes from our divine Nature when It chooses to reveal Itself, and this inner Knowledge is permeated with Bliss. I remember, while feeling the intensity of this unknown "ecstasy," how interesting it was that nothing was happening, meaning that all former intense joy was a result of something outer, food, sex, a new car, or an unexpected compliment. Now it was simply bursting from within for no apparent reason. I was so overwhelmed by all that was happening, so conditioned that happiness came from outside, from things, from people, that it just struck me as odd that this bliss wasn't the result of something exterior. Some in our Western culture are familiar with the ecstasy of St. Theresa of Avila, but other than that, we have almost no awareness of this capacity of human consciousness. But the time has come to hear about it, think about it, and, more importantly, know how to access it.

Swami Muktananda, better known as Baba, was the first living master, first Guru and meditation teacher that I met almost six years after my awakening. He spoke at length about the witness and taught his students that to come to know the witness is true meditation. (More on Baba in Book III) He said over and over that this was the way to access the Self. He told seekers to turn within and see who watches your thoughts from the inside. If you continue doing this, you will come to know the Self. Until I met Baba, I never thought of self-remembering as meditation. I thought that was something people did while sitting with closed eyes. I could not believe that sitting with my eyes closed could be anywhere near as beneficial and practical as practicing self-remembering in the real world, so I had never bothered with it. But hearing him speak of the witness, I knew immediately that it was the same witness that I had discovered with the help of G and his student, P.D. Ouspensky. It was typical of G to make up his own terminology, especially for something as old as meditation, so his students would begin the practice without any particular thoughts or expectations. Baba knew from direct experience and extensive research that one who is able to remain aware of the witness will come to know their true Nature! It is my firm belief that Gurdjieff was very well aware of this truth, and that's why he was adamant about the intense practice of self-remembering, the "state" of being consciously present. The state of knowing what your habitual mind is up to is, indeed, meditation, one of the oldest, most effective, and most enjoyable forms of meditation. As I'm showing, it is not dull, frustrating, or boring!

The Effortless Witness

In this new level of Awareness, as this magical afternoon continued to unfold, I realized that I didn't have to make any effort to stay connected to the witness. It seemed that the Self is the witness, and when I am in the state of the Self, there is no way for me not to be the witness—pure awareness itself. Previously, I'd been struggling to stay anchored in the witness, but this wasn't the case now. You don't have to try and hold onto what you are: pure Awareness, pure and divine Consciousness—your Self!

But at the same time, to give a more complete and honest account, I must say that even being in this State, as just described, my old habitual mind was still there and now a bit active. It certainly wasn't as if it was entirely absent or completely shut down. In fact, almost from the beginning of finding myself in this totally unexpected State, I heard my mind raising questions about what was happening, how this had come about, and how long it would last. This unfolding "experience" certainly was "mind-boggling," but since I no longer identified with this level of constricted and habitual awareness, I, as the Witness, was not disturbed by its inevitable curiosity. I saw it as a natural reaction, something that I should expect from this unenlightened part of myself, what I now thought of as the *mind*. But again, it wasn't surprising at all to me that my *mind* was a little unsettled, because it had never heard of or in any way imagined this immensely advanced and totally sacred level of awareness. But the "I" of this newly expansive and universal Witness was not the least bit concerned about this lower-level activity. It knew that there was no danger, no way that I would or could identify with that level of awareness, especially now. There was just no way that I could take or mistake the old habitual mindset for my real self. I knew, for sure, that all that I had to do was stay "awake," as G said, and everything would unfold as needed and intended! There was nothing to figure out. Figuring—thinking, so to speak, pulled a person back into being identified with this more constricted level of thought and awareness. Again, the witness has no attachment to thoughts and emotions—it's so much more expansive, alert, and emancipated!

Another thing that arose on this lovely and sacred afternoon was the memory of my long-standing and sincere prayer to Jesus for a deeper understanding of this human condition. It was in this connection with the Divine, as I've been attempting to describe, that I felt sure that this blessed "experience" was His response—Christ's answer to this sincerest of desires. I was also sure that this miraculous state of my Self is what He was referring to when telling us that: the Kingdom of Heaven is within us! For me, that understanding was another *given*.

The Pure I AM

After I had been in this divine state for a number of hours and daylight was waning, another precious insight—another pearl of Divine wisdom was revealed. Another unexpected gift, another manifestation of direct Knowledge that came compliments of the Self, was that this pure Self, pure Witness—pure I that was both of these—was none other than the pure I Jesus spoke of—and spoke with—when saying: *"I am the way, the truth, and the life. No one comes to the Father except through me."* John 14:6. In other words, the I that was uttering this Truth was the pure I—the One Self—that exists within us all. Not only is this Divine "I" the highest Truth, but It is also the way to our recognition and experience of our immortal and divine Nature—our true Self. It is this pure I—pure Self within that allows a person to "know"—to experience directly that they are truly a child of God. Again, this is Knowledge in Identity. This insight—this miraculous experience of direct Knowledge, was so pure and powerful that I knew it was the Truth, and I marveled at the blessedness of this State that I was experiencing.

Knowing that what I've just said could be disturbing, to say the least, to many who have not been exposed to genuine spiritual teachings, or to those who are only familiar with orthodox and literal Christianity, I'll just say that I will speak more about this statement and about the *Pure I Am* later on in this account and again in Book IV. And remember: this deepest and purest "I" refers to the divine

Witness, to Divine Spirit, not to my individual mind/body. I'm just saying that this "I", this Divine sense of Self, is what Jesus is referring to. Again, it is not in reference to His personal self! Many great Beings have said as much, but we don't get exposed to them in this fundamentalist-orthodox-dominated culture.

So, I must repeat myself and say: this last unimaginable insight, itself a miraculous experience, was so pure, powerful, and profound that I knew it was true, with every fiber of my being! And it made perfect sense based on my experience of this State. I was humbled and awed by the blessedness of the state that I was experiencing. Then a few minutes later, as I was getting ready to leave for home, another aspect of this holy Truth was revealed: one that was, once again, so unexpected that I hardly dared to acknowledge it—this pure Self, this pure "I" that I'm experiencing, is the Lord Himself!

I Can't Go Back

I returned home, once again, making sure I was just staying in the Witness and not going with the part of my mind that was wondering about these last unexpected "gifts" of direct Knowledge. And I couldn't help wondering about whether I would be in this sacred and divine state tomorrow upon awakening.

When I awoke the following morning, I was pleasantly surprised to find that my internal state was no different than it had been last evening. Maybe not as overwhelming, or should I say subtle—it was both, but the experience of "me," my truest sense of self, being firmly but naturally present in the Witness was still as powerful and steady as it had been last evening. After enjoying my morning walk in this still new and truly incredible state, the railroad called and wanted me to go to work the next day, which was almost a week earlier than I expected. This was fine as I was ready to go. I could not imagine anything interfering with my new state of awareness. I "knew" that I would not and could not go back to the old understanding of myself. The truth of my identity with this newly revealed Self within was more true and more real than any other aspect of my life. A part of me assumed that the awakening must be essentially over because it seemed that there could be no "Truth" deeper, more profound, than what I'd already experienced. I was more than content to simply remain immersed in this pure and joyous inner Self, a conscious awareness that is cognizant of its divine Essence. Even though I was ready to go back to work, I looked forward to another day at the beach!

I enjoyed the beautiful scenery and great weather, but these paled in comparison to my inner "State"—to the peace, serenity, and stillness I was experiencing. While enjoying this ever-so-natural and blissful Presence, the memory of a book I had read only a couple of months earlier came forth. The title was *The Way of a Hindu,* and the author said that he felt that there had been other saints besides Jesus, who had experienced their own divinity and had become established in the highest state—the state of "union" with God, which I now understand to mean union with the Self. Thus, Jesus would not be the only true Teacher, not the only one who was speaking from the divine Self, that is within everyone waiting to reveal itself!

The author writes that he feels it should be fairly obvious to an objective and educated person that all the great religions were founded by beings who were established in this highest State. When looked at with an open heart and mind, they were all basically teaching the same thing—overcome your weaknesses and embrace your goodness, your divine nature. He also pointed out that it did not seem fair or logical that God would send only one savior—one messenger of truth. Cultures were so diverse and changed so much over time that people needed to be exposed to the truth in a way they could relate to. Decades later, Karen Armstrong, author of "*The Great Transformation,*" tells us that essentially all of the founders of the Wisdom traditions did so based on their Transcendent experiences but had no interest in organized religion. Again, these sages, knowing that you cannot describe the experience of the Self, advised people just to follow the golden rule, which will take you to the pure I of your Heart. Joseph Campbell was another scholar and seeker who came to know that all myths, read properly, meaning, not literally, teach about our inner Divinity.

I had enjoyed this book and had intellectually and, years before reading it, intuitively felt the truth of the idea that it would be hard to "identify" with and understand someone who was not a part of their own culture. I had liked it so much that I had recommended it to my mother, who was a struggling and dissatisfied Catholic. Now that I have had firsthand experience of how conditioned we are and how hard it is to comprehend the full depth of our conditioning, I can see that more expansive awareness and understanding are among the greatest blessings we can receive. I could also see how conditioning and different levels of inner development had given rise to many different views and understandings of Christianity. But again, the main point that was now obvious was that this pure I—pure "Self" or Spirit in all is truly the divine Teacher and Source of all the great religions. For me, there was absolutely no question that this one divine Spirit could not be limited to a particular human being when It is fully present in, and the essence of, every human being!

I also remembered reading a book that claimed that the esoteric or original knowledge taught by Jesus was not new or unique, as claimed by most Christians. It showed that this knowledge was possessed by the Essenes, a Jewish mystical community, as far back as 600 B.C.E., and therefore, Jesus most likely learned it from them and thus was not directly from the "Absolute." When I first read this, I knew that I had no way of knowing what to believe. Now I knew that Jesus may have learned a lot from the Essenes, as I had learned from Gurdjieff, but that the only way one could learn—could receive—real Knowledge was to have it revealed by one's pure inner Self. This is where Jesus (and all of the saints and sages) had received His teaching—His understanding, and this is why He told us that the Kingdom of Heaven was within! God IS within.

It now dawned on me that, in a sense, I had gone through this awakening and had arrived at the same basic understanding that I had intellectually and intuitively arrived at months ago, meaning that it made sense to have different teachers—different enlightened beings—to help people of various cultures and different time periods. I had totally and completely forgotten all about this perspective during these miraculous days of transformation, during which I had been under the belief that Jesus was the only savior. I now assumed that it had to be this way in order to truly uproot my deep-seated religious conditioning. I also felt wonderfully blessed not to have to believe anyone any longer. The highest truth was right inside, and that's why many different saints can all speak of the same great truth. It also dawned on me that the memory of these two books and their messages was definitely connected with the revelations of yesterday afternoon, allowing my understanding to deepen and expand a little more.

As I was enjoying my splendid good fortune, as described, I realized that part of that good fortune was being able to spend time on the beautiful beaches of Vancouver. Jogging in my bathing suit and being able to flop into the warmer-than-expected ocean was such a treat. Just drinking water from the public fountain was awe-inspiring, as it tasted better than I'd ever noticed and seemed to refresh my entire being, not just my body. As I was focusing on and feeling the immense beauty of this planet, a thought arose: how does all this diversity and beauty arise, where does it really come from, and what is its essence? Yesterday, I had been so enthralled and enraptured with the revelation of my Self that, you might say, the outer world hardly existed. The inner Experience was so captivating and so stunning that all of my attention was focused within. Now, a day later, this thought of how does all the rest of this fit in or relate to this one Self in all—hardly had finished, when the answer immediately flashed forth: it is the same Self, the same divine Reality that is the source and essence of everything, Yes, the whole universe and everything and everyone in it are manifestations of the same inexpressible and unlimited Spirit.

This experience of "Oneness" is the classical mystical experience: the experience of the oneness of all things! In the yogic teachings, this experience, this direct Knowledge of "Oneness" is called samadhi and in Sanskrit, Lokananda

Samadhi Sukham. This refers to Oneness with the Self with eyes open. The Sanskrit language even has a specific word to refer to the direct Knowledge of the Self: Vijnana—showing that people knew of this divine State thousands of years ago. Sanskrit is the oldest language that we know, and again, it shows that a few of our ancestors were aware of this sacred level of Divine consciousness, where we can directly experience *the oneness of all things*. A truth that we have almost totally forgotten about.

Truth Is Experienced on Different Levels

Now, from this connection to the pure Self—pure Awareness within, I knew that the highest Truth can only come from within, when your Self decides to reveal itself. For me, this revelation was so unexpected. Again, I knew absolutely nothing about the transcendent or spiritual teachings. Throughout my life, I had experienced understanding to be primarily associated with my intellect. Now, I was being shown just how limited the intellect really is, even though I was still aware that our intellects are amazingly miraculous. I could see that it was a combination of my intellect and my heart that forced me to ask deeper questions and seek answers outside of my culture's view. It was also my intellect that helped me recognize the importance of not expressing negative emotions and the novelty and genius of essentially applying the scientific method to self-inquiry, to observing ourselves constantly and as objectively as possible.

I wasn't sure if the intellect was involved in the beginning stages of self-remembering when I realized that the pure awareness of the witness could see me more honestly and objectively than I could through traditional self-analysis. But I was absolutely certain that this exalted level of understanding that came during my experience of the transcendent State was of another order than any understanding that came from my intellect or the wisdom of the heart as well. The image of the caterpillar and butterfly presented itself as an appropriate analogy for these two vastly different aspects of myself. Seeing the caterpillar, how could you ever guess that the butterfly was its potential? Viewing the mind, how could I ever guess that the Self was right within my own being?

Gurdjieff taught that we all have two fully active higher centers within us, but, in our present state of limited awareness and immaturity, we know nothing of the existence of these centers. He referred to them as the higher intellectual and higher emotional centers. I had no trouble accepting the profound and freely given direct Knowledge I'd experienced as being examples of the higher intellectual center and the overwhelming feeling of sacredness and divinity being a reflection of—a "taste" of—the higher emotional center. As I've said, I did not wish to or try to think about or analyze this wonderful new state. I was perfectly content to just remain in the silence and vigilance of the effortless Witness—with which I now seemed to be so perfectly aligned. In this pure State, the normal activities of a day at the beach—walking, sitting, swimming, and playing at the edge of the water—were perfectly delightful and joyful. And as I've said, the Bliss was most definitely beyond this world.

After a number of hours of enjoying this heavenly experience, I got the urge to look for a good bookstore. Not surprisingly, I found one that was just perfect. It had a large section on philosophy, world religions and most importantly for me, Gurdjieff's teachings. I wanted to purchase the first book I had been exposed to on Gurdjieff's teaching, which the school bus driver had lent me. I remembered how strong an effect this book had on me, and was now eager to read this book from my new perspective. This same author, Maurice Nicoll, had written another book, The New Man, which I also looked forward to seeing because it presented the esoteric—the hidden and spiritual—meaning of some of the parables of the Bible, based on Gurdjieff's teaching.

It was while I was at this bookstore for some time that I became aware of a totally new and strong sense of intuition. My impression was that because my mind was so internally quiet and focused, and one with the Witness, versus its former state of continuous internal chatter, a previously unknown power of intuition was now able to reveal itself. This "energy" expressed itself by directing me to and urging me to select books that logically or intellectually I would never have looked at, let alone picked up. Each of these magical selections turned out to be helpful in understanding different aspects of my new state of awareness.

In two of these books, the authors write about a pure and divine "I" within them, which they describe as the Lord speaking through them. I found this quite amazing, since two days before, I did not know such books existed or that the pure Self—pure I existed! This "I" that was speaking through these authors was very consistent with my own inner experience. In one of these books, it proclaimed: *"I am you yourself, your Immortal divine SELF, your true SELF, your 'real' Teacher. I am not the I of the intellect or the body, but the 'I' of your brother and sister and of All Life."* Yes, this was indeed the same "I" that was revealing It-Self within me. It also shared the psalm: Be Still and Know I Am God—again, such was a beautiful way to speak about my own experience, as was the proclamation that: *"I AM that innermost part of you that sits within and calmly waits and watches"*[4] I must say that even though it was nice to skim through these and see how closely they matched my own experience; I was not really that interested in reading through their fairly in-depth teachings. I was more interested in getting it directly from my Self. I wanted to enjoy this pure Self within and let it reveal to me what It wanted to and have it do so whenever it desired. I made my purchases and returned to the beach to enjoy being with myself.

Later, I checked in with the railroad and was delighted to find that I was going to be traveling to Jasper, Alberta, to pick up a train there. I would be able to ride in the club car—a specially designed car for viewing the high mountain peaks and would be paid for this exciting ride to boot! What a way to begin work in the Northwest. Also, I didn't have to leave until early afternoon, which meant that I could spend the whole morning at the beach.

Before I move on with this story of my experiences of the transcendent, I need to say a few things about the vastly different levels of transcendent experience. One could write an entire book on this subject, but I will keep my points short and simple. First, I'm definitely saying that my experiences are of the highest nature, as I've been stating. This level of experience is extremely rare based on decades of reading spiritual literature. It seems that the majority of experiences of the transcendent are momentary and often fleeting. Meaning, they don't stay with one very long, and often come with no warning, but that doesn't mean that they are not powerful and even life-changing. Dr. R. Bucke published a book of people's experiences of the transcendent almost a century ago titled Cosmic Consciousness. It provides us with a wide variety of individual experiences of this forgotten level of ourselves that happened to ordinary folks during all kinds of events in their daily life. Many of these took place in nature and gave them a strong "hit" of the Spirit underlying all things. Based on my own experiences, I'd assume that many of these "nature experiences" occurred when the person was absorbed in the thralls of nature, while their so-called normal mind was still and quiet. But, due to the fact that they had no way, no framework to begin to understand these precious experiences, they could not pursue them as a reader of this account can. But even so, these accounts tell us that the majority of these people knew that the *truth* that they had experienced was far greater than the religion they were being taught and thus dropped organized religion, no longer interested in its limited beliefs. This and other aspects of these stories demonstrate to me that these were authentic experiences of the transcendent, just not the highest levels of it. But, as mentioned, they still often contained a decent hint or "taste" of the transcendent. The point is that a lot of people have had a hit of the transcendent but have no understanding of the different levels of awareness that are possible for a human being, and don't know how to pursue a deeper understanding of these miraculous experiences. Or put themselves in a position to have more experiences of this blessed State. But now, in this great age of information, this is no longer the case!

Being Present in the Club Car

After another precious morning at the beach, I selected a few books and reported for work. Arriving early allowed me to get a great seat in the club car. As the train rolled slowly into the Rockies, the height and ruggedness of these mountains were even greater than I expected. The whole scene was far too engaging and enjoyable to even think about reading.

I felt that I should just allow myself the pleasure of simply staying focused on this magnificent scenery—much the same way I had done when first learning to practice self-remembering. As I enjoyed the beauty of Mother Nature, I could not help but be amazed at how much my awareness and understanding had changed in a week and a half. Now, most of the thoughts that came forth were almost exclusively concerned with insights and musings connected with my new "State" of awareness. The part of my mind that had been so active and truly uncontrollable at the beginning was now quiet and alert. I kept returning to the thought that it was unbelievable that such a revolution in my experience and understanding could come about just by getting in touch with the part of my mind that was capable of observing the habitual and mechanical parts of myself. For years, I had thought and thought about life's deeper questions but had not come to any satisfying answers. Now, just from trying to observe and restrict the part of my mind that wanted to think, think, think, think, I not only had all my questions answered, but opened into a level of awareness and understanding that I never knew was possible.

After supper, as the train wound slowly through the mountains, I enjoyed viewing the various rock formations as well as the multitude of shadows and streams of light that played upon them. I observed that thoughts of youth kept coming up. I felt that this might be due to the fact that I felt that I had found the fountain of youth, and by that I'm referring to the pure inner Self that I was reveling in. Also, my mind could not help but be aware of the importance of this genuine spiritual teaching concerning "know thyself," its understanding of humanity's "predicament," and the teaching about the potential of human consciousness—about our capacity for inner growth and transformation and *rebirth*. I was sure that this information could be a great help to our youth. While teaching high school the previous year, I was reminded of the tremendous enthusiasm and idealism of youth, but also of their naivete, immaturity, and laziness. The ancient Teachings address all of these in a natural way.

Because I wanted my students to learn how to work together, see related aspects of a chosen subject and learn how to research things they were interested in, I instituted what I called "learning projects" for my senior students in physiology and nursing science. They could select any subject matter they wished and then tell me what they hoped to learn by exploring it and how they planned to go about it.

I found that most had a hard time thinking for themselves. They'd tell me they did not know what to do or just pick some not-too-exciting subject right out of their book. I would ask them, *"Surely there must be something that you've heard of but don't really know much about, that you would like to know more about?"* (There were no limits on what they could choose.) When they said "No," I would remind them that, for me, this was a sure sign that their education was a failure! Besides not being able to think for themselves that well, they had a very tough time seeing how their chosen subject connected with other subjects, how it fit into a larger whole. To me, they seemed mechanical, just going through the motions, and, for the most part, quite immature. And I was only 23!

These students were extremely concerned about what others thought or might think about them. They absolutely refused to work in groups not of their choosing, and if required to do so, many were prepared to quit the class. Also, they found it nerve-racking to get up in front of their peers and explain to them how they went about doing their projects and what they learned from the process. Many seemed worried about their self-image and possessed little self-confidence. I tried to get them just to relax and talk to the class as if they were talking to a friend on the phone. Very few could do this, but by the end of the year, they all had improved.

Another pleasant memory that emerged was about their difficulty in understanding the respiration process. I explained that our chest muscles and diaphragm create space within, and the atmospheric pressure automatically pushes air into the lungs. They weren't buying it! They knew from experience that they were inhaling it—sucking it in! Even with further explanation, they couldn't relate because they had no concept or awareness of atmospheric pressure. This memory seemed to be a great analogy of how, by simply opening up to the teaching of self-remembering, I was automatically filled with new awareness and understanding!

As these and other memories surfaced on this magical evening, I once again saw the preciousness of the ancient imperative to "know thyself," and how such self-knowledge and its resulting increased awareness could address so many of the things that our youth were in need of but were missing out on, such as the expanded awareness and understanding of both their inner being (inner life) and their culturally conditioned ego-personality. If young people could participate in self-study in a group setting, they could begin to see how they hate to be judged but often judge others. Same with gossip. If they could discuss their experiences of self-observation accompanied by self-remembering together, it would go a long way in helping their inner and outer natures mature in a natural and healthy way.

I was excited to see Jasper. I had half expected to spend the previous winter there, but things had worked out too well in Vail for me to want to move on. Upon arriving in Jasper, I was not disappointed. The surrounding mountains were beautiful, each different from the other in all four directions. This diversity, along with the tropical blues and greens in the local ponds and rivers, gave Jasper a unique and magical feel to it. It seemed appropriate because that's how I felt myself.

Asleep In Prince Rupert

Later that day, we left for Prince Rupert, a town up near the Alaskan panhandle. Similar to the rest of my travels, the scenery was just spectacular. The land we were passing through was rugged wilderness, providing the perfect situation for me to stay focused inwardly while enjoying Mother Nature's display. As we got further north, there was even snow alongside the tracks.

I found the job of being a chef to be much easier than I had in previous years. Before, my mind was always wishing it were somewhere else, home, at the lake, with my girlfriend, playing golf, etc. Now I was just perfectly content to stay immersed in this indescribable state of the pure Witness. A little work did not disturb my state in the least. As we were pulling into Prince Rupert, a couple of mail handlers, whom I had given some leftover food to, asked me if they could show me around, knowing this was my first visit. Both of these fellows were quite rugged and looked like they probably owned a motorcycle. They wore their hair greased back, had tattoos and had cigarettes wrapped up in their T-shirt sleeves! After suggesting that we have a beer for starters, the biggest fellow said, "Let me check out this bar. I'm not sure that we should go in there, as this is usually a pretty rowdy bar.

As his friend and I waited on the sidewalk, I, my mind, could not help but wonder if these guys were trying to pull my leg, so to speak. It was about 2 p.m. on a Tuesday afternoon, and I could not believe that the bar could actually be crowded and rowdy at this early hour of the day. I kind of smiled to myself and felt that it did not really matter, as all I wanted to do was stay connected to my own deeper Self. After only a moment's look, the fellow said that we should check out another bar, as this one was way too rowdy. As we were heading to the next bar, again, my mind could not help but wonder what could be going on that this fellow would want to avoid. He checked out the next bar and this time said that it was pretty rough, but thought it would be all right.

A Joyous Awakening

Upon entering, I was shocked to see that it was just packed with people, full of smoke, and so noisy that I could barely hear my escorts. Most of the people were flat-out drunk and extremely vocal. I heard myself say, *"I wonder what the other bar was like?"* I found it easy to stay in the witness state because of this incredibly wild scene that was taking place all around me. My mind reminded me that I, too, had been this foolish, in the mid-afternoon once, during Oktoberfest while in college. My guides informed me that most of these patrons were native people who were being taken care of by the federal government. It seemed to me that they were being neglected much more than they were being taken care of. After a couple of beers with these gentlemen, I was happy to return to the hotel for a hot bath and some peace and quiet.

Later that evening, with the images of the bar still fresh in my memory, I decided to review what Gurdjieff had to say about *"sleep."* Sleep in these ancient spiritual teachings always refers to a person who is not consciously present or Awake to their real Nature. These bar patrons had been extreme examples of unconscious people, but based on my experience of the past two weeks, I knew that Gurdjieff was right to say that basically everyone exists in a state of *sleep.* By this, he means that most people are unknowingly trapped in their heavily conditioned ego with no separate conscious awareness of themselves. I picked up Ouspensky and saw his reminder that *sleep* means unawareness of one's self, not knowing what their mind is up to, and no clue of their conditioned nature, and that only by remembering himself does a man begin to awaken.

Being asleep is not caused by something; it is the result of our not developing properly. It is the result of a person not making an effort to know himself, of his failure to enter the state of self-observation and self-remembering. A major cause of being *asleep* is that people don't know that there is anything beyond what they are currently experiencing. They feel that they are already self-aware, already know themselves and are in complete control. And they have no clue that there are higher levels of awareness available to them. This was exactly my state and belief before becoming aware of G's teachings.

Without my own "awakening" to the deeper state of the pure witness and all that it had taught me, I would have thought this talk of "sleep" and lack of awareness and "higher" understanding to be foolishness. But now, based on the perspective of this much deeper, purer, and conscious Identity that I had been experiencing these last few days, I knew that Gurdjieff's teaching was not only genuine ancient wisdom; it was also absolutely true! I also knew that when I was in the witness state—I was "Awake" when I wasn't, I was "asleep." I—myself— was not consciously present! It was that simple.

The Transcendent State

Being the chef with only a few passengers on the train, I had a lot of free time to myself. Remembering that Kenneth Walker had an entire chapter on *sleep* in his book, and still being amazed at how deep my own *sleep* had been without me even noticing it, I decided to re-read this chapter that I had read months before. I was well aware that when I first read this, I was not the least bit conscious and knew nothing about the nature of my mind. I expected that rereading would be enjoyable and fruitful: I never dreamed that it would be basically a great description of my own experiences.

The first thing that really struck me was Walker's presentation of Ouspensky's definition of the word *consciousness.* "Consciousness was not a function; it was an awareness of a function. Some people use the word consciousness as though it were synonymous with thought, but thought could take place without any awareness of its existence on the part of the thinker, and consciousness could exist without there being present any thought." 5 I had experienced the truth and accuracy of this definition myself many times over these last few days, but this was the first time I had seen consciousness defined in this way. My reaction was that Ouspensky, actually Gurdjieff, was just so right on. Consciousness was most definitely an "**awareness**" of a function. Consciousness is our ability to focus our mind, our ability to be aware of being present and our ability to know what our mind is up to! It is Awareness!

Walker describes two distinct aspects of his experiences of the state of the Self. He says that the first characteristic of higher consciousness that people experience is: *"The internal conviction of the truth that they carry with them."* He adds, *"Difficult though the individual may find it to formulate what he has learned, he has no doubt of its truth. It is knowledge which has been reached by a route other than by which ordinary knowledge is acquired… It is direct and immediate knowledge."*[6] I was astonished to find my own experience so eloquently expressed!

Walker's description of the second aspect of the experience of transcendent consciousness is, if anything, even more apt. He writes:

"The small limiting 'self' of everyday life, the self that insists on its personal rights and its separateness, is no longer there to isolate one from everything else… Separateness has gone, and, as the clamor of thought dies down into the inner silence, an overwhelming sense of 'being' takes place. Not only has the head ceased its chatter, but the very words it formally used have lost all relevance."[7]

A Joyous Awakening

Speaking of a person's first experience of their true Self, Walker says: *"One becomes conscious of a unity, an intensity of existence, a blissfulness of 'being' never experienced before."* He goes on to say that the Hindus describe this ecstatic state by the Sanskrit word Sat-Chit-Ananda, which translates, syllable by syllable, as being, consciousness and bliss. I found out years later that this Sanskrit word is one of the more ancient descriptions of the Self, and as Walker said, *"It gives a fitting account of it."* [8]

I was surprised to read a quote by William James, a great original thinker who brought together the disciplines of psychology, physiology, and philosophy pertaining to the subject of consciousness. James says:

"One conclusion was forced upon my mind, and my impression of its truth has ever since remained unshaken. It is that our normal waking consciousness, rational consciousness as we call it, is but one type of consciousness, while all about it, parted by the flimsiest of screens, there lie potential forms of consciousness entirely different." [9]

Walker goes on to point out that James was right, but that he failed to say that there were methods that one could use to break through these flimsy screens that separate one state of consciousness from another. Walker then speaks about his own experiences of self-remembering, saying how this helped him and his fellow students see that they did everything without being aware of themselves while they were doing it. This was exactly my own experience. He then says that it was only after learning to divide his attention, keeping part of it focused back on himself, that an awareness of himself could be maintained. Also, that this division of attention was the gist of self-remembering and that this observing "I" was what Hindu philosophy called the "witness." [10]

At this point in my own awakening, it was nice and reassuring to hear of another who had followed a similar path of awakening. Walker describes how difficult it was to stay *awake*—to remain in the state of the witness, and how this came to an end when he was identified with something because no one was present to act as the observer! Again, all of Walker's points are essentially an exact description of my own experiences of *"awakening."*

To say the least, I had a tremendous feeling of gratitude for being exposed to this precious teaching. It was wonderfully evident how far I had come in such a short time. In my present "state," it seemed that I was the observing "I"—the witness—without really having to make much effort at all. I didn't feel that this was because of any special merit of mine, but that my rapid opening into this rare and holy state had come so quickly and so naturally, as a result of divine grace. (All of the wisdom traditions speak of the need for effort and grace to tread the path of higher awareness and understanding, and grace being absolutely necessary to experience your own true Self.)

I was surprised to hear James say that these different states of consciousness were separated only by the flimsiest of screens. This was an appropriate description for my experience of June 20th, because going from the peaceful and quiet state of the observing "I", to the miraculous state of the pure and Divine "I" had been very smooth and subtle. But I felt that it was ridiculous to say that one's normal state of *unconsciousness* is separated from a reasonable state of self-remembering by only the flimsiest of screens. Walker, Ouspensky, and G's other students, including myself, had all experienced how difficult it was to "*awake*" in the beginning, even for a few moments. In other words, the strength of our own habits, the tendency to be totally identified with our thoughts and emotions, was anything but flimsy.

It seemed to me that a person needs to hear first about higher states and genuine methods to pursue such states to give them the confidence to start participating. It also seemed that seekers should be prepared for the difficulty in trying to "*awaken*." People should understand that this quest is difficult, but they should also know that if they persist, they will make discernible progress. And if they participate with intensity and brutal honesty, as G suggested, they might have the most uplifting experience of their life! This "work," as G called it, is one of the keys to answering humanity's deepest questions about life, as well as giving seekers a direct experience of their deeper nature. (In the years since this awakening to the Transcendent, I've learned that a seeker can evolve more than they would or could believe simply by making small but sincere efforts on a regular basis. This will draw grace to you, and inner transformation will take place naturally, and without any beliefs—this I know for sure.

Attachment Cancels Self-Awareness

Everything about this first work session was very easy for me and went just perfect right up until the end. As a chef, it was my job to provide a complete inventory of stock at the end of each trip. This made it easy to keep track of consumption, discourage stealing, and let the next chef know what he was starting with. While I was doing this final task, I realized that there were six cans of soup that had not been listed. I accounted for them on this final inventory so that the next chef would know that there was plenty on board.

Shortly before arriving back in Jasper, the steward asked me for the inventory book, and sure enough, he noticed that it showed that we had more soup than what we had started with. He told me that he had found a mistake and that I should provide the correct count. I explained the situation, but he did not seem to understand. He just kept saying, *"No, that cannot be. Just change it and put down three."* I thought that maybe because he was French, he could not understand me, so I took him into the kitchen and actually showed him that there were six cans of soup. He still said, now angrily, *"No, no, no, don't try to cause trouble, just put down three, and everything will be right."*

Up to this point, my "state" had been the same as it had been since the major shift of consciousness on June 20th. I had been staying in the witness almost effortlessly. But now "It," my old conditioned personality, who could not stand this sort of person that I was now dealing with, was ready for battle. I recognized this old familiar energy and tried to remain calm and *'awake'* and told him that it would be better to let the next chef know the true number so that these cans of soup could be used up. His reply was still the same. Realizing that he might be afraid that one of the supervisors would notice the discrepancy, I told him that they were looking for people stealing food, not for finding it. Now he was steaming mad and demanded that I just change it, right now.

By this time, I had lost all contact with the witness and was functioning totally from my conditioned ego-personality. This lower aspect of myself was now letting him have it, telling him how stupid he was being and demanding to know what he was afraid of anyway. "It" also wanted to belittle him for his wimpish, fearful, and effeminate nature, but did not dare to do so in this public setting. It was during this immense flash of anger that the witness finally returned, allowing me to realize that I had totally lost it—had fallen "asleep" without even noticing it. Because of this, I was able to drop the anger, change the count, and nicely tell him, *"We'll let someone else worry about it."*

As I was departing from the train, enjoying the beauty of Jasper, I was still amazed at how easily I had gotten sucked into one of my old and powerful "I's"— one of my many aspects of personality. From as far back as I could remember, I had always been very impatient with and hard on people who were hesitant, irrational, and unreasonably fearful. I had been enjoying such a deep state of the Witness these last number of days that I didn't expect or believe this sort of thing could happen so easily and swiftly.

I felt thankful for this lesson as it made me realize that my old self, my old deeply conditioned "I's," were far from being totally passive and dissolved. It also confirmed the intuition that told me that even though it seemed as if I did not have to make the same sort of internal effort to stay connected with the witness, I should continue to do so anyway, as I had seen previously, time and time again, how easy it was to lose touch. I could fall *asleep* without even noticing I'd done it. So, this incident with the steward demonstrated to me the importance of continued vigilance.

The Transcendent State

The whole crew was asked to stay in Jasper so that we could do another trip back to Prince Rupert the next day. This was fine with me as I was looking forward to exploring the Jasper area, and, at the same time, intently making a determined effort to recapture the wonderful state of the deeper and true Witness. I hiked some of the local trails and enjoyed the woods immensely—the stillness and beauty were perfect for my efforts. I had spent a lot of time in the woods in Maine while growing up and had always liked the feeling. I had not thought about those times in years. Now, it dawned on me that during these times in the woods, I had a quiet and focused mind and was almost always anchored in the present moment. From this recognition, I felt that the reason I had enjoyed the woods so much as a child was due to the fact that I was in touch with this pure and divine aspect of my awareness—of my nature. My enjoyment of the exquisite beauty of the Jasper area and the needed exercise from hiking allowed me to return to work refreshed, awake, and determined not to get caught up in the steward's emotional dis-ease.

Everything went fine. The work was easy, and I was able to stay 'awake' in the witness, as I had been these last number of days. The steward was his same nervous self but was not bothering me in any way. What he did was serve as a constant reminder of how easily I had become identified with my old ways. Knowing that this act or habit of identification with one's thoughts was the primary cause of *sleep,* I decided to review G's teaching on *identification.* I started with Walker since I had enjoyed his thoughts on sleep so much.

He defines *identification* as losing all awareness of oneself. He had mentioned this before, saying that when one was identified with something, there was no one left to observe. [11] This had been my experience right from the start of trying to remember myself. I was so used to being totally identified with my thoughts that I lost all awareness of my intent to practice self-remembering, to keep my awareness in the witness. I could easily see that when my attention was on the witness, I was not identified with my thoughts and feelings. But when it wasn't, I was completely identified with them. Thus, I was either "awake" or I was "asleep," identified or not identified; there was no in-between.

Walker pointed out that when your feeling of "I" is in self-remembering, in the witness, you won't get caught up in identification. When one is in touch with the higher and more conscious part of oneself, you don't get seduced into the hypnotizing effects of "identification." Yes, that was my experience exactly.

Another aspect of G's teaching concerning the importance of understanding "identification" and its interference with "awakening" spoke about the habits of: (a) imagining and worrying about what others think, (b) blaming others, (c) judging and running down others and many other expressions of negative and useless emotions. I had seen for myself the importance of not identifying with negative emotions. I had experienced that basically all of these negative emotions were mechanical and conditioned reactions—not conscious choices. From this and my new appreciation of the "Witness state," I could appreciate the truth of G's teaching about the price people pay for identifying with negative emotions and how this holds them in their small and mechanical "I's" of their immature ego's and again, prevents one from being present in the witness. Most importantly, it prevents them from participating in inner transformation as they are meant to.

G defined another aspect of "identification" as internal considering, and this referred to being identified with one's inner state, which, besides negative emotions, also included one's beliefs, images, expectations, fantasies, and wondering and worrying about what others think of you. G's students also pointed out something I had already experienced the truth of many times. *"When one is identified with their inner state, they are completely under its power."[12]* This is especially apparent when your inner state involves depression, anxiety, pride, greed, lust and so on. Since I had just discovered the power of naturally identifying with the witness through the practice of self-remembering, I was a bit shocked to see that so much of my free time had been spent in internal considering, in wondering, worrying, fantasizing, complaining, and doing just about anything but being consciously present in the moment.

What is especially significant about this, as G's students point out, is that while you are identified with your inner "state" and all its baggage, you cannot change, especially when it comes to the understanding of yourself. Until I learned about the non-expression of negative emotions and the ability to be present in the witness, my seeking had produced only minor changes in my understanding. On the other hand, simply by trying to stay connected with the witness, my understanding of myself had expanded immensely, and was predominantly practical versus theoretical.

In fact, during this trip, I was constantly amazed by how clearly I could understand Walker, Ouspensky, and Nicoll, and knew that this was due to my sincere practice of self-remembering and grace. I was also even more awestruck by how clearly and easily the witness could recognize my many and often subtle and deeply ingrained "I's" of ego-personality. For years, I had taken these to be the real "me"! I was also very aware of my great fortune of being present in the liberating awareness of the witness because many of my most conditioned and mechanical "I's" were being stimulated by this steward's nervous and effeminate nature. It was interesting to see how often these "I's" felt obligated to "comment" on their perceptions of his shortcomings, and also how harsh these comments were. I still marveled at how fortunate I was to be given such a precious understanding and to no longer be such an unknowing slave to these lower and mechanical aspects of my mind. I knew that if I had not witnessed all of this, I most likely would have spent the majority of this trip in internal considering, internally running this poor soul down and feeling sorry for myself that I had to put up with him.

When we got back, I was asked to stay in Jasper so that I could run "chef" one more time back to Prince Rupert. This time, I was the only one to stay. Part of me was glad to see this steward go, but another part was thankful that he had helped me further understand how lucky I was to be awakening to the knowledge and understanding that I had sought for years.

I enjoyed the opportunity to spend more time on Jasper's beautiful mountain trails and beside its blue-green waters. After this last trip, I had an even greater appreciation of why G had taught that one had to do this "work" on oneself in the midst of everyday life. And now I was grateful for the opportunity to be alone in such pristine surroundings. This supported me in staying awake in the present moment.

I was excited to begin reading Nicoll's The <u>New Man</u> because Ouspensky and Walker both had mentioned that G's ideas of "*sleep*" and "*awake*" were mentioned in the Gospels but were not understood in their deeper sense. I was interested to see what Nicoll had to say, since I now had such a different understanding of Jesus' teaching based on my own inner experiences. But another part of me knew that that could wait until I started working again and that right now, I should just get some exercise, enjoy the outdoors, and stay vigilantly focused on "the witness."

So that's what I did, and I basked in the great joy and enthusiasm that only this connection can give.

Inner Transformation, Rebirth, and Higher Understanding

The trip north was peaceful and again, was not very busy, so it was easy for me to be centered on the witness. I also started reading Nicoll's book, *The New Man*. In addition to being a student of G's, Nicoll was a psychologist who had studied with the well-known psychologist Carl Jung. For these reasons, I expected a scholarly approach and was not disappointed. One of the first things that Nicoll speaks about is that all sacred writings contain two levels of meaning, one outer and another inner. Behind the literal words lies another range of meaning and understanding, far removed from the literal meaning. Nicoll also says, *"The Gospels speak mainly about a possible inner evolution called 'rebirth.'"*

A Joyous Awakening

Nicoll adds that this inner evolution is psychological. He says, *"To become a more understanding person is a psychological development. A man is his understanding."*[13] I agreed with this statement and the one about "rebirth," even though I didn't know anything about the ancient and hidden language of the parables. Since I was presently experiencing a vastly higher level of knowledge and understanding within myself, I knew for sure that Nicoll was right about the sacred literature containing an inner meaning that is very different from the literal meaning. I also knew that the intent of this literature is to describe the rebirth he mentioned. Rebirth to one's higher, true, and divine nature with added understanding that this pure Spirit is the true nature of all beings. (Years later, I read the works of Joseph Campbell and Karen Armstrong that expanded the deeper meanings of sacred scripture greatly. See Book IV)

Nicoll acknowledges that the question immediately arises—if it's true that there is a higher meaning, why not just come right out and say it? Nicoll then says that understanding anything literally and understanding it psychology, or internally, are two very different things. Then he says, "The idea behind all sacred writings is to convey a higher meaning than the literal words contain, the truth of which must be seen by man *internally.*[14]

It occurred to me that this is the way it is in all epic stories and fairy tales: The literal meaning is connected with the mind, a simple story, but the moral or psychological meaning and interpretation are of the heart. The heart represents the Spirit in the esoteric literature and is most definitely on a higher level, more mature level than the conditioned mind and ego!

Nicoll also says that one reason for the higher meaning being hidden within the stories, myths, allegories, and parables is that this subtler and divine knowledge will not be distorted or destroyed by those who only believe in the literal meaning. Secondly, the higher meaning can only be grasped by one who has already achieved a higher level of understanding through self-inquiry, esoteric teachings, and the inner "work" they require. This kind of attainment takes a long time and the proper setting.

We can understand this concept (problem) when it comes to teaching children—you cannot teach the child the whole truth—the deeper and subtler truth of politics and math, etc. Such takes place over a long period of time and after a lot of education and personal experience. Children's stories are graphic, exciting, and simple so that children can easily relate to them. But when they get older, they recognize that there is a deeper meaning to the story, a moral to the story, and they also, hopefully, begin to realize that there is a deeper side of themselves, one that has the capacity to recognize and resist 'their lower nature and embrace higher principles.

The Transcendent State

Still speaking about the need to hide the true meaning and message of sacred literature, Nicoll continues by telling us that if the higher meaning were stated for all to hear, many people wouldn't believe it; they would think it nonsense. I could easily understand this because I knew that if I told most people what I was undergoing at this time, they would think that I was crazy—literally! So, yes, I could understand that the hidden meanings in sacred literature have to be veiled because, as Nicoll said, *"In order to take in the Truth, one has to be ready to receive it."* I knew that being ready to receive is about higher levels of awareness and maturity, not higher levels of intellect or conditioning!

(In this time of the internet and with so many distortions and outright lies and so many distributors of information, a lot of folks are ready to receive. They are sophisticated enough to hear about their ability and capacity to evolve and mature, to go beyond the childish level of bickering, being selfish, having no compassion or tolerance, and thinking that they have the only truth. Also, knowing that you can no longer believe in the literal interpretation of sacred scripture, seeing how it just doesn't add up—its message no longer satisfies. Also, how it divides instead of unites and enhances one's ego much more than the love in one's heart!)

After speaking about some of the general teachings associated with esoteric teachings, Nicoll speaks about rebirth, saying, *"All esoteric teachings say that he, a human being, is capable of a second birth. But this rebirth… belongs to a man in himself, the internal man, not the man he seems to be in life."* [15] Based on my own experiences, I knew he was correct. The inner rebirth is a much deeper level of understanding than thinking; "accepting" that rebirth is as simple as accepting Jesus as your savior.

As mentioned, I knew that I had experienced a rebirth through the brilliant practice of self-remembering because I experienced a new identity, an entirely new sense of myself. And the Self, revealing Itself to me, represented the genuine "rebirth," the highest and truest Identity of our Being. This level of rebirth was "the Way" to enter the Kingdom. But just having my sense of self move from my highly conditioned ego, my ego-personality, as I came to call it, to my sincere heart was how I became a true seeker of higher understanding. This is in itself a rebirth. Thus, rebirth, like levels of expanded awareness, has different levels of experience and understanding. And it was most definitely the understanding gained from the higher experiences of rebirth that resulted in my new perspective and understanding that made the seemingly impenetrable teaching of the Sermon on the Mount understandable and even possible to follow!

Reiterating that the Gospels refer to what a man is internally and not what he appears to be, Nicoll says that this is why Christ attacked the Pharisees. The

Pharisee represents the outer side of man, the side that does everything for the sake of appearances. [16] This is what we now call and know to be the "ego." The Pharisee doesn't represent people who lived long ago, but the Pharisee in ourselves, our underdeveloped sense of self. Again, I knew, based on direct experience, that this outer aspect, the individual conditioned part of me, was not my truest sense of self. The major point of this is that it—the small ego—is *incapable* of inner growth.

As the train pulled slowly into Prince Rupert, I stood on the platform between the railroad cars, enjoying the breeze, the sunshine, and a gorgeous view. I took a brisk and long walk around the area for some much-needed exercise and to enjoy my inner state and the quite different but still exquisite scenery. I'd like to remind the reader that the vast majority of my time, throughout my *"awakening,"* was spent doing normal everyday activities. The time I spent reading and contemplating represented only a small percentage of my day.

The New Man—Spiritual and Symbolic Understanding

I have chosen to speak mainly about Nicoll's *The New Man* because many seekers are thirsting after a higher understanding of spiritual teachings, and it's helpful to hear from one who has had a direct and profound experience of the truths of these perennial teachings. It's also true that I experienced many other things during this awakening, some of which Ouspensky talks about in <u>In Search of the Miraculous.</u> But most of these things are difficult to speak of, and from trying to do so, I know that it ends up being more confusing than helpful. Knowing that I can only share a small part of my total experience, it is nice that I can share some of the understanding I truly longed for. Also, this new understanding of Christianity and my own true Nature were a couple of the most joyous and wonderful aspects of my spiritual awakening. Again, Nicoll is speaking about the inner meaning of sacred literature, and I'm sharing my experiences that these Teachings are speaking about—no beliefs, just awareness!

On the way back to Jasper, I finished the last part of Nicoll's opening chapter about the ancient language of the parables. Because of the experiences that I'd been having, I was interested in the idea of levels of truth. Especially the teaching that stone, water, and wine actually represented three levels or stages in the understanding of esoteric truth, concerning one's capacity for higher understanding and transformation. Nicoll reiterated that stone *"represents the most external and literal form of esoteric Truth—Truth in its most inflexible sense."*[16] Again, the basic truths about morality and how a person should behave are a necessary foundation and starting point for the quest for higher knowledge and are a part of all the Wisdom traditions. But as we're seeing in the present day, inflexible literal truth causes untold trouble in the Middle East and right here in the U.S.A. It has done so practically everywhere for centuries. And, hopefully, it's evident that this literal interpretation of "truth" that is being preached worldwide by orthodox fundamentalists does not lead to inner growth or expanded awareness or the uncovering of one's ego. Instead, just the opposite! Followers are asked to accept dogmas without question, which results in no self-inquiry or contemplation. The result, then, is the exact opposite of the essential teachings of all sacred literature: Don't believe anything and check out everything for yourself—how you behave is paramount.

Nicoll tells us that while *Truth is not a visible object,* it is represented by visible objects in the ancient language of the parables—in sacred writings. Each object has a deeper symbolic meaning. Nicoll points out that the term *water,* for instance, appears often in the parables and must signify something besides its literal meaning. He cites Christ's statement to Nicodemus, where He tells him that one must be born of water and spirit to enter the Kingdom of God. (John III:5) I had read this before and had no idea what it meant. Nicoll says that we might guess that "spirit" might mean willpower or the most real part of man. Also, we might surmise that to be born does not mean to re-enter the womb. But how, he asks, are we to understand "water" in reference to rebirth? What could this symbol mean?

My own thought was that "spirit" in this passage represents the pure Self. From my perspective, based on my "experience," it was connecting with the divine Self that I truly entered the Kingdom within. But I still had no idea what "water" referred to in Christ's statement to Nicodemus. Nicoll cites more examples from the Old Testament to continue to develop his thought: *"They have forsaken me the fountain of living waters."* (Jeremiah II:13) and *"Whoever shall drinketh the water I shall give him shall never thirst"* (John IV:13–14) Nicoll then says that in the ancient language of the parables, 'water' means a special kind of knowledge called the living Truth. It is living Truth because it makes a man 'alive in himself,' as Nicoll says, "once the knowledge of it is assented to and applied in practice."[17]

It seemed to me that this was a wonderful and accurate description of my experience of self-remembering. The *experience* of pure awareness made me feel more alive than I'd ever felt. Assenting to and applying this practice is what allowed me to "awaken" and become consciously aware of myself. As I'd seen time and time again, this knowledge of how to be the witness had to be applied in practice: it had to be lived to allow a deeper understanding to come forth. And, as I've already said, this practice of being still and alert was what created the opportunity and the atmosphere that allowed the Self to reveal itself to me. From that perspective, the teaching that one had to be born of water and spirit to enter the Kingdom made perfect sense to me.

In one sense, due to the above "recognition," I felt like there was no need to read further, but at the same time, Nicoll's analysis had been so stimulating and interesting that I wanted to see what else he had to say about this ancient language of the parables—the inner meaning of sacred literature. He continues by saying that "stone, water and wine" represent three different scales of meaning of the Truth of man. Nicoll uses another story from Genesis (XXIX 1–3) of Jacob rolling the stone from the well to elaborate on stone and water representing two different levels or stages of truth. Nicoll says that this story of the stone blocking the water is saying that when a seeker interprets esoteric truth literally, he makes it stone, which prevents the seeker from knowing and embracing its living, higher, and transforming aspect, symbolized by water. Once again, my experience exactly! And finally, we hear that "wine" represents the highest level of Truth. There was no doubt in my mind, in my experience, that "wine" is the Truth that is revealed by one's pure Self. And like the wine, direct Knowledge is intoxicating, as I've tried to describe.

Nicoll claims that the Ten Commandments were written on stone tablets to convey that the teachings about higher evolution must rest on a firm foundation. He is saying, like all esoteric teachings, that inner development is only possible for those who follow the basic rules of life contained in the Ten Commandments. Nicoll reminds us that a seeker *"cannot add to his stature, by taking thought."* By which he means following his own beliefs. A spiritual seeker must follow an authentic teaching instead of their own beliefs. Nicoll cites the Tower of Babel as an example of a story about people trying to reach Heaven, the inner Kingdom, through their own knowledge. They use brick, which is man-made, rather than stone, nature's ready-made material, so they had no genuine teaching.[18]

On another tangent, Nicoll says that a person who wants to reach a higher state must know what to ask for. Christ says, *"Ask and you shall receive." But how do we know what to ask for? He continues by explaining that Christ is not talking about seeking help with everyday matters, the "things" in our life, but help with our inner development and understanding."[19]*

This reminded me of my own impassioned quest for higher understanding. Somehow, at the time, it was obvious that what I needed to ask for was a higher understanding. Knowing it was the only thing that would truly stick with me and truly satisfy me. Now, I could see that this desire had come from the depths of my soul. The soul can't ask for things of this life. I could also see that a seeker does need true teachings for guidance along this subtlest of quests and that Christ's teachings are true teachings. The teachings in *The Sermon on the Mount* helped me realize that I needed to evolve to follow Christ's teachings. But as Nicoll is underscoring here, the literal level of these teachings does not provide enough guidance to answer all of the questions that arise in one who is truly seeking and sincerely participating in self-inquiry. This was my experience, completely.

Finally, to end his introduction to the language of the parables, Nicoll tells us that we need to understand the idea of "vineyards," which are the source of the wine, representing the highest level of understanding. Nicoll tells us that in the ancient language of the parables, a vineyard represented a special school that is based on and teaches about this highest Truth and how to experience "That" for oneself. I was sure that Nicoll was referring to an esoteric school that G claimed to have discovered and then participated in as a student. Nicoll then reminds us that this higher understanding of Truth does not arise in ordinary life. It must be learned from a person, a Sage or Guru, who has evolved to the highest level of Truth, symbolized by the wine, the product of the vineyard.

I knew that there was no way that I would have ever discovered the act of self-remembering without help from one who knew it well. I had always taken my thoughts to be my own. Without someone telling me about and instructing me in self-remembering, I was sure that I would never have discovered this on my own. How could I have? Why would anyone? Who could ever consider one's thoughts to be anything but his own? After having received this teaching, I was amazed at how this subtle but significant change in perception had resulted in such a profound change in my understanding, underscoring the absolute necessity of a genuine spiritual path and a genuine spiritual Master!

The trip back to Jasper was just so sweet. I got to spend a lot of time enjoying the scenery, talking to passengers, and almost effortlessly staying in and reveling in the Witness state. Being no longer needed in Jasper, I was sent back to Vancouver. I was excited to view these magnificent Canadian Rockies from the comfort of the club car once again. Being able to view such stunning scenery, in such a wondrous state of being, had to be the best job going. I also looked forward to reading a little more of Nicoll's book, knowing that it was the 'New Man" in me who was doing the reading.

Another aspect of Nicoll's book that struck me on my trip back was his observation that the devil symbolizes the evil force within a person's own nature.[20] These aspects of the mind are expressed as one's self-love, vanity, pride, ignorance, and egotism. That had been my experience when encountering the truth of these various I's within myself and how they hold me at the lower level of myself. But I also experienced that as you see that these I's are not the real you, they begin to lose their seductiveness and power. I remembered that I was taught as a Catholic child that the devil is successful because he poses as your real self—

again, classical esoteric teaching. And I could now easily understand that all of those various I's, all those thoughts, desires, etc., that you always took to be yourself, get in the way of your inner growth. They are not evil—just immature and are ignorant of their true Nature! Once again, witnessing awareness is the key, the way to see for yourself that such I's are not you and to see as well that identifying with these lower I's keeps you *asleep* and prevents you from experiencing the truth of your own Self.

After a good night's sleep and some great viewing from the club car, I again marveled at how peaceful, clear, content, and focused I was. Again, this had basically been my "state" since June 20th, so I was starting to get used to it. However, as mentioned, I was still making sure that I was being very vigilant about participating in the practice of self-remembering. This new "state" was so indescribably wonderful and blessed that I treated it as the priceless pearl spoken of in the Gospels. Knowing that we would be back in Vancouver in a few hours, I decided that I would again enjoy the company of Nicoll and his thoughts about the higher teachings of the Gospels.

Nicoll's chapter titled "The Marriage at Cana" contained a lot of follow-up information that was okay but quite detailed. Being in the "state" that I was, I was not that interested in so much detail that was not well supported by Nicoll's own inner experiences. I knew that if I was not in this awakened state and had not experienced what I had over the last couple of weeks, I might have found the story interesting but not very meaningful. Ultimately, it would have been no real help to me. There is always the question of whom to believe and what to believe. But I was not interested in trying to prove anything or learn all the minor points about esoteric teaching or the language of the parables. From direct experience, I already knew that Nicoll's basic message of esoteric truth—that a person has the ability to transform themselves and experience higher centers within—was indeed factual.

Silence, Union, and Mystical Insight

But there were a couple of things I found especially interesting in the chapter on the marriage at Cana. At the beginning of the chapter, Nicoll says that all the miracles of Jesus take place in "silence." My own miracle, the revealing of my divine Nature, also took place in silence. Nicoll also said that in order to change oneself, silence within oneself is required. [21] I had never heard anything like this before, but I now knew that this was true.

For me, silence represents witness awareness, and it's this unknown and miraculous part of our self, our conscious awareness, that allows us and helps us transform our understanding. Even though the witness is silent, the insights that come from the witness, the inherent wisdom in pure awareness, come through clearly and beautifully. At this stage in my 'awakening', I was highly confident that all I had to do was remain silent and vigilant within myself, and this long-sought higher understanding would unfold in a natural way.

The primary theme of the chapter is that the marriage at Cana is itself a symbol, not of a wedding, but of Jesus' spiritual marriage, his reaching the fulfillment of His inner development and achieving union with God. What signifies that Jesus has become the Master, is His transformation of the water into wine. It is in this State—union with His Self that He reaches the highest level of inner development, the highest understanding of Truth, the goal of the spiritual journey. The *wine* is the direct Knowledge that I've spoken about! Nicoll supported this view by pointing out that the number three in the ancient language represents fulfillment—Christ rising on the third day, Peter denying Christ three times, etc. Nicoll says that this is why it begins with *"Upon the third day there was a marriage at Cana. This signifies the fulfillment of a stage."*

Nicoll also says that the number three can also represent the completion of one stage and the beginning of another, again, the beginning of Jesus' role as Master, as Christ. It can also mean, he says, that the higher level is beginning to be active and the lower is beginning to obey the higher.[22] This last statement is what struck me the most poignantly, as it seemed to describe what was going on in myself. The higher-being, the divine aspect of my nature—"my Self"—the pure universal Witness, and the lower-being, what I always thought myself to be before June 20th. I hadn't actually experienced it as the lower obeying the higher; the way I put it was that the higher, the divine part, was the real me. The idea or image of "union" between the human and the Divine was meaningful and helpful. I certainly felt both aspects of this union. But the higher part, with its expanded understanding and its sacred and immortal Nature, is most assuredly what I truly Am. I was also aware that I was just beginning this journey on the path to union and was not anywhere near the level of a Master.

But once again, I was sure that all the wisdom and guidance I needed were right within me. All I had to do was stay *"awake"* to receive.

I arrived back in Vancouver on July 3 and decided that since I had worked about 160 hours since June 22, I should have a little time off and see some of the surrounding countryside. Even though I had worked a lot of hours, I wasn't the least bit tired and had to admit that I had just experienced some of the best days of my life. I went back to my new residence to get ready for the beach, as it was another beautiful day, and I was excited to frolic in the water. I made sure to bring Nicoll's and Ouspensky's books with me in case I felt like reading later in the day.

I was amazed at how nice the water was and how awesome it was to sit in the warm sand and gaze upon snow-covered mountains that appeared to be still floating in the air. Even though this setting was truly a sight to behold, I knew that the real reason that I was so "ecstatic" was because of my inner state and with that, I renewed my inner intention to make self-remembering my main focus and activity. The frolic at the beach was secondary.

I spent the first few hours playing in the sand at the edge of the beach and enjoying the water. Being in such a peaceful, joyous 'state of presence', I just naturally played in the water, did not really swim, just flopped around, did somersaults and so on. The motion, along with the buoyancy, was delightful. The same sort of thing was true in how I played in the sand. I felt a childlike joy in just pushing the sand around and watching the water invade the patterns in the sand. Just the sensation of the sand between my fingers and toes was fun and pleasing. I truly remembered how great it was to be a child just enjoying nature in the moment! I also enjoyed jogging along the beach, checking out the little sand bars and the vast array of "life" that made up this beach setting. After relaxing in the shade and enjoying looking at the mountains and the sky, I felt the urge to read more of Nicoll's book, <u>The New Man</u>. His next chapter was titled *"The idea of Good Above Truth,"* and I knew that this pure Self that was in me and everyone else was the highest Good and highest Truth. So, I was excited to see what Nicoll had to say. He had been impressive so far.

The Good, the Self, Transcends Truth

At the end of the previous chapter, Nicoll mentioned the 'good', quoting Plato: *"The good may be said to be not only the author of knowledge of all things known but of their being and essence."* (Republic 508,509) Such seemed to be a perfect description of the pure Self. As I've said, shortly after I experienced the Self, I *knew* it was the source and essence of all, both outer and inner, and its Nature was "goodness itself." I experienced the Self as an entirely different level of being, way beyond the do's and don'ts of religious and moral philosophy. It is a "state" of pure Spirit and pure Goodness, beyond anything the mind can conceive or understand.

Nicoll begins by reminding us that Jesus offended the Pharisees by doing good on the Sabbath Day. He healed a man in the synagogue. Nicoll says that such is an example of putting good above truth and that the term 'Pharisee' refers to the inner state of a man who acts only from external laws and feels merit in keeping them, in contrast with that of a man who acts genuinely from what is good. He then mentions the story of the Good Samaritan, this being the classic example of a person acting from the goodness in his heart, as opposed to following the external laws and customs. Nicoll then brings up the obvious but little-mentioned fact that throughout history, all religious quarrels and persecutions have arisen out of conflicts in doctrine, that is, conflicts over which eternal principles (beliefs) are true. It's obvious that if people were in touch with the Good within them, such battles and wars would not happen. Then, Nicoll makes a statement that I had never heard of:

"The end of all knowledge is only one thing: 'What is Good. There is no other end or meaning in knowledge but Good.'"[23]

Again, for me, there was no question that the "Good" stood for the pure inner Self, the pinnacle, and the goal of Knowledge, which is the direct Experience of your own unimaginable Goodness—your own Self! Another related and truly remarkable idea is that when a religious doctrine is taken as an end in itself, instead of a means to a higher truth and good, then it becomes an impediment.[24] This was not only a unique way of expressing the difference between religious (literal) and spiritual (esoteric) teachings, but it was also a reiteration of my own experience. If a person's sense of identity remains only associated with intellectual knowledge, religious beliefs and inflexible rules of dogma and does not encompass their deeper nature, such will indeed act as an impediment to the highest Truth, the Good.

Nicoll makes another important and much-observed point: when one is coming from their self-love, their love of ego, they can easily twist spiritual truths to suit their own vanity. This is what is done by the Pharisees in every age. The TV evangelists and the hard-core fundamentalists of all religions are perfect examples of this. This is also true of many politicians, celebrities, and billionaires. In order to see the veracity of this truth, one must take a sincere look at oneself, and such is not really possible without a firm commitment to self-inquiry and the practice of being consciously present—meditating! In my own case, I became aware of my ego when I began self-inquiry, first turned within, but didn't really *see my ego* until I became wonderfully connected with the witness, and this was possible only after years of self-inquiry and a sincere longing for a higher perspective.

In contemplating this teaching of Plato's "the Good" to represent the truth, I contemplated some of the different meanings of "good." One of the general themes that came forth was how most of us learn the difference between good and not-so-good actions when we are young. Most youngsters are taught basic religious and moral dictates, such as "Don't lie or steal, etc." I know I was encouraged to do the right thing—be the Good Samaritan and treat others as you yourself would like to be treated. One needs to feel the rightness, the goodness, not only in the head but in the heart too. Something that seems right to the mind might support our sense of merit and vanity, as Nicoll described it. One also needed to experience what it felt like when they didn't obey the golden rule, and also, hopefully, what it feels like to experience genuine remorse. Getting in touch with the inner experience is what matters most here.

Outer and Inner Freedom

As the sun was setting and my day at the beach was coming to an end, I remembered that tomorrow was the 4th of July—America's Independence Day. Canada had just celebrated its Independence Day on July 1st. Being very much aware of my good fortune to be free of unwanted and unnecessary thoughts, I appreciated how lucky I was to be able to experience freedom both politically, on the outside, and spiritually, on the inside. I was also very aware of how rare it was for one to even know about the concept of inner freedom, let alone experience it as dramatically as I was.

To celebrate my experience and new understanding of what freedom can mean, I decided to treat myself to a day of relaxation, exercise, and exploration. I went to the beach early to beat the crowds. It was wonderful to feel the un-restrictedness and serenity of the beach in the early morning hours. The light in the sky was a lot like a sunset, and the air was refreshing and truly divine. The stillness and quiet made it easy to remain quiet and focused inside. Jogging along the shoreline while enjoying the breath-taking scenery and the ocean breeze was a joyous way to start off this day of celebration, of the human spirit. After spending quite some time in this idyllic atmosphere, I knew it was time to move on and get some breakfast.

I had no interest in going to a restaurant after working in one and practically living in one for a number of days. I seemed to be only interested in buying picnic-type foods that I could easily carry around with me. During this time period of my "awakening," I was so energized that I never seemed to get really hungry. Mostly, I just ate a little here and there. I did not eat regular meals and had not eaten in a restaurant since I had arrived in Vancouver. During this period, I also noticed that food had a lot more taste than usual. With my mind quiet, alert, and focused as I was eating, I got to experience the texture and taste of the food much more than I usually did. Since I never really focused on the food I was eating while talking, reading, or just thinking to myself, I did not enjoy the taste and texture as I had recently. After running along the beach, I would stop for a drink from the public drinking fountain. Being in a great state of self-remembering while drinking, I experienced that this water not only tasted incredibly wonderful, but it was also extremely soothing to my whole self.

This understanding of the connection between taste and being focused in the moment brought forth the memory of how good food tasted as a kid when you were really hungry. I assumed, but could not truly remember, that at this time of life, there was no internal dialogue while eating. I was just eating, and that was it. The memory that was most vivid of such a time was how great food tasted after picking potatoes. Picking potatoes all day was hard business for a kid, and by the time supper was put on the table, my brothers and I only wanted to eat. Thus, we were totally focused on the food, and this was when the food tasted its very best.

After picking up some food, I decided to drive into the mountains just to experience them. I had enjoyed them while on the train and now wanted to be able to check them out for myself. After some time, I came across a small lake that had a picnic area right beside it. It was a beautiful setting with small mountains surrounding the lake. It reminded me of the lakes in Maine that I had so often enjoyed. I sat at the edge of the lake, trying to just immerse myself in the exquisite surroundings and, at the same time, stay consciously present. I did not have any trouble staying focused in the witness, but my mind kept bringing up memories of July 4ths of the past. I got to witness many pleasant memories of being with family and friends at my 'parents' camp. Memories of the two 4ths of Julys I had spent with Jane came up as well, and I could feel how these memories of her were much different than the other memories coming forth. They still had some emotion attached to them, and I was thankful that I could now look at such thoughts so differently than I did before experiencing this deeper part of myself that was so much freer and unattached. And I also knew that she played an important part in my destiny, being the one who set me off on this journey of seeking higher understanding.

The rock I was sitting on was getting hot, and so was I. Thus, I decided it was time to go for a swim in this pristine lake. As I was standing there getting ready to plunge into the pure, crystalline, clear water, I, the witness, heard my mind say: *Hold it, this looks awfully inviting, but it's probably cold as the dickens in there, with ice water draining in from all sides.* As I experienced this part of my mind, I, as the witness, just kind of chuckled at the realization that this other part of us, which is more childlike, less expansive, always seems to want to question every decision or be skeptical and often afraid. I just laughed at this part of myself that I had gotten to know fairly well over these past couple of weeks, and said to these wimpish I's—too bad I'm not listening to you any longer. With that, I jumped into the lake, making sure I stayed focused entirely in the "witness," so I could experience this event simply for what it was, versus experiencing it through this lower and more sheepish part of myself.

Even though the water was cold, I did not experience it that way. I felt engulfed by its coolness and softness, and this produced a wonderful tingling sensation throughout my whole body. I just felt incredibly alive and joyous as I moved through the clear mountain water. Being totally present without thought,

A Joyous Awakening

I simply enjoyed the motion and the many other physical sensations I was experiencing without any negative vibes whatsoever! I emerged from the lake, thankful that I knew enough about the nature of my mind to prevent it from making me miss out on such a glorious expression and experience of freedom.

I spent some time exploring the edges of the lake and went swimming a couple more times, all the while intently practicing self-remembering. I spent a couple of hours playing and relaxing at the lake. My mind kept bringing forth thoughts on liberty, freedom, and independence. It was an interesting mixture of traditional thoughts on these subjects, along with not-so-traditional thoughts concerning my newly awakened experience and understanding of my ego and some of its cultural conditioning.

One of my prominent and recurring insights was how outer freedoms were minor compared to the inner freedom and emancipation I was experiencing. But I was also aware of how fortunate I was to have been raised in a free country. Freedom of thought and worship played a major role in my inner development. I appreciated that it would be pretty difficult for children raised in a totalitarian state or in strictly orthodox societies to be open to new thinking. I knew that I had been fortunate to be raised by parents who encouraged me to think for myself, but to do so in conjunction with the wisdom of my heart. I also knew that it was this teaching about not being afraid to think for yourself, more than anything else, that allowed me the confidence to seek beyond my culture's understanding for the knowledge I sought. Such allowed me to not only be open to but also recognize something special in G's teaching.

Another thought that kept surfacing was G's statement that one has to realize that they are in jail before they try to escape. From my present state of awareness, I could appreciate the immense importance of being exposed to esoteric teachings, especially hearing about and seeing for oneself how conditioned one truly is. Without such exposure, it's easy and normal to think of our instinctive and culturally conditioned responses as being free. But after participating in self-observation accompanied by self-remembering, one gets to see and experience for themselves that nothing could be further from the truth. There is no freedom when you are under the control of another, even when the "other" is part of yourself, your own mind, even when it's your own ego! It was also obvious at this time that those who were very proud of their cultural heritage and their philosophical and/or religious belief systems would find it very hard, if not impossible, to be open to this ancient teaching that asks one to "know thyself" and evolve towards a higher level of being.

Feeling divinely blessed for the higher awareness and understanding I had received, I continued on my sightseeing drive through the mountains, simply enjoying the overpowering majesty of nature herself. This certainly was a glorious way to celebrate my inner and outer freedom on this 4th of July. As I worked my way back towards Vancouver, thoughts about the movement for increased personal freedoms of the 60's and early 70's came forth. This youth movement, as it was sometimes referred to, felt compelled to speak out about many things, like the freedom to speak out against the government, university regulations, or the narrowness of some cultural and religious beliefs, also, about the freedom to wear your hair the way you wanted and for women to wear pants or quit wearing a bra. I could see that such concerns were a natural progression of freedom and education. They mainly represented intellectual advancement, but these thoughts and demands had a strong emotional charge associated with them as well. Many of the things that were being brought forth, especially segregation, women's rights, and other examples of narrow and prejudiced thinking, were obviously in great need of being exposed. I could appreciate that goodness and higher understanding were underlying many of these movements.

I arrived back in Vancouver in time to enjoy the late afternoon sun and sunset on the beach. Ever since my awakening began, I had treasured the early mornings and evenings, especially the sunsets, because these were wonderful times for feeling the spirit. In this northern setting right on the coast, the combination of the ocean, the beach, the mountains and the prolonged evening light and color in the sky made the sunsets in Vancouver quite remarkable; truly a spiritual experience in itself.

Savoring the last of this magical 4th of July, the connection between discipline and freedom bubbled up into my awareness in the same way many other insights had. This seemed a little odd at first because, like most people, I had never associated discipline with freedom. In fact, just the opposite. But in my present "state", it was obvious that the discipline of self-remembering, the willful determination and constant effort to stay "awake" in the "witness," was what had and was continuing to provide me with the highest and most precious experience of freedom I'd ever had. Freedom from one's mechanical and conditioned nature, plus the total freedom and bliss of one's true "Self," is, without question, the pinnacle and essence of freedom.

The next morning, after my early morning walk around the neighborhood and some quiet time at the beach, I decided to check out the university library. While sitting at a table looking at a number of books that I had selected, I was asked by a sweet young nursing student as to what I was doing with these weird books. I told her that I was having a wonderful experience of what is referred to as higher consciousness and was, therefore, interested in what others had to say about it. She was intrigued by this and also very attractive, so I was happy to try to share some of my basic insights with her. She seemed to find it hard to understand what I was trying to share with her. I told her that it was the same with me when I first began looking at these ideas. It was only after practicing self-remembering and learning to become the watcher of my mind and its incessant activity that I began to appreciate and see the truth of these teachings. She said that she would like to stay, but had to get going. I assured her that if she could just learn to watch her mind objectively—as if it were someone else's—she would learn more about herself and the nature of the mind in general than she would ever believe right now. She didn't look convinced, so I told her not to believe me, just check it out for herself.

Falling Asleep at the Beach

I decided that since I was right here, I would check out the nude beach that was just down from the university grounds. I had heard about this beach from my old girlfriend and felt the desire to experience the freedom of being naked in the great outdoors. When I got there, I found that basically no one was around, which was fine with me. I was aware that being on a nude beach would be a real test for my staying "awake," but I felt that I was now so well centered in the Witness that I would be just fine. I spent quite some time swimming and sunning on a number of little sandbars before returning to where I had left my towel and clothes. Two young ladies and a male friend had settled in right next to my spot. As I was approaching and noticing these naked young women, I immediately said to myself that this could be trouble and could make it tough to stay "awake" in such circumstances. Therefore, I would just enjoy the sun long enough to dry off and then leave. But before I could accomplish this, these young goddesses had engaged me in a conversation about where I was from, what I was doing, etc. They wanted to know all about Vail, Jasper, and Nova Scotia. Talking about myself while enjoying the company of these young people put me quickly into a deep "sleep," where I remembered nothing of the witness.

One of the girls wanted to show me around the city and its many parks, so I spent the rest of the day with her and never did "wake up" until later that night, after the young woman left. Once again, I was truly amazed that, after all that I had experienced, I could fall "asleep" so easily, even when I was aware of the impending danger, and then stay "asleep" for so long afterwards. I realized that this was a great reminder of the seductive power of the senses and that I was not as stable and as *awake* as I thought I was.

Before going to bed, I decided to look at Nicoll's chapter on the Sermon on the Mount—this being the part of Jesus' teaching that had originally made me aware that some kind of change in perspective was needed to follow the Sermon's teachings. I had recognized that this teaching about not lusting or being anxious about tomorrow was hard to understand and hard to follow. But it was this Sermon, and other areas of The New Testament, that somehow had intuitively allowed me to be open to the idea, the belief, that there must be another "way to be." Another level of awareness that would help you and keep you from being pulled into these instinctive responses.

I skimmed through the chapter to see if Nicoll had anything to say about lust specifically, but he did not. I decided to read the first section anyway and was pleasantly surprised right from the start. He pointed out something that I had never heard about or thought of before—the Sermon comes after the teachings of John the Baptist and before Christ's teaching (parables) about the Kingdom of heaven. He claimed that each of these represented a different level of the sacred teaching. For me, this represented different levels of inner experience. Those of the Baptist being the most basic and literal, those of the Sermon being intermediate, about how *to be* versus what to do, and those about the Kingdom being the highest, about the goal of the spiritual quest, about Union. [25]

The idea that the Sermon was about "how to be" versus what to do was a reiteration of G's teaching that Christianity was a teaching about "how to be"— be a seeker of truth—instead of what to *believe*. I had been struck by the awesome truth of this understanding shortly after I had begun the practice of self-remembering, and now, with the experience of this day still fresh, I, once again, marveled at the truth and power of self-remembering and my good fortune to become aware of it. The understanding of "how to be" and why one should strive to do this was, for me, much more of a practical issue than a moral one. I didn't really feel bad about the day's activities, that they were sinful. It was more the case that if I had been "*awake*," the afternoon activities could have been more uplifting and serving. I could also appreciate that it is important to respect the basic rules of proper conduct—if one goes to a nude beach, one probably should expect to become overpowered by one's basic instincts. That's why one should avoid such places. Again, it's not mainly a question of morality. It's a matter of common sense and staying disciplined! As G said, whatever brings you close to your goal is good: whatever takes you away from it is bad—easy to remember the teaching, harder to do it.

A Few More Thoughts on The Sermon on the Mount

This time, Nicoll caught my attention with his teachings concerning the Beatitudes, "Blessed are the pure in heart, for they shall see God." Nicoll says that this refers to "an emotional state that can be reached in which the reality of the existence of God is seen directly from the clear-sightedness of the purified emotional understanding," for we understand not only with the mind.[26] When I first read this, for whatever reason, I thought that it did not really describe my own experience of my "Self"—the "State" where one not only directly experiences the reality of God but also of their deep connection with God. I thought of this "State" as extremely clear, purified, and holy, but not emotional. But after reading further, I realized that Nicoll's fuller description of a pure heart really did match and describe my experience of my "Self" clearly and beautifully!

He goes on to say that when our emotional side is full of various emotions, what one might call human emotions, it "cannot fulfill its rightful function of mirroring the higher level. When cleansed, the heart sees—that is, understands the existence of a higher level, of God, of the reality of the teaching of Christ."[27]

I was already aware that this continuous inner dialogue was keeping my emotional side constantly stirred up and that it was only after achieving a quiet mind and becoming well centered in the Witness, our divine consciousness that is free of emotions, that this so-called emotional side was clear enough and pure enough to reflect—reveal—the higher level—my real Self. Nicoll's thoughts helped me to better appreciate how this continuous internal dialogue was keeping my emotional side constantly stirred up. It was only after a quiet mind and becoming well established in It—the witness—that this emotional side became calm and clear enough, or pure enough, to reveal the highest level.

The next morning, I woke up to a colorful dawn, feeling rested and full of enthusiasm. Last evening's contemplations and insights reminded me of the importance of keeping a focused and vigilant mind. They also helped me gain a better understanding of the wisdom behind spiritual teachings. I could see how Jesus' teachings in the Sermon are consistent with, and an expression of, esoteric teachings. My inner experience was so powerful, sacred, and undeniable that it needed no other confirmation. But it was definitely enjoyable to see how the truth of this inner experience and how to get in touch with it **was** contained in Jesus' teaching.

Because the experience of the "Self"—the "Transcendent I"—is beyond description, the insights that I was gaining through Nicoll gave me a way to have a better understanding of this amazing, miraculous, and mysterious divine energy that had revealed "Itself" within me. I knew that having Nicoll's The New Man and Ouspensky's IN SEARCH OF THE MIRACULOUS was no coincidence— they were just a couple of the many gifts of grace I was experiencing.

I went on my early morning walk to enjoy the peace and stillness of that time of day and to enjoy the precious color of the sky. This setting, combined with an awareness of my bodily movements and keeping focused on the shapes of the houses and their surrounding landscapes, made it easy for me to stay centered in the witness and not let my mind start rattling on. For me, this was the best way to make sure I was truly "awake" before going on to other activities. On this day, I was more than content to do some more sightseeing and spend another sunny day at the beach. It was another gorgeous day in paradise—a saying that I had heard often in Vail. Now, I truly felt like I was in paradise, not only because of the perfect weather and natural scenery, but even more so, because of the beauty of my inner "State."

Wisdom equals Presence of Mind

I returned to the beach in mid-afternoon after another jaunt into the mountains and spent a couple of hours swimming and playing in this seemingly freshwater ocean. Then, once again, I allowed myself the pleasure of seeing what Nicoll had to say about *"The Idea of Wisdom in the Gospels!"* Right from the very start, Nicoll was scholarly and impressive. He tells us that Christ often used a word in His teaching that has been translated as 'wise,' but that is the original Greek, this word: *"meant in its earliest use, being in one's right senses and so having presence of mind."* Obviously, this connection of *presence of mind* and *wisdom* had a lot of personal meaning for me.

Nicoll underscores this point by saying that this word, translated as *wise*, is used in the Gospels to describe the proper actions of a seeker who is longing for a higher understanding of himself. In other words, Nicoll is reminding us that Christ's teachings are about practical actions that lead to inner transformations, as opposed to merely a way to believe.

Nicoll expounds on the idea of *the wise* and *foolish* in the Gospels by analyzing the parable of the ten virgins. Matt XXV, 1–13 His explanation of this parable provided me with an amazing and almost perfect description of how my own "awakening" had taken place and was still taking place. The parable begins, "Then shall the Kingdom of Heaven be likened unto ten virgins. So, from the very beginning, we're being reminded that this parable is about the Kingdom—about one's true "Self" that lies within.

(Remember that parables, metaphors, and myth have to be used because the Transcendent is beyond description! This is true worldwide of esoteric teachings.)

These ten virgins took their lamps and went to meet the bridegroom. Nicoll points out that five of the virgins are called wise because they have oil for their lamps, whereas the foolish virgins do not. So, what is the meaning of the symbols? Nicoll points out that everyone had a lamp, and this means that they had all been exposed to esoteric (spiritual) teachings about inner evolution and transformation. They had heard about and contemplated the teachings; therefore, they had a lamp.

The wise were those who had oil for their lamps. Having *oil* means that a person has done more than just think about the teachings; they have applied the teachings, attempting to live in accordance with this new truth and understanding, not just talk about it. Nicoll reminds us that Christ said, *"Everyone that heareth these words of mine and doeth them shall be likened unto a wise man and everyone that heareth these words of mine and doeth them not, shall be likened unto a foolish man.*" [28] Obviously, the words of Christ refer to the spiritual teachings and spiritual practices that actually transform one, that continue to enlighten us.

(Since my "awakening," this is one of the biggest misunderstandings I see amongst the so-called "new agers" and other spiritual seekers—they talk a lot about this new understanding—about spiritual principles—but they don't seem to be that interested in sincerely knowing thyself and *doing the inner work needed to do so.*)

Once again, this reiterates that sacred writings are about a way 'to be', not a way to think and believe. From my own experience of the past few weeks since leaving Vail, it was obvious that by participating in self-observation and self-remembering, I was being practical and, therefore, wise. This is what had allowed my understanding of myself, and the nature of awareness itself, to undergo a life-changing transformation. If I had just taken G's teachings as a set of ancient ideas that were quite unique and mystical, they may have transformed my thinking and beliefs, but would have done nothing to transform my understanding of myself and of human consciousness itself!

Again, Ouspensky's book contained many other aspects of G's teaching that were very esoteric and which, because of my inner "state," I seemed to be able to follow, but these had more to do with G's extensive and mostly unsupported philosophy. They helped me to understand some of the subtle aspects of G's teachings, but did not produce any inner transformation the way self-remembering did. (In later years, I realized that most of these teachings were not really important and actually can be detrimental in that they may distract the seeker from doing the real inner work. Again, it becomes a way to think and believe versus a way *to be*. Making fuel for their lamp through the effort to stay awake, by intentionally being consciously present, was a great way to speak of my own experiences. This fuel, the subtle energies from the insights and Bliss, is what keeps a person's lamp burning, keeps the light of understanding unfolding and evolving. I was aware that by staying awake in the witness over these last few weeks, my physical as well as my mental energy had changed. I had to assume that I was running on a much higher grade of fuel, and that was why I didn't need as much food or sleep as I normally did. I also assumed that this higher or, better yet, ethereal energy was making it easier to remain in the witness-state and was responsible for the outpouring of bliss that was as profuse as it had been from the start.

Coming back to the ten virgins, let's not forget that this parable is about the Kingdom of Heaven, about the union of the spiritual seeker with God (referred to as the Beloved by many mystics). The message is about the importance of the seeker being ready, being consciously present, when the Beloved comes. Again, if your mind is busy with anxiety, etc., you can miss this sacred, subtle energy. The parable ends with, *"Watch therefore, for ye know neither the day nor the hour when the Son of man cometh."*

The bridegroom and the Son of man, I had and have no doubt that these images both represent the pure Self within us all. As I've said, when my Self revealed Itself to me, I knew that this pure Self is the "I" that was speaking in Jesus' statement; *"I am the way, the truth and the life."* It is the Kingdom within and the supreme Truth and goal of sacred teachings. Such wisdom and enlightenment just go with the *"direct experience"* of the inner Self.

A Delightful Journey to Vancouver Island

The next day, my roommate told me that the railroad had called and wanted me to go back to work. I felt great and had no problem with going back to work, knowing it was not a question of what one was doing, working, or playing—but a question of what "state" one was in while doing so. As far as I was concerned, the only real work was to stay "awake." The fact that tomorrow was my birthday made it an easy decision to take a few more days off and go to see Vancouver Island. Ever since I had arrived in the area, people had been asking if I had seen Vancouver Island and telling me that I must see it before leaving because it was so wonderful. Therefore, it seemed appropriate that this would be the perfect place to spend my upcoming birthday.

I decided that I would go to Vancouver Island via a route that was quite a distance from my house. The drive had been so spectacular that I wanted to see it again and visit one quaint little beach along the way. I arrived at the ferry terminal about mid-afternoon. I was a little surprised to see such a long line, but since I was in no hurry to be anywhere except in the witness, I was not the least bit disturbed about the prospect of waiting. It just so happened that my place in line was right on top of a big hill, which gave me a perfect and far-ranging view of the ocean bay. The scene reminded me of Maine because there were so many tiny islands just off the mainland. I decided that I should make good use of this time and lovely spot to allow my mind to truly become one-pointed on the scenery and myself.

This went well, and for about fifteen minutes, my mind was quiet and focused with very few thoughts surfacing. Then I noticed that a ferry was returning from the island. It was still a long way off and was winding its way through the many little islands. It was not taking a direct route to the ferry terminal but was pursuing a very particular course of its own.

Due to all the happenings and insights of the last few weeks, my mind was primed to perceive things in relation to the spiritual teachings and my own higher nature. Thus, while watching this ferry work its way toward its destination, the image came forth that this was symbolic of one having to work his way around many obstacles before coming in contact with esoteric teachings and finally one's own true Self. Also, from my vantage point high on the hill, I could appreciate that the ferry was heading toward port, even though it was doing so in a roundabout way. This would be much harder to appreciate for someone in the boat. So, having a higher perspective was truly an advantage. Obviously, this is also the case when it comes to appreciating the importance and truth of spiritual (esoteric) teachings. One who has expanded their awareness through sincere self-inquiry and authentic spiritual practices always has an advantage in life, so why not take the advantage?

As I got closer and closer to the ferry, it looked like there was not going to be enough room for me to get on. As soon as this image had registered in my mind, I could feel a part of me starting to get a little uptight and frustrated. I then witnessed myself thinking: *"Oh no, I have waited all this time and now I'm not going to get on."* Once again, I, the "witness," was amazed that such a negative reaction could still be so easily aroused after all I had learned these last few weeks. It was just another great reminder of the importance of being in the witness because one never knows when these deeply ingrained feelings will be triggered by outside circumstances.

So, I just relaxed, being very happy to "know" that it was not a question of getting on, wasting time or being unlucky: it was just a matter of staying in the moment and in touch with my real Self that was happy no matter what. Not surprisingly, after I had surrendered to the situation, I was the last one to get on! The ferry ride was great, and a number of symbolic thoughts kept coming up, like crossing over being symbolic of my inner transformation. But this time, I chose not to flow with them but instead just to enjoy the ride and my innermost awareness that was the source of this transformation.

Once we arrived on Vancouver Island, I hung out at a beach not far from the terminal to enjoy the late afternoon sun, which still felt very warm. Then, I visited a large park near the city of Victoria. It was beautiful and very well taken care of. It was nice to walk in my bare feet while trying to stay one-pointed on the trees, shrubbery, flowers, and my own Self. Keeping the mind quiet and focused in this way allowed me to not only appreciate the beauty and uniqueness of nature, but its inherent divinity as well. I watched the shadows of the trees grow longer and longer, then the sun finally disappeared. It was different than being at the beach but just as magical.

As I was leaving the park, I realized that I had not even thought of visiting Victoria, the city that I had heard so much about, and actually, the same was true for the city of Vancouver. Without really realizing it, I had only been drawn to natural and peaceful places that so perfectly mirrored my inner state.

With darkness setting in, I headed north to find a nice spot along the road to spend the night. I had planned to sleep in my car because I found it comfortable, and I liked waking up at the crack of dawn. This time of the morning is so peaceful and beautiful. By putting boxes on the floor of the back seat and then blankets over them, I came up with a bed that was actually quite comfortable in this sub-compact car. The fetal position was the only position, but this was fine. With my mind being so quiet, my body had no trouble staying comfortably still, also. The conditions in my little room back in Vancouver were also extremely simple. I had a couple of folded blankets for a mattress, and my boxes acted as a table and chair for me. One little lamp for the "desk," and that was it, but I was perfectly content there because of my inner state. The inner dominates the outer. I had known this for a long time, and now these conditions pointed out the truth of this in a wonderfully simple way.

I settled in and read for a while via the small dome light. I was excited about my upcoming birthday. I had always liked birthdays since I was small, and now looked forward to celebrating my birthday in a more conscious state of mind. Thinking about some of my past birthdays, I surmised that because I had always considered them special, I had had more self-awareness on those days. It also struck me that I was finally experiencing life as absolutely wonderful, the way it was and the way I expected it would be when I was a youngster.

The next morning, I awoke at daybreak and just stayed in my car for a while watching the light increase in intensity, and thereby causing the surrounding mountains to present themselves in their glory. The thought came forth that the sunlight represented higher understanding and was necessary to show things in their proper perspective. I appreciated the thought and renewed my intent for this day to be one of pleasant watchfulness and wakefulness!

A Memorable Birthday Hike

After a hearty breakfast at an old-fashioned diner, I headed north to view the huge Douglas fir trees that were in a park at the northern end of the island. I noticed on the map that there was a ski area on the way, and for whatever reason, it struck me sort of funny that there would be a ski area on an island—even though there were mountains everywhere! So, I decided to check it out.

As I was sitting in the parking lot all alone, looking up at the mountain, I decided that I might as well hike up the mountain. The exercise would be great, and this would provide me with something to focus on while I tried to keep my mind quiet. The view from the top would be great, and since it was expected to be another hot day, the temperature would be a little cooler, too. Also, there were plenty of wildflowers of all colors to enjoy. I had taken walks into the forest behind my house on a couple of birthdays, but I'd never climbed a mountain.

A Joyous Awakening

I was in good shape from skiing all winter, so I found the climbing easy, but keeping my mind focused and quiet still demanded attention. I found that really paying attention to where I was stepping and regulating my breath helped a lot in keeping the internal dialogue down. I also experimented with consciously trying to listen to the surrounding sounds more intently and look at the wildflowers more intently as well. Both of these actions helped me stay quiet inside.

By the time I got to the top, I was in a wonderful, heightened state of awareness, both mentally and physically. I sat there for a while, just taking in all the surrounding scenery. It was neat to be able to enjoy the beauty, and, at the same time, kind of visualize what it would be like to ski down these slopes. The area was much smaller than Vail, but still would have been fun to ski. I could now appreciate that one of the reasons that I and many others liked skiing so much was that while the body was enjoying the thrill of motion, the mind was often quiet and alert, in a state of heightened awareness and *presence.*

I was surprised when I got to the top of the ski area to see that there was still a lot of mountain to climb, mountainside that the ski area had never developed. There were even some snowfields visible. This part of the mountain was not visible from the parking lot, so I had not expected it. But I now felt so good from the walk thus far that I decided that I would continue. This only seemed appropriate with respect to my own ongoing transformation: you can't be satisfied with just a high level. If you find something higher than where you are, then you must carry on.

I started out along a road but quickly noticed how hot it had gotten, and after a short time, decided to follow a small stream instead, as I knew it would be cooler there and would help me stay "awake." After traveling a short way along the stream, I realized that it would be easier to just walk in the water and that walking barefoot would make it even easier and more fun. I then decided that, since I wanted to be as aware of myself as possible on this birthday, why not just be appropriate and wear my birthday suit for this special occasion? There had been no other cars in the parking lot, and there was certainly no one fishing this tiny stream, so I had no fear of meeting someone. I knew that walking naked would definitely make me more aware of myself than normal, since I had never done anything like this before.

Walking along the stream bed was easy, as most of the spring runoff was long gone. The warmth on my back felt great, but my feet got very cold if I had to walk in the water for very long. I slowly worked my way up the mountain, trying to stay focused on my immediate surroundings and making sure that my mind did not start wandering around on its own.

Climbing in this manner turned out to be very pleasant. I was hopping from one rock to another. Being naked, I needed to be aware of branches, and this really aided me in staying focused. That, along with all the new sensations that were coming from my nervous system, made it easy to stay in a state of self-remembering because there was very little internal dialogue to witness. The only thoughts that were coming up were remembrances of when I was a youngster skating up a small brook down in the back of our house. Since we were so small, we could skate right under the many branches that were overhanging the brook. That had been a wonderful sensation cruising along, dodging branches, and weaving around snow and rough ice. I had totally forgotten about those adventures and how joyous they were.

Those memories, along with being all alone in the middle of the woods, also reminded me of how much I had enjoyed spending time in the Maine woods as a child, summer or winter. It now seemed that in those times, I was probably in a partial and spontaneous state of self-remembering—I was just being in the moment. I realized that back then, I did not have to try to be mentally quiet; it was just a natural "state" in such beautiful and peaceful surroundings. I thought that this must be why I felt so "childlike" during this entire awakening. It struck me that I could not remember noticing internal dialogue until adolescence, when I started being more concerned about what others thought of me and how I looked!

Finally, I came to a place where it was too steep to climb safely under the circumstances, so I left the stream bed and found the road, actually more of a path, a short distance away. Then, about five minutes later, I came to the snow line! A part of me said *turn back,* and another part said *don't let a little snow hold you back. Your feet will get cold, but you can just witness it, and everything will be fine.* After a short while, I realized that witness or no witness, the body has physical limits, and I've got to get out of this snow.

I noticed off to my right that there was a small pond about twenty yards into the woods, and there was a small sandy beach at one end of this pond. I immediately headed for the sand, knowing that it would be nice and warm. I was not disappointed. It felt incredibly good on my cold feet, which I sank down into the sand so they would be almost completely covered.

Once my feet felt normal, I laid down on the sand to experience its warmth all over. All this while I was still intently staying in the witness, intentionally keeping my mind quiet so I could really appreciate the body's sensations. It wasn't long before I was actually feeling hot, so I stood up to catch a little breeze off the water. As I was looking at the water, I was tempted to stick my feet in the water. Immediately after this thought entered my head, I heard a part of me say, *"Hold it. This is not as good as it looks. It will be too cold—don't do it."* Except for the sandy beach, pretty much all of the rest of the pond was still surrounded with good size snowbanks! My mind also reminded me that the melting snow from up above was draining into this pond. Once again, I had to laugh at myself, seeing how quick and protective the mind was. I knew that if I had been ten years old, I would have been playing at the edge of the water without a thought of it being too cold to touch.

So, I proceeded to ignore the "I" who did not want to experience this lovely little pond, and to my pleasant surprise, I found the water to be very nice. It felt just like the lake I grew up on would have felt in July. After standing there for a while, enjoying the feel of the water and sand under my feet, as well as the sun and a slight breeze on my naked body, the thought arose that I should go in for a swim. Since the water felt reasonable, and the entire setting was so divine, I should take advantage of the moment, especially on my birthday, Celebrate!

Well, wouldn't you know it? Practically before that thought had time to finish, I heard that same meek "I" or one of his buddies say, *"No, no, no, the water right on the edge of the beach might be warm because it's only a couple of inches deep, but the deeper water will definitely be freezing!"* I marveled at how alert and how persistent this part of the mind could be. I figured "it" might be right this time, but I was pretty hot by now and figured a quick swim would feel good, even if it was real cold. Also, the image of bathing—cleansing, leaving the old behind and starting fresh, with a totally different understanding of myself, was powerfully present on this twenty-fifth birthday celebration. This, and the feeling that I could not let such insecure "I's" have their way on this special day, led me to take a couple of quick steps and plunge headfirst into the water. Again, I was rewarded with wonderfully fresh mountain water, whose temperature was just fine. It was definitely a wild feeling to be swimming naked in the sparkling pond lined with snowbanks and snow-covered peaks above while being sweetly immersed in the witness. The eyes (and some "I's") would expect this to be freezing, but as long as you stayed at the top, it was actually warm. Once you went more than a foot down, it got incredibly cold.

It dawned on me that I seemed to be experiencing physically what I had been experiencing psychologically or spiritually these past few weeks. The paralyzing nature of the cold below, being analogous to the limiting nature of one's lower self and the divinity and vitality of the warm water at the top, was symbolic of the unbelievable and unexpected lightness and blissfulness of one's "Self." After this unforgettable swim, I again enjoyed lying in the warm sand.

About the time I was ready to get up, I was surprised to hear voices. I quickly realized that a few people were walking down the mountain. Right away, I heard my mind say, *"What is going to happen if they see me lying here naked, and then realize I don't even have any clothes to put on!"* It made a few more paranoid comments, and I, the "witness," just smiled. Even though I could feel a little tension and some nervousness in my body, I knew that, whatever happened, all I had to do was keep my sense of self in witness, and I would be just fine. Even though I was only about sixty feet from the path, the other hikers were so engrossed in their conversation that they did not see either me or the pond. Now that I knew a little more about the nature of the mind, this outcome did not surprise me. I then decided that I'd let them get ahead, and then, I, too, would descend the mountain.

On the way down to pick up my clothes, I just stayed on the road so it would not take so long and decided that if I met anybody else on the road, I'd just say hello and tell them that it was my birthday. I assumed that it was just the ego that was so bashful, as "it" was so used to hiding behind various masks of one's personality. I, the witness, did not feel the least bit out of place. I had nothing to hide or fear.

I arrived at my clothes without incident and proceeded down the mountain along the main ski run. I hopped in my car and was sure glad to have been able to start the day off in such a unique and memorable way.

Faith, Growth and Transformation

I proceeded to work my way northward, stopping whenever the urge struck me. As I was sitting on a tiny beach overlooking the ocean, a feeling arose that the reason we were born was to experience our true nature—our true "Self." How blessed was I to not only know this for sure but also to experience the truth of this before my 25th birthday! Knowing that I had felt this Truth on that first day of the Self revealing Itself to me. And I also knew that it was my faith in Jesus and my constant prayer for higher understanding that were responsible for these blessings—this "state" that I was so enjoying. So, I decided that it was time to see what Nicoll had to say about *faith* in his little book, which I found so helpful in expanding my understanding of the experiences I was undergoing and how these were closely connected with ancient teachings.

Nicoll's "The New Man" had helped me appreciate that the insights and understanding that had come with the experience of my Self were the true essence of Christianity. As I've mentioned, I'd known this intuitively right from the start, but Nicoll's work was invaluable in putting this feeling/experience, which is beyond words, into context that made understanding and appreciating it easier. I knew that the presence of this book in my life was just another expression of God's incredible grace and love. It was in this mood ("state") that I began reading Nicoll's chapter on Faith.

The first thing Nicoll tells us is that faith, as it is spoken of in the Gospels, is not easily defined. He says that the Gospels divide people into those who have faith and those who do not. He says that contrary to what people suppose, faith is not mere belief. He also says that faith is not based on anything seen. It is not connected with the senses and their resulting experiences: faith is a result of something much deeper in us, which Christ compares to a seed.

Nicoll begins to explore the meaning of faith, according to esoteric teaching, by looking at Matthew XVII:14–21. When Jesus is told that the disciples could not cure an epileptic boy, he answered, "O faithless and perverse generation." Nicoll explains that the word translated as *perverse* from the original Greek, signifies turning in all directions and that such action makes them faithless because they have no one direction to follow.[29] He reminds us that we have all experienced this turning in different directions. One day, we're in a particular mood with accompanying beliefs, and another day we're in a different mood with different beliefs. These can change again and again, depending on the last book we've read or the last opinion we've heard. I had certainly seen the truth of this in myself a number of times.

This image of turning in many directions versus having one direction to follow, not surprisingly, reminded me of self-remembering and how surprised I was to see how quickly and easily I shifted from one "I" to another. I had no real direction, no steady awareness until I recognized this deeper awareness within myself, the awareness that I am calling the witness.

I will interject here some information that I learned from Karen Armstrong, who, from extensive research, tells us that faith in ancient times was centered around faith in your Teacher, faith in the practices that you were given to transform you. This is definitely an important aspect of esoteric teachings by emphasizing the importance of a spiritual master and having faith in the Path that you were being shown. Faith is doing the *work*—not believing a teaching!

Nicoll did not speak specifically about self-remembering, but he did speak about transformation. He points out that this parable about the epileptic boy comes directly after Christ's Transfiguration, which is a demonstration of the possibility of the transformation of mankind. It is at the end of this same parable about the epileptic boy that Jesus relates faith to a seed, saying, "If ye have faith as a grain of mustard seed," The seed is important here because it possesses the potential for growth and transformation. The meaning of *faith* is thus intertwined with this idea of transformation, and *"so is not mere belief."*[30] It is the possibility of transformation, of experiencing new meaning for and a new understanding of one's life. This is what is possible for the real essence of faith.

It struck me here that my faith in Jesus was based upon His being Divine and upon my belief that this divine being would allow me to understand how I could live in accordance with His teachings. Thus, without totally realizing what I was doing right from the start while contemplating the Sermon on the Mount, I had associated faith with transformation. But, again, it wasn't until I was exposed to the teaching about the possibility of inner transformation, and how to begin that process, that I actually began to experience the truth of this for myself.

In part two, Nicoll presents another meaning of faith that I had already experienced the truth of: "Faith cannot be understood unless the idea of levels in man is understood. Man does not live at the highest level of himself… What is higher is in him, but it is as yet unknown, unvisited.[31] My feeling was, yes, how true this is. What is higher in us is unknown and unvisited because our culture, our science, and our religions do not understand the real essence and potential of human consciousness. The ancient practice of meditation, simply being consciously present, allowed me to experience the truth of these statements on faith, and to experience directly the true "Self" described in or alluded to in these statements.

Next, Nicoll made a statement that I could not agree with: "Faith is the absolute certainty of a higher level." This was definitely not the case with me. As mentioned, I had great faith in Jesus, but it was far from an "absolute certainty." Now that I had experienced the great Self within, I could say that I had absolute certainty of the Divine within. I found it hard to believe that anyone could have absolute certainty, absolute faith, without this most precious experience of their true Nature. I've found that the experience of my Self has kept my faith alive and active during dry and difficult periods of my life. This is why I'm encouraging sincere seekers to know thyself, to find out what meditation can do, and to seek a true spiritual Master, as all are keys to the experience of one's own highest level—one's own true Self.

In the second part of the above statement, concerning absolute certainty, Nicoll says that such faith opens one to the influence of a higher level. This was not only something I could agree with, but was now something I could understand in a way that I had not up till now. I could see that I had lost faith in the Catholic Church, in their ability to answer my questions satisfactorily. With that, my understanding and faith had turned within, I had the faith to follow my own inner instincts, follow my heart's desires, and faith that Jesus could show me the way. From my upbringing, I trusted the deeper part of myself that just somehow "knows" right from wrong.

I had naturally turned within and felt the truth and comfort of this deepest part of myself, which I knew to be good, honest, sincere, loving, etc. But not being aware of the nature of the mind—its tendency to identify with every thought and desire had kept me turning in many directions, asking why, why, why, and this kept my understanding from evolving. What changed all this for me was discovering the state of the witness. It proved to be a genuine aspect of my deepest and truest inner being. It turned out to be my real Self.

Another of Nicoll's teachings that spoke to my inner experience was that faith was connected to making things obey. He tells us that the Greek word for faith comes from a verb that means: *to persuade or make obey,* and uses the Biblical parable of the centurion to connect faith with obeying a higher level of authority. It was easy for me to see how obedience couples well with the idea of not going in all directions. As I read Nicoll's discussion, it occurred to me that obeying a higher authority can prompt a person to make their moods, desires, etc. adhere to something higher in them, even if it's just an ideal. In this way, these lesser aspects of a person's mind would be aided by a higher image and goal.

Nicoll said that this aspect of faith—of obeying a higher authority is connected with making all of one's moods, desires, etc., obey something in him because this something is of such a nature that it deprives all these many things of the power to affect him. [32] I thought that this was a great way of describing the witness. It is of such a nature that it does not identify with these types of thoughts and emotions. It doesn't have to try and make hair-splitting judgments—it's just its nature to deprive such things of their power over you. When your sense of self is one with the witness, you just "know" that such things are not you, so you are not attached to them, and they don't affect you—they don't have power over you. The more one knows (from experience) about the witness, the more they can see the importance of identification and attachment, losing touch with yourself and how such allows you to be at the mercy of outside influences and habitually conditioned emotions.

Once again, I headed north, immersed in the wonders of nature, inside and out. I made a few more stops along the way just to enjoy the breeze and all the surrounding beauty. As evening was approaching, I arrived at my destination, a National Park featuring a forest of very old and huge Douglas fir trees. I had heard about the awe-inspiring beauty of these special trees and was excited about being able to experience them while in such a special "state" and, on my birthday to boot. These majestic trees did not disappoint in any way. They were bigger and more powerful than expected. They had such a commanding presence that it was hard to be anything but alert and quiet inside when amongst them. In other words, they demanded all of your attention and awareness, thus making it easy to be in a state of self-remembering. As I was experiencing this type of awareness, I was again reminded that it was due to this type of inner experience that many people experience such tranquility and peace when viewing Mother Nature at her finest.

I walked slowly along the paths provided, viewing the trees from many different angles, all the while making sure I was firmly established in the witness so that I could "feel" the sweet and ever-so-peaceful vibes of this unique spot. Being in such a good state of inner focus, I was also able to appreciate many of the subtler aspects of this glorious forest; the vines, mosses, smells, and one of my favorites as a youngster—the many things that make up the forest floor. This forest was so soothing and comforting that I just did not want to leave. So, I found a nice spot off the paths to view the last rays of the setting sun breaking through the canopy and seemingly being absorbed by the majestic column-like trunks of these silent trees. I stayed put, enjoying the view and the comforting peace as the light slowly gave way to darkness.

Early in the morning, I headed back towards Victoria, and after a number of little side trips, I arrived at Butchart Gardens, the well-known man-made gardens outside of Victoria. The many different arrangements were lovely, and I was reminded that all of nature, not just her grandest displays, was truly an expression of the divine. Being in such a fantastic state, feeling so blissful and free, I decided that before leaving the island, I would treat myself to one last beach experience to finish Nicoll's chapter on faith.

Once again, I was happy to see that Nicoll's thoughts on faith were consistent with my inner experience and were almost a perfect description of my awakening. They also provided me with another way to understand how my own experiences and thoughts were consistent with ancient esoteric teaching. Nicoll reiterates that faith is connected with a level of inner understanding that is not a result of anything outside, i.e., miracles or the outward faith displayed by the Pharisee. He then says,

"A higher level of man can only be reached through a class of knowledge and ideas that must be kept alive by continual effort. Faith is thus a continual effort, a continual altering of the mind of habitual ways of thought, of habitual ways of taking every day habitual reactions."[33]

For me, this idea of continual effort and a continued altering of the mind's habitual ways of thought by taking the stance of the witness perfectly described my quest to awaken and remain in the state of self-remembering. But from the previous day's contemplation, especially concerning levels of man and levels of understanding, I could see that this definition also applied to the beginning stages of spiritual life. One who was trying to follow the Ten Commandments and other basic moral teachings had to make a continual inner effort to alter one's habitual thoughts and actions. A person who doesn't make this effort will not be able to experience the power and persistence of their conditioned thoughts, desires, and actions. They won't begin to get in touch with their heart, their inner being that knows and recognizes the way "to be" or begin to feel the power and falseness of their ego, their heavily conditioned and immature lower nature. But it was also obvious that without knowledge about and directions of *how to* evolve inwardly, it would be very tough to do.

Thus, I could see that from any perspective, faith required being active inwardly, which is very different than passive belief. Faith, in itself, does open one up to a higher level of themselves. But faith, accompanied by the efforts associated with self-remembering and other spiritual practices, can speed up the inner transformation that faith is speaking about and give one a vastly superior understanding of oneself at the same time. This level of participation prepares a seeker for the experience of the Self, and this is the experience that allows them to know for sure that their faith in God is well placed and requires no blind belief, only continual effort

A Trip to Winnipeg

I arrived home late to find out that my boss needed me to go to work right away. It was the busiest time of the year, and many of the older chefs were on vacation. I called in and found out that I could "run chef", as the railroad called this job position, to Winnipeg tomorrow afternoon. I told them that I'd take it. I knew that this trip would be a lot more work than the others because there would be a lot more people on the train, but I felt so good that I looked forward to the challenge of staying "awake" in the hustle and bustle of the workplace. G had said that his teaching, "the work," was meant to be done while living in the real world.

After another glorious morning at the beach, I reported to work about noon in the best of moods. The chef was the first to report, so he could check out the dining car and order the necessary supplies. Right away, I noticed that the refrigerators and freezers were not working properly. The thermometers were registering temperatures off the dials. So, I called maintenance and told them I had to have these fixed before leaving, since this was a long trip and the weather was very warm. I told them we were due to pull out in about four hours and assumed that this would give them enough time. They responded, "No problem, we'll be right over."

After taking stock and placing my order, I realized an hour had gone by and still no help from maintenance. So, I called again and was told that someone was coming right over. Of course, another hour and still no help, so I called again, reminding them that this food cannot handle this heat and that time's a-wasting—same response. Finally, someone shows up about one hour before departure, takes a quick look, and tells me that this would be a major repair and that there is just not enough time to do that before we leave. Thus, we will have to get it done at our first major stop. He said that he would call and make the arrangements.

I was sure that they planned it this way. My mind could almost hear them say: just put him off until it's too late; let someone else do it. I had always hated this type of laziness, and over these past few years, I had spent countless hours ranting and raving, inwardly and outwardly, about this type of work ethic. I could feel this same old energy pattern starting to well up within, but thank goodness I was still wide "awake" and, therefore, did not get caught in this familiar negative energy. I knew it was not my job to wonder and worry about them. Instead of fretting for the rest of the trip, I would just stick with my own "work" and not worry about all the problems associated with this huge company.

Things went along fine, but as expected, when we arrived at the next major stop, we got the same old stalling, the same "there isn't enough time" song and dance. Once again, my mind wanted to attack these lazy goons and let them know what I really felt about them, but the witness was not the least bit concerned or troubled. Basically, the same thing happened at the next major stop. We were now into the second day. Once again, I expressed my concern to the steward and my fear about the food spoiling. Like so many other old timers, he responded that everything would be fine and not to worry about it. I assured him that I wouldn't, but that it was still our responsibility to make sure the food was fit to eat, and that was near impossible when you didn't have a clue what temperature your refrigerators were at.

During lunch on the third and last day, we were due to arrive in Winnipeg about 5:30 p.m.—one of the waiters brought back a beef pot pie, saying, "The passenger is complaining that it is rotten!" I responded that I wasn't surprised and asked him to send in the steward. I told the steward about the passenger's complaint and reminded him that I had warned him of this a number of times. I also told him that it was my responsibility to close down the dining car for obvious health reasons, except for soups and a few things for sandwiches, things I could be sure were still good. He told me I could not do this—no one had ever done this and just hang in there, and we'd be in Winnipeg soon. I said no, it's my responsibility according to union rules. I also told him to have the head engineer call ahead and let Winnipeg know that they were going to have to take this car out of service and restore it with another stocked dining car with the evening meal already prepared, as we would not be able to do so. He gave me a dirty look, shook his head, and left. I told my helpers to give this car a complete cleaning, as I was sure the health inspectors would be coming aboard.

The steward came in just as we were finishing, and I asked if Winnipeg had been contacted, and he said that they had. He looked like he was ready to have a nervous breakdown, so I reminded him that this was not our fault and that we had tried to have this fixed before we left Vancouver. I also asked him if he was sure that Winnipeg had understood that they would have to prepare the evening meal. He replied with a little anger in his voice: yes everything has been taken care of."

We rolled into Winnipeg, and before we came to a complete stop, the Montreal crew had come aboard. A little Frenchman about 5'2" hollers out. "Who is the chef?" I responded, expecting him to inquire about the situation. Instead, he asked me if everything was ready. I thought he was teasing until I saw his eyes bulge out as he saw the perfectly clean kitchen. In a state of shock or hysteria, he kept repeating, *"Everything is supposed to be ready."* Before I could say a word, I saw an inspector that I knew and immediately asked him if they had been informed about the situation. He responded that no one had said anything about anything. I quickly told him the basic story and asked whom I should report to in the main office to fill out a full report. I also told him that he should find out why that dammed steward never notified them. He told me not to worry that I had done the right thing and that he would take care of it from here and probably talk to me in the morning. I did stop by the office, finding it hard to believe no one would want to know what was going on here. I told them of my conversation with the inspector, and they said, *"Fine, let's leave it at that."*

I was amazed that management was taking everything so calmly since this was a major disruption and would result in a major delay as well. I remembered thinking about how working would be a good test to see how well I could stay "awake" in the challenges of everyday life. I felt that the Lord was really trying to test me, but at the same time put me in circumstances so far out of the norm that, in a way, it would be easier to stay "awake."

After a much-needed walk and some food, I returned to my room, looking forward to seeing what Nicoll had to say about the Kingdom of Heaven. I knew that it was this connection with this highest part of myself that had made it possible for me to still be "awake" and feeling quite well, almost like nothing at all had happened.

6
The Kingdom of Heaven Is Within You

THE FIRST THING NICOLL says about the Kingdom of Heaven is this: *"No one can understand the level of life belonging to the Kingdom of Heaven"* [34] Reading that, I thought you surely cannot fully understand it. You certainly can't express it, but you most definitely can experience it. As I said, right from the very first moments when I first experienced my true Self, I knew that IT was what the "Kingdom of Heaven" referred to. I knew that the Kingdom referred to this inner "State" where one becomes automatically aware of their inherent identity with God. This idea that humanity can experience and even attain union with God has been a part of Christianity right from the beginning. Actually, it predates Christianity by many centuries as part of the EETs. I'll speak about this more later, but for now, it was obvious to me that this insight just accompanies the experience of being in this blessed State. An example and expression of direct Knowledge which is not a conclusion, assumption, or belief, is inherent in the State. Nicoll also describes the Kingdom of Heaven as an inner "state", not an outer place. He quotes Luke XVII, 20*: "The Kingdom of God cometh not with observation; neither shall they say, Lo here! Or There! For lo, the Kingdom of God is within you."*

To help better explain and prepare the seeker to understand the mysteries of the Kingdom, Nicoll reminds us that John the Baptist is one who has received the teaching—meaning the spiritual (esoteric) teaching about inner transformation—but Christ specifically tells us that; Luke XVII, 28 *"Among them that are born of women there is none greater than John; yet he that is but little in the Kingdom of God is greater than he."* Nicoll tells us that in the language of the parables, in the symbolism of esoteric (mystical) teaching, the fact that John is said to be born of a woman shows that he has not undergone the rebirth necessary to enter the Kingdom. Thus, John represents one who is aware of esoteric teaching concerning inner evolution, and he is described as the greatest of those at the normal level. But he has not undergone the inner transformation that is referred to as rebirth; he has not directly experienced his oneness with God, his own divine Self. In other words, John has heard about the teaching that speaks of our capacity for union with God, but has not experienced this divine State—he has not experienced the One Spirit in all.

John the Baptist is described as baptizing with water and preaching repentance. Nicoll tells us that *"The Greek word translated as repentance, means 'change of mind' in the original Greek. As we've already seen, water represents psychological truth and inner levels of awareness in this ancient language. Nicoll says that John taught a knowledge that, if accepted, could cleanse the mind and lead a man to repentance, a change of thinking.*"[35] I could see how this could be understood on a number of different levels.

Initially, this call for repentance, for a change of mind, could refer to humanity's not being open to the teaching about being able to evolve. It could be about humanity's capacity to be civilized, which would be fitting in the time of Christ, but also today. If you truly attempt to change yourself—to do what you believe is best, you realize it's not easy to change because your habits and desires are so ingrained. Nicoll is saying—a truth, if accepted, can lead to a change in thinking. This may be accurate, but a change in thinking, in beliefs, is not the *repentance,* the *"change of mind"* that leads to or prepares one for the Kingdom. Based on my own experience, I knew that the change of mind that was necessary to enter the Kingdom referred not to thoughts but to a whole new level of awareness and understanding that comes from the expanded awareness one gains through self-remembering, through meditation.

A few years after this awakening, I came across another explanation of repentance by Nicoll, in his book *THE MARK,* which described my experience of self-remembering remarkably well. According to Nicoll, the Greek word that has been translated as repentance—metanoia—is most accurately translated as: *transformation of mind.* Meta means transformation, and noia means mind in Greek.[36] This translation goes perfectly with my own experience of self-remembering, which transformed my understanding of myself and my understanding of the nature of the mind in general, its lower and higher aspects. Finally, this transformation of mind and identity led to the experience of divine union, the experience of my Self, and that definitely transformed my understanding completely. This is the rebirth that is necessary to enter the Kingdom.

You Can't Put New Wine into Old Skins

Speaking further about the Kingdom, Nicoll reminds us that John the Baptist represents a seeker at the level of the earth. John exists at the ordinary level as opposed to being born from above. In the symbols of esoteric literature, this is shown by his clothes—*"what truth his mind is clothed with."* Thus, John can only understand the new teaching "from the earth level", from his intellect and senses, because he hasn't experienced spiritual rebirth. In other words, John can only understand the new in terms of the old thoughts and beliefs.[37]

Such is the most natural way for all of us to learn. In my education training, I was taught that one had to go from the known (old) to the unknown (new) in order to teach. You have to use the known to uncover and begin to understand the unknown. But in some cases, this does not work; one of the most famous is

The Kingdom of Heaven Is Within You

Einstein's Theory of Relativity. It has to be understood in an entirely new light—not in terms of the old, because it refers to such a vastly different level. This made it almost impossible for most of the older prominent physicists to understand Einstein's relativity because the only way they could begin to understand it was in terms of the old and familiar, which were of no help. Such seems to be the case for John the Baptist and for all of the rest of us with respect to the esoteric teachings offered by Jesus, especially concerning the Kingdom. You must have the Experience to understand!

To support and expand upon this point, Nicoll quotes Luke V, 36–39 and points out that this parable is spoken in direct reference to John and his disciples.

"No man rendeth a piece from a new garment and putteth it upon an old garment, else he will rend the new, and also the piece from the new will not agree with the old. And no man putteth new wine into old wine skins; else the new wine will burst the skins, and it self will be spilled, and the skins will perish. But the new wine must be put into fresh skins. And no man having drunk old wine desireth new: for he saith, "The old is good.""

In light of what's been said above and remembering that one must understand the language (symbolism) of the parables in order to "realize" their true meaning, it's easy to accept that this parable is about not being able to receive the higher teaching via the lower level—the part of us that contains all of our beliefs, prejudices opinions etc. Nicoll tells us that this new garment represents the new teaching, and as stated—it cannot be simply added onto the old because it does not agree with the old, and more importantly—this ruins the new. I had been wondering how Christianity, in general, had missed the true and highest understanding of Christ's teaching. How had the Kingdom that is within you become a place outside of everyone? But with the help of Nicoll and the above parable, I could easily see how this could happen.

Nicoll restates a critical aspect of the higher esoteric teaching by telling us that this new garment—new teaching—must be worn.[38] For me, this means that one has to imbibe the teaching, one has to live it. It is not enough to just think about it or accept it. Nicoll points out that the new must be accepted in its entirety. Also, accepting something you don't understand will not transform you—only confuse you. In other words, if a person takes it in the old way through the intellect alone, as a new doctrine to believe in, instead of directly participating in the "transformation of mind," the transformation of awareness and understanding that's available to them, they will not move towards the necessary rebirth required to enter the Kingdom. To attain the higher inner State, you have to shift your identity to the witness and its expanded awareness and begin to understand the true meanings of esoteric teachings!

A Joyous Awakening

It was easy for me to see how most were content to assume that accepting Jesus as their savior and advocating the basic teachings that accompany this view was all that was necessary to enter the Kingdom, the place of reward for the faithful, the place where God is. Due to a misunderstanding, the Kingdom is seen as a place to go after death rather than a "state" to be sought after and experienced in this life, right here and now! It was also easy to see why the priests and ministers so often focus on the literal doctrines to keep their flock in line, in good Christian standing. This is in contrast to the much more challenging job of helping one truly understand the teachings and how to begin to live according to the teachings. In other words, how to start awakening, evolving and becoming a real Christian—a compassionate and non-judgmental being—and feeling its transformational value.

Those who have really tried to follow Christ's teachings know that it's very tough to "obey" the teachings, especially those that refer to one's inner life, inner thoughts, and emotions. This is when you truly realize that you need more help. This is when a higher level of instruction is needed in order to begin living the teaching. I knew that I was supremely blessed that my own Self was providing the primary help, and G and his students were providing much-appreciated secondary support!

Nicoll quotes Christ speaking to Nicodemus; *"Verily, verily I say unto thee, except a man be born from above, he cannot see the Kingdom of God,"* John III, 3 For me, this is exactly the same as saying— *"only one born of water and spirit can enter the Kingdom, and both are referring to one's 'Self'—one's pure and divine Nature—revealing 'Itself' to you."*

This is the genuine rebirth—compliments of Spirit. It is truly being reborn from above because your true "Self" is absolutely pure, sacred, holy and is definitely on a level far above your normal self. It is this State of consciousness that the Kingdom represents. Being born "from above", being born of the spirit, is when you directly experience the highest Truth, a "State" beyond words and thoughts. It is a spiritual experience—a spiritual "State," where you directly experience your identity and oneness with the Supreme.

Based on my own experience, I could see why one had to enter into a state of a near perfect alignment with the pure awareness of the witness. If you're not in this vigilant, calm, quiet and pure "state", your true Self cannot reveal itself to you. If one's mind is active in its normal manner, this subtlest and holiest of "experiences" can't come through the noise. This is why, again and again in the spiritual literature, you find statements about the necessity of stilling the mind to experience the Truth. There is a classic analogy that pertains to this. It says that only when one's mind is as clear and undisturbed as a perfectly calm pond can it act like a mirror and allow you to see the reflection of your true Self. My own image at this time was that when one was in this pure, still, and alert "State," their mind, their awareness, was like a radio that was perfectly tuned to receive a very hard-to-get station, the "Self." Like the radio signal—the "Self" was always there—you just needed the perfectly tuned instrument to get in touch with it.

As to the idea of the old not being able to receive the new, I like the biblical illustration of not being able to put new wine in old skins. You have to remember that the wine represents the highest Truth, the inexpressible experience of your own Self. So, what's being said is that the highest teaching and Knowledge, which comes forth from within, cannot be put into or received by old containers. Yes, containers like your culturally conditioned concepts and your familiar sense of limited self that holds the habitual I's of ego personality (habitual internal dialogue) that one has always taken to be yourself. The new understanding, this wine, has to be put into fresh skins, and the fresh skins represent one's revolutionary new identity and understanding that comes through the "Experience" of your oneness with the Supreme.

There are a couple of reasons why the *new skins* are absolutely necessary. First, the old skins—old concepts, beliefs, and images of yourself simply cannot contain the highest Truth, the truth of your identity with God's vastness. Yes, this new wine (new revelation) will surely burst the old skins! Secondly, in addition to the state of pure silent awareness being necessary to actually receive the wine, the Self. Again, it is necessary that you have practiced self-remembering (meditation) extensively so that you know, for sure, that the pure awareness of the witness is indeed your real self. Then, when your Self reveals "Itself," you naturally recognize that It is a higher expression of and the source of your conscious awareness. If you are not familiar with the witness consciousness and only identify with your habitual I's, then the experience of your true Self could be taken as something other than your true nature. In that event, the experience could be quite disturbing and confusing; this, too, could burst the old skins.

The Pharisee (the Ego) Prevents Us from Entering the Kingdom

In the last part of his introductory remarks in this chapter on the Kingdom, Nicoll speaks about the Pharisee because the Pharisee shuts himself and others from the kingdom. Let us now briefly look at the Pharisee and what he represents in this ancient teaching. The Gospel shows Christ attacking the Pharisees, whereas He offers almost everyone else unconditional love and compassion. On one level, the Pharisee represents one who does everything for show and recognition and also focuses only on the outer ritual and literal obedience to religious doctrine.

A Joyous Awakening

As a youngster, I could easily see the falseness and self-love (ego) of the Pharisee in the Gospel, and as a child with an open heart, you just knew that this was not the way to be. But now, I could see that when one is not taught about the ego, and how easily influenced it is by peer pressure and cultural conditioning, and the immense power of the senses and the vagaries of your mind, it is easy to fall prey to this weaker side of your nature as you get older. Even after I had begun to recognize the ego in myself, it was not easy to change or catch it at the moment it was taking place. Thanks to G and his students, I finally had some tools for dealing with and exposing it's falseness. From this, I knew that the Pharisee represented this immature and insecure part of my nature that, as Nicoll said, does everything out of self-love. Yoga adds that everything is done out of desire and fear, due to the ignorance of our true Nature.

G taught that this immature part of our nature, which we now refer to as the ego, can't evolve spiritually—can't turn within—can't undergo genuine transformation. This is why the Pharisee in us (our ego) prevents us from entering the Kingdom, but it also prevents us from the experience of the expanded awareness of the witness. Nicoll focuses on the sin of hypocrisy—doing everything for show with no real internal understanding and says that this is what truly dams the Pharisees.[39]

"But woe unto you, scribes and Pharisees, hypocrites! Because ye shut the kingdom of heaven against men, for ye enter not in yourselves." Matt XXIII, 13,14

Hypocrisy keeps a person stuck in their ego, focusing on the wrong direction, without verses within and identified with the lowest part of their nature. But at a subtler level, at the level of the "Kingdom," as I've said previously, this pure "State" cannot be accessed or revealed when one is identified with any of their lower "I's," such as those associated with lust, greed, vanity, envy, anxious thoughts, etc., not just hypocrisy. I had experienced the truth of this time and again over these past few weeks. Inevitably, when centered in the witness, other thoughts, and emotions (other I's) would present themselves—tempting me to shift my sense of self from that of the witness to being identified with them as I had always done before. As I've said, many times they succeeded. But when I was truly centered in the Self, I knew that these thoughts were not me.

I also knew that if I allowed myself to become identified with these old habitual I's, I would lose touch with this most precious and real aspect of my being, my Self. As the saying goes, you can't be in two places at once. I could see that this identification with the ego is how each of us truly damns ourselves and prevents us from entering the Kingdom.

This completed my first look at Nicoll's thoughts on the Kingdom of Heaven and, once again, I was amazed at how easily I could understand him and even more so, at how closely this "teaching" aligned with and articulated my inner experience. I enjoyed a hot bath and got to sleep early, knowing it was going to require a lot of focus to be in the presence of this steward and still remain "awake."

I reported to work early the next morning, expecting that I would have to make some form of report, but I was told that everything was taken care of and to forget the whole thing. I thought that that was good advice because my desire was to just remain vigilant in the present. But shortly after getting back into the kitchen, the old part of me that I'm calling my mind (my ego) wanted to belittle the steward and make him explain why he hadn't notified anyone about the situation at hand. My ego mind also wanted to run the whole organization down—all of the maintenance men who, in my ego's opinion, were too lazy to do their jobs and the management for not wanting to even know what happened. But thanks goodness I was still well centered in the witness and was, therefore, not surprised to see that my mind was playing its familiar role. I remembered that Gurdjieff had taught that it's not really a matter of things being right or wrong, it's a matter of staying conscious.

Things went well at work, with the steward basically avoiding me. The chef who had arrived on the train from Montreal had lunch completely prepared and a good start on the evening meal. After serving lunch, I had my helpers do the few things that were needed to get ready for supper, and I returned to my room, anxious to see what Nicoll had to say about the parables that referred specifically to the Kingdom of Heaven.

Nicoll begins by saying that the first parable given by Christ is that of the Sower Matt XIII, 4–9 and that this is the starting point of Christ's teaching about the Kingdom. Also, Christ Himself says that this is the parable of parables—unless it is understood that other parables cannot be.

The Parables of the Sower and the Tares

Before I begin sharing my insights into these parables, just a reminder that this is not Bible study! We are not talking about beliefs. This is about recognizing that the parables about the Kingdom are indeed speaking about the Teachings that tell us of our capacity to experience union with God and the difficulties and subtleties of following these esoteric Teachings. Also, a final reminder that these parables are aiding me in my attempt at sharing my experiences of the transcendent State of awareness.

The parable from Jesus is this:

"A sower went out to sow. And as he sowed some fell by the wayside; the birds came and ate it up. Some fell on rocky ground, where it has little soil, and it sprouted quickly because it had no depth of earth... Some seed fell among thistles;

the thistles shot up and choked the corn. And some of the seed fell into good soil, where it bore fruit, yielding a hundredfold or it might be sixtyfold or thirtyfold. If you have ears, hear."

Immediately after hearing Jesus say this, His disciples ask, *"Why do you speak to them in parables?"* Jesus replied, *"It has been granted to you to know the secrets of the Kingdom of Heaven: but to those others it has not been granted... I speak to them in parables because, in seeing they see not, in hearing they hear not, neither do they understand."* Jesus then tells His disciples that *"They are very fortunate to hear what they now see and hear, because many saints and prophets desired to hear it and yet never heard it."*

A reminder that these esoteric teachings are not meant for the public. They are for a select few of the Master's disciples. This seems to have been the case with most spiritual Masters for millennia. We are also reminded that many others longed to hear the real and highest meaning of these esoteric teachings that they are about to hear. So, we in the present day have a rare opportunity to listen up and begin participating.

Then Jesus says, *"You then may hear the parable of the sower."* Matt XIII:18

"When a man hears the word that tells of the Kingdom but fails to understand it, the evil one comes and carries off what has been sown in his heart. There you have the seed sown along the footpath. The seed sown on rocky ground stands for the man who, on hearing the word, accepts it at once with joy; but as it strikes no root in him because he has no staying-power, and when there is trouble or persecution on account of the word, he falls away at once. The seed sown among thistles represents the man who hears the word, but worldly cares and the false glamour of wealth choke it, and it proves barren. But the seed that fell into good soil is the man who hears the word and understands it, who accordingly bears fruit, and yields a hundredfold or it may be, sixtyfold or thirtyfold." Matt XIII, 19–23

Nicoll concludes that the parable of the Sower and its explanation by Christ shows that *"Man is sown onto the earth as material for the Kingdom of Heaven; the human race is an 'experiment in inner evolution.'"*[41] From my own experience, I couldn't believe that Nicoll would come to such an odd conclusion! It was clear to me and should be to all that *what is sown* is the *word*, the Teachings—not man! Christ says at the outset: *"When a man hears the word that tells of the Kingdom but fails to understand it"*... Matt, XIII, 19. There is no question that what is being sown is the *word*, the teaching about the Kingdom.

Another thing that isn't mentioned is that the seed and then the word that speaks of the Kingdom both center around inner transformation, the underlying message of spiritual teachings. And it's primarily a transformation in identity, away from being identified with body and mind—the thoughts and emotions of the elementary ego. Whereas the word, the teachings of the Kingdom, shifts one's identity, one's sense of self, to the pure awareness of the witness, to their spirit that can see the falsity of the ego. This is the growth and evolution available to those who seek it. So how did the Kingdom that is within you end up outside, as a place to go after death, I wondered?

Also, knowing that the "Self" already exists within everyone, I couldn't relate to Nicoll's idea that humanity is an "experiment" in inner evolution. Based on my experience and perspective, I didn't see it that way at all. For me, the word that speaks of the Kingdom within is about the possibility of one's own inner evolution, if they are sufficiently mature. As the parable indicates, some are ready, but most are not. Also, it's obvious that most people are not aware of the esoteric teaching about one's capacity to know the Self. Not because this teaching is not available, but because they are not psychologically and spiritually mature enough to look for it and take it in.

Jesus tells us that this parable is about the secrets of the Kingdom that many saints desired to hear but didn't. I'd say this is important enough that we should look closely at Jesus' explanation of the parable of parables—because it's the key we are told. We need to pay attention because it has been and continues to be totally misunderstood and therefore not used to evolve as intended!

Christ says:

"When a man hears the word that tells of the Kingdom but fails to understand it, the evil one comes and carries off what has been sown in his heart. There you have the seed sown along the path."

Yes, for me, this is exactly what happens to many. They hear the *word* about the Kingdom, whether at the orthodox, the spiritual (esoteric), or transcendent level—which is the level the *word* truly refers to—and their heart feels good. Intuitively, they feel the truth of the *word*, this teaching about their divine nature. But, since they do not understand much about the process of inner transformation, they are vulnerable to the ego's desires and conditioning. The evil one, I now realized, represents the ego and its many desires, limited knowledge, and heavy cultural conditioning—all preventing inner growth. This is how the evil one carries off the recognition of the heart.

The next metaphor in this explanation of the Sower, Jesus says,

"The seed sown on rocky ground stands for the man who, on hearing the word, accepts it at once with joy but as it strikes no 'root in him'—he falls away easily when trouble presents itself on account of the word."

Again, we have a person who hears the *word* about the Kingdom and readily accepts it in his heart, even though he doesn't truly understand it. But when a higher level of commitment is required, when the orthodox priest challenges his understanding, when he is experiencing the pull of the flesh or his sense of pride, and so on, he easily falls away. Why? Again, he really does not understand it and thus is not ready.

The parable continues:

"The seed sown among thistles represents the man who hears the word, but worldly cares and the false glamour of wealth choke it."

Again, these just tell it the way it is—it's an accurate description of what happens. It is not easy to understand this teaching and live by its precepts. It's difficult to evolve, awaken, and rise above one's lower nature. As I had experienced, again and again, these past few weeks, it is easy to fall prey to the ego. The ego—our individual and habitual sense of self—never gives up the effort to be in control, which makes it very difficult to hold on to and live the essence of the teaching, outwardly and inwardly. I had not discussed my experiences with anyone because I knew most people were not ready to hear this higher truth about our true Nature. Such a thing causes trouble—Jesus was crucified for it!

Finally,

"The seed that fell into good soil is the man who hears the word and understands it, who accordingly bears fruit, and yields a hundred-fold."

This can apply to different levels of understanding of this teaching of the word about the Kingdom, but for me, it definitely was referring to the miraculous fruit I had been experiencing these past weeks. True understanding, for me, implies knowing what to do, how to do it and then actually doing it, participating in your own inner transformation. This is how you experience and receive the fruitful bounty that is possible for one to receive.

The second parable about the Kingdom immediately follows the explanation of the first. Since I had plenty of time and had never really thought about these parables, I was anxious to see what it said. Once again, I was amazed to see how well I understood these subtle matters I was reading and contemplating. I would have never believed that reading the New Testament could be so fun and enlightening, too!

The second parable begins with a simile:

"The kingdom of Heaven is likened unto a man that sowed good seed in his field; but while men slept, his enemy came and sowed tares among the wheat, and went away." When the blade sprang up and began to fill out, the tares could be seen among it. The farmer's men went to their master and said, *"Sir, was it not good seed that you sowed in your field? Then where have the tares come from?"* *"This is an enemy's doing,"* he replied. *"Well then,"* they said, *"shall we go and*

gather the tares?" "No, in gathering it, you might pull up the wheat at the same time." Matt XIII, 24–30

Nicoll makes a point in his commentary that went well with my own thoughts concerning this second parable. This concerned the statement: *"But while men slept, his enemy came and sowed tares among the wheat."* Nicoll tells us that in the original Greek, this phrase, *While men slept* translates literally as, *"In the sleep of men."* This refers to one's habitual ego and all the other things that I've spoken about concerning *"sleep."* One must remember that the good seed that is sown refers to the teaching about the possibility of man's inner evolution and the capacity to experience one's own Self. The enemy refers to one's own individual and immature conditioned ego. One has to remember that in sacred literature, the symbols refer to you, to different states of awareness within you.

Nicoll makes another important point that I could never have appreciated without him. He tells us that the Greek word translated as tares refers to a weed that looks like wheat when it is beginning to grow.[40] In other words, right after the true and higher teaching about the Kingdom has been given, the ego inevitably contaminates the teachings by sowing seeds of misunderstanding and doubt, which themselves seem like aspects of the teachings. Again, when you are "asleep," you still identify with every thought and emotion that comes up instead of being in the "awakened state." The ego can't help but contaminate and distort the original pure teaching about inner evolution leading to union with God, just as "it" contaminates one's pristine awareness. Today, too many orthodox cultures, Christian or not, consider this teaching about divine union to be blasphemy!

Speaking from experience, I can say that in the early stages, it's hard to recognize the distortions from the teachings, from the truth. It can be quite difficult to differentiate between the wheat and the tares. I certainly experienced this the first eight days of my awakening, but this can also happen at any time when you are not centered in the witness. But at the same time, I was now sure that one did not have to worry— they just had to stay" awake" as best they could, and everything would take care of itself.

Nicoll makes another very important point by telling us that Christ makes many references in the Gospels to the necessity of being "awake" in order to hear and understand the *Word* that tells of the Kingdom. Nicoll also points out that the Greek word translated as watch actually means "be awake." As I experienced for myself and have shown, being awake—being in the state of the witness, is *the key* to truly understanding this teaching. The challenge is to stay awake because, as Christ tells us, in His interpretation of the parable of the sower, the tares are the sons of the evil one—the ego. The tares represent misunderstandings about the Word, the teaching about the Kingdom, and these are sown *in the sleep of men*, when one is at the mercy of their ego and all of "its" stuff. This is something that everyone must experience for themselves. In the pure awareness of meditation, there is no other way!

Finally, at the harvest, when the seed, which is the spiritual seeker's understanding, has matured, when the spiritual seeker knows thyself and, more importantly, knows "Thy Self," it is easier to separate the genuine truths from the ego-made distortions. Again, when one's Self reveals Itself, this level of consciousness, level of "knowing," vastly differs from one's everyday level of knowing, comprised mainly of rational and discursive knowledge. The Truth has nothing to do with beliefs or rational and cultural knowledge. It has nothing to do with rational conclusions or centuries-old religious beliefs. These are the tares, the weeds. The Truth is transcendent—the *state* of one's Self, which can only be experienced within one's own being, is referred to as the Kingdom and many other names. This divine Wisdom that is inherent in your Self makes it easy to know what to keep and value and what to toss.

Feeling awed at how clear my understanding seemed to be, I happily returned to the kitchen to finish preparing the evening meal.

An Unexpected Challenge

There were a lot of people on the train, but everything went smoothly and as was the custom, the employees ate after everyone else was finished. While enjoying the view and the ensuing twilight, I and the others sitting with me heard the steward, who was sitting directly behind us, tell those he was sitting with that he thought that I had prepared yesterday's evening meal for the Montreal crew. And that, *"it just wasn't right to close the dining car down like that; it had never been done before."* He said that there were just too many young people working now, who just do not know what they are doing.

The four of us at the table looked at each other in disbelief. We all knew that the steward had been told why I was taking the car out of service, had been told more than once to call Winnipeg to let them know the situation, and had personally looked at the kitchen after it had been all cleaned up!

Personally, I could not believe my ears. My first *reaction* was to verbally abuse this sorry person so severely that he would either psychologically self-destruct or get up and fight. But I was still partially "awake" enough to know that this would be giving in to my old mechanical self, my ego, and its conditioned tendencies. But the unexpectedness of this personal attack, however, had me feeling quite "identified" with my old self (old I's)—more than I had felt in some time. The un-evolved is just so touchy, so ready to fight!

The Kingdom of Heaven Is Within You

Intent on refraining from falling "asleep," I stood up, looked the steward straight in the eye and told him that it was obvious to me, and to the others present, that he was losing touch with reality.

I told him, *"Everybody here knows why I closed the kitchen down, knows that I told you to contact Winnipeg and knows that you assured me that you had more than once. Everyone also knows that you saw the kitchen after it was prepared for the health inspectors."* I also told him that even though the people in Winnipeg wanted to just forget about this, I knew that it was my responsibility to tell our supervisor in Vancouver the whole story, especially what you just said in front of these witnesses. Turning red in the face, he left the car without a word.

Realizing that I was becoming quite identified with my assessments, I told my second and third cooks to close the kitchen down for the night and I also left without another word.

Considering what had happened over the last couple of days, things went along fairly well the next morning, but the steward was definitely taking every opportunity to show everyone that he was still the boss. It was obviously not going to be possible to deal with him rationally, so most of us tried to avoid him and ignore him. This worked up until the second seating for lunch. The dining room had 44 seats, so the passengers would be given a seating time, eleven, twelve, or one o'clock for lunch. Such made it easy for the passengers and the crew. People were not allowed to come in halfway through the setting to make this routine work. The steward is the one who is supposed to enforce this.

Beginning at breakfast, the steward allowed and even encouraged people to come in anytime. I told him that this was clearly against the rules and that I would not be serving anyone who came in between settings from now on.

To no one's surprise, he allowed a group to come in halfway through the second setting. When the waiter came in the kitchen to put the soup order in, I told him that I had made it clear this morning that I would not be serving people between seatings. Therefore, would he please inform the steward that I will not be serving these folks right now? The steward came in shaking and demanding that I do as he told me. I was expecting this and thus was able to say, from a fairly conscious state, that I was no longer putting up with his childish behavior. He would just have to tell these people to leave and come back at their appointed time because I would not serve them. Looking like he was going to have a coronary, he told me I was fired. He was taking me out of service, and I was to return to my room immediately.

I said fine, handed him my apron, told him he could do the cooking and left.

As I was walking back to my room, I was pleased to realize that I felt fine, felt reasonably "awake" and thought that it was the right choice to stand up to this unstable fellow, stand up for the rules and for the employees that the rules were made for. I also looked forward to just spending some time by myself. I knew before leaving that it would be a challenge to stay "awake" on this return trip but wasn't expecting things to be quite so wild.

More Parables about Entering the Kingdom

After looking out the window to enjoy the scenery and to, once again, get well connected with and established in the witness, I decided it was time to carry on with Nicoll's look at the parables about the Kingdom of Heaven.

The third and fourth parables—the Parable of the Man and the Grain of Mustard Seed and the Parable of the Woman and the Leaven were short and were, again, about taking the teaching, acting upon it, and living it. The parables are these:

The Kingdom of Heaven is like unto a grain of mustard seed, which a man took and sowed in his field: which is indeed less than all seeds: but when it is grown, it is greater than the herbs, and becomes a tree, so the birds of heaven come and lodge in the branches thereof. Matt XIII:31–32

Another parable he spoke unto them: the Kingdom of Heaven is like unto leaven, which a woman took, and hid in three measures of meal, till it was all leavened. Matt XIII:33

Again, this is just what I would expect, a reiteration of the first two parables, about taking the teaching and acting upon it and how this effort allows your understanding of the teachings and yourself to grow enormously. This is exactly what I had experienced this past month. In the ancient language, in the symbols of esoteric teachings, the field represents us and like a normal field this is where growth takes place. Nicoll expands upon this by telling us that in the language of the parables, birds represent thoughts and birds of heaven represent thoughts, that belong to the level of the Kingdom, what I prefer to call insights, and direct Knowledge. Again, my experience exactly! Just by practicing and valuing the teaching the best I could, insights from the Self, the Kingdom, just came to me as described.

I found Nicoll's thoughts on the fourth parable to be very enlightening and in support of my own experience and understanding. Nicoll points out that the woman takes the leaven and hides it as opposed to sowing it. He suggests that this is to distinguish it from the *"leaven of the Pharisees and Sadducees"* that Christ speaks about elsewhere, Matt XVI, 5–12, which, of course, in the language of the parables, refers to their teachings. As before, we are reminded that the religion of the Pharisees was all about outer merit and show, about keeping the literal law, and not about inner transformation.

The Kingdom of Heaven Is Within You

In contrast to the Pharisees, the woman hides the teaching within, takes it and applies it within, instead of boasting, which in turn affects the whole of her being. (The number three in the language of the parables represents the whole or completeness). Again, this certainly was my experience of taking this teaching to heart and working with it within myself. It had affected the whole of me and had raised my level of understanding enormously. Nicoll makes the astute observation that these two parables are also about the two ways of receiving the teaching—through the mind and the heart, and that all four parables together give a good picture of esoteric teaching.[42] The spiritual teaching about a seeker and his/her journey to the Self, the Kingdom within.

I had to agree that it was a good account of the need to truly understand the essence of spiritual teachings, to understand that there are many distortions to the genuine teachings, and to realize that one has to "awaken," make effort and cherish the teaching every day to evolve. Then, one day, you can experience the Truth of the teaching for oneself, within your own Self.

Shortly after I'd finished these contemplations on the parables about the Kingdom, one of the waiters, a college student, stopped by and commented on the craziness of this trip. I agreed with him and said that in the four summers that I had worked, I had never seen anything quite like it. After talking for a few minutes, he told me that he was surprised that I was not angry with the steward for the way he had treated me. I acknowledged that a part of me wanted to feel that way, but recently, I had learned that giving in to anger just held you in a very low and miserable state. I asked him, *"Why should I let someone like him cause me to be angry when I am actually feeling peaceful and happy?"* He responded, saying, *"That sounds good, but how can you realistically do it?"*

I told him that I had been practicing a technique associated with the ancient quest to "know thyself" and that this had allowed me to get in touch with a part of myself I'd never known was there. This deeper part was much more free and joyful, more the real me. But if I allow myself to wallow in anger, I cannot stay connected with this deeper aspect. I told him, *"Since I've been working hard at staying in touch with this more joyous and natural part for some time now, I can ignore the steward and keep in touch with the great vibes I'm feeling inside."*

Not surprisingly, he said that he wasn't quite sure what I meant by the deeper part of myself.

I told him that the best and simplest clue I could give him was to watch his thoughts and emotions as if they were someone else's, someone he wanted to know and understand well. I said, *"That part of yourself that can watch your thoughts is the key to this inner freedom."*

He wished me well and said he'd think about what I'd said and try it, but it was now time to get back to work. Right after he left, the thought came that I was not embroiled in anger because of taking the teaching to heart and practicing it intently. But from another perspective or level, it was also due to the fact that I could not forget or deny that the "Self" was not only the essence of myself but of the steward as well. I knew that this was one of the great fruits of truly valuing and practicing the teaching about inner transformation.

I took advantage of this unexpected free time to practice self-remembering and read some of Ouspensky's book. I had one of the cooks bring me some food, so I would not have to be exposed to the negative vibes of the steward. Just as it was getting dark, I decided to read a little more of Nicoll's book—realizing how lucky I was to be able to see that my own experiences were in agreement with the spiritual (esoteric) meaning of Christ's teaching. I was finally beginning to understand Jesus' teachings!

The Parables of the Hidden Treasure and the Pearl of Great Price

The next parables show the seeker how to enter the Kingdom of Heaven. These parables are about the hidden treasure in the field, the pearl of great price, and the need to sell all that one has in order to buy the treasure. Matt: XIII 44–46. Nicoll says these parables are about inner selection—what a person must do internally to attain the Kingdom. This does seem to be the case, as we'll see shortly, but as I read these parables that particular evening, I was immediately reminded that when I first experienced my pure Self within, one of the initial images that just came forth on its own was that this sacred and divine Self was *the pearl of great price*. As mentioned, right from my initial experience of the Self, I knew this is what I am, what I truly am, and all that I thought I was before—assumed I was before—had to be viewed in a new way. Again, the experience of one's Self is so pure and powerful that there is no question that it is your true Nature. It's like waking up from a dream and immediately being able to let go of all the images, situations, and conflicts, and so on that seemed so important in the dream but that you now know are irrelevant and unreal. This makes them easy to let go.

On a different level, the treasure or pearl refers to the authentic teachings about inner evolution and how important it is to take them in and let go of the lesser teachings, which are contaminated with manmade distortions.

And, as Nicoll says, it is about inner selection, the process of inner transformation that takes place when you take the teaching and put it into action. As I've described, this started happening to me at a remarkable rate when I first began practicing being consciously present in the witness. I easily found that the witness part of my awareness was (is) extremely adept at knowing what to keep and what to get rid of. Through this inner *work*, as G called it, the witness guided me to the experience of my true Self.

Nicoll points out that in each parable a person must sell all he has in order to buy the treasure. This is a major point in these esoteric teachings about the Self, the pure One—the treasure within. It refers to what a seeker of Truth must do within oneself to experience the state the Kingdom represents. To *sell all that you have* means to get rid of your wrong images of yourself and of your culturally conditioned belief system, and even your sense of individuality, the belief that you are your body and your personal history. This is not done through philosophy or religious doctrine but through turning within and getting in touch with your truer self through the witness and then your real Self through grace. Meditation shifts your sense of self to pure awareness—the one Consciousness in us all. This is how you loosen your sense of individuality and experience your connection with humanity! In order to evolve inwardly and ultimately reach the goal of the spiritual journey, you have to sell, discard—all of your limited beliefs, misunderstandings, negative habits, and attachments—all of which are associated with your small individual ego. This is impossible to do through will-power alone, especially for a person who still is attached to their small ego.

But one who is in touch with the witness does this automatically, by not identifying with any of these thoughts or images. As I've said repeatedly, I found it becomes easy not to be attached to the mental conditioning associated with my culturally conditioned ego-personality when my sense of self is truly centered in the witness—the part of our awareness that is separate from our conditioned mind. This is what has been missed for millennia—it's why authentic meditation is unappreciated and totally misunderstood. It's essentially the same with respect to contemplation where the seeker holds a subject of interest in their silent awareness and allows their deeper consciousness to reveal what it may at that time. Thus, another way to connect with one's deeper Consciousness.

Of course, becoming fully or permanently established in the state of the witness is a process that is accomplished with much effort over time. To become established in the Self is another thing altogether—some say lifetimes for this perfected State! Therefore, even when you have experienced getting past certain ego patterns, some are so stealthily ingrained that they will surface when certain situations come up. This is why the continued practice of self-remembering, being consciously present as best you can every day—is a must.

Nicoll also points out that, in Luke XVIII, 22, and XII,—33 Christ reiterates the teaching, "Sell all ye have" and says that one of the things that must be gotten rid of is anxiety, and in addition to this almost impossible task, Christ in the

A Joyous Awakening

Sermon on the Mount, asks us to pass no judgment and to always treat others as you would have them treat you. Anyone who has sincerely tried to keep these teachings, in thought, word, and deed, knows how difficult this is. Again, my experience showed me that while my everyday mind could not keep these teachings, the witness could do so without effort!

Shortly after these parables, Christ says in Matt XVI, 24–26:

"If anyone wishes to be a follower of mine, he must leave self behind, but if a man will let himself be lost for my sake, he will find his true self."

This is just a reiteration of this ancient teaching that says; you must leave your old self, old beliefs, and understandings behind. Your sense of self must become free and pure in order to experience your true Self. This teaching (the Word) can be a little hard to understand until you actually take the teaching in, learn to turn within, and put it into practice by participating in self-remembering in your daily life. Then, once you are familiar with the witness, it's easy to see the need to go beyond one's old self by embracing the guidance and deeper understanding that the witness, the pure Spirit, provides. For me, this is the most natural and quickest route to the inner transformation that the esoteric teachings speak about. Getting to know yourself through the witness's perspective lets you to see your ego and its childish ways right when they are happening. This lets you see for yourself what needs to be sold—gotten rid of—and also what needs to be retained and expanded—awareness!

This teaching is hard to understand because most have never been taught, have never heard anything about our need and capacity to know ourselves. Most people have never heard about their capacity to transform, about higher states of consciousness, or about the Self. They are only familiar with the literal, the most basic and elementary aspect of religion and sacred literature.

I would like to offer the seeker another perspective that I experienced, which is connected with this principle of selling all that you have so that you can buy what you value most. G taught that to "awaken" and make progress in the quest for inner evolution, one had to conserve energy by not wasting it on conditioned and mechanical behavior, outwardly and within one's own being.[43] Once I was established in the witness, I was able to begin to quit identifying with many of the thoughts and emotions that continually kept coming forth on their own accord.

As I got better at this, I realized that I had a lot more energy available to me, and this energy allowed—helped me—to stay better connected to the witness. This made perfect sense because I wasn't throwing it away on so much thinking and pointless internal dialogue. I was saving my energy by not identifying my sense of self with these many and ever-flowing thoughts and emotions. I was *selling* or letting go of my old habitual self. This allowed me to buy or hold on to what I valued the most, which was the witness state, the state that was responsible for my inner transformation. Yes, inner selection and inner awareness are very important in this ancient and mystical teaching.

As I thought about this further, I could see that what I was doing in this regard was making oil for my lamp! As mentioned, this energy savings also expressed itself as not needing as much sleep as I normally did and not requiring as much food either. Even though this was the case for weeks, my energy was clearer and more robust than ever before, and of a higher octane. Again—come see for yourself—you will not be disappointed.

The next morning, I woke up with the dawn and was happy to see that we were in the heart of the Canadian Rockies. The vistas, as I described before, are just gorgeous and the perfect setting for the practice of self-remembering. My mind was very peaceful and focused while enjoying the spectacular scenery. Thoughts about the Kingdom, mainly concerning last night's contemplation, were about the only thoughts coming forth. They were mainly reminders about how fortunate I was, and how my understanding of the Kingdom, religion, and of myself had been radically changed, and that all of this change had come from within myself—via effort and Grace.

I went to breakfast in the best of moods, determined to stay "awake," knowing we would be back in Vancouver just before noon. Everything went well. Except for some cold looks, the steward ignored me. The other employees were very friendly and eager to tell me what a jerk the steward was being. I reminded them not to let this poor, disturbed soul get to them. We were almost home, and I was going to talk with our supervisor about this trip and about this fellow running in charge.

After spending about an hour in the dining car chatting with employees and tourists, all the while making a determined attempt to stay "awake," I returned to my room to finish Nicoll's last section in his chapter on the Kingdom, which I had enjoyed so much on this most unusual of trips.

Have Ye Understood All These Things?

After giving the last of the parables about the Kingdom, Christ asks the disciples if they have understood all these things. They answer yes, which Nicoll says is *extraordinary*. I had to agree with him, since it was clear to me that the teaching cannot be understood through intellectual concepts alone. Nicoll points out that this new teaching from Jesus must have been especially difficult for His disciples to understand because they expected the Kingdom to be a literal place, something that Jews had been expecting for centuries. I felt the same. Surely, it would be impossible for His disciples, who, we assume, have just heard these parables for the first time, to have even a basic understanding of the Kingdom. Or about the inner transformation that leads to the state of the pure Self, let alone to take in all of its subtle and mystical meaning. Again, participation in the teachings is a must before you can *know and understand* yourself.

Nicoll supports his view by pointing out that, in His response, Christ refers to householders who mix up the new and the old. This refers to what was said earlier in reference to John the Baptist about mixing the new with the old. Remember he was speaking about trying to understand something new through the old and how this renders the new powerless. As I pointed out earlier, it is completely natural for a person to try and understand something new in relation to their present concepts and beliefs. The only way around this fact, this teaching, is to actually participate in the quest to know thyself via self-remembering (meditation) so that you can begin to see for yourself your own conditioning and ego. Remember too that this same age-old principle of mixing the new with the old, and thereby contaminating the new, is kind of the essence of the first two parables about the Kingdom. The 13th chapter of Matthew ends with Christ returning to His hometown and being rejected by the local people. Nicoll says that this is just another reiteration of the principle that the old cannot receive the new.[44]

This made perfect sense to me because throughout this "awakening," I had wanted to share my new understanding and joy with my family, but knew there was really no way to do so. This new way of seeing and understanding is not something that can be grasped with just an explanation. Even with Nicoll's book, how could anyone understand or believe my perspective without first intensely participating in self-observation and self-remembering for quite some time? I certainly was not overly concerned about this; it just seemed natural, however, that having found this hidden inner treasure, I would want to share it.

We arrived in Vancouver on time, and even though I was looking forward to being at the beach, I knew I had to talk with my supervisor. I was in a great mood and a good state of self-awareness, and I was determined to remain *awake* while giving the basic story of this wild trip. I also knew that my old tendencies would be to become quite "identified" with all of my anger and concerns about why this company puts up with so much incompetence. At first, I did fine giving him the basic gist of how things had unfolded. But when I heard that he didn't even want to talk to the steward, I pretty much immediately lost it, fell "asleep." I instantly identified with my old views and feelings, and started complaining about how lazy and irresponsible people were, how this company was run so poorly and foolishly that it was disgusting, and so on.

My supervisor sat there very relaxed: he smiled at me and told me that I should be glad that I did not have to work here all my life like many of these guys had to. He said that many of these old guys had had it pretty rough and were almost finished working, and he thought it best to leave them alone. I asked how he could put up with this week in and week out? He responded by telling me not to take all this so seriously. Everything was going to work out, and I would be gone soon anyway. *"Just forget about all this,"* he said, *"Enjoy your visit here."*

When he said that, I began to "wake up," realizing that he was right and that I had succumbed to my old feelings without even noticing! I told him he was right and thanked him for his time and fatherly advice. As I left his office, I had to laugh at myself, knowing that he had been more "awake" than I was and that he was right; I didn't know half of what these fellows had been through or how this company was really doing. I did know that I was glad that this trip was over and that I could now spend some time outside—at the beach.

A Deeper Experience of Oneness

It was another perfect day to be at the ocean; the sun, sand, and water felt great, and the feeling of unrestricted movement was a treat after being on the train for a couple of days. I was thoroughly enjoying myself throughout the afternoon, but was a little surprised to observe that I was experiencing quite a low level of energy—something that I had not felt in quite some time. My "mind," as I had come to call it, still wanted to complain about the steward and the railroad in general. I had not been buying into these old patterns but realized that this past trip and the feelings that were aroused from it had taken more out of me than I had realized. I had to assume that this was why part of me was feeling a little low. I knew that all I had to do was keep my awareness, my sense of self, in the witness, and everything would be fine.

I woke up at dawn feeling great and immediately went on a walk to make sure I got well-centered in the witness before the "mind" could fall into its old habits. After breakfast and a little reading on the porch, I headed to one of the local beaches, knowing it would be awhile before the crowds arrived. By early afternoon, I was ready to just sit in the sand, focus on the picturesque surroundings and enjoy the deep serenity that I was experiencing.

As I was sitting there, practicing self-remembering, as I had done for weeks now, being perfectly contented as I was, I once again, through no effort of my own, entered into a very deep "state of the Self." This state was similar to what I experienced on June 20th. But the experience of this day was different than anything I had experienced previously. The feeling was that this was just a deeper experience of the Divine within or another facet of this sacred Self. There is no way to describe such an experience adequately—describe the "Transcendent State." But, I will say a few things here to try and give a little feel of how it differed from the experience of the "Self" on June 20th.

On this day, the state that I experienced was one of perfect inner stillness—a seemingly total absorption in my pure Self. Rather than the awareness that the Self and I are the same, I experienced such a deep immersion in the Self that my core sense of identity was that of the true Self. My individual self was barely existent, way less than before, but the witness was still there, like a faint shadow. Again, this "State" was so pure, clear, blessed, harmonious, sacred—what words can I use?—that I knew that I could easily remain here for eternity. When I say here, it refers wholly to the Self—nothing of my body or "mind." I can't say how long this state of consciousness lasted, as I don't wear a watch, and there is a profound sense of timelessness in the state of the transcendent. This reconnection with my Self, at this new, unexpected, and unimagined level, reestablished me in an extraordinary state in which I felt vividly "*awake*" and bursting with inner bliss and wonder. The level of inner joy, bliss, and gratitude that is uniquely associated with the Self is nothing like the joy and happiness that are associated with the senses and the intellect. Years later, from studying Yoga philosophy, I realized that this experience was very similar to what's known as samadhi, nirvana, and the pure "I AM" consciousness, all of which refer to a profound experience of the Transcendent State of consciousness.

On that afternoon, my experience was so all-encompassing that when I began to emerge from its deepest levels, I still had the feeling of being perfectly aligned with the pure Witness. My "mind" wanted to start asking questions and speculating about this "state" that I had just experienced, but as the Witness, I had no interest in this. I was content to just enjoy the inner quiet and peace, and the unimaginable bliss and contentment that accompany such a state—such an experience.

A number of hours later, still infused with the energy of the Transcendent, I picked up Kenneth Walker's book *A Study of Gurdjieff's Teachings* and skimmed through the chapter titled "The Search for Self." Walker starts by talking about G's teaching concerning one's many "I's"—how one's every thought and feeling claims one's sense of self—sense of I. Walker mentions the Scottish philosopher David Hume's search for a self and how Hume had seen some of his many "I's, and Walker repeats Hume's comment that: "*I can never catch anything that I can call my I,*" acknowledging that he, like most of us, was just a bundle of surface impressions. My own thought was that it was too bad that Hume did not understand the part of himself, the pure awareness that was able to observe these different perceptions, these different "I's." There was no question in my mind that if Hume or anyone else perused the "witness" as I had done, they would come to see the witness as part of themselves, as their real self, and then later, God willing, as their true Self, because that's just the way it is!

Looking at what Bertrand Russell, one of the West's most distinguished philosophers, had to say about a permanent self, Walker observes:

It must be borne in mind that B. Russell is one of the philosophers—I quote his own words, *"Who confess frankly that the human intellect is unable to find conclusive answers to many questions of profound importance to mankind but refuse to believe that there is some 'higher' way of knowing by which we can discover truths hidden from science and the intellect."*

In other words, "Russell bids us be content with science as our guide and warns us against asking unanswerable questions… Ever since man was capable of thought, he has been seeking to know what Russell proclaims as unknowable."[45]

I quote this passage for two reasons. First, the intellect is indeed incapable of providing satisfying answers to man's oldest questions. The German philosopher Immanuel Kant proved this beyond doubt over a hundred years before Russell. Secondly, not just Russell but practically all scientists, philosophers, and clergymen refuse to believe or even be slightly open to the *fact* that there is a higher way of *knowing* and human beings *already possess this capacity.* This unenlightened belief is why these well-intentioned but misguided people keep telling us to quit asking the most common and profound questions of life. And who tries to convince us that there is no absolute Truth—just relative truths! This is one of the primary reasons that we have lost touch with the true essence of sacred literature, and more importantly, lost touch with our true Self—our Divine Nature.

Walker goes on to say that the most exact accounts are given by the Eastern philosophers, who, like G, teach that when a thought wave arises in our minds, our small ego sense immediately identifies itself with these thoughts, good or bad. Our true Self, on the other hand, remains free from these thought waves and the resulting reactions, because the very nature of the Self is enlightened and supremely free. As long as we continue to be identified with these thought waves—with the ego sense that takes them to be oneself—we cannot know our real Self. My reaction was yes, yes, that's exactly what I experienced—the true Self cannot come through—reveal itself—if one is completely identified with one's lower level, one's normal ego sense.

Walker continues, still referring to Eastern philosophers, saying that: *"knowledge of the Self is direct knowledge as opposed to knowledge gained through the senses and the intellect."*[46] Again, my experience exactly—besides calling it "direct knowledge," I have also referred to it as a "knowing" that affects every fiber of your being, a "knowing" that has nothing to do with the intellect, and a "knowing" that is so powerful; profound and sacred that you spontaneously accept that it is the Truth.

Saying that we are fortunate that we possess facilities that are capable of opening us up to new levels of truth, Walker closes his chapter *"The Search For A Self"* by quoting the *Katha Upanishad*, a Hindu text:

"The secret Self in all beings is not apparent, but it is seen by the means of the supreme reason, the subtle, by those who have the subtle vision."[47]

Once again, I found my own experience being described perfectly—though rather than calling it *a subtle vision,* I would have referred to it as *subtle awareness.*

Feeling totally regenerated and with an expansion that cannot be put into words, I headed back to my room as darkness started to settle over the land. There was a message waiting for me that they wanted me to go back to Jasper the next day. My reaction was, *"No way. I need more time off."* But witnessing this, I knew that such was just an old perspective, and the truth of the matter was that I felt rested and elated. So "I" decided that I might as well go back to work and see how well I could stay *"awake"* this time.

The Soup Steward and the Preacher

After spending most of the day at the beach, I reported to work in the best of moods. As I was settling into my quarters on the train, I asked one of the other crew members if he knew who the steward was for this trip. I told him that I'd had a couple of humdingers lately. He pointed to the other end of the car and said, *"Here he comes now."* My mind immediately said oh no—not again! It was the first fellow I'd had a run-in with—the one that had demanded that I falsify the soup count! From the look on his face, I could tell that he was having about the same "reaction" to the thought of working with me.

Fortunately, I was wide "awake," and I allowed the witness to remind me that I was responsible for my own state of awareness. I did not have to be influenced by someone else's negativity if I was alert and awake. In a light and humorous way, it also seemed appropriate to find this steward on this particular run because this is the way it had been going these past number of weeks. Each time I experienced a powerful inner awakening, afterwards, I seemed to be tested to see if I could put my new understanding into action. Could I live it?

I knew I would do just fine on this trip as long as I kept my awareness in the witness, instead of my mind's old ways of perceiving.

The ride through the Rockies was as gorgeous and stimulating as ever—especially from the club car, with its huge windows. With darkness covering these spectacular views I decided to read some more of Ouspensky's book, *IN SEARCH*

The Kingdom of Heaven Is Within You

OF THE MIRACULOUS, mainly because I was in such a miraculous state. The part I was reading was about the creation of very subtle energies needed to experience one's true Nature, the Self. I enjoyed the presentation immensely because I could appreciate how what was being described seemed to be an accurate description of what was taking place within myself.

The part I want to share here is my realization that the final conclusion of a person's spiritual awakening—spiritual journey—was the complete merging of their being with the divine Being of God! My mind had been wandering about where this "awakening" that I was experiencing would finally lead. Now, I understood, at least intellectually, what the final goal was. This was G's way of speaking of what others called union with God again, something I was not familiar with before my awakening. I thought, what a beautiful ending. I also knew that the experience that I'd had at the beach was a decent "taste" of what this State is like—a *State* where one could easily exist for eternity. All of this put me into another indescribable state. I felt overwhelmed with the recognition of the mystery and sacredness of my own inner Nature.

It was at this time that I looked back and counted how many days it had been since I had begun this miraculous journey. I was very surprised to realize that I was now just about to begin the 40th day! My mind immediately recalled Jesus' 40 days fast, Noah's 40 days on the water, and the Jews 40 years in the desert! I knew that the number forty represented transformation and that the transformation I had experienced in both understanding and inner identity since the beginning of this awakening was truly beyond imagining or describing.

It was nice to be back in Jasper, as it was so beautiful there. After a very short layover, we were once again on the train heading to Prince Rupert. I was pleasantly surprised to find out that my second cook was a Bible student who would be starting his final year of study in the fall. In previous years, I would not have looked forward to a situation like this, as I had no interest in being subjected to what I considered a narrow and dogmatic view of religion. But in my present "state," I truly looked forward to hearing what he had to say, knowing it will be interesting to see where he is coming from, and also to expose any of my own religious conditioning that I still have not recognized. I also had a slight hope that he might be familiar with one or two of the concepts that I had learned about and seen the truth of in the last six weeks. Not surprisingly, such was not the case.

As part of the normal small talk that takes place when meeting a new person, I asked how he happened to become a Bible student. His was a tale of being very down and out as a teen and young adult. He had no real friends and no training with which he could get a decent job. He was quite depressed until some Christians took him in. It was after he had accepted Jesus as his savior that he felt that he had truly been born again, and shortly afterwards, he decided that he wanted to become a minister. He asked me if I had been born again in Christ Jesus.

Not wanting to say anything about my awakening, I just told him that, in a way, I had been born again as well. I explained that for years, I had asked Jesus, whom I did believe was a divine being, for a greater understanding of His teaching and of this wild and crazy world. Just recently, I said, He had answered my prayers.

The Bible student didn't ask me anything about my experience, but as I soon found out, he was elated to have someone to preach to!

Being Born Again, Salvation, and the Acceptance of Literal Beliefs

As we headed north, the preacher began sharing with me all of his recently acquired knowledge, which centered on quoting the Bible and explaining what it means. Due to my past experiences and present state, I did not find his literal interpretation of scripture interesting or believable. His enthusiasm, on the other hand, was wonderful. I was happy to be able to listen and try to stay awake.

He kept returning to the idea of being born again because, he said, it was the only way to get to heaven. After about the fourth time, I reminded him that I had accepted Jesus years ago and that I had just had a very powerful re-connection with Him, realizing that it was possible to experience and live a much deeper understanding of His teaching. I also had an intense experience of my personal relationship to Him, and thus, in my mind, had already been *born again*.

He was not the least bit interested in my experience or even the idea of personal spiritual experience. For him, the only way to be born again was to accept Jesus Christ as your personal savior and accept his understanding of the Bible, a conservative and literal view of the Bible. Actually, I'd rather not say "his understanding" because, from my perspective, it had nothing to do with understanding. This young student believed what he had been taught without contemplation; he had accepted it whole, on blind faith.

Just for the fun of it and to see how he would respond, I kept subtly trying to see if he might in any way be open to the idea that there are different ways to understand and worship God. Surely an all-loving God would not expect all of his children to worship Him in the same exact manner. What about the Hindus, Muslims, and Jews? Don't you think it's natural and proper for them to worship the way they were raised? Nothing doing! There was only one way and that was the Christian way.

I told him that I had just read a great book by an English psychologist who taught that there was a deeper psychological meaning hidden in the stories and parables in the Bible, and that his explanations made a lot of sense to me. Again, without asking or caring what my experience was, he told me, in no uncertain terms, that this sort of stuff was to be strictly avoided. It was the work of the devil (trying to confuse people). The Bible was easy to understand—to question it showed a lack of faith. With that, I could not help but ask him what it meant to— don't look here or there; the Kingdom of Heaven is within you. He said that that was not important—the only important thing was to accept Jesus as your savior— that was the way to heaven.

During these types of interaction, I could not help but be reminded of how lucky I was that my faith was based on personal inner experience versus simply accepting someone else's understanding and beliefs—unquestioned! I knew that accepting Jesus and the basic Christian teachings was a good beginning; it had served me well, but as I had experienced for myself—there was a major difference between "knowing thyself" and experiencing the Kingdom within versus a belief system that does not encourage or allow one to grow and mature inwardly— spiritually. I felt that to value Jesus' teachings, one must sincerely contemplate them. Then, as G said, one must keep His precepts. Based on personal experience, I knew that if you were honest with yourself—if you're paying attention to yourself—you'd see that it is not so easy to follow Jesus' teaching. In fact, it is often tough not to be anxious, greedy, vain, jealous, judgmental, lustful, etc. Realizing my own hypocritical nature and lack of control over my inner responses or reactions resulted in my becoming a seeker of a higher understanding of myself. Thus, I knew that the standard Christian teaching was fine, but if one does not sincerely contemplate it and try to live by it, rather than preaching it, then one will never come to know its true value.

Upon arriving in Prince Rupert, the crew, except for the young minister-to-be, was anxious to head for the very active bars. I told them that I had already checked them out and was looking forward to other things—like time alone, exercise, and some long, hot baths.

The next day, getting ready to head back to Jasper, everyone on the crew had their stories of the fun and excitement they'd had in the famous bars of Prince Rupert. This got the young preacher all fired up. He started telling them that if they did not change their ways, they were all going to end up in the fires of hell. I could see that he was no longer just "preaching," He was now really getting angry with these people who were not interested in his message.

It was easy to see that there was no love in him, in this particular setting anyway, let alone any awareness of other people's inherent worth.

I tried to change the energy by telling him of my experience of reading the New Testament, of how I was reminded that Jesus' life was about loving and accepting others as they are and encouraging them, in a positive, respectful way, to rise above their lower nature. I also said that following His teachings should bring forth a feeling of love and tolerance, not hatred and anger.

Unfortunately, he wasn't able to hear this and just kept saying that if they did not repent, they deserved to go to hell. It was easy for me to see that his self-righteousness was connected with and dependent upon his rigid beliefs, which kept him totally focused in the wrong direction and thus at the mercy of outside influences—just like G's man at breakfast! It was also easy to see that he was still very immature and a perfect example of one putting truth above Good, his beliefs above the natural goodness of the heart.

Due to a lack of teaching about how to turn within, how to work on oneself, and the deeper meaning of sacred literature, there was no way that this well-intentioned fellow could begin to understand how his anger and judgments were holding him in his lower nature. I thought how ironic it is that he can't see that he represents the modern-day Pharisee, the one person that Jesus was really down on! Like the Pharisee, this fellow's intense identification with his narrow understanding and his need to force this upon others was preventing him from knowing himself. In Biblical terms, he couldn't get the log out of his own eye so that he might be able to help others.

Seeing his self-induced misery, I wanted to reach out to him, but I knew that he was not ready. I also knew how rare it is to have a direct experience of the true essence of sacred literature. Once again, I was very appreciative of the great blessings I'd received and still was receiving.

Righteousness Versus Self-righteousness

Everyone was happy to arrive back in Jasper, as the atmosphere in the dining car was anything but peace and harmony. I was looking forward to reading Nicoll's chapter on righteousness that I had skipped earlier. The strong and very self-righteous emotions of this young preacher had made it evident that it was time to see what Nicoll had to say in his: *"The Idea of Righteousness in the Gospels."*

Nicoll begins by quoting Jesus:

Except your righteousness shall exceed the righteousness of the scribes and Pharisees, ye shall in no wise enter the Kingdom of Heaven. Matt V:20

Nicoll reminds us that in its everyday meaning, the term *righteousness* refers to one keeping the laws and customs of his society, and that for the Jews *righteousness* means strict adherence to all the details of the Levitical law. Also, he points out that Christ attacked the Pharisees a number of times for their outward show of righteousness.

The Kingdom of Heaven Is Within You

Nicoll then says that the word *exceed* in the original Greek implies *over and above or uncommon and remarkable.* Therefore, the level of righteousness needed to enter the Kingdom must be higher than that of the Pharisee, whose righteousness is external and that is performed *before men.*

From my own experiences of the past few weeks, it was easy for me to see how the feeling of merit and pride that comes from keeping the letter of the law holds a person in their lower self, their conditioned ego. To go beyond this better-than-thou feeling, a person has to evolve to a higher level of self-awareness. I couldn't imagine a better way to achieve this than self-remembering!

For the first time, I could appreciate why I had always viewed the righteousness of many politicians, preachers, and others of strong religious persuasion with a wary eye. To me, it looked like self-righteousness. It was funny to think that I'd so often seen self-righteousness passed off as righteousness that I had lost respect for righteousness! The best way to go beyond what we might call ego righteousness is to connect with their deeper self, the witness, the part of themselves that is free from prejudice, judgments, and all of the other unfortunate mindsets that self-righteousness carries with it.

In order to further explore this idea of righteousness, Nicoll quotes Christ as saying:

"Take heed that you do not your alms before men, to be seen of them, else ye have no reward with your Father. When therefore thou doest alms, sound not a trumpet before thee, as the hypocrites do in the synagogues and in the streets, that they may have glory of men. Verily, I say unto you, they have received their reward." Matt VI:1–4

I had remembered this teaching a number of times these past few weeks. Looking at it from the perspective of the witness as I was, it was easy to see that when we try to receive credit for our good actions, as we all do at times, we hold ourselves at the level of ego-personality even when our intentions may be sincerely altruistic.

I also knew that this teaching doesn't only apply to outer praise. It includes our innermost thoughts as well. Our inner voice that congratulates and praises us is still an aspect of our individual ego. We must be careful only to witness and not identify with such praise, or that praise will be the only reward we receive! As I had experienced many times, identification with my thoughts always disconnected me from the witness state. Just the thought *of what a good soul I am!* can cause the person who indulges in it to become disconnected from the more expansive awareness of their true spirit deep within themselves. And, as I've said, this is not only true for the outward show of meritorious deeds; it is also true for the cardinal sins of lust, greed, envy, and so on. The silent witness has no desires or judgments—it is simply pure intelligent awareness, free from identification of any sort.

In this chapter, Nicoll reminds us of Christ's promise in the Beatitudes:

"Blessed are they that hunger and thirst after righteousness, for they shall be filled." Matt V, 6

Nicoll says that to be *blessed* is to attain bliss. I thought, *"He is definitely right about that."* The experience of your pure Self, the one Spirit within, is unspeakable bliss. The satisfaction of the senses does not compare at all and shouldn't even be called bliss because it is such an inferior experience of joy. Nicoll also makes the astute observation that as long as a person feels righteousness as they are, they cannot change.[48] Reading that reminded me of the young Bible student; he thought he knew the true word of God, and he saw no reason to change. He had never heard that sacred scripture's essential message is about our capacity and potential for inner growth and transformation.

After a great layover, I wasn't exactly excited about listening to the Bible student's self-righteous preaching. I realized that when a person isn't aware of the higher teachings, it's difficult for them not to be self-righteous. So, when he started with his preaching, I asked him, now that he knew that no one else was interested, why couldn't he be content with his love for Jesus and leave everyone else alone? Also, I asked him how he could love God in a state of anger? And wasn't Christianity supposed to bring forth love, not hatred?

He said that I just didn't understand. Of course, I felt that I understood perfectly—preaching and judging made one's sense of self and one's ego feel very important and superior. But he took the hint and basically kept to himself, which made the trip much easier for everyone.

Temptation

Just before we arrived in Prince Rupert, the train's only waitress asked me, once again, where she could have met me before. She had been asking me this same question ever since we had met on the last trip. I had told her that there was no way we could have met, as I had only been in Vancouver a short time and had been working and sightseeing alone ever since my arrival. This time, just to stir things up a bit, I told her that she must have seen me at the nude beach in Vancouver. This got a rise out of both her and the preacher. With a big smile, she said, *"I'll bet that's exactly where I have seen you, as I go there often."* The preacher could not help but remind us that such behavior would condemn us both to hell. Before he could say more, Rosa told him to please leave us alone and save his narrow beliefs for someone who might be interested.

The Kingdom of Heaven Is Within You

Rosa and I chatted for a while about the normal sort of things when people first meet, and then she asked me how I could be so relaxed having to work with this jerk, the preacher. I told her I was very content within myself and, therefore, why should I let this poor, misguided fellow bother me? Just because he is angry doesn't mean that I should follow his unhealthy example.

"That sounds fine," she said, "but how do you do that? It seems so natural to dislike a person like him." I told her that for me, the question wasn't about him; it was about me. By keeping track of myself, by paying attention to my own conditioned emotional reactions and not letting them take over, I could keep free from another person's negative energy. This demanded a lot of attention and willpower, but the rewards were well worth it.

She said that she had sensed something different about me, and now she knew why. She added that she did not really understand how one could pull this sort of thing off. I told her the key to this was the ancient call to "know thyself." She said she would like to hear more about that, so I asked her if she would like to have dinner with me that evening. She said that would be great and had a couple of nice places she would like to show me.

With a little manipulation from Rosa, we ended up in adjoining rooms that shared a common bathroom in this old C.N. hotel. I had just gotten settled in when I heard Rosa call from the bathroom—asking if I would please help her wash her back. While talking with Rosa earlier, I had "witnessed" some of my old familiar "I's" come forth, all with their own desires for this beautiful young woman. Right then, I decided this old, mechanical, hormone-induced pattern was not going to lull me to "sleep" once again. This had happened when I had visited the nude beach that I had mentioned to Rosa.

So, with the utmost determination to stay "awake," knowing this would be another severe test, I told her that I could probably handle such clean work. She responded that it would be appreciated, but please don't get any ideas. I thought to myself, that's exactly what I'm going to try and do—not get any ideas! But when they do come, as they inevitably will under such circumstances, I will just have to "witness" them and let them go. I do not need to let them grow! I completed my task and told her it was time to leave before my mind started to get any ideas and expectations.

I got cleaned up, and we headed out to dinner. She had on an outfit that was so striking and revealing that no normal guy could walk by her without at least wanting to look back. I commented on how nice she looked and teasingly asked her if she was sure about not wanting me to get any ideas. I could not help but think that once again the Lord was really testing me to see how well I could do, how well I could stay awake in such an outlandish situation.

A Joyous Awakening

As we were cruising around trying to decide on a place to eat, I was trying to focus all of my energy in the witness, not her outfit. Then, in a flash of recognition, it came to me that the feelings, emotions, and experiences that I had been having over the last six weeks were far superior to anything I had ever experienced through sex or any other sensual delight. This helped me keep the conversation with Rosa on the topic of the mind, its nature, and its cultural conditioning. I tried to keep it light and about things everyone has experienced—like the story about the man at breakfast.

While we were waiting for the check, a young fellow who obviously knew Rosa came over and joined us. We decided to stay and have a drink together. While he was getting the drinks, Rosa told me that she met him on the train and had offered to let him sleep in her room, as he was heading to Alaska and was getting very low on cash. She said that she did not want to "sleep" with him but figured that he had gotten other ideas. I smiled at her, looked pointedly at her outfit, and told her that I could understand how that might have happened. She asked what she should do now, and I told her the most important thing was to be honest with herself, do what you know is best for you, and let him know how you honestly feel. *"If you do that,"* I told her, *"everything will be fine."*

After finishing my drink and wanting to stick to my desire to remain "awake," I told them that it was time for me to call it a day, as I had been up very early this morning. Rosa said that she was also tired and guessed that she would go back to the hotel with me, and told the other fellow that he could have her key and just come in later and crash on the floor. He said that he had a big day ahead of him tomorrow and should get to bed early, too. Rosa looked at me with upturned eyes as if to say, *"What have I gotten myself into?"*

When we got back to the hotel, we chatted for a few minutes in Rosa's room. I recognized that part of me really wanted to make a move for Rosa, but I was determined not to give in to these old, familiar patterns. While the other fellow was in the washroom, Rosa whispered to me, saying she was afraid to stay alone with him. I told her just to make sure she was honest with him right from the start—then there would be no trouble. I told her to give me a holler if she was having any trouble. Once the guest returned, I wished them a pleasant evening and went to my room.

I went to bed right away, feeling good about how I had handled this very tempting situation. Moments later, Rosa came into my room and asked if she could stay with me, saying that she trusted me. I told her that would be fine. She hopped into bed and snuggled up close to me, making it impossible for me not to be aware of her naked breasts on my chest. Then she immediately tells me— reminds me—that she doesn't want to "do anything." I said that was fine, but then asked her if she realized that her body language was saying one thing and her mind was saying another. She said, *"I'm just afraid."* I responded that there was nothing to be afraid of and asked her why she thought it was so hard for human beings to just say what they felt. Why do we so often pretend and play games with each other? She said I don't know, you tell me, you're the one who is supposed to know about the mind.

I said it was the same thing I've been saying all along about our minds. We just don't know ourselves. I told her that it was too late for this now. We can talk more about this tomorrow. I also told her that I was fully prepared to go to sleep, but could not do so with her youthful body so close to mine. She propped herself up with her left arm, looked me in the eye, and said, "I know that I don't know myself all that well. But you're right, I do know that I definitely want to make love with you," and then kissed me in a manner that was consistent with her words.

We woke up the next morning feeling great and happy to be with one another. We both expressed how much we had enjoyed each other's company—right from the beginning when we had first started talking on the train. It seemed hard to believe that it hadn't even been twenty-four hours yet. I told her that I felt that the Lord had rewarded me with her presence because I had not entertained any lustful thoughts towards her, which was something new for me. She said that maybe that's why she felt so comfortable with me and so attracted to me. I told her that it was so nice to be able to talk to someone about the great things that I had been experiencing lately. I also told her that the great love we were feeling right now was a reflection of the great love and joy that exists deep within everyone. We spent the rest of the morning together until it was time to report back to work.

It seemed that the crew had enjoyed our long layover in Prince Rupert as everyone seemed to match Rosa's and my upbeat mood. Everyone except the preacher, who almost immediately started condemning all of us for our sinful ways. He had been getting more and more belligerent during our time together so while we were in the kitchen alone, I finally told him, who was, after all, my second cook, to leave the crew alone. I reminded him that he was here to work, and that included getting along with the people he was working with. Instead of preaching, he should look at himself and try and see how self-righteous and judgmental he was being.

He said that he wasn't judging them: he was only trying to save them. I told him that it was fairly obvious that they did not believe him, most likely due to his anger, better-than thou attitude, and the severe, relentless judgments he kept making about everyone's behavior. I told him that he showed no love, no sign of forgiveness and no evidence that his faith or religion had made him more understanding, more tolerant or happier.

He said that religion is not about feeling good—it's about accepting the Truth, which, I believe, to him meant accepting his literal understanding of dogmatic rules and beliefs! He quieted down for a while, but you could see that he was still steaming inside.

The rest of the day went smoothly, and the evening sky was a sight to behold—truly a divine display!

Rapture Versus Unconditional Love

He started talking about the rapture and how they were all going to be sorry soon. He had mentioned this before, but since I was not familiar with this, I had not inquired about it as he was fired up enough already. When I first heard the word rapture, I immediately thought of the miraculous experience I had the day before I left on this trip. With the memory of that divine experience still fresh in my mind, I asked him what was this rapture stuff all about. He told me that the Rapture was the day that all of the faithful born-again Christians like himself would be magically transported to heaven. Then, basically all hell would break loose on earth. All sorts of awful things would happen to punish us terrible sinners for our lack of faith and of course our sinful ways.

As he was describing this scenario and providing support for it via his conditioned understanding of the Bible, it was easy to see how this made him feel important and superior and even happy at the thought of seeing so many sinners suffer! He showed absolutely no love, forgiveness, compassion, or interest in ninety-something percent of the world's population! Here was a vivid example of self-righteousness, egotistical fanaticism, and hatred based on religious dogma that has been around forever. He was happy playing the role of judge, jury, and executioner. I thought: *"No wonder we've had so many religious wars!"*

It was also impossible for me not to realize that his beliefs were pretty much the opposite of Jesus' teaching about unconditional love and almost unlimited forgiveness. What happened to *"love thy neighbor as thyself"*? This whole scene seemed to be another bizarre reminder of what can happen when a person is not taught about the importance of "knowing thyself," about sincere contemplation, and about the deeper meanings of sacred literature.

At the same time, the preacher's judgments reminded me of the importance of staying in the witness state and not getting caught in my own judgments, along with the worrying and critical tendencies of the mind. From personal experience, I knew that this type of relentless mental judgments and attachments prevented a person from the experience of genuine rapture—the experience of their own Divine

Nature. Therefore, with this renewed dedication and attention to my true "work," as G called it, the rest of the trip went smoothly. They did not need us in Jasper, so we boarded the train for Vancouver.

I spent most of the time with Rosa, talking about some of the things I had learned recently that had really helped me to come to a new understanding of my awareness of human awareness. I told her about things like the non-expression of negative emotions and what it's like to be the witness as opposed to being trapped in the normal chatter of one's mind. I showed her the part in Ouspensky's book where he talks about his own first experience of self-remembering and gives his arrow diagram, pointing out the need to have part of your attention focused back on yourself to accomplish this unfamiliar task—this unfamiliar state of awareness. I told her that this was the key to the ancient quest to "know thyself" and the reason for doing so was to release a person from all their misunderstandings and the misery that accompanies many of one's thoughts. Also, and more importantly, it was to pave the way to a direct experience of their own true Self—their own divine nature—a truth that we have totally lost touch with.

Having just recently become lovers, we were not only happy to be together but were also feeling very honest, open, and sincere with each other. Such made for this perfect type of interaction. Unfortunately, the steward was not sharing our bliss. He was constantly bothering us, saying that Rosa was not supposed to be in my room because it was against the rules to have a woman in your room. I told him: *That rule was made for passengers, not for other crew members. I said that when this rule was made, there were no female employees. At this point, to not allow her to sit and talk with me would be a clear case of discrimination.* Of course, he didn't care about that. He was so upset and worried that we were going to "do something" that he would not leave us alone. Finally, right in front of the Engineer, I grabbed him by the coat and told him to quit harassing us, or I would file a formal complaint.

This really upset Rosa, and now she was worried that she was going to get in trouble. I assured her that nothing would happen, as the railroad never looked into anything. Thank goodness we were only a few hours from Vancouver. Before we arrived, I decided that I had had enough of this and told Rosa that I would explain everything to the boss in Vancouver, who knew me well. I also mentioned that I planned to retire from the railroad and take a little time for myself before starting grad school. I tried to get Rosa to have dinner with me that evening, but she said she couldn't and didn't know if she could see me again because she had other commitments.

This time, when I talked to my boss, I felt no anger or frustration. Afterward, I happily left the railroad for good and headed straight for the beach by my house.

I put all my attention and efforts into staying in the witness state just as I had every time I had been to the beach this summer. Once again, I thoroughly enjoyed myself.

Another Expression of Oneness

The next morning, I headed to one of the few local areas that I had not visited yet, a lake that was southeast of Vancouver. It was a gorgeous Sunday morning, and I was in the best of spirits, knowing that I had almost a whole month to myself before starting grad school. I arrived at my destination—a beautiful, deep blue lake with huge, golden sandy beaches and surrounded by the majestic Canadian Rockies. I knew right away that this would be a special day and that the unique beauty of this place would help me stay "awake."

While floating on my back, looking at a huge tree on one of the mountain peaks closest to the lake, I had my first and only out-of-body experience. As I was looking at the tree, using it as a point of focus while focusing my attention on the witness, suddenly, I found myself looking down at the lake from the vantage point of this tree. There was no question that I—my conscious awareness—was on top of this mountain and was vividly aware of the surrounding mountains, other trees, and the lake far below. My state of self-remembering had not changed, and I had no sensation of having physically moved, but I was definitely experiencing a sudden and unexpected shift in my perspective and physical space. I don't know how long this lasted, but I don't think it was more than ten seconds, then I was suddenly "back in my body," looking back at the very spot that I had just been looking from! Again, I felt absolutely no sensation of physical movement.

Unexpected as this was, it wasn't at all disturbing to my state of pure awareness. As I sat on the beach afterward, I was witnessing all of the thoughts that this experience generated. Not surprisingly, it generated a lot of thoughts and a lot of questions, too. For me, some of the most meaningful and helpful were connected with the idea of the One source of all—the unity behind diversity. As I've mentioned, when the Self had first revealed "itself" to me, there was a subtle but unmistakable awareness that this divine Self, which was my own and everyone's true essence, was also the essence of Nature and the whole universe. G taught that everything is Consciousness, all forms simply vibrating at different frequencies and levels of subtlety. I assumed that I just had a dramatic experience of the truth of this pure Consciousness, pure Self, that is the source and essence of all things. This experience demonstrated, once again, the wonder and mystery of this divine Consciousness and how being centered in the witness can suddenly connect you to this pure Consciousness that lies within.

Another image related to pure Consciousness that came up for me was that of a prism, demonstrating how the one supreme light is refracted to become many. Without a medium like a prism, how would you know that light comprises many colors, many wavelengths? Likewise, without the experience of the witness, the experience of meditation, how could a person truly know about themselves, know their ego and their pure awareness, at different levels? Without help, who would ever think that the key to the highest Truth would come from simply keeping one's mind, one's awareness in an alert but thought-free state?

The final insight that came forth that afternoon was the awareness that I had now been in Canada for forty days. Again, the number 40 representing transformation, I knew that my previous feeling that it was time to move on felt correct. And that if I left tomorrow, I would have time to visit Vancouver Island one more time, see the Redwood forest in Northern California and still catch my brother, who was going to be in San Francisco for a few days. I had the awareness that my timing and my alignment with the universe were still in perfect sync.

Listening to My Inner Being

When I got home that evening, one of my roommates told me that Rosa called. With my extraordinary experience that day, I had totally forgotten about her. Remembering my very special feelings for her, part of me wanted to stay and spend a few days with her, but my deeper self that was (is) associated with the witness knew that it was time to move on and keep with the schedule that was presenting itself to me. I called her, and she was excited to tell me that her boyfriend would not be back for a while and that she wanted to spend a few days with me before I left. I told her that it was great to feel her presence again and that part of me truly wanted to be with her also, as the love I experienced with her was definitely genuine, but I had had another unbelievable day—another incredible experience of my deeper Self and from this, I knew that it would be best if I left tomorrow as planned.

She reminded me of how special and perfect our relationship was and that it just wouldn't be right not to see each other at least one more time. I again assured her that under normal conditions, I would never leave without seeing her, but as I had told her, things had not exactly been normal for me lately, and I knew that I had to respect and follow my inner being. I reminded her that I, too, felt that our relationship was so sweet and in tune physically, mentally, and spiritually that spending a few days together would make it very difficult to leave one another. She said that she realized that, but it would be worth it to her. I reiterated to her that I knew exactly what she meant, but that she should remember and be open to the fact that what we were both feeling and in touch with was the pure goodness and pure love that exists within and is the true essence of everyone.

I ended by asking her to please forgive me and to remember that the pure love that she is feeling now is coming from her and is a reflection of her true Self. My pure Spirit is helping her experience "that" but again, it's not coming from me. It's coming from her, and that by getting to know "thyself" via self-remembering, she could stay in touch with the sweet love she was now experiencing without me. I reiterated to her once again that I loved her for her unique self, but I just knew that our time together was perfect, appropriate, and very serving to both of us. But it was now time to let it go and not let it become something that might drag us down to less lofty aspects of love. She said a part of her knew I was right, but that she was not as strong as I was. I assured her she was and reminded her that this pure love existed in her boyfriend, too and that I hoped that she could experience the same love with him. We shared our heartfelt good-byes, knowing that we would probably not meet again.

A little while after speaking to Rosa, I was somewhat amazed that, once again, I had done the right thing concerning Rosa. I had followed my deeper self instead of my old self. Who would have stayed until her boyfriend returned and then "thought" about her for months. I was delighted that it now felt natural to follow the wisdom of my true self and know that's what I really wanted. It was not a moral question, but a question of being in touch with yourself. I knew that my time in Canada had truly been a miraculous time of profound and irreversible transformation, and now I was excited to visit Vancouver Island and then travel along the coast all the way to San Francisco.

While passing through Oregon, again using the extreme beauty of the coastline to help me stay centered in the witness, I heard my mind express dismay at how they could allow so many junky shops to sort of ruin the natural beauty. Moments after this thought, a higher inspiration sprang forth. We, humans, are like the coastline—we start out pure, but slowly we accumulate the not-so-pure "I's" of ego that cover over and hide our genuine inner goodness. One needs to remember that, in spite of the chatter and distractions, our true Self, like the beautiful landscape, is still there. You just need the proper focus—the right presence of mind to see it!

I arrived in the San Francisco area on a bright and sunny afternoon. Even the Golden Gate Bridge was completely free of fog. I thought, how appropriate, since I feel so bright and sunny and so crystal-clear inside. I also knew that I had found the "golden gate," the "priceless pearl," the "philosopher's stone" right within myself! This was, of course, the "Witness, the Self—the true essence of my own awareness. Our natural and authentic Self that is always present and available, if we just remember to be with it."

The directions to where my brother was staying were vague because he had not been there himself when he had given them to me. I decided that since my deeper self was connected to everything, I would, just for the fun of it, let it guide me and see what happened. Normally, my intellect would have been my only guide, but now I knew that my deeper being was much wiser than my intellect, so why not take its advice—that of pure intuition, when there was no way to be sure. Not surprisingly, I joyfully arrived at the right address without one wrong turn. This was a great lesson to make sure and listen to my deeper self when there was no way to be sure.

I was excited to see my brother and certainly would have loved to share my great joy and new understanding with him, but knew that this was just not possible in the couple of days that we were going to have together. We hadn't been together long when he commented that I must have had a good time this summer, as I seemed to be bursting with great energy. I told him that it was true; I had never been happier or more pleasantly energized in my entire life, but unlike other times when he had seen me in a joyous mood, this wonderful energy had nothing to do with outer things. The bliss I was enjoying right now was coming deep within me, from a place that I never knew existed, and was not dependent on any outer thing or circumstance. I also told him that much as I'd like to, there was no way—no words—to really tell him about it. I told him, as weird as it sounds, our culture is not aware of this, so this makes it tough to share right now. Let us just enjoy this divine energy and our time together, and sometime later I will try and share what I'm experiencing. We spent a couple of fun days together, and it was wonderful to know that the intense love I felt for him was the pure Spirit ("Self") in me loving the pure Spirit ("Self") in him!

I spent a few extra days in the Bay Area and then headed up into the mountains, destined, once again, for Colorado. I intended to sleep in my car, but the desert sky was so bright and so awesome that after lying in the back seat looking at it for a while, I knew that I was just too energized to sleep. So, I decided to skip it and just enjoy being so wonderfully awake. After a little car trouble and some help from my friends, I arrived in Vail and spent about five perfect days there. Again, the energy that I was experiencing each day was just perfect. There is no other way to describe them.

I decided to visit the Black Hills of South Dakota before booking it back East. As I was traveling through Wyoming, about ready to stop for the night, I struck a deer. The radiator was broken, so I knew that I would be spending the night right there. I was not the least bit upset; I actually thought it was kind of funny that the car had finally gotten fixed earlier today, and now it was basically totaled. I casually opened my trunk, took out a book that I had been wanting to look at, and prepared to read in the back seat for a while before going to sleep. I realized that, in the past, I would have been bummed out by this situation, and my mind would have been worried about all kinds of things. This realization, along with my present state of unattachment and complete contentedness, let me know that I had found a part of myself that was incredibly valuable and that this was the breakthrough I had been sensing and hoping for when I had left for the West at the beginning of June. Without a doubt, I had found it, had experienced it, and it was much more than I could have ever expected.

BOOK III
Shaktipat Awakening: Phase Two

"Honor your own Self

Meditate on your own Self

Worship your own Self

Kneel to your own Self

Understand your own Self

Your God dwells in you as you—for you"

Swami Muktananda

7
The First Years After the Awakening

M Y FIRST YEAR OF DENTAL school went along about as expected, an awfully lot of work, but I was happy to finally be there. Until spring, I was able to stay quite positive and keep my sense of "I" in the witness. My hold on that state wasn't as strong as it had been in the summer, but considering the circumstances, I did quite well.

Tufts Dental School in Boston had moved from the traditional four-year curriculum to three years, graduating the first three-year class in the spring, a few months before I began. The school was not pleased with the results, so starting with my class, they compressed the first half of the four-year program into the first twelve months. We went all year round. Obviously, this meant that in the first year, there was an incredible amount of work, and by spring, the pace finally took its toll on me and many others.

Because we were being asked to take in way too much material in such a short time and because we were being treated more like junior high students, instead of the graduate students we were, a number of first-year dental students became quite negative, disappointed, and angry. I could certainly sense what was happening to my classmates and me and knew that I should not let myself become identified and affected by this energy. But, for many reasons, including the constant and overwhelming negative atmosphere and my own low energy, I couldn't seem to do otherwise. The witness aspect of myself would often remind me that I should not let my "mind" and my emotions rule. But in G's way of putting it, *"I just did not have the energy to stay 'awake.' Knowing the basic principles involved in this quest and the added advantage of having the direct experience of the truth of these still was not enough to recapture my 'great state' of the previous summer. Even though I could not practice self-remembering the way I had before, never once did I question the validity of my 'awakening,' or the truths that it taught me."*

One thing that I did enjoy in this first year that helped keep me in touch with my spiritual energy and perspective was trying to share some of the things I had learned with my older brother, whom I had spoken with in San Francisco. He was the only person I attempted to do this with because I found it very difficult to express most of what I had experienced. (I didn't find out until years later that basically everyone who has experienced the "Transcendent State" has had difficulty in speaking about it.)

One of the aspects that I could easily address was the nature and effects of our culturally conditioned mindset. In addition to talking about how conditioned we are and how little we notice this, the other thing that kept coming up when trying to share my experience of the Self was the intense awareness of the One behind the many. Again, the classical mystical experience. Since I lacked a vocabulary and the framework of spiritual teachings, I found it tough to share the essence of my experiences in a meaningful way. But this effort to share did help to keep me in touch with these most precious experiences, and this in itself was very helpful and enjoyable during this extremely busy time.

Because I didn't feel comfortable speaking about my transcendent experiences with the people directly around me, and especially with a couple of fine women I most likely would have otherwise gotten closer to, I ended up feeling somewhat isolated. This was a totally new situation for me. It seemed ironic because from my contact with the "transcendent state," I knew that all people had this pure Self within. But how could I tell people that when my spiritual experiences were so far removed from people's normal waking reality, and when our culture is so unaware of esoteric teachings and the expanded states of awareness they speak of?

One result of this isolation was that it was difficult to find a mate, a relationship I surely wanted. It felt weird not to be able to be totally honest about who and what I was and what my goals were. I had no real interest in material life, and no easy way to talk about the most powerful and influential experiences of my life. My brother made an insightful comment about this situation, by saying that it was like the well-known T.V. game show Jeopardy, in that I had the answer but was not sure what the question was. I'd had a powerful experience of the transcendent, but I knew nothing of the history and the ancient wisdom traditions that would give perspective to this little-known level of awareness. Nor did I know that most people who experience spiritual awakening do not remain in that state for very long and must perform years of spiritual practice before they are ready to live in that expanded "State."

Coming across Joseph Campbell's teaching on Mythology would have helped put my experiences into context, but it was not my destiny to discover Campbell's writings until years later. So, I continued on with my dental training, which was not that tough for me after the first year. I was fairly content knowing that my spiritual pursuits would have to wait until I graduated and had more time to myself.

Midway through my final year, my friend Doug asked me to return to Vail upon graduation and help him start a little restaurant. In return, he would remodel my dental office, build the necessary cabinets, and let me live with him cheaply so that I could afford to make this move. At first, I didn't think this would be possible, and no one else did either, but the more I thought about it, I realized that this was the best thing I could possibly do.

What interested me the most was the prospect of getting back into the state of self-remembering—getting reconnected with my true Self. Since Vail was the place where I had first begun this magical journey, it just seemed perfect that this should be the place I would go to reconnect. Going back to Vail was an unexpected dream come true, and it eliminated the problem of what I was going to do after graduation. The excitement of it, and the pleasant memories of how much I liked the Vail area, made the end of my dental school experience a pretty good one, despite some aggravating medical problems I was experiencing at the time. I spent a couple of well-deserved months off with my family in Maine before moving to Vail in August of 1978. I arrived in Vail feeling very upbeat and full of confidence that I would be able to reconnect with the deeper and truer part of myself that I had so enjoyed before starting grad school.

The first few months went very well, and I got my Colorado dental license. The remodeling of the office went along smoothly, and the weather was just perfect. Everything seemed to support me nicely in recapturing the positive and enthusiastic attitude that I had enjoyed while living here previously. In November, I opened my beautiful office feeling optimistic, even though I knew that Vail had too many dentists already. The office had such a nice feel to it and a great view as well. Thanks to Doug and a conservative upbringing, my monthly expenses were quite low, giving me every opportunity to succeed. But truthfully, I was not the least bit worried about anything because I felt that it was my inner and sacred energy that had brought me back to Vail and that this inner divine nature was going to be with me no matter what happened. I could also appreciate that building up a practice slowly would make it easier to get re-established in the "witness state" in self-remembering. I remember clearly that, before ever seeing a patient in my new office, I reminded myself that this pure and divine Self exists in everyone. Therefore, I should always remember who I am really working with and try to treat them accordingly. I knew that if I could do that, things would work out fine professionally, and this perspective would help me remember my own Self as well.

Just as my friend Doug was getting geared up to start construction on his crepe shop, his older and only brother died unexpectedly. This, along with being a perfectionist and making the mistake of thinking drug use would help with the stress and grief, put a great strain on our relationship. I finally moved out of his condo, knowing that there was no possibility of recapturing the close friendship that we'd had, mainly because of the drugs. Also, I knew that the atmosphere around him, like the dental school atmosphere, was not conducive to getting in and staying in touch with my deeper and truer self.

I made a number of new friends, and things went well for the first couple of years. I went out with a few women, but still could not seem to allow myself to get involved with them the way I had with my former girlfriends. My younger brother moved to Vail right out of high school, and it was really sweet having him around. As with so many others, I wanted to share with him some of the great insights and experiences of my spiritual awakening, but again, I found it very difficult to do so in a way that truly communicated what I had to share. But basically, things were going very well; I was enjoying my dental practice, learning about holistic health from some of the many new-age people in Vail, and reading books like *The Tao of Physics*, by F. Capra, which showed that the principles of modern physics seemed to support the spiritual perspective.

During graduate school, I had thoroughly enjoyed all of the science courses covering the different aspects of the human body, because I could see how this great, divine, and supremely intelligent energy that is the core and source of our being expresses itself in the miraculous construction and function of the human organism. Gary Zukav's wonderful book, <u>The Dancing Wu Li Masters,</u> was another powerful and enjoyable book for me. Like <u>The Tao of Physics</u>, it said things that I had been longing to hear, to connect with, in order to help me better understand the transcendent state I had experienced within myself. Speaking of this state, Zukav says, *"Enlightenment entails casting off the bonds of concepts (veils of ignorance) in order to perceive the inexpressible nature of undifferentiated reality directly." "According to mystics from around the world, each moment of Enlightenment reveals that everything—all the separate parts of the universe—are manifestations of the same whole. There is only one reality, and it is whole and unified."*[1] Both of these statements—descriptions—came very close to describing my own experience of the inexpressible nature of undifferentiated reality and the "Oneness" of all things.

These two books about the new physics and its connection to the spiritual (mystical) teachings of the East, along with Franklin Merell-Wolff's <u>Pathways Through to Space</u> and Joseph Pearce's <u>Exploring the Crack in the Cosmic Egg</u> and <u>The Magical Child,</u> were my favorite and most helpful books. I enjoyed Pearce because he spoke about how conditioned we are and also about our awesome potential, both of which I had experienced the truth of during my own spiritual awakening. In fact, it was my love for Pearce's work that finally resulted in meeting my first authentic spiritual teacher—Swami Muktananda.

I had encouraged my older brother to read Pearce's book <u>Exploring the Crack...</u> to try and help him begin to realize his and everyone else's heavy cultural conditioning. Not having the advantage of deep spiritual experiences, he could hardly read it, let alone get much out of it! But when he heard that Pearce was coming to his hometown in Northern California, he was interested to hear what Pearce had to say about child development and human potential. Thus, he took the weekend seminar that was being offered. Afterward, he called me and told me whom he had just seen and asked me if I had ever heard of Swami Muktananda. I said, *"No, why do you ask?"* He said that at the end of the seminar, Pearce told them that if they truly wanted to know more about human potential, they should see Muktananda, as he was a great spiritual Master from India, and he was human potential personified!

Meeting an Authentic Spiritual Master

Having no other options that I was aware of and knowing that I needed a true spiritual teacher, I told my brother that I thought we should check this fellow out, *"See if you can find out what Muktananda's schedule was and let me know."* This was January 1981. He called about a week later and said that we could attend a two-day 'Meditation Intensive' on the third weekend in February.

My brother also said that a good friend of his knew a woman in the Los Angeles area, where Muktananda was currently, who had reluctantly agreed to see him because her Hatha Yoga students kept bugging her to do so. After reluctantly attending one evening program, which seemed to be no big deal to her, Muktananda started appearing to her in her room, which she could hardly believe. But he spoke to her about very deep and personal things that she had been pondering for years. This went on for a number of nights, and what he said had great meaning and insight for her. I said, *"That sounds pretty wild. Let's go and check this fellow out."*

I left for California with a fair amount of excitement, but at the same time, no major expectations. I guess I just did not quite believe that one could find a true spiritual Master by going to a paid weekend program. Gurdjieff had spoken about such masters, and I had often thought that, like him, I should go to the East and seek one out. But at the same time, I knew that such an adventure would be too expensive and that such an endeavor would be difficult and would also have little chance of success. But here was a candidate almost at my front door.

So, I was looking forward to seeing my brother, to hear what Muktananda had to say, and to learn about meditation as well. At this time, I still did not realize that G's self-remembering is just another name for classical yogic meditation.

The weekend with Muktananda—"Baba" as he was lovingly called—was a lot of fun, but neither I, my brother, nor his friend, who shared the story of the yoga teacher, had any extraordinary meditation experiences. Even though I really didn't know what to expect, and wasn't trying to expect anything, I kind of expected Baba to be serious, quiet, and holy-acting. He turned out to be very sweet, light, gentle, enthusiastic, and so, so funny. Baba and his supporting teachers, who gave talks in the Intensive, kept the 1,200 people there laughing for much of the weekend, something I was not expecting at all.

That weekend, I chanted for the first time, which was nice, but what truly caught my attention was Baba's primary teaching,

Honor your own Self

Meditate on your own Self

Worship your own Self

Kneel to your own Self

Understand your own Self

Your God dwells within you as you—for you. [2]

I knew that the Self represented the pure and divine One within us all and that this teaching was the truth. It was what I experienced for myself. The statement: *God dwells within you as you—for you,* was also my exact experience and a perfect way to express this inexpressible mystical experience. I was also absolutely sure that this teaching was the highest Truth. The command to honor, kneel, and worship our own Self was just so perfect because, as I've shared, the experience of your own Self is so supremely sacred and holy that one cannot help but want to honor and worship the One in all. Also, the call to meditate and understand your own Self is something that I had done and truly could not help but do since my Self had revealed itself to me. So, for me, it was perfect that this would be Baba's essential message, and it made me want to become familiar with all of his teachings. I bought a few books and left California feeling good and very excited as well.

Even though I did not have any inner experiences that would compare with my previous ones, I was pretty sure that Baba knew a lot more about the Self than I did. He was impressive in person, as Joe Pearce had told us he would be. I had no way to know if he was a genuine Guru, but at this point, that wasn't an issue. What I did know was that he was the first living person I had met since my awakening who claimed to know about many things, and I had been waiting for almost six years to know more about him.

I landed in Denver and decided it was time to buy another car. I was still driving the old junker I had in dental school. With the help of my newly acquired enthusiasm, I knew that a change in transport was now appropriate. Thus, I headed up into the mountains in my almost new, powder blue B.M.W., anxious to get home and see my girlfriend. For about nine months, I had been trying to share my spiritual insight with her, but to no avail. Now, hopefully with Baba's help, my ability to communicate the highest Truth might finally improve. As I was approaching the Eisenhower tunnel, which marks the continental divide, I had the inspiration to stop after passing through the tunnel and get out and enjoy the sky and the symbolism of crossing into a new era of my life. As I looked at the beautiful night sky, a flood of blissful energy engulfed me. It was clear to me that this was the divine energy of the Self, the divine energy I had been waiting and hoping to experience for a long time now. It was also clear that this experience was connected to Baba, that it was a gift from him.

After this experience, I was able to stay connected with the spiritual energy for quite a while, but the constant negative emotions that arose from my relationship with my girlfriend, spending more time with my other friends and living with my own lack of discipline, I slowly but surely fell back into my old state. Even so, I could not forget Baba or my renewed desire to learn more about the spiritual teachings and lead a more spiritual life, knowing this was the thing that would truly make me happy and contented.

In the spring, my girlfriend decided to move back East, which I knew was best for both of us. Her departure would give me another chance to see if I could recapture the state of self-remembering and, ultimately, my own Self again. It was at this same time that I committed to spending the month of September with Baba, as this would be his last month in the U.S.A. He was offering a month-long course, and I felt that this was an opportunity that I could not afford to pass up.

To prepare myself for this unique adventure, I decided to give up all forms of intoxicants and remain celibate for at least forty days (the transformation number) before heading to the Catskill Mountains in New York to be with Baba. I had talked my good friend and roommate, Dr. Bob, into accompanying me to New York for the month. He had a genuine desire for the spiritual life but drank too much and was too angry with the "establishment" to make any real progress. My hope was that a month in Baba's ashram doing spiritual practices and listening to spiritual teachings would provide the needed energy for both of us to begin living spiritual lives verses just talking about it.

Being with Baba Muktananda in the Catskills

The summer went well—summer's high in the Rockies is ever so sweet—and before we knew it, we were at the ashram just in time to catch the last hour of a Supta—the chanting of God's name for an extended period. There were hundreds of people present, including Baba, and as the chant built towards the finale— getting louder and faster—I felt very naturally pulled into the high and wonderful energy pervading the room. What a way to start this spiritual retreat. I found that this sweet and joyful energy was present throughout the entire stay.

The daily schedule, which everyone staying in the ashram was expected to follow, started off with early morning meditation from 4:40 to 5:30. The day carried on with chanting sessions, courses in yoga, meal times, study and personal time throughout the day, lights out at 10:00. Bob and I took every course we could. Not only were we very busy, but we even had homework and tests to take!

The highlight of each day was the evening program. The evening programs were hosted by an emcee, who was generally someone light and humorous. They usually started off with an experience talk by someone who had been spiritually awakened, initiated by Baba. These accounts were unique to the individual, and these accounts were tremendously varied as well. Then there would be a short talk on one of the main themes of Siddha Yoga, which is what Baba called his spiritual path, the collection of practices and teachings he gave to students. Everyone would chant and meditate for a while, and then Baba, who had joined us earlier in the program, would give a talk on some aspect of the ancient teachings of yoga. The term "yoga" refers to the yoking or union of the individual soul and the Supreme Soul. The concept of union with God was an important part of Christianity for centuries and is the major teaching of all the wisdom traditions.

After only a few days of participating in the daily schedule, I began to notice that the energy I was experiencing was very similar to that which I experienced during my spiritual awakening in 1975. I hadn't felt so spiritually connected and joyous since that time, except for the brief experience I'd had after returning from my first meeting with Baba. Because of this powerful and uplifting energy, I found it easy to follow the ashram's daily schedule, but sitting for meditation for almost an hour was not easy for my body or mind.

The courses were taught by Baba's monks and lay people who were well educated and natural in the way they presented the material. The teachers were all well prepared and funny—and another thing that really impressed me—they started right on time! But even without that, I would have found these courses exciting and uplifting. I'd been longing to hear these ancient spiritual teachings about the Self for years. These courses in Baba's ashram not only helped me to better understand my own experiences of the Self, but they also provided me with the framework and history of the spiritual teachings I need to help me move forward.

The evening programs were definitely the highlight of the day for me. In these evening programs, most of the people giving these experience talks were, just like myself, everyday people who had had very powerful spiritual experiences. Theirs had come through Baba's gift of initiation. It was great to hear about other 'people's experiences of this subtle terrain I'd been exploring, and it was powerful, too, to chant with hundreds of people. But, without a doubt, being with Baba was oh-so-precious and the highlight of the day.

Baba's talks were light and funny, yet at the same time, they were always about some aspect of the Self that most could easily relate to. One of the reasons I found his talks powerful was that it was obvious that he was speaking from personal experience, not from a belief system. He quoted from the scriptures of India, both Vedanta and Kashmir Shaivism, yet he made it clear that he wasn't espousing a particular religion. He based his teachings on the experience of the Self, and yet he made it clear that this experience is verified by the mystical scriptures of his tradition and that he used both and needed both to articulate his experience.

Baba was so sweet and emanated so much joy, love, and wisdom that there could be no doubt that he was in a very high state. Every day in his ashram, every moment in his presence was magical and most enlightening. I was really glad that I'd taken the time to be with Baba.

The Teachings of Yoga Match My Experiences

The teaching that Baba emphasized over and over again through his courses and in his talks was that the Self—the Supreme Being—dwells within us all and is truly what we are. Since this was precisely my experience, it was easy to accept Baba's teaching and his claim that it was coming from his own direct experience. Another of his basic teachings that fit perfectly with my own experience is that: "The Self is already attained." By this, he meant that the Self is already fully and perfectly within us and that spiritual practices are necessary to help us experience this reality for ourselves. As I've said, when I first experienced my Self, I knew that it had been there all along and that it is always present in everyone. Also, there is Baba's signature teaching, which I thought was the perfect way to express my own inexpressible experience: *God dwells within you as you, for you.*

It was exhilarating to have the direct experience that Baba's teachings are the Truth and that I had finally met a real spiritual teacher. In addition to being fully and permanently enlightened, Baba had studied the yogic scriptures extensively and had practiced years of austerities and discipline—hatha yoga, Ayurvedic medicine, and gardening were also extensive.

Another thing that Baba emphasized was the connection between the mind and the Self. This was a topic that I was dying to hear about, something I'd always thought that a spiritual Master would speak about. Baba taught that classical yoga is the science of the mind—the science of human consciousness. Yoga psychology was discovered and formulated by the ancient Sages and Seers from their own experience of the Self. Like G, Baba teaches that yoga is "real psychology" because it speaks about the mind and the Self.

The basic premise of yoga psychology is the necessity of stilling the mind in order to experience the great Spirit within, your own Self. As I mentioned earlier, Patanjali, one of the most widely known and respected of the ancient yogic sages, expresses this in his *Yoga Sutras* when he says that once you still the modifications of the mind—his term for your thoughts—then the Self will reveal Itself to you.

When I first heard this teaching in a course on yoga in the ashram, I knew immediately that this was a good description of what had happened to me, could happen to anyone, and that it is the Truth. I want to reiterate here that the one pure Self, the pure Self that revealed these truths to Patanjali, to Baba, and to other yogis, also revealed them to me. This is the understanding that is missing from orthodox religion—literal religion. The religions that I know don't tell people that God will reveal the highest Truth right within their very own being—this is the essence of the Word!

This leads to another of Baba's teachings that I recognized the truth of from my own experience: the Self lies beyond the mind. Yoga psychology teaches that the mind can contemplate the Self but cannot know the Self, because the Self is that Supreme Consciousness from which our limited consciousness, the mind, derives. I know this may sound weird and even contradictory, but as I've repeatedly described, the aspect of my consciousness that was able to see what my habitual and often uncontrollable mind was up to was obviously separate from my habitual and conditioned mind. Otherwise, how would it be able to look at the mind? It is the Self that is known as the witness, actually we should call it the Witness when referring to the One Self in all. The Self is pure Consciousness itself. Thus, it is clear that, since the true Self lies beyond the mind, the mind cannot know—cannot encompass—the Self within its thoughts. I am fully aware that this is new and hard to accept, hard to fathom, but this is one aspect of the transcendent experience that has been experienced by many from all cultures over thousands of years. A big part of the problem is that we in the West have been taught that the intellect is supreme, so we automatically doubt knowledge that transcends the intellect, goes beyond rational thought, except for religious belief, of course. But remember, we are speaking about direct Knowledge—not beliefs!

As I've said before, I experienced being in a state where my mind was perfectly still and silent. It was also alert and stable in its focus on the witnessing aspect of my consciousness. I was in this vigilant state when the Self revealed itself to me. I've also spoken of how my experience of the Self was beyond all previous concepts and imaginings. From the experience of the Self, I just knew that it was beyond the capacity of our rational mind, it was a higher order of understanding and awareness, and only possible through Grace! From the very beginning of this miraculous experience, I knew that one could never know one's own Self from reading and contemplation, from thinking, or from any other means that I had ever expected to know the Truth. I had always expected to understand the Truth through my intellect, through lofty and beautiful concepts. Again, once I'd experienced my Self, I understood, without words, how and why our normal everyday mind cannot know the Self.

I'll say it one more time: the mind must be totally clear, pure, and still for the Self to shine through and reveal itself. This experience, which is felt throughout your entire being, is nothing like the intellectual insights or understanding you might have of other experiences through the workings of your mind. The experience of the Self is totally beyond what we refer to as the *mind*. Yoga psychology teaches: *"The mind can contemplate the Self—but cannot know the Self—because the Self is a matter of experience, not of intellectual thought."*

Another tenet of Baba's teaching on the mind, and yoga psychology in general, that I recognized from my experience of the Self is that the primary obstacle that prevents a person from knowing the Self is **the mind**! The main obstacle is our own mind! As I've mentioned throughout my awakening, it was my own seemingly uncontrollable mind that kept me from being in the present, from being in the witness state, and so kept me from knowing my own Self, and then from staying connected with it.

My experiences of self-remembering also allowed me to see the truth of another of yoga's teachings about the mind: The mind is not only our worst enemy; it is also our best friend. My mind was acting as my friend when it pointed out that there had to be better answers for my and many others' deepest questions. Also, it helped me recognize the importance of Jesus' and G's essential teachings. However, it was my enemy when it kept me from being in the present moment, as I described it doing many times in my story of awakening. I also knew that when my mind was under the control of my ego-personality, or sensual desires, it was not usually my friend. Thus, it is not really the "mind" that's the problem, but the one "who" is using it—one's ego or the deeper part of oneself represented by the watcher or witness of the mind. Thus, it was easy for me to grasp and appreciate the yogic teaching that the mind cannot know the Self, but, at the same time, the mind is the vehicle or means to know one's Self via its power of will, focus, and desire to know the truth.

Yoga psychology teaches that the mind is the most important thing for seekers to *work* on, not the Self, because the Self is already present within. The practices of yoga purify the mind so the Self can shine through and can reveal itself. Baba's primary methods for this are meditation and chanting.

Another of Baba's primary and essential teachings is the importance of meditation on the Self, on the pure One within. Before he left on his second world tour, Baba said that he wanted to start a meditation revolution. Therefore, he had many things to say about meditation. What I'd like to focus on here is the aspect of his teaching on meditation that relates to my own experience of the practice. I am speaking of self-remembering or, as Baba put it, getting to know the *knower* or *witness* of the mind.

In one sense, I was quite amazed that Baba's teaching about meditation, about putting one's self in a position to experience one's own Self, was so similar to my own experience. But knowing that, truly, this is just the way it is—just the nature of human consciousness itself—it was not really that surprising. Like many other spiritual masters, Baba tells us to turn within to get in touch with that part of ourselves that can watch our thoughts and emotions. Baba's teachings that match my own experience exactly are:

"Turn within and see who watches your thoughts from the inside. If you keep watching in this way, you will come to know the Self."

"If you want to reach the Self, you have to meditate on the Self. You have to meditate on the witness within. If you do not understand the witness, you will go in the wrong direction in your meditation."

"When meditating, as a thought comes up…the one who makes you aware of that thought or image… is nothing but the Self, the witness… To know the knower is true meditation." [3]

There are a couple more of Baba's teachings in which I saw my own experience of the Self. Baba tells us to see God in everyone. As I've shared, this is one of the most profound and surprising truths that only the Self can reveal. He also tells us that a direct experience of the Self, receiving direct knowledge of the Self, is the rarest and most precious gift possible and can be experienced only through the grace of God. Again, all of the above describe my own experiences and insights perfectly. Many great beings have expressed these profound Truths and based on my own experience, I can say that such grace is available to anyone who truly seeks it, who has the sincere desire to experience the goal of human life.

Keeping all of the above in mind, let me say one more thing about the teachings of yoga psychology that I could relate to absolutely perfectly at this time: Once you experience the truth of the Self, even for an instant, you can never forget it. Your identity shifts from your ego to the pure "I" of the Self. Once you truly experience the Self, you can no longer think of yourself as an individual that is separate from God. You know with every fiber of your being that you are a child of God.

There is no way to express in words how precious, exciting, and satisfying it was to see how closely and perfectly Baba's teachings on meditation and the Self related to my own direct experience. It was pure joy for me to finally meet someone who not only understood my experiences but also could put me in touch with these ancient teachings of this little-known spiritual journey. Everything I think of saying about this sounds to me like a gross understatement. It was literally a dream come true for me to know more about the foundations of G's teachings and their origins. I had come to believe that the ancient teachings that G's system was based on had been lost. I felt that the genuine teachings probably still existed in the hidden esoteric schools of the East, but there was realistically no way for me to find them.

Now, thanks to Baba, I was sure that G's teachings were those of classical yoga.

Another Gift of Grace

I knew that being able to examine these sacred teachings for myself, with the help of Baba's writings and references, was another gift of grace. There were a number of parallels that I found in Baba's and G's teachings. Of course, these are some of the most basic teachings of yoga—teachings of an authentic spiritual path. Based on my own experiences, they surely reflect authentic spiritual experience and Knowledge.

Both Baba and G encouraged the seeker of truth to "awaken," to become aware of your own predicament, as G would say, become aware of the nature of your mind, and your own ignorance. Ignorance in yoga is defined as our lack of awareness of the Self, and I would add, our pervasive mental conditioning. But, for both Teachers, what is most important is that you know your highest nature, your true nature, your own Self. Both teach that one of the major keys to experiencing the Self is not to waste energy and not to be at the mercy of outside influences. Do not identify with all your thoughts and emotions, especially anger, pride, self-pity, and so on. Instead, put your energy (efforts) into self-observation and self-remembering, into expanded and detached awareness by being the witness of your mind.

Both encouraged the seeker to do their daily "work"—one's spiritual practices, with conscious awareness. Both suggest that we do our practices in the midst of our ordinary lives, and let the awareness of our certain death be our advisor. This way, you can focus on what's really important to you. These are the ways a sincere seeker can make steady and meaningful progress on the spiritual path.

Another parallel is that they both distinguish between witnessing and judging oneself. Both teach that while you need to watch, to observe yourself, it's important not to analyze and judge your efforts, your actions, and your meditations. They both indicate that getting the feel and experience of being the watcher or witness is the most important thing. This is what allows you to see how you really are! I was sure that they both knew from personal experience that when a seeker perseveres as the observer, the rest would just take care of itself.

They both taught that a human being consisted of four bodies, the fourth and highest of these being analogous to the single and pure "I Am"—one's true Self. Also, all who permanently attain this highest level of consciousness have the exact same understanding. In other words, there is only one Truth and all enlightened beings, no matter what their background, their cultural or religious upbringing, all live in the experience of this one Truth. After having the experience of my own Self, I felt absolutely sure that there was only one Truth. The Self, the one Spirit, is the Truth, and there could be nothing higher. It was exceedingly clear to me that the Self is a universal experience and the Essence of human consciousness. Both teach that the Self has nothing to do with religion, philosophy, or any other beliefs. The Self, the one Spirit in all, is beyond all thought and all concepts.

Another thing that they both were very clear on is that to make real progress in this highest and most subtle of human endeavors, it is necessary to have a true teacher, a genuine spiritual Master. Also, it is not enough to agree with the master's teaching, or believe in it—it is necessary to put those teachings into practice. First, the seeker needs to be exposed to real knowledge, knowledge about the nature of one's mind and the Self. But then, to truly progress on the path, one has to put this knowledge into practice and keep putting it into practice. Only then will your understanding begin to transform.

With all the instances where G's and Baba's teachings were essentially the same, and there are many others besides those that I've mentioned, their teaching styles could not have been further apart. G liked to keep things mysterious. He would present little pieces of the teaching here and there, but never give one a real overview of the entire landscape of what he was saying. This, Baba, did with great clarity and enthusiasm. G seemed to want make things difficult so that the student would have to struggle. On a personal level, he wasn't known to be friendly or easy to get along with. In contrast, I could see that Baba was very friendly, accessible, joyous, and humorous. His teachings were available to all, straightforward. They spoke about all aspects of the spiritual journey with clarity.

A Joyous Awakening

Baba emphasized everyone's greatness and worthiness, the presence of one's true Self, and their capacity to experience this Truth. G focused mainly on one's present state, one's mechanicalness, and one's predicament, being at the mercy of one's ego and its foolishness. In hindsight, it is interesting that G never said anything about initiation, an extremely significant aspect of all the wisdom traditions. Baba called his yoga Siddha Yoga, by which he meant yoga under the guidance of a Siddha. He taught that a Siddha is a fully enlightened human being and that a Siddha Guru is a perfected Master. He said again, and again, that it is only this level of teacher, the true Guru, that is able to give genuine initiation. Baba spoke of this initiation as *shaktipat, literally the descent of Grace.* He was a *shaktipat Guru,* an authentic Guru who initiates a seeker, thereby giving them spiritual awakening. Baba was initiated and made a Guru by his Guru Bhagavan Nityananda, an important part of the tradition.

Baba made it very clear that his own attainment was the result of the grace he received from his own Guru, Nityananda.

In fairness to G, I must say that he specifically stated that the fourth state, the transcendent state—the Self—is the ultimate goal, but that his teaching was strictly about the third state. The third state is the state of being consciously present, the state of expanded awareness, the experience of self-remembering. I believe G taught this way because he knew that one had to become familiar with and well established in the third state in order to have a chance to enter the fourth state. From the way I read G, he wanted his students to see, for themselves, their own lack of self-awareness and their minds' heavy conditioning. Again, these efforts and exercises are what begin to transform a person's understanding of themselves. Based on these experiences, they will be in a position to see why they need a spiritual Master, one who has completed the spiritual journey to the Self.

From my own experiences, I knew G was right, but once I had experienced my Self, G's teachings were not much help to me in understanding this totally new and unexpected state in which I found myself, or the nature of the spiritual journey I was on. Again, this is why I was so ecstatic to realize that Baba's teaching not only presented the entire teaching about the spiritual path but also contained its ancient sources from a number of different cultures.

For years after my awakening, I had often wished that I could have spent some time with G, but now, I was very happy to be with Baba.

For me, it was clear that Baba was a much better teacher than G. It was great to hear Baba say that he was speaking from the state of his own experiences of the Self, not something he believed in, and that he was not interested in religion; he only taught about the Self, the one Spirit in all. It was so evident, from his teaching and his behavior, that he was a very advanced being. I never saw G talking about his own experiences of the Self, or even about his own experience of awakening to the third state.

In the Presence of the Master

There was no question in my own mind that what I experienced in the summer of 1975 was true spiritual initiation. This fact was the only thing that did not seem to fit into Baba's teaching that a person could only receive *shaktipat* from a Siddha Guru. As I've said, I felt that my awakening was due to self-effort and grace.

One of Baba's teachings that I wasn't yet able to understand is that the Guru is not this fellow that we can see and talk to; the Guru is a manifestation of the supreme Principle, the Holy Spirit manifest in human form. If I had been able to take in this teaching, there would have been no conflict for me, but, like many other seekers at this time, I was focused mainly on the physical form—on Baba himself. Thus, I was perplexed and wondered how I could have gotten shaktipat when I certainly had no Guru, except possibly Jesus.

Baba also spoke about the inner Guru, your true Self, and how the inner Guru and the outer Guru are, in fact, one. In other words, there is only one Self—one Supreme Principal, and that is called the Guru. I had experienced the presence of the inner Guru, so I knew that was true. What I didn't know was whether or not the outer Guru was a full, complete, and perfect manifestation of this inner divine Principal. I had no way to really judge this, and truly, there was also no reason to make such a judgment. I was having a great time. All of Baba's teachings that I could comment on were in perfect agreement with my own experiences, and I was feeling some very special energy—energy that was very similar to what I had experienced during my initial awakening!

At this time, I asked Baba for a spiritual name. A name that represents our spiritual nature. He gave me the name Lokesh.

As my stay was coming to a close, I couldn't resist asking Baba about my awakening in 1975. I was absolutely sure that it was the real thing, but I was still interested to see what Baba would say. Up to this point, I had not spoken to Baba personally. So, one day during darshan, the ancient tradition where the seeker attending the evening program is able to greet Baba personally. I presented a few written questions to Baba through one of his translators. The first question was: Should I consider my spiritual awakening in the summer of 1975 to be my shaktipat initiation? Then, if the answer was yes, whom should I thank for this great gift? If the answer was no, then how should I understand that blessed experience?

A Joyous Awakening

Baba was looking directly at me, and I at him, as the questions were being translated. To the first one, with a very sweet and loving face, he laughed and said in English, "Yes, of course," as if to say, you already knew that; what else could it be? To the second question, he replied in Hindi, and the translation was this: *"Thank God, it was through God that you received* **shaktipat** *awakening."*

Feeling unimaginable gratitude and grace, knowing Baba's words were true, I started to leave. At that point, Baba spoke again, and the translator said: *"And don't forget to thank your own self."* I looked back at Baba. He was still looking right at me, radiating so much joy and love, smiling and nodding his head. I went back to my seat totally infused with love and gratitude, with joy and awe.

There is no real way to convey all that I experienced while standing in front of Baba. What I can say is that while looking at Baba, I had the distinct impression that he was looking right through me, that he knew me cold. Everything. Past, present, and future. This feeling was very strong and also something that I had never felt before, even remotely. Over the years, I've heard many others say almost the exact same thing about being in Baba's presence. This experience, my sense of being seen by him, along with my instant and intuitive recognition that he was speaking the truth, made this encounter with Baba unimaginably powerful.

As I settled back into my seat, pretty much blown away, as we used to say in those days, I wondered if Baba's final comment referred to my ordinary self or my true Self. At first, I assumed it had to mean my ordinary self, in that if I had not pursued deeper understanding for years and self-remembering intently for days on end, I wouldn't have experienced this "awakening." But then, I remembered that, in another sense, "I" had nothing to do with the Self revealing itself. At the time, I experienced that my Self had chosen to reveal itself to me, totally on Its own.

After contemplating both of these feelings for a short while, I was pretty sure Baba was referring to both of them because together, they represent effort and grace. Both are necessary for a true awakening, and they're both me.

So, being with Baba was much better than I could have hoped for. I learned more and felt happier than I would have dared to dream I could. Even though the above only presents a fraction of the things I learned and experienced during this almost month-long stay with Baba, it still gives one a decent feel of what it is like to be with a true spiritual Master.

I headed back to Vail with Bob and my girlfriend, feeling that I could now finally carry on with my life. I now had a way to not only understand my spiritual awakening better, but also to speak about it with others. After years of longing to know more and having to keep it all inside, I could finally learn more about it; I was finally in a position to learn about and talk about this life-transforming experience. And I truly wanted to share this greatest and most profound experience of my life.

It's Still Awfully Tough to Stay Awake

After returning to Vail, I was able to hold onto the spiritual energy—spiritual perspective and experience fairly well for a while. However, the hope I had that my girlfriend and I could live in harmony and enjoy the love that we truly felt for each other was not to be. Even though she had had a Meditation Intensive with Baba, she had done it mainly to please me. She'd had a couple of great experiences where she got to see the foolishness of the ego, and the mind's tendency to be judgmental, worried, etc. But still, she could not stand to hear me talking about the witness or the insights that had such a profound effect on me.

My girlfriend and I mutually decided that this relationship had to end. It was obvious to both of us that neither one of us was going to change. I was happy not to be embroiled in arguments on a daily basis, but I still had the demands of work and keeping active with my other friends. Bob and I held weekly satsang gatherings to introduce people to Baba's teachings and the practices of meditation and chanting. But I couldn't seem to make time to chant or meditate on a daily basis, even though some part of me wanted to do so. I read Baba's books and still continued to practice self-remembering every day.

What I mean is that I made a determined effort to stay in touch with the witness every day. I knew that self-remembering was a form of meditation and that it was a much more powerful and rewarding one for me as compared to traditional meditation. Self-remembering was now a natural and permanent part of my life.

I guess I was satisfied with this level of yogic practice. Or perhaps I should say that I knew that this was the best I could do at the time. Again, I still felt a little guilty about not being a better student of yoga, but also knew that feeling guilty or unworthy was only another set of thoughts and judgments. I witnessed this tendency in myself and knew from experience not to become identified with these negative emotions, as they would only make everything worse.

I also knew that living alone was not that good for me either. There was no question in my mind or body that I needed a mate. I felt that if I had an appropriate mate—one who was interested in the spiritual life and the great outdoors, then I would be able to settle down and pursue the spiritual life more earnestly. For this reason, I made a very deep and sincere prayer to Baba and Jesus to help me with this, as I was tired of being single and doing the things most single guys do to find women! I knew God was right within me and was thus sure that He knew exactly how I felt. So, I told Him that since He knew that I sincerely wanted to know Him and experience Him more, why couldn't we quit wasting time? He should just let me meet a woman with whom I can get along with and who has similar goals for her life.

Finally, the Right One

My prayers were answered. A couple of months later, I met my future wife. My relationship with Pam began on June 21, the summer solstice. This day, with the most light of any in the year, is a perfect time for a new beginning. Like many others, this relationship started with lots of social and romantic activity. Pam joined me in Maine for a vacation with my family and friends. It made for a great beginning, but, as I was trying to fit in as many things as I could during this stay, it wasn't anything like my normal routine.

As the vacation was winding down, I let Pam know that this was not my normal pace and that partying and carrying on were fine for this vacation time, but were not something that I was really that interested in. I told her that I was drawn to other things that were quite different in nature and difficult to explain. These were really what my life was about. She responded, saying she was also having a great time with my family and friends but that she had done plenty of partying and socializing in her life and knew that she wanted and needed something more genuine—even though she wasn't quite sure what that was. I told her that when we get back to Colorado, and the timing feels right, I'd start sharing some of the things that have had a very powerful effect on me, things that I couldn't help but pursue.

Pam decided that she would really like to see a moose before leaving Maine. I told her that she would have to get up before sunrise to have a good chance to do so. She said, "Let's do it." Early the next morning, we drove in a little fishing boat to an area of the lake where I grew up, where there used to be a lot of moose. When we arrived at our viewing spot, I just spontaneously suggested, while we were waiting, to just focus on the surrounding beauty, the exquisite morning sky, and the perfectly calm lake, which was only a few feet deep in this section.

"Most importantly," I told her, "try and keep your mind silent." I encouraged Pam to truly look at the many old stumps, the driftwood, the different plants, the bushes growing in the water, and the birds that were all around. I reiterated that while she was taking all this in, try to stay silent inside, with no internal talking. "If it starts up," I said, "just let it go." Put your attention into being totally present in this wonderful and magical moment." Without planning to do it and without putting a label on it, I was teaching Pam how to meditate—how to participate in self-remembering.

The First Years After the Awakening

It wasn't any more than a couple of minutes after these instructions that a big bull moose, which we had not noticed, lifted his head out of the water and stood up straight, showing off his magnificent form as he slowly looked around. He was not that far from us, making it easy to see him and even easier to feel his presence. Moose had been protected in Maine for decades, so they were not the least bit afraid of people. As we were enjoying this picturesque sight, Momma Moose and her baby came strolling out of the woods to join Papa Moose for breakfast. All stayed for several minutes, making this early morning adventure in the Maine wilderness truly a memorable one.

Afterwards, Pam told me that in the minutes before the bull moose rose up, she had experienced an inner stillness and peace that she had never known before. She said this experience was something she had always longed for. I responded that the experience was precious, more significant than seeing the moose, an experience of meditation, of the great joy and peace that lie within us all. I also told her that inner experiences such as this were what most interested me in my life, that I found them more satisfying and knew that they were more real, more lasting, than other, more mundane things. I said that this was what I was talking about earlier, when I said that my real interests were not in socializing and partying but quite different things.

Pam said, *"If this is a preview, then I know this is where I want and need to go. I just feel so good right now."*

Back in Vail, our relationship flourished. We played a lot of golf together, and I continued to encourage her to try and stay in touch with the inner silence and the part of her awareness that could see what her mind was up to. Things went so well that we decided to return to Maine for the fall foliage.

It was a perfect year for the leaves. They were so bright that they almost looked like they were spray-painted! Compared to the summer, the pace of this vacation went at an easy pace, with us playing a little golf together and picnicking with my parents in different areas where we could enjoy the spectacular fall colors. The fall had always been one of my absolute favorite times because it often brought forth the most lovely feelings in the heart, making me so appreciative for just being alive.

So, this vacation was romantic, although in quite a different way from the one in the summer. I remember thinking that I could marry this girl, but felt that I should give it some more time to make sure that these deeper interests of the heart were sincere and not just a passing fancy that often went with the initial great feelings of falling in love. Remembering how quickly Ustrid could shift from the heart to the mind and its many needs made it almost impossible to make a commitment quickly.

A Joyous Awakening

Just before heading back to Vail, a friend called me to let me know that Baba Muktananda had passed away the previous day. The news neither shocked me nor made me sad. I firmly believed that Baba was an enlightened being and also believed that—actually, from my own experiences knew that—all of our final destinies are to merge fully with the Supreme Being. How could one be sad about such an event, whether you thought of it as a great ending or a new beginning? My own experiences with my divine nature—with my Self—had shown me how indescribably and unimaginably joyous and blissful our true nature really is.

So, instead of feeling saddened by Baba's death, I was powerfully reminded of my own true Self and my own and everyone else's great destiny. I also felt grateful for listening to myself or my Self, and making the time to be with Baba. I'd realized that he was getting old, and this might be my only chance to be with him. Now I realized how fortunate I had been to be in his presence for almost a whole month.

So, again, I just felt a very deep sense of gratitude to God for allowing me to experience my own divine Self and for allowing me to meet a being like Baba, who had helped me understand my own spiritual experiences much better by describing his own and by putting me in touch with the wisdom teachings that are the foundation of all true spiritual paths.

Pam and I had been attending our weekly meditation gatherings, so she had been slowly introduced to Baba's major teachings and, through the practice of meditation, had begun to see how difficult it can be to focus the mind. Baba's death provided me with the appropriate atmosphere to speak about my own spiritual experiences and how they related to Baba's teachings. The timing was just perfect for this, coming at the end of such a wonderful vacation and just as we were starting to live together for the first time. We went skiing together and spent a lot of time talking about spiritual teachings and why they were so important for us to pursue. Besides attending weekly meditation and chanting sessions, we didn't do any other spiritual practices. But, in hindsight, I realized that skiing, discussing the spiritual teachings and our own spiritual experiences are truly spiritual practices!

Pam had a major breakthrough on our first Valentine's Day together. Being in her mid-twenties, from California, and going out with a young dentist, she envisioned a great dinner at a fancy restaurant, at least one expensive present and who knows what else her mind may have created. For me, Valentine's Day just represented another commercial event and thus had no real significant meaning. I had not planned a thing and had not even thought of buying Pam anything. I knew that we would get together and do something, but again, it really wasn't that much different than any other day for me.

We saw each other in the late afternoon, just talking in my car in one of Vail's many scenic spots. Once she realized that I had no big plans, she got quite upset, assuming that this inattention meant that I didn't really care for her that much. At first, I was a little surprised at this, but then I realized, from my past experiences with other girlfriends, I should have known better.

So, I told her that I was sorry and that my lack of planning was not a reflection of my feelings for her but of how I felt about genuine love. For me, love doesn't depend on material expressions, especially when related to commercialized events. For me, love was a condition of the heart, the blissful and awesome feeling one has when one's sense of self is in touch with that pure and divine space deep within one's self. I reminded Pam of how she felt just before seeing the moose in July and when she was looking at the brilliant leaves in October.

Then I told her about a couple of my own experiences in 1975, when I had first experienced this deeper understanding of love. I spoke of my understanding that this state of pure love exists within each of us as an expression of our true Self. I told her that I was sure that this state was what Jesus was speaking about in referring to unconditional love: a love that was at the core of our being and did not depend on outer conditions. This pure love is what we truly are. This inner love is so perfect and so miraculous that what most people think of as "love"— love connected with the material world, simply can't compare.

Because I was reflecting on my own highest experiences of genuine love, I was able to speak very passionately about it and also reconnect with that "pure state" in this very significant moment. My high energy and the beauty of the mountains during sunset resulted in Pam experiencing a flood of her own divine and blissful inner love. As she listened to me talking about that state of love, she was experiencing it herself.

From her perspective, this experience of true love—a "taste" of her own Self, was the best Valentine's Day present she could have possibly received. Thus, the two of us proceeded to have the best Valentine's Day anyone could ever have— one that was better than anything I could ever have planned.

Returning to the Ashram, July 1983

In the spring of 1983, when the Siddha Yoga summer calendar came out, I decided to return to the Ashram in New York to take a follow-up course to the one I had taken with Baba. Just before his death, Baba had installed Swami Chidvalasananda, who is lovingly referred to as Gurumayi, as the Siddha Yoga Guru. I had known Gurumayi as Baba's translator; the first time that I laid eyes on her, I'd felt that she was a divine being. But this visit was to be my first encounter with Gurumayi as the Guru. Also, I was hoping to reconnect with the pure energy of the Self I'd experienced when I was last in the Ashram with Baba. Also, this visit seemed to be the perfect way to celebrate the eighth anniversary of my spiritual awakening. I felt it would be an opportunity to move onto a higher level of spiritual experience and participation.

So, I left for the Ashram that July with the firm intention to practice self-remembering as intensely as I had eight years before. I hoped that the intensity of the practice in the ashram setting would allow me to become well established in the state of witness consciousness.

Flying into LaGuardia, I was supposed to land in time to take the last bus up to the Ashram. The plane was late, however, and after a wild and expensive taxi ride from the airport, I arrived at the bus station in Manhattan to find that the bus was full! If I wanted to get there today, I'd have to find another way. The ticket agent gave me a couple of phone numbers to try.

I wanted to get to the Ashram that night so I could participate in the Intensive that was starting at 8 am the next day. Being quite emotional after the high-speed taxi ride, and when neither of these phone numbers would work, I got pulled into a state of overwhelming frustration. After the second number didn't work, I slammed the phone down hard enough to break it. Luckily, at that very moment of intense anger and frustration, the "witness" aspect of myself took over and allowed me to fully experience what was happening here and to detach from it. Also, it vividly reminded me that just being "awake" in the moment was all that was required to get in touch with the "state" I was seeking. I heard, *"Just do this, and the Intensive will start right now, and it won't matter when you get to the Intensive hall."* I immediately recognized the absolute truth of this insight, and because of this and my past experiences, I was able to completely let go of this negative and angry energy and be wonderfully established in the peaceful and conscious energy of the witness. In this totally new state, I walked back up to the bus ticket counter to see if they had any other advice, and the agent told me that they had one more seat and to hurry, as it was literally starting to leave. I immediately thanked the Lord for such divine advice and such a timely lesson. A lesson I will not forget.

The intensive is a two-day program, designed by Baba to help seekers get in touch with their own Self through a combination of meditation, chanting, scriptural teachings, and personal stories about experiencing the Self within. Yet the main point of a Siddha Yoga Shaktipat Intensive, and this remains true today in 2024, is that a participant receives initiation—*shaktipat,* which means awakening of the spiritual energy, through the intention of the living Siddha Yoga Master. In authentic spiritual traditions, the seeker of Truth has to receive

The First Years After the Awakening

Initiation from a spiritual master before they can truly begin their spiritual journey. The Intensive was designed by Baba as a vehicle through which the Guru bestows this miraculous gift of grace. To my knowledge, mass initiations of this kind had never happened before. By the end of Baba's life, untold thousands had been awakened through his grace. This alone made it obvious that Baba was a very rare and special spiritual Master. And now Gurumayi was continuing as the Shaktipat Guru.

(I have personally talked with dozens and dozens of people who received initiation from Baba and Gurumayi and also have read hundreds of other's accounts; and, based on my own experiences and understanding, I know their experiences are indeed authentic. I also realize how difficult it is for a beginner to open to this truth, but all one has to do is begin the practice of self-remembering to begin *to know*!)

From my own perspective, being able to attend this unique program was in itself a boon. And to be in the Intensive while I was already in such a great state, just made the whole experience that I was already immersed in much more powerful and enjoyable. What a way to begin another spiritual adventure.

It just so happened that the 4th of July fell on a Monday following the Intensive. After traveling and sitting cross-legged for a couple of days, it was great to just have a day off and be outside. The weather was just perfect, so it was a treat to be on the grounds of this beautiful place. My experience of celebrating this day of freedom was completely centered around the freedom and bliss of the inner Self. I was reminded of the 4th of July I'd spent just outside Vancouver, B.C., in 1975 and how excited and joyous I was on that day, how privileged I had felt to find out and experience what genuine freedom—inner freedom, really meant.

So here I was eight years later, one octave later, still marveling at what I was learning and how things were magically unfolding. To borrow an image from music, it seemed to me that from my experiences of Siddha Yoga practices and my continued practice of self-remembering, I had moved up an octave—moved up a discernible level from where I had been in the years after 1975. I was ready to pursue the spiritual journey with the same excitement and energy that I'd felt during my initial awakening, but thanks to Baba, with a lot more understanding of what the journey entailed.

The Courses

The advanced Siddha Yoga course started off by reminding us that the ashram was designed to help us focus on our spiritual practices and remain aware of our own inner Self. I was touched and impressed, and felt that this was a perfect start because this was exactly why I came here. I wanted to understand my own

A Joyous Awakening

Self better and thus wanted to understand yoga better because it is the science of the Self. We were told that the word yoga comes from the Sanskrit root *yuj*, which means *to bind together or yoke* and refers to the yoking—union—of the individual soul with the Supreme Soul. Yoga is considered a science, not a philosophy or religion, because it comes from enlightened beings, from their own direct experience of the "Self, as a means for others to have the same experience.

We were taught that receiving the teachings of such beings creates the proper atmosphere in which to do spiritual practices. You could say that the ashram is where the teachings take place, but you could also say that they truly take place in the opening of one's heart, which is the only place where the teachings can be understood. This is the place where I learned yoga, through the direct experience that the individual soul and the supreme soul are not different from one another.

We also learned that Siddha Yoga is a yoga that takes place under the direction and guidance of a Siddha Guru, a fully enlightened master who teaches and oversees spiritual practices that are designed to help one experience union with one's own Self. Yoga is a way to purify one's mind and body so the seeker can have the experience of their own Self that is already within them in all its fullness. We were taught that while the goal of yoga is mystical—beyond thought—the daily practices to achieve this most precious of goals are basic.

These practices include becoming familiar with the Guru's teachings, applying them in your life, and participating in spiritual practices, such as self-inquiry, self-remembering, meditation, and chanting, to truly transform your understanding. Again, the enlightened Master provides the basic knowledge and guidance, but if the student does not work on him/herself via the practices, then the teaching just becomes another philosophy, another belief system that is incapable of transforming you, of enlightening you.

Another of yoga's most basic teachings that was described in the advanced Siddha Yoga Course is that a seeker must be detached from mental flux, from all the thoughts and emotions that continually move in the mind. Yoga's answer to this dilemma is to "know the Knower," which is another way of saying that we should focus on the watcher or witness of the mind instead of our many and often contradictory and unwanted thoughts. As I've already described, this subtle change in focus was the key to my own spiritual awakening. Since meeting Baba in 1981, I had heard and read this teaching a number of times, but I still marveled at how fortunate I was to know its absolute Truth. As I've mentioned, Baba talked specifically about the importance of the witness.

Another aspect of yoga that I really needed to hear, to be reminded of, was that yoga—spiritual transformation—was a process that takes place over a long period of time. One should not become discouraged by temporary failure, laziness, or judge oneself on how they were progressing. I'd been experiencing some mental flux recently; I had to admit that most of it was due to being too hard on myself for not being more disciplined and more "spiritual." Instead of just being the witness—being detached from my thoughts and emotions, something I knew the truth of so well from direct experience—I had identified with my judgments. Thus, I was not practicing yoga, not staying awake, not really observing myself or remembering myself.

When I was at the beginning of the spiritual journey, knowing that I didn't know anything, I had abandoned all thoughts and just stuck with the witness. Now, years later, I was remembering just how important witness consciousness is. It was this straight-forward practice that was key to my initial awakening and, thus, my way back to my essential Self.

The course also addressed the question of "kundalini," the latent spiritual energy that lies latent in all human beings. We were reminded that almost all religions and spiritual traditions speak of this miraculous power. In Christianity, it is known as the Holy Spirit, the Japanese call it "Ki," the Chinese call it "Chi", and the Kung people of the Kalahari Desert call it "N/UM." The Jewish mystical tradition knew of it, as did some of our Native Americans, the Australian Aborigines, and the Aztecs and Mayan's of ancient Mexico. So did some of the earliest Christians, the Gnostics, and the Desert Fathers.[4] It's also interesting to know that on the original altar of the Church of Saint Ambrose in Milan, in the 4th century, there is a carving of a serpent coiled three and a half times—exactly the same symbol for Kundalini used by the ancient Indians, from India.

The above is but one small but prime example of the quality of the courses, which were every bit as good as they were in 1981 with Baba. Between these courses and the Ashrams' daily schedule, I was again feeling the special energy of the Self— great bliss, happiness, contentment, enthusiasm, and love.

Another Nectarian aspect of ashram life is the long evening chants. These chants, which took place from about seven to ten, were held on many of the nights I was there. Before coming, I hoped to be able to deepen my meditations to get in touch with the divine energy within. What turned out to be was that these evening chants were much more powerful than my morning meditations, and I could now see why Baba had said that in this modern era it was easier to still the mind and become "enlightened" through chanting than it was through meditation.

Seva, Chanting, and More

The seva, the selfless service, that I was assigned in the ashram was to water the surrounding lawns in the evenings while the chants were in progress. I loved this seva because I got to run around the lawns in my bare feet in the warm, moist

A Joyous Awakening

New York air, a treat that was indeed rare in the Rocky Mountains. I would leave the sprinklers in place for an hour before moving them and would attend the chant in between moves. Because of my great inner state and the high intensity of the chants, I found it very easy to become totally absorbed in the chant. This was my first experience of reaching such a deep level with chanting. Being one-pointed on the chant had the same effect on me as being in deep meditation, in that my mind was extremely focused and quiet.

Time and again, after I had moved the sprinklers, I would return to the chant and almost immediately become absorbed in it. Then, after what seemed like only a few minutes, the deeper part of myself would inform me that it was time to move the sprinklers. I would feel like—*it can't be yet as I just barely sat down*—but I would glance at the clock, and sure enough, every time it was right on the money. Every time, I would be amazed at how the time had just disappeared. My meditations were never this good, my mind was never this one-pointed, and this is why I found these evening chants to be so magical and blissful.

As July 19th approached, I remembered that this was the eighth anniversary of my coming to understand the goal, and that the final resting place of my being was full union with God. This understanding had come forty days after the start of my "awakening" and thus, for me, was symbolic of a great transformation in understanding. This date had come to symbolize the end of the first octave—the first stage of my spiritual work and understanding. Being in a good state of the witness, I could see how "my mind"—my ego wanted a powerful meditation experience or some significant breakthrough in insight, to propel me into this next octave of experience and understanding. Seeing this as a normal aspect of "the mind" and its many desires, I just witnessed it and tried to make sure that I did not buy into these desires and did not identify with these thoughts. When such thoughts would arise, I would just be amused by them and their persistence. Again, I knew that such was to be expected because the mind does not give up easily on its desires.

On the day of the 19th, things went along fine, but nothing out of the norm. I was feeling so good that I no longer had any desire for something special. The courses and chants were special enough. So, I went to bed that night feeling perfectly contented. In the middle of the night, during the state of deep sleep, I was awakened by an explosion of energy at the base of my spine, which roared with so much power that it literally lifted my entire body, except for my feet, completely off the bed. By the time this ball of energy reached my head, I was easily a foot off the bed. I felt the energy explode, and, with my mind's eye, I saw a halo of beautiful sparkling blue energy completely covering what seemed like the inside of my skull. Even though I had come directly from deep sleep into this inner event, I still knew for sure that I was being blessed with a direct experience of my sahasrara—the highest spiritual center where the individual soul merges with the Supreme Soul. In the yogic tradition, various energy centers known as chakras are identified in the subtle body. The center at the top of the head is considered the highest of these chakras and is where the seeker experiences their oneness with God. In paintings, a halo signifies that the center is active. I assume that this experience did not last long in terms of physical time, but afterwards, to say the least, I was wide-awake.

I was able to recognize this experience because I had heard similar stories from other Siddha Yoga students about their experiences of the Sahasrara, most of them taking place during *shaktipat* initiation. I had also read about and heard descriptions of the sahasrara in the Siddha Yoga courses. I must also say that from the very moment I awoke, I was wholly centered in the witness and so experienced this rare and blessed event through that expanded and elevated awareness, with no thoughts, fears, or worries. This experience of the sahasrara was the same as my experience of my Self—peaceful, pure, holy, sacred, and serene. Being immersed in such divine feelings, I just sat on the side of my bed in awe of what I had just experienced, and I also felt tremendous gratitude for so much grace. A thought of Gurumayi came forth, and I assumed that this was a gift of her grace.

I remained in this pure, clear, and quiet state for quite a while. Then it struck me that, taking the time difference into account, this inner "event" had taken place almost exactly at the same time as my enlightening breakthrough eight years earlier. This sent another wave of amazement, reverence, and gratitude through me, as I realized, once again, the awesome power and supreme intelligence of the divine energy within. This reminded me of the importance of just staying in the witness and not listening to the many desires and worries of my "mind." During my initial "awakening," it was so clear to me that if I just stayed in self-remembering—in witness consciousness, the inner energy would reveal its secrets—its divine insights—when the timing was right. This was just another perfect example of this basic yogic truth.

The awareness that such a powerful and holy experience could and would take place exactly eight years later, almost to the exact hour, astounded me all over again. The symbolism of moving up to a new octave was not only signified by the eight years but was also signified by the sahasrara, sometimes called the eighth spiritual center, representing the goal of the spiritual journey. I wasn't established in this state, but here I was, having the experience again. Just as I'd had eight years before, I'd had a dramatic awareness of the resting place of my true being, but now on a different level. This insight made it clear that I was indeed entering a new octave, a new level of spiritual experience and understanding.

Benefits of Being in the Guru's House

In the finale of the Teachers Training course that was held at the end of my month's stay, the instructor asked the participants to share what they had gotten out of the courses and their stay in general. I was one of the last people to share, so before I spoke, I had some time to contemplate the question. I said that before coming, I had hoped to have a real Siddha Yoga meditation experience—the kind that we had all heard about in the experience talks, hoping that this would help me do the practices daily. Then I told them of my classic Siddha Yoga experience, the explosion of energy at the base of my spine—describing it pretty much as I have done here. I said this experience had been wonderful, but that overall, this visit had helped me to realize that the most important thing about spiritual practice was to simply live in the present with the awareness of the teachings and what one's own mind was up to at the very moment. I shared with them the challenge with the ticket in the bus station on my way to the Ashram, and how that helped me get centered in the witness.

I said that all the different aspects of the ashram schedule, especially chanting and the courses, had helped me stay in touch with the witness much better than I was able to at home. I said that I now realized that this was my real reason for coming here and truly was the essence of my *shaktipat* experience. Finally, I said that it was now obvious to me that just a normal life with this heightened awareness and understanding was much superior and more beneficial than sensational experiences in helping me achieve my long-term goals. But, at the same time, I was extremely grateful for a glimpse of the sahasrara. The instructor, along with many others, nodded her head and agreed that this is what the ashram and the Guru do for us all—put us in touch with our Self in a natural way.

So, I had another uplifting stay in the Siddha Yoga ashram in the Catskills. During this time, I felt that I was so in touch with the true Self that I knew it was time for me to get married and that Pam was the right one. I told my mother, who had been waiting for years to hear this, but did not propose to Pam as I wanted to get a ring first and make the occasion one to remember. So, feeling fantastic and wonderfully excited, I headed back to Vail.

On the plane ride from New York to Denver, I had a very interesting experience. Early into the flight, I realized that my body was running a high fever with an intensity as great as I'd ever experienced. I say my body because I—my feeling of self—was not the least bit agitated or distraught in any way. Actually, I felt terrific—in a state of spiritual bliss, so I was surprised to realize that my body had such a fever raging inside it. At first, it seemed remarkable and a little weird that my body felt like it was burning up, yet I could be so ecstatic at the same time.

Slowly, it dawned on me that I was experiencing the Kundalini Shakti working intensely within me. This divine energy had been described in the courses as a "fire" performing internal purification. I found this development, this situation, to be quite interesting, particularly because I had just said that I could see that dramatic spiritual experiences were not really necessary. But at the same time, it seemed that all of my most intense spiritual experiences took place in my normal waking state—not traditional meditation.

My underlying intuition was that this was a going-away gift from the Skakti—to assist in my inner purification. Knowing this was a gift of grace, I could just enjoy the miraculous nature of the experience and marvel at the intelligence of this holy energy and how one never knows when it may manifest. I just knew that the more I tried to stay in the witness, the more the Kundalini Shakti, the Holy Spirit, manifested in me. This continued for a couple of hours, and all the while, I remained perfectly content and perfectly amazed that the Shakti would give me such a tangible experience of Its presence. I had left for the Ashram wanting vivid and explosive experiences of the Shakti to help me get back in touch with my true Self and get me fired up to live a more spiritual life, and now I was returning literally on fire!

Pleasant Surprises

When I got back, I told Pam all about my trip and how it was much better than I could have hoped for, but I didn't say anything about getting married, as I wanted to get a ring and propose in a traditional manner. I wanted it to be a memorable occasion. Little did I know that destiny and the Shakti had already taken over. A few days after I had gotten home, I awoke early one morning, meditated for a while, and then went back to sleep.

Baba appeared to me in a dream that was unlike any dream I ever had. The experience was so life-like that the word *dream* does not seem to apply. Baba appeared to me in a way I had never seen him in person: in a long cotton shirt, with no teeth, and a long beard. He sat down on the bed and, without saying a word, started rubbing my arms and chest gently. This sent incredible and indescribable waves of heavenly bliss throughout my entire body and inner being as well. With each touch, he would send wave after wave of the most awesome joy clear through me, all the while looking at me so sweetly and lovingly, but again, saying nothing. This had the effect of putting me into a very blissful but extremely calm and focused state—a profound experience of the witness state. My mind was perfectly still, and I just lay here absorbing this miraculous energy. This continued for about four or five minutes, then Baba rubbed my legs and then got up and left. As far as I could tell, I awoke immediately, feeling exactly the same as I had in the "dream." My body was still vibrating with Baba's shakti, his divine spiritual energy. I was just amazed that something like this could happen and have such a powerful effect on me in the waking state. I had heard others talk about similar occurrences with Baba appearing to them in dreams or meditation, so I was not that dumbfounded about it, just a little shocked that I should be so lucky—so fortunate. I sat up, still amazed that I felt exactly the same in the waking state as I had in the dream—the intensity of the experience had not changed at all.

Knowing that this was no dream, that Baba had actually been there in his subtle form, I wondered what the purpose could be. Not that there had to be one, but it was so vivid and so extraordinary that I could not help but wonder about its significance. The only answer that came to mind was that this was just another form of purification and another demonstration of the power of the Shakti, and the intensity and generosity of Guru's love and grace.

Pam woke up shortly after I had, and I simply had to tell her about this unexpected and miraculous experience. She was able to pick up on the divine and blissful energy that I had received while listening to me describe the experience. I told her that I thought that this was just another blessing, like the beneficial fever on the plane, another reward for sincerely pursuing the spiritual life, and also another form of purification, like the fever I had on the plane. This "visit" from Baba was just another blessing for putting the spiritual life first. After sharing with each other how fortunate we both felt to know about the "Self" within, to have Baba's teachings, and each other—feeling great love—we decided to get married! Again, not quite the proposal I envisioned, but way better than anything I could have planned.

When I proposed to Pam, I told her that I had decided to propose while at the ashram and had already told my parents and ordered a ring! I also told her that I had heard that one should be careful what they wish for in the ashram, because it may come true sooner than they think. I'd known I wanted to get married and have a family, but wasn't expecting the floodgates to open quite so fast. I let her know that I considered this another gift of grace.

We joyfully made speedy arrangements to get married in Maine in September, one of my favorite times of the year. The wedding day turned out to be warm and sunny, just what we wanted. The setting was also ideal; my parent's pool patio, surrounded by a lush grape vine with clusters of grapes hanging down from a little sun shelter where the ceremony was to take place.

The sun set just after the ceremony ended, and the loving atmosphere seemed to be palpable for everyone there. The reception and honeymoon both went extremely well. Pam went to Los Angeles to take the Siddha Yoga introductory course, the same course I had taken with Baba in 81. We both felt that this was the perfect way to celebrate and provide a great beginning to our family life. I was happy to return to work and let my partner, who had just gotten married the day after us, leave for L.A., with his new bride, to join Pam and a few other of our friends for the retreat.

The fall and winter went by extremely fast, and the day after the ski season ended, we were blessed with a beautiful, healthy, blue-eyed baby girl. We named her Natalia and found out later that in Italian (Pam is 100% Italian), Natale means "the Christ." That just reminded me of the blessed circumstances leading up to her conception and my own experience of being shown that God is truly the essence of everyone. Natalia turned out to be the perfect little baby, easy to care for, and oh-so-much fun to be with.

8
Mystical Insights

Addressing a Time of Baffling Unease

The next couple of years went smoothly. Pam and I both enjoyed each other and our sweet little daughter, who entertained us and amazed us almost every day. We were holding weekly satsangs at our home—spiritual gatherings to chant and meditate. We also enjoyed reading Baba's books. We were not practicing traditional meditation each day as I had always hoped. I was still practicing self-remembering as much as possible, knowing that the witness is my true self, my trusted awareness. Also, this practice of G's is truly a form of meditation.

Things were going so well that we decided that it was time to try for another child and to start making plans for a new home. We started working on some designs that we thought would fit well with the land I already had, and even had an architect draw up some preliminary plans.

As we were doing this, feelings kept surfacing about whether this was the right thing to do. It costs a lot to live in Vail, and I wondered if I should spend this much money on a house. At first, I figured that such was the nature of the mind—to question everything and that my conservative upbringing might have something to do with it too. It seemed appropriate, however, to proceed with caution and to put a lot of forethought into such a big undertaking. I had worked hard for years to get into this financial position, and I felt fortunate to be able to build a new house in such a beautiful area. But even though I knew that getting a bigger house was the natural and expected thing to do and that it was something I could afford, still, some doubts and uneasy feelings would not go away.

I tried to just witness these feelings and be detached from them, but I just couldn't seem to shake them off. And I couldn't enjoy this process of planning a new house without these feelings pulling at me.

After the ski season, we went to California to visit my two older brothers, and in talking about our plans for the house with them, these lingering doubts seemed to finally dissolve. When we got back to Vail after a relaxing vacation, we were excited to finalize the drawings and get ready to build. On my first day back at work, I went to lunch with a couple of doctor friends, and all they could talk about was this speaker they had just seen. He was talking about the upcoming and unavoidable financial crash the U.S. was about to undergo because of the huge deficits. This type of talk had been going on for years amongst the New Agers, so this was nothing new to me. I had been aware that views such as this were

207

probably causing some of my doubts, but I also knew that such talk had been going on for decades.

On this day, however, listening to my friends share and discuss this fellow's main points, I had to admit that his arguments made a lot of sense and seemed almost impossible to refute. My brothers and I had talked about the deficits and agreed that they did not make sense and that someday they would cause trouble. Now, I was having a vivid picture painted as to what that trouble would be like and of course, it was not pretty.

Having just returned from vacation, I was able to laugh at the irony of this. I had just finally gotten to the point of feeling great about going forward with this big project, and these little worries and hesitations that had been pulling on me were finally put to rest. Now, on my very first day back, I have to listen to all of this! I knew this kind of talk, especially with such convincing arguments, would most likely renew the old feelings. So, I decided that this had to be a sign that I really needed to do some sincere soul searching, some serious self-inquiry, to get to the bottom of this pattern.

After about a month of persistent self-inquiry and finding out that Pam was pregnant again, it was perfectly clear to me that the absolute most important thing for me was to get back in touch with my true Self, the way I had been during my awakening in 1975.

Each time I contemplated, What did I really want? What did I want most for my growing family and me?" The same answer would eventually come through— to lead a truly spiritual life, a life guided by the witness's expansive awareness, not my conditioned ego. I knew that this was the only way I could ever be satisfied and truly content. Having tasted so strongly the true Self, the One within everyone, how could I settle for anything less? I had been given an incredible opportunity to experience the true goal of life, and I didn't want to waste it by relaxing into an easy life in Vail. I knew that if I were on my deathbed and had not made a sustained effort to become reconnected with my true nature, I would have profound regrets.

It had been more than ten years since my Self had revealed itself to me, and in that time, I had never once questioned the validity of the Self or that the Self was the goal and Truth of human consciousness. I knew for sure that a big house or a great dental practice in Vail wouldn't give me the genuine satisfaction and contentment that I knew was possible. Once again, I knew that all I wanted and needed was to get back in harmony with the pure, vigilant awareness of the witness. There was no doubt whatsoever that witness consciousness was the key that would reconnect me with my divine Self. Quite frankly, it was baffling to me that I could have so many powerful experiences of the Self and still be living the way I had!

I wasn't all that sure how I could best achieve this goal that I so clearly saw for myself. But I felt that the Vail area was no longer the right place. Vail offered so many things to do and such great weather to do them in that this was often difficult for me to make time for laundry, let alone spiritual practices. But I also knew that in many ways, Vail was an ideal place to experience the Spirit. It was where I first learned to value being in the present moment, and I had truly reconnected with my spirit and the joy that the spirit elicits. Thus, I knew I could not blame my lack of focus entirely on the area. The problem was me, and my own lack of discipline. But, then again, it wasn't just me. Another thing I saw was that practically everyone I knew was primarily interested in exercising and socializing and all that went with it—not the sincere pursuit of inner transformation that takes you beyond the conditioned ego.

So, with this contemplation, I saw that it was probably best to acknowledge my weaknesses but be smart enough to minimize them. I felt that by moving back to Maine, I would be putting myself in a better position to achieve my deepest and sincerest of goals. Being around my family, especially my father, who was such a great soul, always evoked my spiritual nature versus my ego-personality. Also, living in a rural area and taking some time off from work would give me a chance to focus totally on getting back in touch with the witness, the way I had in the summer of 1975.

This would also give me more time to learn about the spiritual traditions I had been exposed to. And finally, it would give me the time to begin writing about my own spiritual experiences—something I had wanted to do for years but could not seem to make the time to do, always too busy—so hard to break from "the routine."

My insights seemed valid, and my conclusions felt right, but I knew that I should not make any hasty decisions. So, I decided to continue to contemplate this question and wait until the baby was born and see how I felt then. I was happy that I had taken the time to contemplate this issue in depth. I was very sure about my innermost feelings, and also content to wait and see how things would unfold, knowing that the nature of the mind was almost always to second-guess itself.

The summer and early fall went by without much change. We were enjoying our daughter immensely, and the pregnancy was going along just fine, as was work and everything else. Then, without any change whatsoever in my outer world, my inner world took a complete U-turn. I started feeling empty inside, and after about a month of this, I had to assume I was experiencing severe depression, even though I had nothing to be depressed about. I was physically healthy, happily married with an incredibly lovely daughter, and another child on the way, which Pam and I both wanted. Business was fine, and I did not feel any pressure about moving as I was still content to wait until the baby was born before making any final decision.

My depression, however, seemed to get worse and worse as each week passed, and I became more and more befuddled as to what was happening to me. Each time I would contemplate the situation, trying to get a clue as to what was going on, the only thing that kept coming up was my sincere longing to get back in touch with my true Self. This was not the least bit surprising since it was the most awesome experience of my life and one that was full of joy, bliss, and great love.

It was, as a matter of fact, just about the polar opposite of the way I had been feeling lately. The inner desire for the experience of God within continued to grow in intensity, right along with my feeling of nothingness on the outside. I continued to perform my daily duties, hoping that this inner desolate and empty feeling would pass once the ski season got in full swing and the baby was born.

The birth of our first baby had been such a spiritual high; I assumed that this next one would be the same. I was so inwardly dead that I never even thought about trying to do more spiritual practices to lift me out of this new but awful state that I found myself in.

December 31, 1986

Pam's due date was January 1, 1987. My parents, who had recently retired, and my younger brother had come to spend the holidays with us, hoping that the baby would be born before they left. Pam, too, was certainly hoping that the baby would come early, as she was more than ready to get this pregnancy over with and, hopefully, see her new son. December 31st had been designated as a day for world peace, with a world meditation set for noon Greenwich time, which was 4:30 a.m. Colorado time. I jokingly said that this time would be the perfect time to come into the world, and the tax break would be perfect as well.

To our pleasant surprise, our son, Robert, was born just after 4:00 a.m. on the 31st, and Pam, Robert and I were all back in Pam's hospital room in time for the 4:30 a.m. meditation! Pam and I both felt incredibly blessed in many, many ways.

On my way back to the hospital later that morning, after breakfast with my family and other guests, I stopped by the office to check the recorder. I had a message from my tax attorney about my year-end tax planning, so I returned the call, knowing that the rest of this precious last day of the year was going to be very full. Mainly, he wanted to know if I was serious about selling my business this upcoming year or if we were talking a few years down the road. The question was unexpected. Almost immediately, I remembered that I had said that I would decide about making this major life change after the baby was born. I felt like the Lord was asking me to make this decision right now, on this truly auspicious day, just hours after my son was born. Knowing that there was absolutely no question about what I really wanted and needed, I told him that I was ready to sell and that I was sure that it would happen within the year.

When I talked it over with Pam, she was in complete agreement. So, we put my dental practice up for sale. We both looked forward to the new opportunity we were creating for ourselves and our families. Moreover, we knew that we were both coming from the same genuine place in our hearts. We were both comfortable and had no second thoughts.

Making this decision, along with having a great time with our divine children, helped me feel a tiny bit better through the winter than I had leading up to the birth of our son. But even with the excitement of new opportunities, a great family life, great friends, patients and employees, and what appeared to be the near-perfect buyer for my practice, I was still very much aware that the emptiness inside was still there, essentially, all the time.

It was not so utterly overwhelming as it had been, but it was still noticeably present every day. I had been hoping to recapture my great enthusiasm and this feeling of gratitude and joy with which I had started my time in Vail before leaving the area, but I just could not seem to do so. I commented to one of my good friends that now that I had an appropriate buyer and was almost on my way to something I truly wanted, you'd think I could finally recapture the natural joy and love that I had enjoyed for so long, but such was just not the case. I still couldn't, for the life of me, imagine what was really going on.

An Unexpected Clue

I did get a tantalizing clue about what was happening to me, and it came from an unexpected source—astrology! Through my friend Bob and a few patients, I heard about a remarkable astrologer who had just recently come to Vail. Some people I knew were totally amazed by how insightful and accurate he was. You could easily tell from talking with them how excited and amazed they were over these astrological readings. After my deep experiences of the Self, I never had much interest in such things and, initially, had no desire to see this fellow. However, he ended up living next door to me on the other side of the duplex.

The first time I met my new neighbor, he told me he had a broken tooth and wondered if I would consider a trade, as he was trying to save enough money to get to his next destination. I told him that I'd be glad to fix his tooth, but that I didn't really care if I got a reading. He insisted that he would have to compensate me for my services and that his reading was probably not what I was expecting. So, I provided him with my birth date, time, and place. The only other thing he knew was that we were planning on moving back East after the practice was sold. He knew from Bob that we were both interested in spiritual ideas. That was all he knew about us.

He ended up doing a reading for me, Pam and the kids, too. Our readings were as amazing as the stories of the other people had been. I will only go into a few of the highlights. Still, before doing so, I must say that when we—Pam and I—first listened to these readings, knowing each other quite well by this time, we both recognized right at that moment that this was indeed quite amazing that he could be so accurate without knowing us at all, really. So let me present a few of the things that relate to this story that I'm telling.

He pointed out how my chart showed that I had made a major decision concerning my future direction in 1986 and also that I had been under quite negative energy patterns for quite some time, especially at the end of last year. He said that this negative pattern was coming to an end soon. He said that the chart showed that I had a strong and passionate interest in speaking about ancient wisdom and sharing these ancient and profound truths in a way that modern seekers could relate to, a way that would help them better understand these subtle truths. I hadn't quite dared to acknowledge this to myself or to think of it in such a bold way, but I felt it was true. I thought that I had this potential, only because of my own profound spiritual experiences.

Landis, the astrologer, also spoke about how it was so symbolic and traditional to be returning to the East for spiritual contemplation and to be taking time off from the normal pace and demands of life for spiritual solitude and practice. This was the type of thing all great teachers had done.

Another thing that he spoke of that really stood out to me was the mention of an upcoming change in my marriage. He took this to be about my relationship with Pam and, looking at her, said that there would be some new challenges there and that we should always remember what brought us together in the first place. I knew that the upcoming move would most likely bring some new challenges to our marriage, but from the moment I first heard the word *marriage*, I immediately thought of the spiritual marriage—the union of the individual soul and the Supreme Soul. I felt certain that the upcoming change in my marriage was definitely referring to the relationship to my own Self, to the spiritual marriage. I had no idea, however, what this might mean. There were a number of other uncanny insights, mostly about things that had already happened, but those mentioned above were the most meaningful and surprising for me.

The sale date was set for August 1^{st,} and I planned to pull out of town on August 15th in a rented truck with all of our worldly possessions, hoping to get back East in time to see my brother and his family, who were visiting from California. With these dates in mind, I made arrangements to take the last two Intensives of the summer in New York with Gurumayi. I thought that this would be the perfect way to begin my new life back East. I knew that these inspiring programs would be the ideal way to recharge my spiritual batteries and start the process of trying to recapture the witness state.

Even though I had had some very good experiences with Gurumayi, as described, I did not think of her as my Guru or Siddha Yoga as the answer to all my questions and aspirations. What I did know was that being in the ashram had, in some very wonderful ways, uplifted my spirits and put me back in touch with my Self. It had put me in touch with a number of precious scriptures as well. And where else could I get this kind of help? Nowhere that I knew of!

Returning to the East to Take Time for the Self

I felt so fortunate to be able to be home in time to visit with my older brother and his family before they returned to California. When they first told me about this trip in the spring, I told them that, most likely, I would not get back East in time to see them. So being able to enjoy them and the last of the summer in Maine was the perfect way to begin my life's newest adventure. Everything connected with the move had gone easily: the sale of the practice and the move across the country. I found myself telling my family how the timing just seemed so perfect; my astrologer could even see this in my chart!

I found it interesting that the actual move had taken place during the Harmonic Convergence. This represented a special time period and, according to the Mayan calendar, the start of a new age. The Harmonic Convergence had gotten quite a lot of press then, in the summer of 1987, so I was aware of the dates but had not planned to make the move at this time. But the way circumstance unfolded, it sort of dictated that it happen at that time. But, for me, regardless of the stars, it certainly did seem to be perfect timing.

My older brother and I were talking about the spiritual path when he told me that he thought I had a lot of guts to walk away from such an ideal situation—good practice, lots of free time in such a beautiful place to live—to follow my spiritual inclinations. I told him that from my perspective, it felt more like God, my own inner Self, had thrown me out of the Vail Valley. I had been so miserable, depressed, and empty and knew that the only thing that would satisfy me was to take some time off and try and get back in touch with myself—the way I had been in 1975. Without any pre-thought on my part, I told him that no one expects to plant a seed one day and harvest the fruit the next and that the spiritual journey was similar. You had to hang in there, and, in time, things would take care of themselves. I was a little surprised to hear myself say this, as I had never really thought of the spiritual journey in this way before.

I continued by telling my brother I was confident that this was the right move for me. Now I was happy to be able to honestly say that I felt great, that the empty and terrible feelings of last fall were entirely gone. I repeated that I knew the timing of this move felt perfect for Pam and me.

While preparing to head to the Ashram, I noticed that the theme of the first Intensive I was taking was on *time*. I had not noticed this or had forgotten, but now it seemed like another reminder of how perfect the timing was for this life change. It also seemed that my upcoming trip to the ashram was perfectly timed to get my spiritual energy flowing and to renew my enthusiasm for making every effort to stay "awake." I want to reiterate that I was going to the Ashram to get the spiritual energy flowing and re-energized; this is all I felt I was going to the Ashram to do. Again, despite the many wonderful experiences I'd had with them, I still did not think of either Baba or Gurumayi as my Guru. The Guru for me was my own inner Self—that's all I was absolutely sure of.

Returning to the Ashram, August 1987

As I was driving to Shree Muktananda Ashram, a six-hundred-mile trip, I heard my mind wondering what time I would arrive. Immediately, the answer of 10:00 p.m. came up. I thought this was pretty interesting, as it clearly wasn't a calculated response but an instantaneous reply. Knowing the approximate mileage, I calculated an estimated arrival time and agreed that it would be pretty close to that.

Just before arriving at my destination, I had to go through two stoplights, and each time, just as I was beginning to stop for the red light, it turned green. Again, the thought of how perfect all my timing seemed to be lately was present. As I was pulling into the registration area, I happened to look at the digital clock and it read 10:00 p.m. not 10:01 or 9:59, but exactly 10:00. Once again, I could not help but think how interesting this was but also reminded myself not to read too much into this—just stay in touch with the witness and don't start *thinking, thinking, thinking.*

The Intensive on Time

In the morning session of the Intensive, one of the things that really struck me and brought up a lot of energy for me was the idea that once you have wasted your time, you can't get it back. I felt that I had wasted a lot of time in Vail by giving in to sense pleasures. I had been playing as opposed to studying spiritual teachings and putting a *super effort*, as G described it, into staying spiritually awake.

As I thought of this, I didn't feel guilty about it. I could see that, in terms of my spiritual search, part of the problem was that right after my awakening, I'd begun grad school, which took up a tremendous amount of time and energy. G's teachings were vague in many ways, and, besides that, I'd had no real teacher to guide me, and I'd ended up in a lot of bad habits. But I also had to admit that even when I had found a true teacher in Baba and had been given access to true teachings through him, I still wasn't able to do a whole lot better. Fortunately, I was now able to recognize this and was trying to change.

One of the first themes of this Intensive on Time concerned the esoteric teaching about *using death as an advisor* because life is shorter than most people realize. I could easily relate to this teaching that I had first heard from Carlos Castaneda's Don Juan. I felt that if I did not make a serious effort to follow my inner truth, I would truly regret this on my deathbed. I knew as well that I'd had incredibly good fortune in this life. It is rare to have such powerful experiences of your divine Nature as 'I've had. Also, how divinely lucky I was to have learned the truth of spiritual teachings from my own inner Self. I knew it was because of my awareness of what I had already received and how divine and miraculous it truly was that I had dared to leave my easy life in Vail and strive to get back in touch with my true nature once again. At the same time, this acknowledgement of how fortunate I had been made it even more baffling for me to understand how I could waste so much time and be so easily influenced.

A theme in the Intensive that was very easy to identify with was that the time to make a change and pursue the spiritual path with renewed effort is now. That's right *now*! Rather than making this something we try to fit in when we feel that we have the time, *now* is the time to make this a priority. I felt blessed that I had felt the truth of this months ago and had actually done something about it. Now, because of that, I was going to have the chance to really pursue spirituality, not just try and do it sometime in the future.

One of Baba's teachings is that we should do spiritual practices now, and not put them off until we are old and retired with lots of time on our hands. No one knows how much time they have in this life, and besides, when you get older, your mind and energy are not nearly as strong as they are when you are younger. Also, most people need to do spiritual practices for many years to truly evolve, the way we are capable of. I remembered that I had thought about this last year and knew that to truly make the effort I truly needed and wanted to make, I needed to do it while I was still young and had the energy and the burning desire to do so. Once again, I experienced gratitude for having had the experience, the understanding, and the grace to have this insight and act on it.

Another pertinent point that was made in the Intensive was how this modern era is such an intense and challenging time, and yet how, simultaneously, this very intensity makes it easier to turn within and experience your own true Self. This reminded me of the beginning of my spiritual quest, which was, in part, initiated by realizing how screwed up and unjust this world can be, and wondering how it could be this way if there really was a God. I was driven to undertake self-inquiry by the experience of my own fickle and hypocritical mind, something I always detested in others. I knew that in order to be content, I needed to find satisfying answers to the deeper questions of life. This effort taught me quite a bit about myself and eventually led me to G and the practice of self-remembering, which led me finally to my Self. So now, with plenty of time, plenty of experiences, and the ancient teachings of yoga to guide me, I was glad to be reminded that the present time is the best time to turn within and get in touch with the Self.

Following the afternoon session, I made a number of entries in my tape-recorded journal. I was feeling extremely good, the most predominant feeling being immense gratitude for all the understanding and grace I had received in my life. I felt especially grateful for my initial spiritual awakening and the intense experience of my Self that accompanied that. I was also grateful for Baba and the Siddha Yoga path for helping me to come to a greater understanding of these experiences.

In Sync—Perfect Timing

Saturday was the first day of the Intensive. That evening, Gurumayi spoke about how, when nothing seems to be going right, you should know that you are out of touch with your inner Self. Likewise, when everything is going your way, when everything just works out with no great effort on your part, know that you are in touch—in sync—with your inner Self.

Hearing this, I had to acknowledge that lately, things certainly had been going my way, almost uncannily so. Just a couple of hours ago, while taking a shower to get ready for this evening's session, I had been reflecting on how, during the last few months, everything in my life had been working out so easily and perfectly. Before leaving for the ashram, Pam and I had found the perfect farm and farmhouse to purchase. Even the meditation sessions of this Intensive were examples of perfect timing. In each session, once I'd realized that it was time for me to stop meditating and just relax, the gong would sound to signal the end of meditation. These are just a couple of the many synchronicities that happened at this time.

During the Intensive talk on Sunday morning, one of the swamis, the monks, spoke about the importance of sustaining daily spiritual practice. Hanging in there through the highs and lows of the spiritual journey. He said that this is the only way to transform your understanding and reach your goal of union with your Self. To illustrate his point, he reminded us that no one would expect to plant a seed one day and harvest the fruit the next day, and between those two actions, time and transformation must take place.

Later that morning, Gurumayi reiterated that: when everything in your life is going along perfectly, know that you are in touch with your Self. I had a distinct and unmistakable feeling that this message, this understanding, was specifically meant for me. I also felt that I'd have to be an idiot not to recognize what the Shakti, the spiritual energy, was telling me. My experience was that my timing was so right on and that this was so blatantly obvious that my mind couldn't possibly question it. I marveled at the mysterious intelligence and ways of the Shakti, the Holy Spirit. I also marveled at how I could feel so fantastic and blissful, and feel it so quickly. I had not felt this good—this spiritually energized—since Baba appeared to me four years before. What a contrast this was to how I had been feeling just months ago!

During the last session of the Intensive on Sunday afternoon, I had a subtle and compelling meditative experience that was a first for me. Initially, the meditation did not seem or feel any different from my normal and typical meditation experience. But as it progressed, it became apparent that my own inner sense of self had merged with, reconnected with, my true Self—the one great Self within all.

There is no way to describe this or to explain it. The seeker has to accept that such is just a gift of grace, just part of the mystery of meditation and of human consciousness itself.

During the meditation, I became aware that the grace that so gently and lovingly put me in touch with my Self was a gift of Gurumayi's grace. This was another mysterious but unquestionable given. How I knew this, I cannot say. That I knew it is undeniable. I must say that this surprised me, in that during my original spiritual awakening, I had the feeling that a super effort was required. This effort, along with grace, had allowed me to come into and stay in contact with the pure Self within. But now, here I was in the same "blessed state," but this time with no obvious effort on my part at all. I had to assume that it was just another demonstration of this miraculous timing and another example of just hanging in there. We can never know when grace will descend—when the Lord, the Beloved, will commeth!

Something else that was a first for me took place during this same meditation experience. After the awareness, as mentioned earlier, an inner voice instructed me to get the book <u>The Dark Night of the Soul</u> and read it. This voice was perfectly clear and distinct, but it was not the voice of my mind, and it was so unexpected and happened so quickly that I had no chance to recognize it. I had heard of this title but had no idea what the book was really about or who the author was. (As we'll see shortly, this was a perfect book chosen just for me by Shakti Herself!)

After the Intensive's culmination—I hesitate to say that it ended—I sat in my car, feeling immense and profound gratitude for this totally unexpected reconnection with the sacred and holy state of my Self. Using my hand-held recorder, I started to record some of the insights I'd experienced during this divine day. Before I could say anything about the experiences I just mentioned, the very first thing that came up was a very deep and intense awareness that this was my personal Easter Sunday. I had risen! I had the image that I had just spent the last twelve years in the Dark Night of my Soul.

That phrase came up because the image of the book title was still fresh in my mind and seemed to provide an appropriate metaphor for the lack of connection that I had felt in the years since my initial awakening to my true Self. And now, the feeling of having risen—of having reconnected with my Self, arose in me all on its own. It was quite a surprising image, but it described perfectly what I was experiencing—years later, I saw that others have had the same experience—the same image.

Intertwined with this amazing insight was the faint but distinct memory of my brother's comment about "leaving all behind" to seek a deeper experience of my Self. I had never quite thought of it that way, but that perspective allowed me to recognize that I had indeed made a major decision and effort to seek God first, to put God first. This answered my feeling of: *"Why me? How do I deserve such blessings"?* Another memory arose: Seek Me first, and all will be added onto you.

Another powerful feeling that came up immediately and without any thought on my part was that I was picking up right where I had left off twelve years earlier. The end of August was about the exact time of year that I started graduate school in 1975. This particular feeling of picking up right where I left off brought forth an amazingly appropriate memory.

This memory was about how the book <u>Jonathan Livingston Seagull</u> was written. Its author, Richard Bach, told the mysterious story of how this book came into being in a seminar that I attended in Denver, Colorado, in the early 80's. He told us that one day, he heard a voice tell him to take down the following story.

He was writing while the voice dictated the story, word for word, and just as the story was getting really good, the voice just stopped.

Bach waited and waited, hoping to hear the rest of the story, but nothing came. Figuring that it might be finished later that day or tomorrow, he went back to his normal affairs. For months, he hoped the voice would return, but to no avail. Finally, he tried to finish the story himself because he knew it had great potential, but it just would not work; it was obvious where his writing began and just did not do justice to the original. So, he finally had to give up on this idea and just forget about it. Sometime after he did so, the voice returned and told him, once again, to continue, and the book was finished on that day.

I was reminded of this surprising story because my own experience of Shaktipat awakening seemed to be following a similar pattern—picking up seamlessly, right where it left off long ago. Again, how do such things work? Concerning the story of Jonathan Livingston, who knows, but with respect to my own story, there was no question that it was Guru's grace. The feeling was unmistakable. Remember, the Guru is not an individual; it is the living Spirit— also known as the Kundalini Shakti.

Another thing that was unmistakable and unquestionable was that Gurumayi is a true Guru. Now, I accepted her as my Guru.

A Perfect Manifestation of My Own Self

As I was making my daily recordings, I was still in a state of awe at what I had experienced and had been freely given. I spoke spontaneously into my voice recorder, just letting my inner being present me with images and insights that could help my mind better appreciate what was unfolding for me. It was in this manner and in what seemed like perfect alignment with my own Self, that one of the great mysteries of the spiritual journey was revealed to me. This was the awareness that not only is Gurumayi a genuine Guru, but she is also a perfect manifestation of my own Self, the one Self in all! In other words, the inner Guru (my own Self) and the outer Guru (the living Master) are "One" and the same— Divine Consciousness.

Again, this understanding came as direct Knowledge and had nothing to do with my intellect: nothing to do with conclusions I'd reached through some thought process. It was a revelation, another gift of grace, similar to my original *Shaktipat* experience in 1975, when the Self, of its own choosing, revealed itself to me. This sort of profound mystical experience takes place in the "transcendent State" and is just another example of the Self revealing more about itself when the time is right for the seeker.

Mystical Insights

The whole experience of reconnecting with my pure Self was as awesome and sacred as it had been in 1975. And this new awareness of the nature of the spiritual Master was just as surprising and humbling (why do I deserve such profound blessings) as when the Self first revealed itself to me.

I had just come here to relax and recharge my spiritual batteries. Even though I had heard some amazing stories in Siddha Yoga, I never once thought about or dreamed about getting reconnected so quickly, simply, and smoothly. I knew the purpose of the Intensive was to awaken a seeker's spiritual energy or enhance that energy if it had already been awakened. The purpose is to give a seeker an experience of their Self. But I certainly never entertained the idea that this exalted state could take place as easily and effortlessly as this.

All of this just reminded me of how loving, profound, blissful, and unpredictable the Holy Spirit (spiritual energy) is. Also, again, Baba and the Yoga scriptures teach that the Guru is not a person. The true essence of the Guru is not a physical being—He/She is a pure manifestation of the Shakti, the divine spiritual energy that is One, that is in Union with God.

I knew that this Intensive, with all of its insights and experiences, was offering me a great and miraculous new beginning for this phase of my life, better than I could have ever wished for or entertained. And, as I had during my initial awakening, I knew that *Shaktipat* is the beginning, not the end, of the spiritual journey. It is a spiritual rebirth, a spiritual baptism that allows a seeker to experience their Oneness with God directly and dramatically. For me, it was this profound and sacred experience I had in 1975 that has kept me treading the spiritual path all these years. Now, I was, once again, experiencing the fruit of this sustained effort.

I remembered hearing that in ancient times, the seeker had to work for the Guru for twelve years before the Guru would give them initiation, a direct experience of their divine Nature. Now, it seemed appropriate that, having met the inner Guru, having experienced my own divine Self twelve years ago. I would have to demonstrate my sincerity, desire, and perseverance in order to reconnect with the divine Self and also to understand that the outer, physical Siddha Guru is genuine. And, even more amazing, to understand that the outer Guru is One with my own Self, a very ancient mystical Truth! A twelve-year cycle was completed— with impeccable timing, once again, right in perfect harmony with ancient traditions.

After I had finished recording my experiences and insights, I decided to go swimming since it was really warm and had been since my arrival. I went to a small pond that was near the ashram that I had been to before. As I was standing on the shore enjoying the beautiful colors of the sunset displayed across the sky, I felt like a monk about to take his ritual bath before dedicating his life to God. Experiencing powerful feelings of purification, rebirth, and deep gratitude for all the blessings I had received in this life, I dove into the water, knowing this act was a metaphor representing my diving in, re-committing to the spiritual life.

It was time for me to make the sincerest efforts I could to hold onto this awakened State by staying in touch with my inner Self via the witness and following the teachings and practices given by the Guru. These were the two wings that would carry me to my goal of spiritual Union.

Monday

On Monday morning, I moved out of the Ashram, because I wanted to be completely free to do as I wanted. I had brought all the things I would need to sleep in the back of my station wagon and camp out because I had had a very distinct inner urge to just be by myself during the week between the two Intensives. This deep calling, which took place before I left Vail, was to just truly relax, sightsee, and try to recapture the essence of my "awakening" in the summer of '75 by making the same effort to stay in witness consciousness as I had then. Now that this pure state of the Witness—pure state of the Self—had just been handed to me by grace, I knew that my job—responsibility—was to enjoy it and also hold onto it.

After scouting around a little, I found a sweet little campground about a half hour from the Ashram. I then proceeded to spend a number of hours checking out the beautiful woods and fields that made up this rural area of the Catskill region, all the while making sure to keep a close "eye" on myself to make sure I was centered in the witness. This seemed to take no effort, but knowing how rare and blessed this "State" is, I felt it prudent to continue to maintain a conscious awareness of my mind. I wanted to make sure I stayed "awake" just in case my mind started to wander and wonder. I had wanted and waited a long time to reconnect with this true state of my Self, so I wanted to honor It and enjoy It the very best I could. Spending time alone in nature was a perfect way to do both.

Later in the afternoon, I returned to the Ashram so I could spend some time in the Temple, enjoy their vegetarian food and check out a local bookstore to see if they had the book <u>Dark Night of the Soul</u>. I was surprised that this book was written by St. John of the Cross, a name I was familiar with and that it was over 400 years old. I certainly felt that my soul had experienced a dark night in the late fall and early winter, but again, I had no idea what this book was really about.

While I was eating supper, it was announced that it was seva night—seva being selfless service to the Guru and everyone was invited to help in an area that was being re-landscaped. Even though I had told myself that I was not going to do any seva this week, except read Baba's autobiography and now St. John's book, I decided that I would help, as it was such a beautiful evening, and I was in such a great state. But by the time I finished eating and was ready to do seva, my inner being reminded me that the campground gates closed early, and I had not taken a key, as I had expected to be back early. So, it turned out that I did not have time to help. This just seemed to reiterate that my job this week was just to relax, read, enjoy, and continue to listen to my inner being.

I returned to the campground just before dark and was surprised that there was no one near me. I prepared the back of the car for sleeping and then sat in the front seat to take a look at the new book I had just bought—feeling excited to finally get a glimpse of what this Dark Night was all about and why I was told to read it. Looking at the contents, I saw that the beginning of Book it was addressed to beginners. Knowing that the "State" I was now in was not that of a beginner, I just quickly skimmed these first chapters, knowing that they did not apply to me right now. Chapter VIII of Book I is where St. John begins the explanation of the Dark Night, saying that it is a contemplation and a purgation—a purification. Knowing that I could easily relate to both of these terms, I looked forward to tomorrow's adventure with St. John. But now it was time for some rest.

I got out of the car to get into the back, where I had made my bed and literally, just as I closed the door, it started to rain—a real torrential downpour that is not that uncommon in the Catskills during the summer. In some spiritual teachings from India, rain represents blessings. Feeling as I did, this torrential rain seemed the perfect thing to symbolize the numerous blessings I had received, both recently and in a very real sense, throughout my life. The timing of the rain, right to the n-th degree, as we used to say, was another reminder of how in sync I was, even with nature.

The Dark Night—and—Now The Dawn

I'm going to speak in some detail about my experience and understanding of St. John's <u>Dark Night of the Soul</u> because it was one of the greatest and most emancipating experiences of my life. Being in such an uplifted "state" of consciousness while reading it, it not only explained to me but also allowed me to experience the answer to why I had to go through the terrible, empty period in the preceding year. This book also explained many of the other seemingly inexplicable things during these past twelve years, the time since my initial awakening.

There is no way for me to express the unfathomable emotions and profound enlightenment I experienced in reading this book. Even so, I feel a fairly detailed description of the most important points is warranted because of the rarity, importance, and mystical nature of the spiritual teachings that St. John is speaking about. One must remember that I'm still only presenting the most essential and profound points to help one better understand the level of spiritual awakening that I was undergoing at this time. St. John's describes this level as a highly secretive and mystical aspect of the spiritual journey. St. John's explanation of the *Dark Night* is perfectly consistent with Muktananda's classical teaching of kundalini yoga.

St. John begins his explanation of the *Dark Night* in Book I, chapter 8, by telling us that,

"This night, which, as they say, is contemplation, produces in spiritual persons two kinds of darkness or purgation, corresponding to the two parts of man's nature, namely the sensual and the spiritual"[5]

He goes on to say that the *dark night of sense*—the cleansing of one's sensual nature—naturally comes first, and since there has been a lot written about this, he will only speak of it briefly. Then he speaks in much greater detail about the *dark night of the spirit,* which he says is "the portion of very few," and which "very little has been said of this, either in speech or writing and very little known of it, even by experience." He further explains that this *dark night of the spirit* is necessary to raise one to a higher level of love and understanding, and ultimately prepare one for complete UNION with God. [6]

I was elated, but not that surprised, to learn that the *dark night* pertained to divine union," that is, to complete and perfect union with the one Self in all. This is the main topic of his book. I was surprised, however, to see that his description of the *dark night of sense* described some of my deeper emotions and experiences of this past year remarkably well. St. John says that such a one finds no attraction or sweetness in anything, feels that they are not serving God and has anxiety about not failing God. During the worst part of my own *dark night,* I found sweetness only in my family, and I was experiencing a lot of anxiety and depression concerning this empty state I was in and also guilt about failing God by not following my own inner Truth. I knew that I had received immense grace and wisdom, but for some unfathomable reason, I could not live the life I felt I should.

At the end of his description of the *dark night of sense,* St. John says that an "abominable spirit" is allowed to molest the seeker in order to test them. When this happens, the seeker is filled with perplexities so confusing that they feel that they can never be satisfied concerning them and also have no possibility of help. I recognized that this was a pretty decent description of how I had felt last fall— confusion and despair with no clue as to how or why this had come upon me and with so much force. I also felt that no one could help me because inside, I was sure that all of this was connected with my deep longing to get back in touch with God—with my true Self, and so any medical or psychological help would be useless. But until now, I had no clue as to what was really going on. All I knew was that after careful, sincere, and thorough contemplation about what direction my life should take, realizing that I wanted to reconnect with my Self first and foremost, and then, apparently for no reason whatsoever, I fell into deep depression.

So now I knew that the *dark night of sense* is connected with sincere contemplation and is a time when an abominable spirit is allowed to molest you—to test you—to see if you are ready for the *dark night of spirit*. St. John reiterates that the terrible feelings of confusion and the sense that no help is available are some of the severest horrors of this *dark night of the soul.* And these travails are closely akin to that which passes in the dark night of the spirit.

The Dark Night Of Spirit

In chapter I of Book II, St. John once again reminds us that God brings the soul into the terrible Night of contemplation that he calls the *dark night of the spirit,* so that: "He may lead it to divine union." Each time I read St. John's words on this terrible night of contemplation, I would remember how awful it was, but now I could also easily identify with the "state" of divine union, because of the blessings that I was now experiencing. St. John says that this dark night of the spirit refers to the "progressives," those souls who have come a long way on the spiritual path. God has to bring about this intense purging in these souls because they still have imperfections, and for divine union—for full enlightenment, all imperfections must be cleansed. God must accomplish this cleansing through Divine grace—because the individual soul can't do this for itself.

There is no way I can possibly share how amazed I was to find out that this terrible time of contemplation, a horrible time of anguish and despair, was the work of Divine grace! Who would have ever thought it? Who would ever believe it? But, because of the state of grace I was in while reading this, thanks to Gurumayi, I "knew" with the direct Knowledge that's associated with the Self, that St. John was speaking the truth.

Expanding on the level of advancement that these souls have made, St. John mentions that they have gained fortitude from the sweet and delectable communion with God, and that such is necessary to provide them with the strength to withstand the violent and severe purgation of the spirit. This description of the sweet communion with God made me think of my original *Shaktipat* awakening. Without a doubt, this experience, along with others that followed, is what gave me the strength to carry on and not forget my goal or, ever once, question the validity and truth of this sweet communion—that my Self was my true nature and was also God. This shows the immense importance of the direct Experience of the Self—it gives you the Trust to keep going forward because you know the goal is real and your destiny.

I could also understand that this level of spiritual experience—the direct Knowledge and the bliss of one's Self—is not only needed for strength and commitment but also is necessary to produce in one an unquenchable burning desire to reunite with God. This *dark night of the spirit* wouldn't be so horrible and probably couldn't exist at all if one had not already experienced the unfathomable bliss of communion with God. In other words, in order to experience the pain of separation, one must first experience the ecstasy of divine union. Once again, learning that the terrible emptiness, confusion, guilt, and despair I had experienced was divine grace for the purpose of spiritual purification removed the weight of guilt and misunderstanding I'd been carrying. This unexpected lightening of my psychic load magnified my present feelings of communion with God many times over and intensified my love and gratitude for Gurumayi as well. I knew that, if it were not for her grace, none of this would be happening.

In Book II, chapter IV, before presenting his explanation of the *dark night of the spirit*, St. John says: *"I went forth from myself, that is, from my low manner of understanding."* Shortly after St John states,

"My understanding went forth from itself, turning from the human and natural to the Divine, for, when it's united with God by means of this purgation, its understanding no longer comes through its natural light and vigor, but through the divine wisdom with which it has become united."[7]

Then he says the same thing about his will. For me, there was no question that St. John is stating here that the discussion to follow is not from his own beliefs or conclusions but from God because he has merged with the Divine, thus with Divine Wisdom itself. In yogic terms, he has merged with his divine Self, and therefore, it is truly the divine Spirit that is presenting this explanation. Baba Muktananda says the same for the Siddha Yoga teachings, and as we'll see shortly, both of these Saints are speaking about the same extremely rare knowledge and "Experience."

St. John starts the actual explanation of the *dark night of the spirit* by saying that it is an inflowing of God into the soul to purge it of ignorance and imperfections (Book II, chapter V). Then, God secretly teaches the soul and instructs it in the perfection of love, without the soul's having done anything to bring this about or even understanding the means of this contemplation that has been infused into it. St. John asks, why is the Divine light which illuminates and purges the soul of its ignorance, here called by the soul a *dark night*? He answers this by saying that the divine light is so high and lofty that it transcends the talent of the soul and is, thus, darkness to it.

Knowing that this is not easy to grasp, he gives us an analogy to understand this obscure point. He says that the more directly we look at the sun, the greater the darkness in our visual faculty. The pupil constricts in direct proportion to the amount of sunlight it's exposed to. Similarly, this divine light of contemplation (purgation) assails the soul, which experiences this as spiritual darkness. St. John continues by saying that:

"The mystical theologians call this infused contemplation a ray of darkness for the soul that is not enlightened and purged—for the natural strength of the intellect is transcended and overwhelmed by its great supernatural light."[8]

Due to my present connection with my Self and my familiarity with the mystical teachings of yoga, I knew for sure that St. John's presentation was a perfect description of Baba's and Gurumayi's teachings on *Shaktipat* initiation. This rare, secret, and ancient initiation is also described as an infusion of divine grace, which proceeds secretly and mysteriously to purify the soul, slowly preparing it for union with God. The entire process takes place beyond the range and understanding of one's rational mind. Knowing how rare, precious, and blessed this divine initiation is, I experienced unspeakable gratitude for the supreme grace I had received and was receiving.

Having just spoken about God entering the soul through divine grace, St. John now describes what effect this grace has on the soul, and how the soul experiences this divine light. He reiterates that this divine light, which is truly wisdom, is experienced as a terrible darkness by the soul. Over the next few chapters, St. John speaks of the various trials, tribulations, and afflictions the soul suffers in this horrible *dark night of the spirit*. He says, *"So many and so grievous are the afflictions of this night…that time and strength would fail us to write of them."*[9]

Assailing it with divine light, he says," leaves it not only dark but empty." He also reiterates that these afflictions are not experienced as a result of divine light but as though they are coming from *weakness and imperfection*. I could see that my own experiences matched St. John's almost perfectly.

St. John points out that the seeker has much spiritual despair due to the fact that the divine light makes it possible for them to see their weaknesses, shortcomings, and inconsistencies. This reminded me of how many times I had railed at myself because I wasn't able to live up to my understanding and experience of the divine light. This is what confused me and troubled me the most. I often thought of the lament of St. Paul; the things that I should do, I don't, and the things that I should not do, I do!

Now, thanks to Gurumayi's grace, my own Self, and St. John's *Dark Night of the Soul*, I was finally beginning to understand some of the reasons behind this previously unfathomable situation. St. John specifically says that during this period of the *dark night,* a seeker cannot even take the advice of a spiritual master.[10] I'd recalled that during that time, I'd had no energy and no desire to do any of the spiritual practices that I had been taught. It also struck me that even though I knew that I'd experience *shaktipat* and was quite familiar with Baba's teaching about *shaktipat,* and how this infusion of grace works to purify seekers without their being aware of it. Still, I was not able to see any of my trials as the work of this divine energy. Instead, I felt disconnected from God and, like Job, as quoted by St. John, wondering, "Why hast thou set me contrary to Thee, so I am grievous and burdensome to myself." But now, I had absolutely no doubt that all of my spiritual "stress" was, indeed, the work of the divine light, or to take terminology of yoga, the play of the Kundalini Shakti.

St. John made it clear that this is done "in order to grant the soul favors, not chastise it," and similarly that "God greatly humbles the soul in order that he may afterwards greatly exalt it." Now that I was experiencing the bliss of these favors and the Divine light itself, the afflictions of the dark night seemed like a small price to pay for the Gifts received. The light of the Self, oneness with the Divine, is so miraculous that any darkness one has felt in coming to it seems like nothing in comparison.

I must reiterate here that I did not think of my divinely given "state of illumination" as full enlightenment or union. I saw the divinely given state I was enjoying as a continuation of my *shaktipat* awakening, another experience of divine grace, another powerful experience of my Self, a further awakening to a higher level of understanding. This higher level of understanding was allowing me to know and experience for myself two of spirituality's most profound mysteries: first, that the spiritual Master is a full and perfect manifestation of the one true Self in all. Secondly, the darkness, confusion, and deep longing one experiences in the depths of their soul after *shaktipat* is the work of divine grace to benefit the soul, not to chastise it.

I would like to underscore that all of this wonderful and truly divine insight came to me as I read about eighty pages in a few hours spread over Tuesday morning and afternoon, with a number of pleasant walks interspersed. Again, there is no way to possibly share the feeling of divine bliss and the depth of inner healing I experienced at this time. I felt that, not only was the timing absolutely divine, but that St. John had written this book just for me—describing my situation almost perfectly.

The Magical Evening Satsangs

I went to the evening program, referred to as satsang, on Tuesday night, feeling tremendous reverence for and gratitude towards Gurumayi for all the blessings I had received over these past few days. At the end of the program, they had darshan—the ancient practice of going before the spiritual Master. I was particularly excited because this gave me the opportunity to thank Gurumayi personally after such a miraculous day, knowing that she is a living manifestation of divine grace. Again, this was another example of something that almost seemed too good to be true—but true it was! I had experienced a similar feeling during darshan at the end of the Intensive on Sunday while experiencing immense gratitude for being reunited with my true Self. Now, it seemed unbelievable that such love and inexpressible gratitude could be magnified a number of times in just a couple of days!

This gives the reader a little feel of how I felt as I showed Gurumayi St. 'John's book and said, "Thank you very much for my deliverance, it has been just incredible." As I spoke, she looked up from the book, beaming ecstatically as our eyes met. In that moment, I experienced a touch of the purity, bliss, and harmony of a Siddha Guru's divine inner State.

It was in this blissful state that I headed for supper. As I left the hall, a thought arose about going to the bookstore, but since it was getting late, I decided that I should eat first. As I was walking by the bookstore, I looked in to see a striking picture of Gurumayi, about 15 x 24, with her looking directly at me, beckoning me with her index finger in the universal pose to "come here." I had to go in because the picture was so enchanting and so alive. Because of my present " connection with the Self, I felt as if the Guru Principle, the divine Shakti Herself, was inviting me to unite with Her. I immediately decided that I should buy this picture as a perfect and permanent reminder of what I had learned and experienced during these past few days. Then I realized that I did not have any money on me, but, at the same time, I "knew" that this picture was for me and that it would be here when I got back from supper. It was, and I bought it.

Another session with St. John

After finishing my morning spiritual practices, I looked forward to exploring some more of the local area. It was another picture-perfect day, and while I was walking through the woods and along the fields, I kept experiencing wave upon wave of love for Gurumayi sweeping through me. I knew that Baba had expressed his love for his Guru, Bhagavan Nityananda, over and over again, and now I was beginning to understand why. It was in this state of immeasurable divine love that I eagerly returned to St. John's *The Dark Night of the Soul* and his description of the mystical journey to God.

I began with Book II Chapter II, with St. John continuing to speak of the soul's experience of being "keenly and sharply wounded in strong Divine love, although it understands nothing definitively," being still in darkness. This divine love is, however, not only infused with vehement passion but also has in it something of union with God. Thus, even though the soul has the feeling of having lost touch with God, of abandonment, unworthiness, and guilt, nevertheless, it has *"the strength, and is sufficiently bold and daring, to journey towards union with God."*[11]

I hadn't really thought of it quite this way, but now I could appreciate that it was my deep and relentless passion for God, the passion to reconnect with my true Self, that allowed me the strength and courage to boldly seek God above all else. Now, even though I had just barely begun the second leg of this journey, He was revealing Himself in many wondrous ways, proving the ancient teaching that if you take one sincere step towards Him, He will take many towards you.

In this same section, Book II Chapter XIII, St. John speaks of some of the "delectable effects, which are wrought in the soul by this night of dark contemplation." He says, *"The soul can become enlightened during this time of darkness and the 'mystical intelligence' flows in different ways."*[12] Most certainly, I had experienced the truth of this many times over the years since my initial *shaktipat* awakening, especially when I was with Baba in 1981. But, as described, it was pretty much the same with Gurumayi in 1983 and was often the case when reading Baba's and other spiritual books. I also felt *mystical intelligence* when trying to share my experiences and understanding with my parents and other family and friends. These, along with many other wonderful experiences, especially of nature in Maine and Colorado, I could easily recognize as signs of the presence of God. In truth, I had many of these experiences over the years, and this is important for the seeker to remember—the spiritual journey is not all dark and gloomy—there are many sunny days as well, and these do remind you of why you are treading the path.

St. John reiterates that during this dark night, the despair and misery one experiences are due to the secret work of divine grace, which is preparing the soul for union with God. One of the main reasons that the divine wisdom has to work in secret is so our own passion and ignorance—our ego won't get in the way. In chapter XVII, St. John says,

"This happens secretly and in darkness, so as to be hidden from the work of the understanding and of other faculties…not only does the soul not understand it, but there is none that does so, not even the devil; inasmuch as the master who teaches the soul is within it, in its substance."[13]

These two images of the infusion of divine wisdom and the master teacher being within the soul both refer to the supreme inner Intelligence, the Holy Spirit, or the inner Guru. St. John's statements are perfectly consistent with the mystical teachings of kundalini yoga and other mystical traditions. As I experienced for myself, the highest Truth and wisdom lie within and are definitely beyond the range and scope of the rational mind. St. John says that it is not only secret during the *dark night* but "equally so afterwards in illumination." Where it *"can find no suitable way or manner… to describe such lofty understanding and such delicate spiritual feeling."[14]*

Yes, every genuine mystic, everyone who has experienced the highest levels of the Transcendent state, says that there is no way to accurately express this "State," that transcends all experience and concepts. St. John and others are forced to use metaphors and myth in order to give some inkling of this blessed "State." St. John himself says how difficult it is to describe something that has not come through the senses. This point is extremely important for the seeker to understand. The highest truth and wisdom only come from within via the master teacher—the Holy Spirit—and not from the intellect, through philosophy or theology.

St. John also speaks of this divine grace as ascending and descending and compares the inner purification to a fire. This, along with the above-mentioned concerning the limits of the intellect, are all aspects of kundalini yoga, the yoga that Gurumayi teaches, and more importantly, gives to seekers as direct experience through the infusion of divine grace. This was something I was presently experiencing in a very dramatic way.

The State of the Union

In Book II, Chapter 18, St. John explains that this infusion of divine grace is like a ladder, and that this secret contemplation is called a ladder for a number of reasons. By means of this divine grace, *"The soul ascends and climbs up to a knowledge and possession of the good things and treasures of Heaven."* As I have shown before, *"Heaven and its treasures refer to the state of union with God."* This state, the purpose of human existence, is the goal and culmination of the spiritual journey. It is spoken of in all the great religious traditions from around the world.

Then, to make sure that there can be no doubt that he is speaking about full and complete union with God, St. John states that, at the summit of this ladder, *"the soul will have attained to God and become united with Him."* He says,

"The tenth and last step of this secret ladder of love causes the soul to become wholly simulated to God, by reason of the clear and immediate vision of God which it then possesses."[15]

This is a reiteration of what has been said earlier about God's illumination of the understanding with supernatural light. This means that our human understanding, when blessed with this State, becomes divine through union with the Divine, and *wholly* means completely!

Thus, there can be absolutely no doubt that St. John is speaking about the spiritual journey leading to and culminating in enlightenment, in union with God. The problem for the modern seeker is that this teaching about the spiritual journey and about its goal, realization or enlightenment, has been basically lost and forgotten in the West for over four hundred years, since the Renaissance and the time of St. John and St. Theresa of Avila.

The symbolism of full union taking place at the summit of the ladder is synonymous with full enlightenment taking place in the sahasrara, the crown chakra or the top-most spiritual center. This is where one experiences the highest state of consciousness. This perfect union, this perfect marriage of the seeker with the Beloved, where one is fully merged with their divine spirit within, is the perfect description of the state of a genuine Saint, Sage, and enlightened Being. The West does not understand or accept such teachers because, again, our culture has become almost totally ignorant about the spiritual journey and the human capacity for Enlightenment. But now, thanks to Gurumayi and others, things are changing.

By the time I had finished reading this Divine book, I was experiencing waves and waves of spiritual energy vibrating within me. I felt tremendous gratitude and amazement that I could be shown and directly experience such deep and rare spiritual truths. I also experienced a powerful resurgence of gratitude and love for Gurumayi, who was the source of this divine grace. I felt so blessed to have the Lord provide me with a book, like this one and also *The New Man,* which made it possible for me to better understand the grace that I was receiving, and what my experiences meant in relation to the spiritual journey.

It was gratifying for me to know that my *shaktipat* initiation was now continuing and the latest infusion of grace was opening me up to a new level of direct knowledge and understanding. As I've said, I could see that I had a true spiritual master in Gurumayi and that Siddha Yoga was an authentic spiritual path. This is what I wanted, had wished for, and knew that I absolutely needed since my awakening twelve years before.

There is an ancient teaching that says, *"When the student is ready, the teacher will appear."* I could see that this is true and that it refers both to the inner and the outer Guru, both manifestations of the transcendent One.

I wasn't sure, but felt that most likely my present state of union was only the temporary experience of the Self one gets during shaktipat initiation. So, I promised myself that no matter what happens in the future, I would remember this divine experience and know that grace is still working within me. I would remember not to ever feel abandoned or rejected, to keep my eye on the prize, and to never get attached to my mental chatter and outer circumstances.

Another Divine Book

After finishing St. John's book, I spent the rest of the morning and a good part of the afternoon enjoying the natural beauty of the Catskills. Before heading back to the ashram, I decided to look at Baba's spiritual autobiography, Play of Consciousness. I had brought this book to re-read, not having looked at it since reading it in the summer of 81. I had wanted to refresh my memory of Baba's spiritual awakening and subsequent journey, and now that the spiritual energy had dramatically reconnected me with my own spiritual unfoldment, I was excited to revisit Baba's remarkable story. Now, I was particularly interested to see what Baba had to say about the Guru.

In *Play of Consciousness,* Baba speaks about how the Guru, by blessing the seeker with divine favor through shaktipat, turns their ordinary life into a sacred existence. This had certainly been my experience, both currently and during my awakening in 1975. In this chapter titled, *''The Greatness of the Guru,' Baba says that the Guru cannot be understood by the ordinary intellect and then later adds that the Guru can lead his disciples to the vision of God without severe asceticism."* [16] Reading this, once again, I marvel at the blessings I have received and am still receiving. When I first became aware of these teachings on the Guru, I didn't know what to think. Now, thanks to divine grace, I knew that both of Baba's teachings were absolutely true. When my Self first revealed itself to me in the summer of 75, I knew that this experience was definitely beyond the intellect, way beyond the rational mind. Now, I knew for sure that the Guru could lead one to the vision of God without severe asceticism because I was living proof of that! Writing and talking about this can only pass on a tiny fraction of what it's like to experience these things. Divine grace surpasses the intellect and its logic by such a degree that one's rational mind cannot begin to fathom the difference.

A Joyous Awakening

It was in this rare and uplifted state that I attended the evening program with Gurumayi.

Patience

In Baba's autobiography, he has a chapter on *"The Importance of a Siddha's Abode,"* and now, feeling as I did, I could understand why he lavished such praise on the Guru. Each time I had come to the ashram, I had experienced a strong connection with my inner being, had a great time, and learned many valuable lessons about the spiritual path that I had not been able to learn elsewhere. At this time, the fact that the spiritual energy was joyously and vibrantly pulsating within me made it very easy to be aware of just how momentous it is to be in the presence of a Siddha Guru.

The Siddha Yoga evening program is known as *satsang,* and *satsang* is a Hindi word meaning *"in the company of the Truth."* Certainly, being in the presence of a living Siddha master is being in the company of the Truth. Like many spiritual terms, *satsang* has other levels of meaning, one being *"the conscious effort to stay in touch with your own inner Truth when in the presence of others,"* which, for me, is also a good definition of self-remembering. I had the fortunate opportunity to greet Gurumayi at the end of the program, when we were all invited to come forward for Gurumayi's darshan.

I had spoken to my wife that morning, and during that call, my three-year-old daughter asked me if I had asked Gurumayi if she would give her a little gift. I told her no, not yet, and she proceeded to remind me that I had said I would. So, I told her I would keep my word and ask her soon. Waiting in the darshan line, I was reminded of the astrologer's prediction concerning a change in my marriage. I certainly hadn't tried to tell my wife all the things I was experiencing, knowing one had to be in this state of grace—state of the Self—to truly appreciate such things. So, I just told her that I was having some really good experiences. But now, I realized that what I was experiencing was truly a spiritual marriage—a spiritual union. This was the marriage in which there was a change for me; my intuition about the astrologer's reading had been right! For me, this was another example of divine grace in action.

When I came before Gurumayi, I spoke to one of her assistants and explained my daughter's request and the fact that she was three years old. He relayed the request to Gurumayi and then turned back to me and said that she had heard the request and that I should sit off to the side of her chair. I gladly squeezed in with the Swamis and others who were there. I felt so fortunate to be close to Gurumayi, knowing that she is a fully enlightened being. Baba had talked about the importance of meditating on the Guru—on One who had become established in their Self. So, this was a perfect opportunity to practice this intently while others came forward for Gurumayi's darshan.

After another half hour of sheer delight, darshan ended, and Gurumayi then casually conversed with a number of different people. She asked her attendants if there was any other business to be done, and they told her no, so she slowly got up and left the hall. When she had asked about any further business, I wasn't about to say anything, but I now asked the attendant if he was sure that Gurumayi had understood my daughter's request. He assured me she had, and I responded that since that was the case, I assumed that I need not ask again. He agreed that such would not be necessary.

I left the hall feeling absolutely ecstatic. Being able to sit so close to Gurumayi had been an unexpected treat, and the fact that she had not responded specifically to Natalia's request did not mean a thing to me. I knew that the Guru does not always respond in obvious ways and that Natalia might receive a gift years from now. Whatever the case, everything was just perfect as it was, and I never gave it another thought.

Thursday

On Thursday, I greeted another spectacular day and looked forward to spending some more time enjoying Mother Nature. While chanting the Guru Gita, the primary early morning chant that takes place as the morning light begins to awaken the new day, an inner feeling came forth that the Guru was telling me to be patient, peaceful, and joyful. And to just let things come to me as they will. From my original experience of *shaktipat* and my experiences of the last number of days, I knew that this was timely advice, and I planned on taking it.

After a long walk, still being very careful to remain in the witness state, I read the beginning of Baba's book *"Play of Consciousness—The Importance of God Realization."* I marveled at how fortunate I was to know for certain the little-known fact that to experience one's Self is to experience God. This is the experience of God Realization, and for me, this is a reiteration of the direct Knowledge of your "oneness" with God and does not necessarily mean that you are fully enlightened. Baba opens by saying that though God exists in all beings in the form of their Self, there are not many who know him. Again, I was astonished that I knew the absolute truth of that statement.

Years later, I studied Kashmir Shaivism and learned that Abinavagupta, considered one of the foremost Sages of Shaivism, taught that if a person knows for absolute certainty that their highest identity is the Self, they are Realized and, as Baba and many others taught, "God Realized." But there is a significant difference between Realization and being fully Enlightened! Ken Wilber is the only one I have seen who speaks about this. He points out that just because someone is God-Realized, that does not make them a saint! As I'm sharing here, this miraculous Experience is a gift of Grace but for many seekers, it's only temporary, and we still have a lot of purification to go through. Again, this is the natural unfoldment, natural purgation, as St. John calls it, of the spiritual journey. Therefore, as Wilber rightly claims, it is wrong to assume such seekers should not show any signs of their foolish ego still functioning! Again, this is why I'm sharing in such detail, sharing how the spiritual journey tends to unfold. It is absolutely normal to experience your true Self long before you reach full and permanent Enlightenment—this is something sincere seekers should contemplate often.

I read a little more of Baba's book, meditated joyously, and went shopping and bought my first CD's before heading back to the ashram, looking forward to another gourmet vegetarian meal on the deck. As I was finishing my meal on the beautiful new deck of the Amrit Café, a lady asked me if I could help in the kitchen for a little while. I hesitated for a moment, but then said yes, as I figured I would still have plenty of time for reading and relaxing after a little work.

I was given the job of separating the good spinach from the not-so-good-looking spinach, which would be used for cooking instead of in salads. The woman instructing me was very sincere and thorough and told me that one had to use great discrimination in performing this seva. My first thought was that this did not really require that much discrimination. I had done this many times before in my job as a cook. But then, I looked at this from the higher perspective, that everything is a manifestation of the Shakti, and thus took this as another teaching from the Shakti; in your newfound state, use great discrimination. Again, instantly, I knew that this was timely advice!

I enjoyed the seva and was feeling immense gratitude for all the lessons and insights I had received in my life, and especially those of the last few days. As I was reveling in this blissful state, the lady who had originally asked me if I could help out now started questioning me with great zeal about where I was supposed to be now and what seva I was supposed to be doing now. I knew that everyone living at the ashram is supposed to have a seva assignment; this is one of the expectations of everyone living in the ashram.

I had just moved back in, which my name tag had indicated—the opportunity to live in the abode of a Siddha was just too sweet to pass up. But had not gotten a seva assignment. Because, as mentioned, I deeply felt that I already had one! After trying to beat around the bush for a brief time, which she wasn't buying at all, I finally looked her right in the eye and told her that I had a private seva from Gurumayi, and that's what I have been doing. I knew that she would assume I meant that my seva had come from Gurumayi, and while this wasn't strictly true, I felt that I did have a "private seva"—reading and relaxing—following instructions from my inner Guru, my inner Self. I didn't mind giving this seva supervisor the impression that my seva was from Gurumayi, knowing for certain that the mystical truth that my Self and the Guru are one.

The woman looked at me with surprise and maybe a little anger, and promptly told me that Gurumayi never gives out private sevas and that she was going to check into this. She wrote my name down and tromped off, clearly irritated.

This unexpected challenge and touch of negative energy gave me a little adrenaline rush, but inwardly, I was not disturbed because I was 100% sure, not even an iota of doubt, that my intuition to relax was from my true Self. And I knew that Gurumayi, as a fully realized spiritual Master, is indeed one with my true Self.

I finished my kitchen seva, went for a walk in the country, and then sat down and started reading Baba's description of his *shaktipat* initiation. I had read this account a few times, but not for a long time. Since I was experiencing an extension and deepening of my own spiritual awakening, I decided to look it over again just for the sheer enjoyment of it. Baba writes so beautifully and reverently about this sacred event that took place through the blessings of his Guru Bhagawan Nityananda.

After receiving *shaktipat*, Baba says he was overcome with wonder, asking internally how such a blessing could have happened to him. I could easily identify with that sentiment, as I had been wondering, *"How is it that I'm so fortunate to experience so many rare and miraculous things?"* I could also identify with his description concerning his state of mind after receiving this supreme blessing from his Guru. Baba said that his mind was a little active but had none of its former frustration, anxiety, stupidity and so on. Instead, there was *"ecstasy, rapture, zeal and enthusiasm."*[17] That is how I felt in 1975, and how I was feeling right now.

A short time after this experience, Nityananda, his Guru, told Baba to go to his place in Suki and do his spiritual practices there. Baba says that as soon as he arrived in Suki, he experienced a change in his inner state. Now, instead of bliss, he was experiencing anxiety and worry, and wondered where his ecstasy had gone. Not having read this book since 1981, I had not remembered that Baba had gone into this negative state shortly after receiving *shaktipat*. Thus, I was surprised to read this and was curious to read more about this unexpected turn, but it was now time to attend the divine evening program.

A Blue Pearl and a Crystal

Each evening program followed the same format and, like the others, this one aroused many wonderful feelings, especially gratitude. It was in this state of gratitude and awe that I happily waited in line to come before Gurumayi during darshan. I had purchased a small meditation blanket and wanted Gurumayi to bless it along with a couple of other things. I planned to hold the blanket outstretched between my hands, like an altar, with the other items resting on it. I also wanted to thank her for all the grace that I had received.

When I came before Gurumayi, trying to stay as conscious as I could, I asked her to please bless these items and, looking into her magical eyes, I also thanked her for the grace and the lessons on patience and discrimination. She looked at me with such pure love and responded that it wasn't necessary to thank her. I said, *"I know, but I just wanted to."* She smiled, and just as I was ready to leave, one of her attendants placed some things on my blanket. Due to my eye contact with Gurumayi, I could not see what they were. I returned to my sitting space and looked down to see a small, ordinary crystal, about two inches long, and beside it lay a beautiful and unique blue pearl necklace. The necklace was a silver chain with a fancy silver heart holding a blue pearl in its center. The blue pearl is the mystical symbol that represents the true Self.

I was a little stunned by these unexpected gifts. When I went up to see Gurumayi, I had completely forgotten about the previous night's request for my daughter Natalia. Now, I wondered whether these gifts were for my daughter or for me.

Could this beautiful necklace be meant for Natalia, who was, of course, only three? Then it struck me that the crystal was similar to one that a massage therapist had shown Natalia, telling her that it was a magic healing crystal. After that, Natalia showed a special interest in crystals. Immediately after that memory, one of Gurumayi's attendants came up to me and asked me what my name was. I told her my first name, never thinking to give her my full name, and she returned to her place near Gurumayi's chair.

I was deeply moved by this gift from Gurumayi. In Siddha Yoga, the blue pearl is a symbol of the true Self, the pure "I" consciousness—the state I was experiencing at the very moment the blue pearl necklace was put on my meditation blanket. And the state I'd been in since Sunday's Intensive. As I sat there, a little stunned by these unexpected events, I immediately wondered if the reason the young woman asked me my name was to see if I was the one who had said that I had a private seva from Gurumayi. Also, by this time, I felt pretty sure that this blue pearl necklace was given to me because it is a symbol representing the pure Self. I took this to be Gurumayi's way of telling me—demonstrating to me that I was indeed experiencing my divine Self. I didn't really need confirmation, as I've been sharing, but it was still nice to have.

At the same time, but from a slightly different perspective, I also saw it as a gift for trusting completely in my inner experience and understanding, when being challenged, knowing, without doubt, that I was in touch with my true Self, and for having absolute confidence that my Self and Gurumayi are ONE. I felt this was her way of letting me know that I was indeed connected to the pure "I," to my Self. Therefore, I didn't need to listen to the part of the mind that always questions. I just need to enjoy it, be patient and use great discrimination! And the last aspect of this same perspective was that the Guru, this time the physical living Guru, versus the inner Guru, was confirming that I was to continue the seva of reading, contemplation, and simply relaxing.

A few other long-time devotees, after asking about this one-of-a-kind blue pearl necklace and hearing my explanation as given here, told me that I should not ascribe motives to the Guru who is in a State that we can't possibly understand. But this never deterred me or made me question my understanding of this unique event. Again, when a person is in this exceedingly rare state of the pure "I"—the state of the Self, doubt does not enter. Just as there was no doubt that my Self and the Guru, Gurumayi, are one and the same, there is only one Self!

Years after this experience, I read a talk by Gurumayi that was reprinted in Darshan magazine, where she spoke about meditation, the witness, and the blue pearl. As I read this article, I immediately thought of the miraculous time that I had received the blue pearl necklace, and these thoughts were accompanied by a wave of pleasant and reverent energy. Speaking about meditation, she said that one technique is to become a witness of the mind. She also mentioned that people often wonder, *"How can I become a witness when my mind is full of thoughts?"* Then Gurumayi essentially presents the great esoteric teaching that says, *"We are not the "I" that we identify with, not the I of our thoughts."* Then she tells them that they are the I that they don't know they have. Reading this, I promptly thought that this was a great way to describe my original shaktipat experience. The "I" that I never knew I had was, of course, the witness, and it was via this pure "I" of the witness, along with grace, that allowed me to experience my own divine nature—my own Self.

Gurumayi continues referring to this "I" that is the witness—it is also called instinct, intuition, and the inner guide as well. Then Gurumayi tells her students that this is the "I" they need to become aware of in meditation, so that in time this "I" becomes the I that you identify with as you. Then she tells everyone that this "I" is the blue pearl! Reading this, my whole being lit up knowing *that was my experience and understanding when I'd received this precious reminder—this precious gift!*

(The above is a paraphrase of Gurumayi's talk, which I have been exceedingly careful to portray accurately. I talk more about this pure "I" in the section on Kashmir Shaivism in Book IV.)

Friday

After the morning's spiritual practices, breakfast, and more exploration of the local countryside, I continued reading Baba's autobiography, *The Play of Consciousness.* Baba describes many amazing meditations in which he experienced spontaneous yogic movements in the physical body, the vision of lights associated with the different states of consciousness, and many other extraordinary things.

I had never had any meditations of this kind. As I've said, all of my profound meditation experiences had taken place while being in the witness state, when I was fully awake, while driving, working, reading, etc. Even though I had some very good meditations during the Intensive on Time, it was my experiences while reading *The Dark Night of the Soul* and while attending the evening programs that were the most powerful and enlightening for me.

I remembered that while I was with Baba in 81, he had said that the seeker should not judge their meditations or get too caught up with visions or expectations. He said that the highest form of meditation is understanding, in the form of knowledge of the Self, and that the goal of meditation is to merge with your divine Self. Knowing that I was experiencing both of these in the best of ways, I certainly was not envious of Baba's visions and other experiences in meditations.

After another pleasant stroll in the countryside, I was excited to read more in Baba's autobiography about the return of his anxieties, as I was surprised that I had completely forgotten about this part of his story. Baba tells us that just after arriving in Suki, he started having experiences in meditation that seemed to threaten his integrity as a monk. Now, instead of ecstasy, he was experiencing worry and anxiety.

Terrified and feeling unworthy to continue the quest, he took off his monk's clothes and fled. Later the same day, in a remote hut kept by a farmer specifically for wandering mendicants, Baba received inner instruction right after essentially being forced into sitting for meditation, telling him to open the cupboard and read the book that was there. At first, he ignored this, but after the third time, he opened his eyes and noticed the cupboard, took the book out, and opened it. He tells us that it opened to the very page that described all the things that he had been experiencing! It explained that all of these experiences that he was having were due to the divine grace that he had received from his beloved Guru.[18]

I had completely forgotten that this had happened to Baba, and immediately after reading this, I was astonished to realize that I had just received a similar "gift" concerning my own inner instructions to read the *The Dark Night of the Soul*. It was from *The Dark Night* that, like Baba, I'd learned that the confusion and frustration I'd been experiencing were due to divine grace doing its secret inner work! Baba says after reading this, *"I became supremely happy, in a moment all my anguish, confusion and worry disappeared."* Yes, I knew exactly how he felt, and, once again, there are no words to express my amazement that my second phase of *shaktipat* initiation was so similar to and in sync with Baba's. And like Baba, I was amazed that such great blessings were happening to me.

During this time, I had also become aware that Baba's initiation had taken place on August 15, 1947, which meant that I had left Colorado for my new life in the East on the 40th anniversary of Baba's *shaktipat* initiation without even knowing it! Another sign of divine timing. The number 40 symbolizes great transformation—Jew's 40 years in the desert, Jesus' 40 days in the desert, and Noah's 40 days on the water, etc. Another example of the symbols of myth and parables. When I first committed to this life change, I had been hoping for significant transformation, but I'd never imagined that it would take place so quickly and that its effect on me would be so profound.

The Sheep Dog

As part of my rest and relaxation therapy, I had made arrangements to tour an old-style organic farm. When I first saw this at the local information center, something about it really attracted me, even though I couldn't say why. Since my inner intuition seemed to be so in tune with the shakti, the spiritual energy, I decided to go with this inclination to see what lesson it had in store for me. I called ahead to make sure the tour was still on, as it was about one hour away, and was told that I was the only one interested: to do it just for me, they would have to charge forty dollars. I told them that number forty was one of my favorite numbers, so it seemed like the perfect price and that I'd be happy to have a private tour.

On my way to this 19th-century-style farm, I felt sure, with the number forty involved, that there was another lesson in store for me. I reminded myself that my job was to stay in the witness state during the tour. If I forget and go unconscious, I could miss what I was there to experience.

I was greeted by a young fellow who was apprenticing on the farm. He showed me how they kept the bees, gathered the honey, plowed the fields with horses, planted and harvested the crops, etc. Then he took me for a ride around the farm in an old buckboard wagon drawn by two beautiful workhorses. Being in such an ecstatic state from this morning's reading and, really, the events of the whole week and with the weather and the scenery both being so perfect, I felt this was probably how Baba felt when he visited heaven in his meditation! I was so high, so peaceful, and so full of gratitude and awe that I assumed that this divine experience must be the reason I was meant to be here today. It was easy to see God in all things on this ride.

After we finished our round on the farm, my guide told me that he had one last thing to show me. He took me to where the sheep were kept and told me that in the ancient lore of sheep herding, the dog and the sheep were originally considered one species! This, he said, was why the sheep dog could direct and guide the sheep. He explained and demonstrated the different signals the dog would respond to. He also pointed out that while the sheep dog was on duty, he would <u>never</u> take his eyes off the sheep. He would stay focused on the sheep—no matter what.

Not only did I find this trait of the sheep dog extremely impressive, but I also immediately "knew" that this was the lesson I had come for. In addition to my lessons on patience and discrimination, I had now received one on the importance of one-pointedness. It was clear to me that the one-pointedness of the sheep dog was a metaphor for the seeker's need for one-pointedness on the Self. I knew this also referred to one-pointedness on the witness and on the Guru too. One-pointedness is one of Baba's major teachings and was eloquently demonstrated by this intense, sharp, and well-trained sheep dog. I knew that this image would stay with me for years, and it has.

I returned to the ashram feeling more blissful than I had all day. Earlier, I wouldn't have thought it possible, but such proves that divine grace can always expand. I bought a light pink, nine-sided crystal that looked a little like the Washington Monument, to give Gurumayi during darshan. For me, this crystal represented my immense gratitude for all that I had received and was symbolic of a few different things. The first was that the number nine represented the divine grace I was profoundly experiencing. And the crystal also represented the hard shell of my ego and the ignorance that needs to be overcome through grace before a seeker can experience the great Spirit within.

The crystal also represented what St. Teresa of Avila called the *Interior Castle,* which, for me, symbolizes the pinnacle of the inner life where one experiences different levels of bliss and understanding leading to union with God. I had seen St. Teresa's book while looking for *The Dark Night of the Soul* and immediately felt that the castle she writes about symbolized the inner grandeur where union is experienced. Later, I realized that St. John and St. Teresa were contemporaries, and both were talking about union with God.

Finally, this beautiful crystal represented a prenuptial gift to the bride, symbolic of the inevitable time when the spiritual marriage—the merging of the disciple and the Guru—the individual Soul and the supreme Soul, will take place.

I gave this crystal to Gurumayi after another great evening satsang, understanding that I had no idea when this union would happen, but knowing for certain that someday it will.

A Wild Ride to the Airport

Immediately after darshan, I left for JFK to pick up my friend Dr. Bob, who had not been to the Ashram since being with Baba in 1981, six years earlier. I'd called him after the Intensive and told him that he should try and make it to the last Intensive of the summer, and, feeling my bliss, he decided to go for it. He was supposed to land about 10 p.m., which meant that I had just barely enough time to get to the airport.

Even though I had directions, I got lost and lost—again and again! After a number of wrong turns and really having no idea where I was, my "mind"—the old part of me that would get wickedly upset in such circumstances—was doing its absolute best to get me frustrated and angry. I, the witness, was doing my absolute best to resist and not fall prey to this old and deep pattern. But with the time frame and the traffic and not being able to get any help, it became an extremely intense battle to resist the immense negativity I was feeling. But, because of all the things that had happened this week, I was determined to hold onto the witness and not give in.

Finally, about midnight, I arrived at the airport just barely hanging onto the witness state—and I do mean barely! As I was coming up to the airline that Bob was flying on, wondering whether I should park in front or proceed to short-term parking, I saw Bob walking to the middle island. Surprised as could be, I honked and then stopped right beside him. When he saw me, a smile of relief came over his face. I assumed that his troubled and tired look was from waiting and wondering if I was ever going to show up. He threw his bag in the back seat and jumped in, saying that he was sorry that he was so late! Mildly shocked, to say the least, I told him that I was just going to say the very same thing, as I was just arriving myself! He gave me a funny look and said, *"You mean that you are just now arriving?"* I said yes and followed with the same exact question. He also responded yes and said that he had literally just walked out of the terminal, wondering how he was ever going to find me, and in the next moment, there I was.

Instantly, I realized that, once again, even though it seemed that I was way off the mark, I was actually right on schedule—right to the very second, just to make sure I wouldn't miss it! I told Bob about my "struggle" to get to the airport and about all of the divine timing I was experiencing recently. Due to our own divine timing, he immediately felt the miracle of it all for himself.

I shared some of the many things I had experienced during the last week, with a special emphasis on St. John's *The Dark Night of the Soul*. Because Bob, like me, had experienced a lot of spiritual frustration over the years, I knew he would be happy to hear that this was the work—the blessing—of divine grace! Knowing that no one would ever expect or suspect such a thing, I had him read some of my highlighted passages in St. John's book while driving back to the ashram, knowing that this would be great preparation for tomorrow's Intensive.

Saturday

I entered the Intensive hall with no expectations and was pretty much perfectly content with all that I had received this past week. And from the events of last night, I knew that my timing was still in perfect sync and that I was still in touch with my true Self. All I had to do was stay awake in the expanded sense of that term and enjoy whatever comes forth.

Everyone taking the intensive is assigned their own space, and my spot for this Intensive was marked F16. Thinking of the hi-tech, high-speed plane with the same marking, I thought that this seemed appropriate since I had been flying so high lately. Later in the day, I realized that F was the 6th letter of the alphabet, and thus, this marking could also be seen as 616, and this had even more significance for me. It had come to me while eating lunch, and with no contemplation on my part, that the spiritual meaning or mystical meaning of the number 6 corresponds to the Guru, the enlightened Master who, being in complete Union with God, is perfect inwardly and outwardly. So, I saw the marking 616 as symbolic of Baba and Gurumayi guiding me, also as the inner Guru—my true Self, and the outer Guru—as two different expressions of the Guru—two expressions of divine grace, helping me reconnect with my divine Nature.

This intensive was called the Maha Intensive—the great Intensive and presented the classic Indian epic, the *Mahabharata,* which is a story about striving to lead a righteous life in the face of the eternal battle between good and evil. The *Bhagavad Gita*, one of India's best-loved scriptures, comes from the *Mahabharata*. The *Gita* is where Lord Krishna teaches Arjuna the highest truths of life, the ancient and mystical teachings about the Self, as the two of them stand on the battlefield, waiting for the fighting to begin. In the Intensive, this tale was presented as a play, with the Siddha Yoga Swamis playing all the roles. I found the play entertaining and also effective in helping me stay in touch with my higher nature. It was also a great reminder that our true nature has many divine qualities and that our lower nature has many truly despicable ones!

As with all other Intensives, there was an hour-long meditation period in the morning and afternoon sessions. During both of these meditations, my intention to focus on the witness was very strong, at least partly because my mind had been more active that day than it had been all week. During the play, I found that my mind was trying to extract special messages or lessons to go with the others that I had received. I was also wondering if I was getting close to enlightenment. This particular time period had been so incredibly powerful, blissful, and full of grace and had so many examples of perfect timing (most of which I have not included). I must admit that, in regard to my own state, I wasn't entirely sure what to think. But in this atmosphere, the witness aspect of myself was present enough to recognize this "mental activity" as the normal play of the ego, so I was able to stay separate from it.

I was a little surprised to see how active my mind was because it had been so quiet this past week. I remembered that someone had asked Baba what the mind was like after enlightenment—did the unasked-for internal dialogue continue? Baba smiled and said yes, but that his "state" was such that he never identified with it—he remained perfectly in the witness. Due to my firm resolve and the abundant grace I was experiencing, I was able to stay focused in the witness quite well in both of the meditation sessions, in spite of some thoughts.

Since there was to be an evening session in which Gurumayi would speak, the emcee asked everyone to try to stay connected with the inner energy and focus we were experiencing by eating lightly and talking as little as possible. I was happy to take this advice, as my only goal was to stay in the witness state. I was really looking forward to being with Gurumayi and wanted to be "awake" as much as possible while listening to her talk.

After eating, I decided that reading Baba's autobiography would be a great way to maintain contact with the shakti. I was still reading about Baba's meditation experiences and continued with chapter 27, "The World of Ancestors," which I had no memory of reading in years past. Near the end of this short chapter, Baba says, *"As my mind became stabilized in the Blue Pearl, Witness consciousness would come to me. This kind of meditation can be called samadhi. In it one remains fully conscious... This is the samadhi of the Siddha Path, where witness-consciousness remains fully active."[19]* I was surprised because, in my limited awareness, I had understood genuine *samadhi* to be a total absorption in God in which one has no awareness of the world.

A Joyous Awakening

Now, I immediately recognized I had, and was currently experiencing, some level of *samadhi*! (I say "some level" because even though I wasn't perfectly clear about the level of the Self that I was experiencing, I didn't think I was fully enlightened.) I did know that I was experiencing true Witness consciousness during my so-called normal waking state, just as I had in the summer of 1975. Right from the first moments that the Self revealed itself to me, I knew that this state of divine presence and the insights it brought were the highest Truth.

Still, in the years since this initial experience of my pure Self, the pure "I" of Witness consciousness, I never considered that this might be samadhi, because I was wide awake! To be told this now by Baba—to be so movingly reminded of how fortunate and blessed I was to experience such rare and miraculous states—was overwhelming. It's impossible for me to express the gratitude and profound awe I was experiencing at that moment.

It was in this most wonderful of states that I headed back for the evening session of the Maha Intensive.

Now more than ever, I was excited to see Gurumayi, knowing that she is always in the state of Siddha *samadhi*. To my delight, but not surprise, the way things had been going, Gurumayi's talk focused on the mind, the witness, and the inner Self. She said that in meditation, one's physical posture is important; one must have a straight spine and be comfortable, yet truly, your inner posture is the essence and key to meditation. By inner posture, she meant your focus on yourself—knowing what your mind is up to!

With humor and lightness that made her message easy to take in, Gurumayi pointed out that you should not let your mind falter or wander in meditation. And that the means to maintaining this inner balance and focus is the witness of the mind! It was wonderful to hear Gurumayi speaking about the importance of inner posture, the nature of the mind, and the significance of the witness. She also spoke about the importance of the intensity of your focus, and how one-pointedness is necessary for you to experience your own Self. I could not help but think of my own initial experience with witness consciousness and the intensity it took to hold onto it. I also remembered the sheep dog that exemplified these characteristics perfectly!

Finally, I was aware that this talk by Gurumayi, coming as it did right after reading Baba's words about witness consciousness, once again, demonstrated the uncanny interconnectedness between my two stages of *shaktipat*, my two experiences of the descent of grace. For me, it was also another demonstration of the perfect timing—synchronization that just happens with the state of the Self.

After the evening program, I read some more of Baba's book, wanting to finish it before heading back to Maine. I also updated my journal and again was awed at how much Baba's and St. John's books had helped me further understand the spiritual experiences I was having. It occurred to me that this had also been the case in 75 with Ouspensky's, Walker's, and Nicoll's books. Such is the supreme intelligence, generosity, and sweetness of grace.

Sunday

Bob and I chatted a little before and during breakfast, both of us acknowledging how great the first day of the Intensive had been and how much we were looking forward to seeing the end of the *Mahabharata*. We also spoke about how impressed we were with Gurumayi's talk the previous evening. It was easy to see that Bob's energy level had been raised a few quantum leaps since he arrived.

Later that morning, the story of Krishna and the Pandavas brothers came to a rousing end. With the quality of the acting, it felt like we were attending the best show on Broadway, and yet, because of the nature of the story and the energy of the Intensive itself, I think each person there couldn't help but feel the great qualities of their own heart. The emphasis was clearly on our higher nature and the virtues that are contained within it. It was in this enthusiastic state that we prepared to listen to Gurumayi's morning talk.

On one level, it seemed a reiteration of the talk she'd given the night before. She spoke again about the nature of the mind, the Self, and the importance of the correct inner posture—the importance of the witness. On Sunday, however, I perceived one major difference: Gurumayi was not just speaking about these subtle and mystical teachings. She was also giving everyone a direct experience of them. Speaking in a gentle, soothing voice, Gurumayi would present some information and instructions, and then, for a short time, she would close her eyes, apparently withdrawing into the stillness of her own being. Then she would speak about another aspect concerning the nature of the mind or the witness, and then, once again, she would turn within for a short while.

In this way, she guided me and, I would presume, everyone else in the hall into a profound state of the inner witness. Through the power of her will and the miracle of her own state, Gurumayi led a roomful of her students to the experience of the inner posture and perfect stillness of true meditation. This level of teaching is a beautiful demonstration of the way a genuine spiritual Master can work with her students.

The morning session ended right after this divine meditation with Gurumayi. I turned to Bob, who was sitting just a little behind me, and could tell from the look on his face that he, too, had experienced the miracle of witness-consciousness. There was no need for words as we were both still reveling in our own inner stillness and bliss. Still, in complete amazement at how this meditation had unfolded, I was reminded that Gurdjieff had said that a genuine spiritual teacher could, as an act of their own will, give the seeker an experience of their own true nature—their Self. The purpose of doing this is to provide the seeker a glimpse of the goal of the spiritual journey and thereby help them to persevere through the most difficult of passages of this challenging process.

Now, not only had I experienced the truth of this in both Intensives, but I also realized that an enlightened Master could do this for many seekers at the same time!

After lunch, people in the Intensive were invited to share their experiences and personal revelations of the preceding day and a half. One woman spoke about how, for years, she had been collecting psychology books so that she could better understand herself, and now, thanks to Gurumayi's talks and guided meditation, she had realized that she must go beyond all book knowledge and put her efforts into getting in touch with her true Self. She would be able to do this now, she said, because she now knew where the experience lies.

Hearing this reminded me of my own initial awakening, where, like this woman and most Westerners, I had expected that what I was seeking would come in the form of intellectual understanding. But, as described in this story of my awakening, basically, all of my divine insights and major shifts in understanding came about by simply staying in the state of witness consciousness. Now, I realized that others could be exposed to these subtle and almost forgotten truths that exist within us, just by attending an Intensive with a Siddha Guru. The experience of the Self is so exquisite, suffused as it is with unconditional love, that I couldn't help but wish everyone in the world could experience it for themselves.

As the last meditation session began, once again, I was inundated with thoughts of the possibility of my becoming enlightened in the near future. There had been so many things that had happened over these last nine days (many of which I have not mentioned here) that I wasn't sure what to think about what was happening within me. Once I was able to become truly anchored in the witness, once I got into meditation, I was aware that these thoughts of enlightenment contained traces of wanting to be recognized for these great and rare experiences I was having. The witness in me could see that my ego was coming up with these desires, and so I knew they should not be taken seriously. In terms of recognition, the Guru rarely acknowledges people in an outer way because doing so would only enhance their ego. The Guru's job is not to strengthen the seeker's ego but to help them go beyond it. This and the awareness that I had received more than I could ever have wished for or possibly imagined allowed me to turn within and experience a pleasant and still meditation.

I came out of meditation because my knees and hips were sore from sitting so much over these last few days. Recognizing this stress in my body, I thought, I guess it's time for meditation to end now. I was thinking of my own meditation, but the instant the thought came to me, the bell sounded to signal the end of meditation!

Even with all the things that had happened since arriving at the ashram, I was still awe-struck to see that the Shakti's timing was still unimaginably and unfathomably perfect. What a way to end the Intensive, knowing that I was still wonderfully aligned with my Self. What a way as well to head home to begin the new life that I wanted to be more spiritually centered.

The Autumn

Pam and I rented a cottage from an old neighbor on the lake where I had spent many wonderful summers as a child. We stayed there a couple of months while waiting to buy a sweet little farmhouse that my wife had fallen in love with. Mist would rise from the lake each morning, and our time there was both beautiful and extremely peaceful. The fall colors were spectacular, and our young family enjoyed many walks into the Maine woods to enjoy the fall foliage. Both Pam and I saw the brightly colored leaves as symbols of spiritual energy. I've always loved the autumn, and this time with my wife and two young children, in the fall of 1987, was the best ever.

I found myself yearning to go to India and spend some time with Gurumayi. I wasn't hoping to receive more. I wanted to be with Gurumayi, to see India, to be in the ashram in Ganeshpuri that I had heard so much about, so I could offer my services there in thanks for all I had received. As it turned out, we were able to get passports and join some other devotees on a chartered flight to India in the first part of December. I was so excited to go to India and so amazed that instead of going in search of the truth, I was going out of immense gratitude for what I had already received.

The couple of months that I spent in Gurudev Siddha Peeth—the ashram in Ganeshpuri, India, were like being in paradise. The grounds were beautiful, the weather was perfect, and the Shakti was truly amazing. Right from the very first morning, I awoke early and was enthusiastic about doing the early morning spiritual practices. This lasted the whole time I was there. This wasn't quite the case for my wife at first, but after about a week, she got acclimated and was very happy to be there, as were the children. We were both able to take an Intensive and a few short courses that were offered as part of the Christmas retreat. This helped Pam align with the Shakti and feel more at home. This made for a magical and divine stay for both of us.

A Joyous Awakening

One of the things that I enjoyed immensely was spending time with Gurumayi in the ashram's courtyard. Being able to go for darshan and then meditate in the Guru's presence, usually in the late morning, was precious and truly indescribable. In this idyllic setting, it was easy and natural for the mind to be quiet and indrawn and the heart to be open and full of the sweetest love. It is similar to the *love* one experiences when falling in love with another. But your own pure Self is not *other,* and it is not all in your heart—this love spreads to everyone and everything! All things are a manifestation of the one Self. On many of these occasions, I was content to meditate with my eyes open—just purposely staying in witness-consciousness—and enjoying all the different aspects of this truly divine setting as I meditated, as I was immersed in and suffused with divine love.

This stay with the Guru was exceedingly joyous and blissful, but there were no major revelations or insights as there had been in New York. These feelings of bliss, which I experienced as Oneness with the Shakti—the Divine spiritual energy, however, were just as powerful, just as much my own Self, as the understandings that had come to me earlier in New York—they just took a different form. I had very little direct contact with Gurumayi, but again, I did not come to India to be with Her personally. The relationship with the Guru is your vibrant connection with the one Self in all. Again, it's not about another. What I had wanted was to be in the presence of Her divine grace, which, as I'm saying, was easily felt.

I did have one experience with her that, to say the least, was utterly amazing. I was heading up to the housing office on the second floor through an enclosed stairway that made a 180-degree turn. As I made the turn, I encountered Gurumayi coming down the stairs. Naturally, I moved to the back of the platform, up against the wall, to let her pass. We both acknowledged each other with our eyes without speaking, and just as she was passing by me, I felt a blast of energy hit me right underneath my heart. The energy was so strong that I think if I had not been standing against the wall, it would have knocked me over. Gurumayi passed without touching me or giving any acknowledgement of this unexpected infusion of energy.

Without question, I was surprised but was not the least bit hurt by this surprising bolt of energy. I wondered if Gurumayi had done this intentionally or had the shakti just leaped forward on its own? Of course, it really didn't matter. What I was certain of was that the Shakti was removing one of the blocks in my subtle body as a form of purification. In fact, years later, I saw a picture of the major chakras in Baba's autobiography, of all places! And there was one in precisely the place where I felt this energy enter.

After finishing my errand, I came downstairs to find Gurumayi already in the courtyard. I went for darshan, and, again, neither of us spoke, and I proceeded to sit for meditation in the divine courtyard. After a few minutes of sitting, I became aware that the whole top of my head felt like I had been injected with Novocain! I had never experienced anything like this in meditation before, and I had the impression that it was a result of the infusion of Shakti I had just received. I assumed that the energy was so powerful that "It" had traveled all the way up to the crown chakra—the highest spiritual center at the crown of the head. My mind was peaceful and alert, but there were no other manifestations that I was aware of. I speak of this experience not because it is any big deal, but only to make the seeker aware that one never knows how the shakti may manifest in the presence of an enlightened Being. This is something we in the West have essentially no understanding of. In the past, people would cherish some relic that supposedly belonged to a saint for its energy, its shakti, but this is nothing compared to the living saint Herself!

To describe what it is truly like to be in the presence of a saint is not possible, because it's of the transcendent. What I can say is that I left Ganeshpuri in early February feeling so much love and gratitude for being able to spend some time in paradise. I looked forward to keeping my spiritual practices active and holding onto the great bliss that I felt in my heart. I was also looking forward to finally starting my writing, knowing that I now had a real ending to my story of spiritual awakening.

Instant Karma

Shortly after returning home, I found out that I had had a sizeable amount of money embezzled from me. I knew that karma had its good and bad aspects. I had experienced so much good karma lately that to experience some not-so-good karma was not that surprising. Still, I did experience great confusion and a lot of guilt at allowing myself to be put into this position. In hindsight, it was easy to see that my long-held beliefs in a world recession and a healthy dose of spiritual pride contributed to this situation. Basically, I had been thinking that because I was in such good touch with my Self, I knew more than other people. So, instead of just witnessing these thoughts that came to me, I acted on them.

A few years later, I read a warning from Baba that when you are experiencing a connection with your Self, you should be leery of your inner voice because it is exceedingly difficult to distinguish between your pure I of your Self and the small I of your ego-personality—until you are fully enlightened. I remembered that I had been cautioned to use "great discrimination," but obviously had forgotten to do so. Later, I discovered that the money had been embezzled the very day that I arrived at the ashram in India, which underscored my sense that this was karma that could not be avoided.

Baba does say that whatever happens after Shaktipat cannot be avoided and can be understood as part of the purification that must take place. In the past, however, I have had many tests and challenges that I have not handled especially well, and I don't believe that this was all unavoidable karma. I possess free will and could have acted differently—especially if I had been paying closer attention to my thoughts and desires, to the teachings, and to the witness that I know is the key. At the same time, I have been sincerely trying to stay connected with the spiritual teachings and my Self. It is just that I get carried away by my senses and by the subtlety of the ego, and I just don't recognize what's really happening on a deeper level.

Gurumayi says that as you move forward on the spiritual path, don't think that the tests get easier—they get harder! I have found this to be the case. This is not an excuse for some of my poor decisions—some of which I can hardly believe myself! Based on my own experiences, I just have to accept that some of my karmas—some of my long-held tendencies towards ignorance—are so deep and so subtle that even though my heart is in a good place, I still make foolish choices. I do not want to dwell on this, but the sincere seeker should know that the spiritual path is not all rose buds and that to make discernible progress, you have to deal with the thorns. You have to hang in there through the good, bad, and the ugly! Seeking to come closer to God and, ultimately, experience union with Him is the greatest of challenges and cannot be achieved without complete purification. This is why most of the stories about the great beings who achieved union or enlightenment describe the almost unimaginable hard ships they had to endure. It's important to remember the teaching of St. John and Baba Muktananda—all of these afflictions, poor choices, or divine happenstance, are still the result of divine grace that's secretly but surely taking you to your goal. To truly experience this, versus just believing it, the seeker must put a super effort into their spiritual practices—especially meditation with eyes open and closed. They should also seek out the help of a genuine living spiritual Master.

The Master's Eyes

Before I left for India, I had specifically asked God to bring on my karma, knowing that one had to burn all their karma in order to complete the spiritual journey. At that time, I offered the prayer, and I felt that I could handle anything. When I returned from India and began to go through the problems of being an embezzlement victim, I was not feeling quite so strong. I knew I had to witness and ignore my "mind" that wanted to berate me and pull me into its harsh negativity. This made it difficult to focus on my writing, and it also let me know that it was time to practice dentistry part-time. I had always intended to do that, just maybe not quite so soon. So, it was a bit of a struggle because of my inner state, but essentially things went well.

Shortly after opening my practice, my family and I went to New York to be in the presence of Gurumayi and to participate in the annual celebration of Guru Purnima. This is the most auspicious day of the year on the Indian calendar to pay homage to one's spiritual master. I looked forward to being in the ashram's vibrant atmosphere and being able to see Gurumayi, especially on Guru Purnama during darshan. I knew that having Gurumayi's darshan would help me feel more focused on my own Self and, hopefully, help my judgmental "mind" to calm down.

We had the good fortune of being able to see Gurumayi during darshan the very first day we were there. She welcomed us and asked how we were doing and how long we were staying. We responded that everything was fine, which I knew it was, even though my mind was doing "its" thing, which, from my experience with self-remembering, I knew was normal and to be expected. As we were leaving, Gurumayi's attendant said to remind him of our departure the day before we left. As expected, we had a pleasant stay and Guru Purnima was far better than I could have hoped for. As my family came before Gurumayi for darshan, she gave us such a long and loving glance that Pam and I both were vaulted into a state of profound inner stillness and experienced a wonder-filled connection with our own Self. This unexpected moment just shows the importance of spending time with the Guru.

On our last day there and our last darshan, Gurumayi showered us with gifts and, again, the most captivating and loving smile. We all felt drenched in her love, love so palpable that you cannot possibly miss it. At that moment, I witnessed that part of my mind was still feeling some guilt at the way I had handled my business affairs. That part of me—that I—felt I did not deserve so much love—even though my family certainly did.

After I had been home for just a few days, I realized that all of the guilt, remorse, and tension that I had been feeling for these past months was completely gone! There was no doubt in my mind that it was due to Gurumayi's grace. I could also see that in my darshans with her she was letting me know that she loved me unconditionally. One of the gifts that Gurumayi gave me was a hand-carved, heart-shaped jewelry box that says *I love you* written across the top. Now that I was in touch with my Self in a much fuller sense, again, thanks to Gurumayi, I realized that, once again, she was totally aware of my inner state. I firmly believe that is why she wanted to know when we were leaving. She wanted to be able to shower us with her divine love. She also wanted to remind me that she loves everyone unconditionally. What I know for sure is that by stepping in as she did, she gave me the grace to move on.

The miracle of this event, for me, was both an outer and an inner, something that I cannot adequately express in words. This sentiment applies to all the events I've attempted to describe during this miraculous visit. One of my major reasons for sharing my spiritual experiences is to give sincere seekers even a glimpse of how much they can receive from a spiritual master and how exalted the state of a true Guru actually is.

Gratitude, Gratitude, Gratitude

I returned to the ashram just before Labor Day 1988, to catch the last of the summer retreat programs and celebrate the one-year anniversary of my deeper understanding and connection with my beloved Guru and my beloved Self. I was feeling so good, and so thankful to God for all that I had received in this life that I asked Gurumayi if I could return to India to continue with the work I had been doing at the beginning of the year. After asking about my writing and my family, and being assured everything would be fine, she indicated that I was welcome to come. I arranged to leave in November and stay three full weeks in Gurudev Siddha Peeth, and, as before, I had a truly indescribable and miraculous stay.

A few days after I arrived, Gurumayi announced that there was going to be chanting in the courtyard every night to help raise the energy level of the staff to prepare for the upcoming Christmas retreat. Gurumayi led the chants, and all I can say is that not only were they uplifting, but they were also absolutely divine. I experienced that we were all being purified at a very profound level, at the same time, we were being supercharged. I felt pure and one-pointed and was sweetly and vibrantly aware of the Self. I also felt strongly that I had come all this way just to chant with Gurumayi in this divine setting and that it was well worth it.

I was able to participate in some of the courses that were designed for the staff. These, along with the chanting and the divine atmosphere of the ashram, elicited a sense of gratitude so deep and all-encompassing that it is impossible to explain. A feeling of gratitude at this level comes only from the transcendent Self, and I experienced this level of gratitude almost every day I was there. I never expected this; in fact, I never knew that such was even possible. It is just another example of the unexpected grace that comes from being in the presence of an enlightened spiritual Master.

As another expression of this divine grace, I would wake up naturally every day at about 2:30 a.m. and go through the entire day until around 9:00 p.m. without being the least bit tired during the day! I did this for three weeks and never felt the need for additional rest. My day would begin with the morning Arti—traditional morning worship by the Brahman priests, then my sitting for meditation in Baba's Samadhi shrine from 3:15 to 4:00, simply practicing witness-consciousness with my eyes open. Then I would go to the Meditation Cave for formal meditation from 4:00 until 5:00. After a short break, we chanted scriptural and devotional chants until 7 o'clock. It's hard to believe that a person could keep such a schedule and not get tired, but that attests to the power and support of the Shakti in the house of a genuine saint.

It is said that since the enlightened Master, a genuine Siddha Guru, is fully immersed in their own Self, even their normal mundane speech is charged with or saturated with Shakti and, as such, can have a profound effect on the disciple. I had a very dramatic experience of this on the last day of my stay. I had been contemplating whether or not to ask Gurumayi about a question my wife had brought up with her in July, while we were in New York. My wife and I had decided to ask Gurumayi if it would be in the best interests of our sadhana—our spiritual pursuits—to have another child. But when in front of Gurumayi, my wife Pam simply asked her if it was OK for us to have another baby. Gurumayi said sure and looked at my son, who was two and a half, and said, in a humorous way, he wants someone to fight with! While everyone was laughing, I was thinking that this was not the question we—actually, I—had felt we should ask, and thus, I had not really accepted her answer. Thus, I thought that I should ask the question again—properly—to make sure we received the appropriate response. Then, on the final day of my visit, I decided that I did not need to speak to Gurumayi about this. I had had such an incredible stay, and like many disciples of a true master, I experienced that Gurumayi had done so much for me these last few weeks that I was completely full. All I needed to do was listen to my own true Self, and that would be the same as talking to my Guru. Since I was in such high spirits—in such good connection with my Self—that would not be hard to do.

So, as I was on my way to my final darshan of this visit, I decided that I would just try to be fully awake in Gurumayi's presence and see what came up.

As I made the turn to head up the aisle to her chair, I heard Gurumayi say, *"So you're leaving tonight."* I had not been looking at Gurumayi, who was about fifty feet away, but instead, I had been looking at the entire setting of this divine courtyard. Thus, I did not immediately realize she was speaking to me. I had heard her clearly and had instinctively looked at her, and then was quite surprised to realize that she was looking directly at me. She was speaking to me! I responded that, yes, I was leaving tonight. She asked me if I had had a good time. I smiled, knowing that she was well aware of how good—of the unimaginably great—a time I'd had. I said, *"Yes, I had a wonderful stay."* Then Gurumayi proceeded to ask me if I had worked with various people, all the while making jokes, teasing many people, and just having the best time. Those who have had the great fortune to spend time with Gurumayi know how light and joyous she can be when she's simply being her joyous self. As this was going on, I, like everyone else, was thoroughly enjoying her playful spirit. I was also surprised and amazed that this was happening to me—that Gurumayi and I were joking around and just laughing and laughing.

Finally, I said to Gurumayi that since we were just chatting, which certainly had never been the case before, did she mind if I asked her a question. She said no, of course, go ahead. I told her about my wife's question last July and what we—I—had originally intended. She laughed and said that my wife and I should get clear between ourselves, and that we should both write to her. Of course, I said fine, and about this time was feeling a little guilty about the amount of time I had been with her and thus, said, *"Thank you very much for having me,"* and started to go and sit for meditation. (When I got off the plane a long, long day later, my wife greeted me, saying, *"I'm pregnant!"*)

I was more than a little charged up from this magical encounter with Gurumayi. After sitting for a few minutes, just trying to stay in the present—in witness consciousness, I became aware of an indescribable sensation throughout my entire being. I say *being* because it was not just my body—it permeated the whole of me, my body, mind, and spirit! I had never experienced anything quite like this before, and yet I knew that this was just another experience of the Shakti—of the grace of the Master. It was as profound and as dramatic as being hit by the bolt of energy—grace—that had ascended to the crown of my head during the last time I was with Gurumayi, and yet this time it was totally different in its effect. I was experiencing this in a great state of witness consciousness, and marveling at the powerful effect that the shakti was having on my entire being.

Then I remembered the teaching that even the mundane words of a Siddha Master are charged with divine Shakti and thus can have a profound effect on one who is subtle enough to experience them. Having experienced the vibrations of my Self many times before, I knew for sure that this blessed experience had nothing to do with my ego. It wasn't just that I was proud that I'd gotten to spend some precious time with Gurumayi. On the contrary, I felt that I was able to experience this so fully because my heart had been opened so dramatically, and I had experienced so much purification during these last three weeks.

This feeling stayed with me for quite a while, and as I went about my day, preparing to leave, the sensation was rekindled a number of times by people coming up to me and saying what an incredible darshan I had had. Each time I would say to them, *"Yes, isn't it amazing what can happen in the Siddha's abode."*

Each time that this happened, I was reminded of the absolute blessedness of my own Self and the Siddha Guru, which are, of course, one and the same mystery.

Since that exchange with Gurumayi in December of 1988, I have had a number of wonderful encounters with my Guru. Each has been different, and all of them have had a incredible effect on me. So, I can truly say that being in the presence of a Siddha Master is both a unique and a divine experience. Ultimately, every spiritual seeker can't be in the presence of a Siddha Guru. But, at the same time, I remind seekers that the spiritual teachings say that the only way to know the Guru, to experience the Guru, is to know your own inner Self. I know that this teaching is true because I've experienced its truth for myself!

It is possible, however, for anyone interested in studying the Guru's teachings to follow the spiritual practices that the Guru recommends, and in this very lifetime to realize the unconditional joy of their own divine Self. This I know, is what truly matters. And remember the Guru is not an individual. The Guru is an embodiment of the one supreme Spirit, the divine Self in all, manifesting as an individual in order to help others achieve the same blissful state. I write more about this in Book IV. Even though I love being in Gurumayi's presence, I understand that the only way to truly know the Guru is to know your own Self.

BOOK IV
Teachings Of
The Great Beings

"When a man knows his true Self for the first time, something else arises from the depths of his being and takes possession of him. That something is behind the mind, it is infinite, divine, and eternal. Some people call it the Kingdom of Heaven, others call it the soul, and others again, Nirvana. Hindus call it liberation. You may give it what name you wish. When this happens, a man has not really lost himself; rather he has found himself."

Ramana Maharshi

9
Experiences and Expressions
of the Truth

THE FIRST THREE SECTIONS CONTAIN the full story of my spiritual awakening. I've presented it in detail so that its authenticity may be clear, and I want to underscore that nothing in this account is contrived or made up. This is what happened to me, and it happened primarily as a gift of grace. Though there were clearly actions I took and attitudes I assumed that drew grace to me and opened me to receive it, ultimately, what happened to me was not of my own doing. A person cannot make such a thing happen as an act of will. To be awakened in this manner, by grace, is not a common occurrence. As mentioned in the Preface, I feel that such an event deserves, actually needs, to be shared for the benefit of sincere seekers of Truth. Again, during my spiritual awakening, I had the clear understanding that I was to share this miraculous experience so that other seekers could use the account to guide themselves in getting started on the quest for inner transformation and expansion of awareness. My hope is that this work will be instructive to seekers in the initial stages of their journey, helping them to begin on the right foot, so to speak.

Before getting more specific, I want to remind everyone that the major topics of Book IV: The mind, Meditation, The Self, The Witness, and The Ego are all dynamically interrelated and simply different manifestations of the one divine Consciousness that is the source and Essence of everything. Because this divine Consciousness is beyond all thoughts and concepts and is of such a miraculous nature, this Mystery cannot be described or defined. This has been the case for thousands of years; the above subjects—witness, meditation, and so on, are ways those who have had profound experiences of this Supreme Mystery have chosen to try and give us some feel for It. Thus, as you read this account, try to maintain an awareness that these seemingly separate distinctions are just different facets of the Divine Mystery that transcends thought, words, and symbols!

In this fourth and final section, I explore how my own experiences of awakening are consistent with the teachings of the ancient wisdom traditions. I want to make it clear that what happened is not just an interesting experience for me but is rather a classical expression of spiritual awakening. Aldous Huxley calls it the perennial philosophy, by which he means these attempted descriptions of the deeper states of consciousness are, throughout time, remarkably consistent. Perennial means reoccurrence and this refers to the fact that esoteric Teachings keep arising in different souls again and again throughout history. Again, the

A Joyous Awakening

Truth always comes from within—always! From my perspective, seeing the uncanny consistencies between my experiences of awakening and the essential teachings of ancient wisdom brings what happened to me into focus. Many of the *experiences* provide good examples of what these Teachings are really telling us. Book IV gives my experiences a place to stand in tradition, and it brings ancient teachings to life in the present day and shows that they are not beyond our comprehension or beyond belief, and they are *practical, sensible and inclusive!*

My awakening is a classic experience of the Transcendent—of the one Self that exists in all, and that is the source of any authentic mystical experience, and any profound transcendent insight. The Truth that others and I have experienced is inherent in every human being. The seeker must remember that the goal of the wisdom traditions is alive, conscious, and present in everyone and is awaiting discovery! Thus, it is possible for anyone to experience these transcendent states. My hope is that with the help and perspective of my story of awakening, these essential truths of the wisdom traditions, which emanate from genuine transcendent experience, will come alive for more seekers, who will see these truths and will experience these truths for themselves. Therefore, they will be more meaningful and useful, and less mystical! Also, my hope is that once sincere seekers of Truth become aware of the possibility of experiencing their own essential nature, their oneness with the Absolute, they will be prompted to make efforts similar to what I did to become open to experiencing these higher states of awareness that exist in the consciousness you already have!

One of my main purposes in this section is to discuss in greater detail the major topics I've introduced throughout the book, such as the witness, meditation, and the Self. Since my spiritual journey began with witness-consciousness, I will start there. It's also my goal to show readers where they can go to learn more about these topics. So, in this section, I quote a number of fully enlightened teachers, who are spiritual Masters and Siddha Gurus, and I also present the teachings of some contemporary Westerners, teachers who may or may not be fully enlightened but who write accurately and in a familiar vernacular, about such topics as the witness and the Self. I say that these writings are accurate based on my own experiences. Since I had these experiences before I'd ever even heard of the wisdom traditions, I know for certain that what I perceived was not colored by someone else's dogma or ideas.

As I said, several times in this account of my awakening, the experience of your true nature, the one Self in all, is so profound and inherently sacred that the experience itself lets you know that it is valid and that it is the ultimate Truth. Nonetheless, it was enormously satisfying and also very helpful, for me to find that these experiences are in alignment with the teachings and insights given by

Experiences and Expressions of the Truth

those whom I know to be enlightened spiritual Masters, and I want to share these sources of knowledge so that seekers can look at these writings, many of which are sharings—for themselves, for their subtle insights about Consciousness and to stimulate enthusiasm too.

At the end of this section, I share more thoughts on my good fortune of being a disciple of a genuine living spiritual master, a Siddha Guru. Even though many thousands of Westerners have met Baba Muktananda and Gurumayi Chidvilasananda, and many thousands more have read their books, still, in the West the Guru-disciple relationship is unusual. We are familiar with Jesus and His disciples but know nothing of how this, this relationship between disciple and Master, fits into and *is* a major part of these esoteric teachings.

Many, possibly most, Westerners hold the belief that there is only one genuine spiritual master, Jesus, who lived two thousand years ago. According to this viewpoint, there is not even a possibility that a true master might espouse a path other than orthodox Christianity or that a contemporary seeker might meet a living master who could lead them to the experience of union with God while living—rather than in some remote heaven. The wisdom traditions teach that it is the birthright of each human being to know their Divine nature and that an authentic spiritual Master can lead a seeker to this Experience. For those who are sincere seekers, I would like to reiterate that my first teacher, Gurdjieff, and the first Siddha Guru I met, Baba Muktananda, both taught that seekers who want to make real and sustained progress on the spiritual path need a living Master.

According to a Buddhist proverb, *"When the student is ready, the master appears."* This was my own experience, and while I'm sure that it can be yours as well, I also appreciate that you will walk your own path in your own way. At this time, it is no longer possible for the mildly curious to meet the Siddha Yoga Guru. I would say that "mildly curious" is a fair description of my own orientation when I first encountered Baba Muktananda, and I know that if I were in that place right now, I would not be able to meet Gurumayi. I would, however, be able to read her books, I would be able to participate in a Shaktipat Intensive, I would be able to attend a Siddha Yoga meditation center or chanting and meditation group, and truthfully, any of these options might be more than enough to get me started on the spiritual path. The key in any spiritual endeavor is to have a burning desire *to know* the Truth, or even a much higher level of understanding, and a firm faith that grace will support you in this. Ultimately, you must remember that your own inner Self, the inner divine Master, is within you already, waiting to reveal Itself. Again, it has been said that when the student is ready, the master will appear! But remember, the Master is already within and thus, have Faith and Trust!

A Joyous Awakening

Again, my goal is to help readers further explore their own inner terrain. Even though I can't say what another person's spiritual path will look like, based on my experience, I will tell you that if you turn within and become acquainted with the witness of your mind, with the **awareness** that your thoughts arise into great things, it will happen. Of this, I am certain.

10
Witness Consciousness

MANY AUTHENTIC WISDOM TRADITIONS SPEAK about the need for a seeker to practice witness-consciousness or mindfulness and to come to know the Knower, the Witness of the mind. This is one of the major keys to genuine inner transformation and to truly knowing thyself. Based on my own experience, this has not been truly understood by most seekers of Truth. Witness-consciousness is true meditation, connecting with a part of our own awareness that helps and allows a seeker to become aware of their own deeper and more expansive consciousness, more expansive awareness. This is how I came to honestly *know myself* and then the one Self in all.

I am certain that the practice of witness-consciousness—of genuine open-eyed meditation—will allow a sincere seeker to prepare themselves for an awakening, for a wonderful and understandable increase in awareness on a number of levels. This will help them to begin to understand the teachings of the wisdom traditions in a way that is clear, practical, and enlightening. I know that the most significant action I took in support of my own awakening was first becoming a genuine seeker of truth. Secondly, getting familiar with self-inquiry and actually doing it honestly and sincerely. Thirdly, were the attempts I made to stay spiritually awake, to maintain a state of self-remembering, the "state" of being consciously present! It was in this way that new insights came to me and were of the most amazing quality and practicality.

For this reason, if you haven't actually tried self-observation and self-remembering for yourself, I would strongly recommend that you do so now. I mean, right now! We Westerners often think that we can understand all manner of things just by reading or hearing about them. In receiving knowledge about the highest Truth, however, the wisdom traditions tell us that a seeker must experience the Truth in order to have any real understanding of it. Such an experience can come through witness-consciousness and, as I'm stating, possibly in a much shorter time than you would believe. Where else can you get these kinds of results? Remember, increased awareness and understanding are available and are your birthright.

The term witness refers to the aspect of human awareness that is able to watch the antics of our habit-driven and mostly uncontrollable mind and emotions with complete detachment, which is just the nature of the Witness. This level of Awareness has also been referred to as the Experiencer and the Knower, but I will continue to use the Witness as I have throughout. It is the witness-awareness that the seeker needs to get to know, needs to connect with again and again, over an extended period of time. You can do this through meditation, either open-eyed or in-drawn—and truly, you should do both. When you're engaging with the world around you, this process is what Gurdjieff calls *self-remembering* and what Baba Muktananda refers to as *witness-consciousness*. As my own experiences show, it is by becoming aware of this deeper witness, this generally unnoticed part of ourselves, an aspect of our *own awareness*, that you can radically and honestly change your understanding of yourself, the mind, and the nature of awareness itself—for the better, in a very short time!

It is through witness-consciousness that you can begin to open yourself to a spiritual awakening, an awakening to a more expanded experience of yourself and, possibly, to the ultimate level of the witness, the Witness, which is the Self, the pure "One" in all. As the witness is always present in all of its levels—in the consciousness of every human being, this "Path" or "Way" is available to all seekers. You just have to begin—you just have to participate in whatever way you can to get started!

From reading the literature that talks about the transcendent, the mystical experience, I can see that many enlightened beings have spoken quite specifically about the mystical nature of Witness-consciousness, the awareness of the *conscious Presence* within us all.

Ramana Maharshi, a highly revered master from South India who recommended self-inquiry as the fastest means to liberation, describes the Witness in this way:

"That inner Self, as the primeval Spirit, eternal, ever effulgent, full, and infinite Bliss, single, indivisible, whole and living, shines in everyone as the witnessing awareness." [1]

Thus, the Witness is the Self, the innermost essence and awareness of all beings. As I've said, when the Self revealed itself to me, I no longer had to try and stay connected with the Witness; it was just there in a fuller and vastly more expansive way. I could say that it was still the witness as I had come to know it, but now it contained an unmistakable awareness of my own Divine nature and the oneness of my nature with God! It was a vastly different state of consciousness, one that was permeated with the sacred and the Universal. When Ramana Maharshi, Shankara, Baba Muktananda, and Bhagavan Nityananda tell us that the Witness is the Self, which is God. this is the level of the Witness-Awareness that they are speaking about. But you must remember that the conscious awareness that is readily available to the seeker right from the start, the witness in everyone, as I experienced for myself, is still an aspect of the great Spirit; it's just not a full expression of that Spirit—yet!

As I've said several times, I experienced that the Self reveals itself of its own choosing. A seeker, no matter how strong their motivation may be, cannot bring the Self into their awareness as an act of pure will. But they can, as I experienced and as the wisdom traditions teach, cultivate a still and alert mind, a state that encourages the great Self to reveal itself. Here is what Gurumayi has to say about how to achieve an inner state of alertness and stillness:

"In true meditation, consciousness is fully active, but the mind is quiet. Meditation should never be inert. When you meditate, your entire being is alert, vibrating with awareness. You watch your mind, you witness your mind, but you don't buy into its comings and goings."[2]

As I've described, when I first started the practice of self-observation and self-remembering, which is an advanced form of meditation, I found it difficult to stay present in the witness and not buy into my mind's comings and goings—not become identified with every thought and emotion my mind generated. And yet I had such fun with this enlightening practice! Being able to observe and experience that I was different from my thoughts and emotions was incredibly emancipating and truly was the master key to my spiritual awakening.

Because I was consciously present—in the midst of my daily activities, as best I could be, I quickly and naturally perceived the antics of my undisciplined mind and the pervasive cultural conditioning of my ego, my individual sense of self. All of this was shown to me because, for the very first time in my life, I wasn't buying into my mind's habitual comings and goings. I was keeping my sense of identity in the one watching the mind, in the witness—the witnessing-awareness. This practice brought me so much long-sought insight that it was easy for me to be enthusiastic about wanting to continue doing it with enthusiasm. Ultimately, it was this simple, enjoyable, and yet profound practice that assisted my highly conditioned and unruly mind in becoming still and alert and allowed my Self to reveal itself to me!

The Buddhist Teaching of Mindfulness

In his book *Mindfulness in Plain English*, the venerable and contemporary Buddhist teacher Henepola Gunaratana has this to say,

"Vipassana is the oldest of the Buddhist meditation practices. The method comes directly from the Satipatthana Sutra, a discourse attributed to the Buddha himself. Vipassana is a direct and gradual cultivation of mindfulness or awareness."[3]

Gunaratana also says that *Vipassana* is a term from the Pali language meaning *insight meditation*, which refers to insight into the process of perception—into the very nature of reality. From this and from Gunaratana's further descriptions of mindfulness, it seems clear to me that the act of awareness he is speaking about is what I'm calling witness-consciousness. For instance, he says that mindfulness is free from criticism and judgment and has nothing to do with thought or analysis. He says it is simply pure awareness that is both deeper than thought and prior to thought. He says that mindfulness is a moment-by-moment examination of the very process of perception itself. And, further, he says that it is a process of ever-increasing awareness that has the power to reveal the deepest level of reality available to human consciousness. Here, Gunaratana refers to Self-realization or enlightenment, the goal of both Buddhist and yogic practice, as well as esoteric Christianity, and *union with God.*

When I first realized that the Buddha taught the same act of awareness that I learned from Gurdjieff as *self-remembering,* I was a little surprised. Since this is, however, the nature of human consciousness, it is to be expected that it would appear in various paths to enlightenment. What I found most interesting is that the Buddha did not explain but instead asked the seeker to "come see." As the sage Sutralamkara explains it, this means that a seeker must participate in the act of awareness; they must experience for themselves this deeper level of consciousness. He writes:

"The Truth indeed has never been preached by the Buddha, seeing that one has to realize it within oneself."[4]

Coming to that realization is, of course, quite challenging, but human consciousness is designed to meet that challenge. Gunaratana says that one of the great difficulties in the practice of mindfulness is remembering to be mindful. He says that most of the time, we are not paying close enough attention to realize, to directly experience, that we are not paying attention! He adds that the way you can cultivate mindfulness is by constantly pulling yourself back to the state of mindfulness. He describes the practice of mindfulness as a living activity, an experiential activity, one that can be done anywhere and anytime if you can just remember to do it. Gunaratana adds,

Don't get discouraged. Realize that you have been off track for such and such a length of time.... There is no need for any negative reaction at all. The very act of realizing that you have been off track is an act of awareness. It is an exercise of pure mindfulness all by itself.[5]

His encouragement is, I think, enormously useful and accurate. The difficulties he describes were my own experience in attempting to become consciously aware, and I think, if you look with honesty, you will find them to be yours as well.

Mindfulness, Gunaratana says, is not the same as either concentration or willpower. True though this is, it seems to me that these three have a strong connection. As I experienced, mindfulness is relatively easy to connect with but hard to hold onto. Staying with mindfulness requires both concentration and willpower, which are, therefore, absolutely necessary to one who wants to be mindful at the level of awareness the great beings are speaking about. And *intention* is another facet of focused awareness that needs to be reemployed again and again.

Many seekers have a strong desire to know, but this yearning alone is not enough to bring quick and significant progress. In my own life, I found that it was important to learn that a capacity for transcendence was present in me and to learn, as well, how to recognize and engage this capacity. So, the authentic instruction I received in self-remembrance—in witness-consciousness—was vital. For me, all of Gunaratana's instructions are authentic—come see!

In this regard, another of the Buddha's teachings is: Not putting any head above your own. What this means, I believe, is that we should not blindly accept what others say to be the truth. Gurdjieff has another way of putting this; he tells us that faith is not required, instead one must verify for himself what he has been told. Once a seeker directly experiences the inner witness, then belief is not an issue. In order to achieve this level of experience and insight, however, the seeker must muster sustained will, intention, and concentration in order to make the effort that's necessary for inner *work*. Most people find it much easier to simply believe the words of another, to have blind faith, and to be passive instead of consciously active. As I learned from reading Gurdjieff's student Maurice Nicoll so many years ago, it is concentration and willpower that provide the fuel to keep your lamp, your light of inquiry, burning ever brightly.

Advaita Vedanta and the Self as Witness

Having shown that the Buddha, who lived in the 5th or 6th century BCE, speaks about the importance of practicing the awareness known as mindfulness or witness-consciousness. Now I would like to move forward some thirteen hundred years to Adi Shankaracharya, a legendary sage of India who lived in the 8th or 9th century and who gave very similar advice about dealing with the mind. Both of these sages of yore have huge followings to this very day. Shankara forged the monastic system of which Baba, Gurumayi, and all Siddha Yoga swamis are a part, and he is the most famous exponent of Advaita Vedanta—a system of non-dualism based on the teaching portion of the Vedas, India's Most ancient scriptures. Non-dualism refers to the one Self that is the Source and Essence of all. Gurdjieff expressed this saying; Everything is consciousness. Franklin Merrell-Wolff gives Shankara's teachings credit for his *"Awakening."*

When Baba and Gurumayi speak about the witness, the teachings they give are not only expressions of their own experience, they're also expressions of Vedanta. Bear in mind that Vedanta, Buddhism, and all of the world's wisdom traditions were originally inspired by the experience of the Self, the one supreme Spirit in all. Here is what Adi Shankara says about the Witness in his *Crest-Jewel of Discrimination*:

"By allowing the purified mind to come to rest in one's true nature, the Witness, which is nothing but Consciousness, it gradually guides the mind to a state of stillness."

I quote this in hopes that one can appreciate how accurately it describes my experience of the witness—how it allowed my mind to come to a state of stillness in a completely natural way. Here is another quote from Shankara in his same Crest-Jewel.

Who but the Atman [the eternal Self] is capable of removing the bonds of ignorance, passion, and self-interested action? ... The Atman is the Witness of the individual mind and its operations. It is absolute knowledge. ... [6] And Shankara tells us,

"The wise man is one who understands that the essence of Brahman [the eternal ground of all existence] and Atman is pure Consciousness, and who realizes their absolute identity. The identity of Brahman and Atman is affirmed in hundreds of sacred texts." [7]

This sage is unequivocally saying that only the Self can remove our bonds of ignorance, that the Self does this as the Witness of the mind, and the direct Knowledge that it provides the mind, and that this Self is one with God. Shankara adds that this final truth is affirmed in *hundreds of sacred texts*, and yet we in the West are largely unaware of them.

Recently, I've learned from a great being and author that Shankara wrote many sacred texts himself, many too deep for most seekers. But in the end, this is what Shankara had to say:

"Here is the gist of all the scriptures in half a verse. Your inner Self is the Lord Himself, the Supreme Being Himself, and never forget this. The realization of this truth is the only worthwhile goal of life."

Modern Authors' Recognition of the Witness

Over the years, I've been delighted to discover that besides these and other classic references to the Witness, there are a number of contemporary Western authors who write on this same subject. I'd like to mention two in particular, Ken Wilber and Deepak Chopra, who are among the most prolific and popular writers on spirituality today. In his book *A Brief History of Everything*, Ken Wilber speaks in some detail on aspects of the observing Self. Posing the question, *"Who is the one who witnesses?"* Wilber posits that it is not the body, mind, or ego, nor our senses or our thoughts, because all of these aspects of ourselves can be seen by the observing witness. Wilber raises the question posed so often by the mystic Ramana Maharshi,—"Who am I?" This is what Ramana once said in response:

"I am not the body, not the organs of sense perception... not the thinking mind or the unconscious state. Having rejected all these as not "I", he says, 'That which remains separate and alone by itself—that pure Awareness is what I am.'"[8]

Wilber states that we are pure awareness and not anything that arises in that awareness! Of course, as I've been saying, we naturally identify with all the things arising versus our inherent awareness itself. This happens because, when we are children and as we become young adults, we are not told about our awareness's deeper capacities because our Western culture is not aware of them. Thus, we continue to identify our sense of self with what is arising—**instead** of the Consciousness that is observing or simply *aware* of what's arising. As Ramana tells us: *"Pure Awareness is what I am!"* Yes, not all of the conditioning and overlays covering and distorting—our pure *Awareness!*

One extremely significant point that Wilber brings up is the distinction between being a participant observer as opposed to being an academic observer. This really hit home for me because it's my observation that the West has been stuck in the intellect for so long that we've lost touch with higher levels of awareness and higher, more conscious levels of participation. Most people in the West don't understand and don't even accept the existence of higher levels of human consciousness. Wilber demonstrates that he is a participant-observer by telling us that the witness is ever-present, unvarying, never tempting, and never consoling. Since I, too, am a witness participant, I would add that the witness is never judging or complaining as well.

Wilber adds that the witnessing Self has a pervasive sense of freedom; in other words, when you are in touch with witness-consciousness, you are not bound by anything you are witnessing. Then he tells us that when we—what I've called the ego-personality or simply the mind—identify with what arises in our awareness, this identification itself cancels any sense of freedom. We are then identifying the Knower, the Witness, the Self!—with "things" that can be seen and heard, tasted, and felt, again, all of which can be observed. In my own experience, it was *always* my identification with thoughts or emotions that made me lose touch with the pure Witness and all its divine qualities.

This loss of pure, untainted awareness, Wilber says, is a loss of freedom and the beginning of bondage. He quotes the sage Maharishi Patanjali's classic description of bondage, which is *"the identification of the Seer with the modifications [the thoughts] of the mind,"*[9] instead of the awareness wherein these arise. This is, basically, everyone's experience and has been for thousands of years! Thus, in our everyday state of mind, where we are completely identified with every thought and emotion we have, we are not able to experience the watcher, the pure Awareness, the Witness. Because of this, we are not able to directly experience that we are vastly different from and vastly more than our heavenly conditioned minds!

Now, coming back to the original point, one reason for being a participant observer, rather than being just an academic observer, a contemplator or *thinker,* is that when you are consciously staying connected to the observing self, this very effort can give you a direct experience of your own bondage. I first experienced the truth of this as my mind having a *mind* of its own! The bondage comes from your identification with your thoughts and emotions, your being at the mercy of your cultural conditioning and base instincts, and, most importantly, your being totally unaware of your true, divine essence. Ramana's: *"Pure awareness is what I am."*

Now that he has described some of the qualities of the observing Self and has described what it is not—the body, the mind, the emotions, and so on—Wilber poses a question: *"What if you push beyond or behind the mind, into a depth of consciousness that is not confined to the ego or the individual self?"*[10] Of course, the entire thrust of the book you are now reading, and of spiritual writings from all epochs and cultures, is to pose and answer this very question! For his own response, Wilber puts forward one of the most renowned answers of all time, a passage from the *Chandogya Upanishad:*

There is a subtle essence that pervades all of reality. It is the reality of all that is, and the foundation of all that is. That essence is all, that essence is real. And thou—thou art That.

When I first awakened to the Self, I had the spontaneous experience of this statement of truth in that I simply *knew* that this pure Witness that I was experiencing was—is—my own true essence and the essence as well of everyone and everything! This particular wording, *Thou art That,* is one of the *mahavakyas,* the "great statements," of Vedanta. It is one of the supreme realizations that comes from the one pure Self!—as direct Knowledge. It is yet another confirmation that the individual soul and the Supreme Soul are One, the teaching that is repeated continually in Eastern scriptures and the Perennial Philosophy. Actually, I love Baba's way of putting it the best: *"God dwells within you, as you, for you."*

Another of the points Wilber makes that I resonate with very strongly is that the wisdom traditions are based on experiments in awareness and personal experiences that are repeatable and reproducible.[11] These are significant criteria for validity in science. It isn't enough that a certain set of conditions brings about certain results once. If it's a valid scientific finding, if it's true, then the experiment must be repeatable, the results reproducible. It's the same, Wilber is saying, with spiritual work: Because of the validity of the spiritual experiments in contemplation and meditation that are described by the wisdom traditions and many of their sages, these exercises in heightened consciousness have been successfully repeated over the centuries by countless seekers of Truth.

In the West, as I've said, both religious and secular authorities tend to deny or ignore the existence of higher states of consciousness. They have mistakenly thought these states were religious instead of psychological capacities of our own consciousness. Or better yet, our consciousness's natural state. This makes it doubly important for those of us who have experienced these states to acknowledge that we have been able to repeat and reproduce the experiences of the ancient sages by following the "experiments," the teachings and practices they've put forward. In time, our sheer numbers will make the authenticity of our experiences hard to deny. And the potential for significant numbers is definitely there.

As I've said, another of my spontaneous understandings when I first experienced these states of higher awareness was that I knew with complete certainty that this inner Divinity was not particular to me. I knew that everyone has this same potential, this same possibility of repeating and reproducing these exalted spiritual experiments—because the Self is already fully present in everyone!

Wilber goes on to say that, as the wisdom traditions tell us, Spirit is the essence of the entire process of evolution itself, at all levels of the universe. At the highest stages of this process, Spirit becomes conscious of itself and begins to recognize its own true nature.[12] A number of authors have spoken of this. One I have found particularly compelling is Eckhart Tolle, who is introducing millions to their own capacity for higher consciousness through his writings. Too often, these higher states can seem mystical, remote, even unobtainable to seekers. But these states aren't remote at all; they're already within us—again, get to know the consciousness *you already have*! And they aren't unattainable either; the process of spiritual realization has been reproduced and repeated again and again over the centuries. It's just that you have to be willing to participate intensely and sincerely in the experiment. When you don't understand something or trust its validity, it's hard to participate intensely. This is why a seeker must—"Come see." And to experience the ultimate results, you have to have a guide.

The final insight that I'll mention from this section of Wilber's writing is the need for the seeker to integrate and consolidate after peak experiences of pure Awareness. He says that these experiences are enormously exciting, and yet what matters most is the seeker's development and evolution. [13] Personally, I found it very helpful to integrate my own deepest insights and highest experiences with the teachings of the wisdom tradition. I often did this with the help of the talks and writings of Baba Muktananda and Gurumayi, who both advocate contemplating your spiritual experiences—over and over again. Both also provided examples of Saints and sages from all the wisdom traditions to assist these contemplations. And both are only concerned with the inner experience of the Self—never with religion. I've found that one of the best ways to integrate my own experiences of the witnessing consciousness is to study the teachings of those who are well-versed in this subject, those who have themselves studied, contemplated, and experienced the highest possibility. And, rarest of all, mastered this mystical state. As I have said many times, I have been helped tremendously by the writings of Maurice Nicoll, P. D. Ouspensky, St. John of the Cross, Ken Wilber, Franklin M Wolff, Plato, Jacob Needleman, Karen Armstrong, and so many others.

In fact, this fourth and final Book is meant to help the reader integrate and put into context what they've read and are hopefully checking out for themselves. The idea of reading other people's experiences and understandings of the spiritual path is not a substitute for your own contemplation; it is an aid. Reading what others have to say about spiritual experience and inner *work* is a way of reminding us of our own; it's an inspiration to us to further explore our inner knowledge. In my own experience, the most profound insights have always come from within myself, and real consolidation involves taking the time to recall these insights, to record them, and to consider how they fit with the spiritual teachings and apply them to my life, minute by minute and hour by hour. The watcher of our own mind is always available and is so pure and alert that it can provide the essential insights that will substantially increase your understanding of yourself and others. This happens with no thought involved, no cultural conditioning, no identification or contraction to distort—just pure awareness unfolding toward higher understanding. Again, this is how inner transformation takes place, and in the West, this is what is missing and has been missing from our understanding of human consciousness for eons. But for those who really want to know and are ready to listen, the information is readily available.

The contemporary philosopher Deepak Chopra writes about the role of the inner witness in his book *The Book of Secrets:*

"The silent observer is the simplest version of me, the one that just is... There is real joy in finding this version of yourself because it is already at home. It lives above the fray, totally untouched by the war of opposites. When people say that they are seeking, it is this level of themselves that is calling to them in its silent, untroubled way." [14]

Witness Consciousness

Chopra goes on to speak about the importance of being and staying connected with your own center, pointing out that the ego's sense of "I," "me," and "mine" is false. Chopra asks, *"If the ego is not our center, what is?"* Deepak points out that the center of our being is not a place but is an experience, and that experience is a focus of attention. I understand this to be our innermost awareness, our consciousness itself. This is the awareness of the observing Self, the silent witness. As Chopra explains:

"You can't summon the silence witness, but you can place yourself close to it by refusing to get lost in your own creation.[15]*"*

In my awakening, I saw again and again that getting lost in your creation, in your mind's comings and goings, is extremely easy to do and cancels whatever level of mindfulness you have been able to achieve. Mindfulness—our witnessing-awareness-functions from a position of detachment. Thus, we find that this deeper focus of attention (what I would call another, more conscious level of awareness) is always calm, alert, and detached. He calls this second or deeper perspective our center and says that it is a close encounter with the silent witness.[16] I was struck by his description because it is so similar to the way I've described what I experienced during and since my own awakening.

What I find particularly significant here is Chopra's implicit point that the second perspective, or witnessing-awareness of the mind, is available to us through our interest and effort. Becoming firmly immersed in the witness of your own mind can put you into a state of awareness where the one silent Witness in all may reveal itself to you. Therefore, the sincere seeker who truly wants an experience of their own great Self should make whatever effort is needed to become aligned with the witness of their mind so that they are actually watching their participation in life and not playing in the pathways of their minds. This is, of course, easier said than done, and my advice to those who truly wish to experience their own divine Self is that they need to make this wish, as G called it, their number one priority. And they should get initiation from a genuine spiritual master. I speak more about that at the end of this section.

In the introduction to *The Book of Secrets*, Chopra begins by mentioning that the greatest hunger in our lives is not for money or success; it is for the secret that is hidden inside of ourselves. He says that in the ancient wisdom traditions, this quest is likened to searching for a "pearl beyond price" and that this is said to be accomplished by plunging deep into one's being. As I've said, when I first experienced my true Self, I instinctively knew that this was what these traditions were referring to, and I also knew that my unrelenting desire for true understanding was the primary reason I'd been given this Divine experience. Chopra also says here that he takes the New Testament literally when it says, *"Ask, and you shall receive, Knock and the door will be opened.*" I believe that Chopra is saying that when you truly want to know the highest Truth, it can and will happen for you if you sincerely Seek. This is my understanding as well. I also believe that, like myself, he is saying, "*One of the best ways of plunging deep within is to become acquainted with the witness of our own mind.*" [17]

To put it another way, one of the oldest, most popular, and most efficacious ways to satisfy the deep hunger we have to experience the profound beauty and depth of our own lives is through the practice known as meditation!

11
Meditation

I EXPERIENCED MY TRUE SELF, the great Spirit within, through the open-eyed meditation known as self-remembering, even though I had absolutely no awareness of witness consciousness, no expectations of this practice, and no knowledge that it is a form of meditation. Thus, I experienced the goal of meditation, the goal of the spiritual journey, without knowing that I was meditating and without any particular desires or beliefs pushing me forward. Again, I was only looking for a deeper understanding. I wasn't looking for the Self because I was completely unaware of its existence, and yet when I experienced It, I knew that It was a natural part of my awareness, and the essence of my own being. Thus, I know from direct experience that the Self is the essence of what we are as human beings, that this core identity can be known through meditation, and that experiencing it requires no beliefs whatsoever!

I also learned from the practice of self-remembering that the witness is a natural part of everyone's awareness. It is a part of our consciousness that has always been there, but that we have never been taught about. More importantly, we have never been taught how to recognize it. But once you do become familiar with this ability to be the watcher or witness of your own mind, you will see for yourself that it is just you; it is not a philosophical concept, an idea, or a belief. Having naturally discovered the witness state through the dogged desire to simply become consciously present, I recognized that the witness is just a deeper part of myself, and it was due to my becoming familiar with this expanded and unattached state of awareness that allowed me to recognize my Self as another aspect of my own consciousness and its capacity for unbounded awareness.

Thus, once again, I know from my own experience that the Self is our Source and Essence. The Self is the true nature of Consciousness. The mystics and saints have said for thousands of years that the way to experience the Self is to become consciously still and quiet, and let your consciousness be drawn inside your being. You have to be conscious of what your habitual mind is up to; you have to be consciously present—you have to *meditate*!

Speaking about the goal of meditation, Baba Muktananda, often described as a master of meditation, put it this way:

"If you want to meditate successfully, you must first understand what it is that you are to meditate on... If you want to reach the Self, you have to meditate on the Self. You have to meditate on the witness within. If you do not understand the witness, you will go in the wrong direction in your meditation." "The truth is that when most people meditate, they do not meditate on the Self. Instead, they

pursue the mind, trying to eradicate its' thoughts... during meditation, something comes up inside. You identify it as a good thought or a bad thought, an image, or a fantasy. The one who makes you aware of the existence of that thought or image... is nothing but the Self, the witness... To know that knower is true meditation." [18]

Learning to observe from the perspective of the witness of your mind is, as I've been saying, an immensely practical form of meditation that can be practiced both in seated meditation and throughout your daily routine.

"The inner witness is of the highest importance, and a meditator should meditate on the inner witness. It is that inner witness, which is the goal, the object of meditation. The sages say that the inner witness is without attribute; it is pure consciousness, the Lord Himself." [19]

The Inner Witness Is Pure Consciousness

Baba Muktananda often spoke about the nature of the witness that the meditator is to focus on:

As I've said, the pure universal Witness is known as the Self. There are a number of places to focus your attention in meditation, and Baba makes it exceedingly clear that he is advocating meditation on one's Self. The experience of your Self, your own divine nature, is the goal of all the wisdom traditions. Baba states that if you're going to reach that goal, you have to meditate on the Self. He and others tell us to focus on the witness because the Self is *"transcendent— beyond thought altogether."* Another spiritual Master from India, Ramana Maharshi, puts it this way:

"Meditation on the Self, which is oneself, is the greatest of all meditations." [20]

But hearing that they should meditate on the Self, their own divine nature, most beginning meditators have no idea what to do, because meditation is so foreign to our culture. Baba explains precisely how to do this by saying that you must meditate on the witness within! In other words, put your attention on the Self that is constantly witnessing your thoughts.

Over the years, I've noticed that most beginners feel that they cannot meditate because their minds will not stop being active, even for a moment. Knowing how this works and how this can result in a wrong understanding and giving up before realizing that they are actually doing fine, let me tell a story about a beginning meditator's conversation with a spiritual Master. After sincerely trying to meditate and finding that his mind would not stop for a second, the novice meditator tells the meditation Master of his experience and asks for help. The Teacher tells him that everything is fine, just keep practicing. The young man responded, no, seriously, I've really tried, and I just can't do it. You've got to help me. Again, the Teacher tells him that everything is fine and to just continue what he has been doing. Once again, the meditator reiterates how sincere his intentions are and how hard he's tried and pleads for help. The Teacher then asks him how he knows he's doing so poorly. He repeats that every time he sits for meditation, his mind just won't stop—which is basically everyone's experience. Then the Teacher asks him, how does he know this? He, feeling a little awkward, replies, *"I just know it, that's what I experience."* The Teacher tells him that this awareness of what his mind is up to shows that he is meditating, just keep focusing on this part that knows what's happening, and in time your mind will quiet down, and you will experience the deeper meditation that you seek.

For me, this story, along with my own, should demystify meditation and allow the beginner to relax and know that as long as they are paying attention, as long as they are consciously present, they are meditating! Again, just get to know the "knower"—the one who knows what's happening, which can be nothing but our own Awareness! Sincerely, the only tough thing that one has to do is to remember to stay present, be the Witness that is always beyond and separate from thought. Don't be carried away by your mind's comings and goings!

Don't Fight with Your Mind—Just Watch Its Play

Both Muktananda and Gurdjieff, my first two spiritual Masters, tell us that in meditation, you should neither wrestle with your thoughts, analyze them, or judge your efforts. They're saying, don't fight with your mind, and don't fret over its unruly nature. Because then you are identifying with your thoughts instead of just watching the play of the mind and, most importantly, getting to know the one who is capable of watching that play.

Another thing that we are not taught to contemplate is: Who is capable of easily uncovering our individual ego and its conditioning? We see the ill effects of conditioned ego in others, but leave it at that with no further curiosity or contemplation! What most of us have done for the majority of our lives is to identify with all of our thoughts and emotions, having no clue that we have any other choice! As I've shown, what we need to do is place our attention on the witness of all those thoughts and emotions. As you learn to keep your sense of self focused on the one who is watching your thoughts, in time, you'll see that the witness never becomes trapped by your thoughts. Never! Being trapped is synonymous with being *identified* with your thoughts, which keep you bound to your elementary ego and all of its *stuff*.

The paradox of being told not to wrestle with our thoughts is that the great beings of all of the wisdom traditions tell us that stillness of mind is of the greatest importance on the spiritual path. They say that if a seeker can transcend the restlessness of the mind, they can experience their own Self. Of course, as anyone who has tried to still their own mind has experienced—and as these same teacher's acknowledge, achieving stillness of mind is enormously difficult. Based on my own experience, I believe the easiest way to still the mind is for the seeker to put all their efforts into keeping their sense of self in the witness. This is so much more natural than trying to force the mind to stop thinking. The witness is naturally silent, vigilant, and focused. The witness isn't affected by the mind's unruliness or restlessness even for a moment! You just have to persevere to experience this Truth for yourself.

If a beginning seeker tries to stop their thoughts, they will find they cannot. And if they try to force their mind to be one-pointed on a candle flame, or some other image, I feel that they are setting themselves up for frustration and likely failure. Such is fine for one when just starting, but why not just focus on *the one who knows* what is going on in your awareness? My experience of getting to know the witness, which is authentic and practical meditation, is a less frustrating and more enlightening practice and one that's accessible to everyone. And with the right attitude, it can be quite entertaining and humorous!

And even if you could hold your mind still as an act of pure will, your understanding wouldn't mature as quickly as it does by being consciously present during your daily routine. And if one learns to hold their mind still, via will, that has the possibility of enhancing their ego instead of uncovering it! Every spiritual Master I'm familiar with—the Buddha, Shankara, Ramana, the Saivite Sages, and my Siddha Gurus Baba and Gurumayi, to name a few—encourage seekers to pursue uninterrupted mindfulness. This is true meditation, and this is meant to be our natural state.

Our natural state is pure vigilant awareness, not the conditioned awareness that we end up with by the time we become young adults. But, since we've lost touch with the traditions that speak of this situation—**this predicament**—these superimpositions overlaid onto our pure awareness seem to be *us*. We are not able to recognize this *situation* until we are told about our witnessing capacity and shown how to experience this for ourselves. Again, no beliefs are required; only effort and perseverance are required. As we see worldwide, cultural conditioning is unimaginably pervasive, deeply ingrained, rigid, and almost impossible to uproot through education and logic—no matter how good. We've seen this time and time again and are still seeing it vividly today, pretty much worldwide, and it's usually quite ugly. In other words, thoughts can't uproot centuries of conditioned beliefs or the feeling that we are our thoughts and emotions that comprise our own individual lives. But meditation, our ability to take the stance of the witness, the stance of pure awareness itself, has the power to emancipate us from our conditioned and limited thoughts and emotions—our habitual mind. Meditation—our witnessing-awareness, can uproot these ideas and beliefs because the part of us observing them is separate from them and not the least bit attached to them. You, as the witnessing-awareness, realize that *you* have indeed been heavily conditioned, but the pure awareness that you are looking with—looking from; has not and is not! Again, the pure witness is never *identified, attached,* or *conditioned.* Period!

This transformation of identity, from habitual thoughts to the pure awareness of the observer of these thoughts, is the best, most natural, and practically the only way to uproot and move beyond the limiting conditioning that every human being must go through in order to reach adulthood! This form of meditation allows us to experience our observing awareness and our ability to be consciously present. We need to become familiar with all these aspects of ourselves in order to resist the old ingrained mental and emotional habits and quit taking them as *Me*! This is the beginning of *awakening.* This is why all of the wisdom or esoteric traditions taught and encouraged meditation, because the saints and sages of these Traditions knew the nature of human consciousness. Thus, they also knew that in order to align with our natural state, you have to uproot and shed these limited and conditioned views of yourself and your culture's beliefs. The greatest Teachers have told us that meditation has the ability to empty the mind of its delusionary contents. Now, hopefully, you can understand how this is accomplished through your own witnessing-awareness! So, for me, the word *meditation* has been misunderstood or better yet, not understood in its higher and intended meaning and potential.

Our consciousness already has this ability as a natural aspect of our normal awareness. We just have to learn how to recognize it and how to connect with it. It takes some effort, but so does almost everything else in growing up, in becoming a mature adult. Meditation, as I'm describing here, is the most natural way to unfold our potential, to unfold our being as it was designed to do, so we can eventually experience our Self, our truest Essence and its Divine Nature. No BELIEFS required! Remember, this Divine Consciousness knows how to unfold itself—there is nothing to figure out—just stay present in the witness.

Don't Be Anxious or Feel Hopeless—Don't Judge

This practice of vigorously trying to stay present and in touch with the deeper level of awareness known as the witness is unquestionably demanding. Its reward, however, to one who is persistent, is a much higher level of awareness, contentment, and freedom. What is it that contracts and enslaves us? Being anxious, envious, fault-finding and judging others and ourselves as well. Also, lusting for or wanting something or someone and feeling left out or underappreciated are only a few of the ingrained traits of the immature ego that begin to be exposed and fall away for the person who makes mindfulness a part of their daily routine. Once I got in touch with this much more conscious and freer level of awareness and experienced the immense benefits that came with this focus, the lightness and freedom that came with it, I could easily accept the validity and truly amazing practicality of this practice. The wisdom traditions tell us not to gossip—why? When you are gossiping, you are identified with your and the other people's thoughts, not the watcher of these thoughts! Your sense of self is in the wrong place. I believe this is the answer to why we should not gossip, judge or be anxious. Similarly, it's only the immature ego that's interested in these kinds of thoughts. A person with a pure heart who sees the divine in all is not interested in gossiping or judging others. I realized that this teaching is not strictly a moral issue—it's a question of where your sense of self is—are *you* your thoughts, or the awareness they are arising into?

My experience was: once I experienced witness-consciousness as myself, there was no going back. *Ignorance* means not knowing something, and in this case, once your ignorance is uncovered, you 'cannot return to the state of not knowing, even if you wanted to! Seeing for myself the pervasive cultural conditioning and unruliness of my mind, from the detachment of the witness, was indeed the beginning of uncovering and going beyond the ignorance of my rigid beliefs, etc. It was easy and natural, no beliefs or assumptions required, to know, to directly experience, that I was the observing awareness, the conscious presence that was witnessing my habitual thoughts and emotions. This radical change in perspective, in understanding and expanded awareness comes from simply turning within. Watching yourself like a hawk allows you to begin seeing how bound or free you really are. This is not radical, not mysticism, not foolish, nor a waste of time. It's the beginning of meditation! As you do this ancient practice, you will come to know the witnessing awareness better and better, and you will know—for sure—that you are becoming freer and freer. And, even more importantly, that this consciousness-awareness is your true essence—your true identity.

Being at this miraculous level of awareness cleanses and purifies your mind by exposing its unnoticed and unconscious patterns. These are almost always culturally conditioned and egoistic in nature, and some are karmic as well. Directly seeing these tendencies and seeing that they are different and separate from the real "you,"—the one who is aware of them, allows you to stop identifying with them and, in time, leave them behind and become free of them by transcending them. As I experienced, this is a slow process, but it happens naturally—because human awareness is made for unfoldment. But, as I experienced, this can be quite fast when it becomes a priority and grace smiles upon you. Perseverance and sincerity are what the sages tell us draw the grace.

Remember, it is a general principle of consciousness that increased awareness yields increased understanding. Such is the nature of—and natural evolution of—consciousness.

Do You Love Your Mind?

Now let's turn to a benefit of witness-consciousness that's not so obvious. Deepak Chopra says that he has asked many people, *"Do you love your mind?"* He says that the answer is always no. [21.] I find this very interesting. Many people that I have spoken to feel that their minds are too active, too emotional, too needy, and not easy to satisfy, and this, too, I find interesting, but not surprising or bewildering.

People's attitude towards their mind suggests to me that many of us are in touch with the same level or aspect of awareness that the spiritual Master called to the attention of the novice meditator, who knew that his mind wouldn't stop thinking. This underlying awareness is, of course, what I've been calling the witness as well as the knower, mindfulness, open-eyed meditation and so on. People's attitude toward their mind shows me that they are aware of what Gurdjieff called their predicament, what the Buddha called human suffering. It also seems that they are aware that they need help. Unlike the novice meditator, however, most people do not know that there is an ancient and reliable remedy for their dilemma!

Personally, I think that people would be more likely to participate—to practice witnessing their mind in their daily lives—if they would only realize that they are already familiar with the witness and with the deeper awareness that it represents. And more familiar with the esoteric Teachings that speak about this state; fairy tales, myths, and some Christian parables, even if they only recognize these vaguely. Often, patients would come in to my office saying, *"My mind just won't stop worrying about what you're going to do to me today—even though I know everything is going to be fine."* Their awareness that their mind and or emotions are out of kilter is absolutely correct, and where did this awareness come from? It didn't come from the mind, as I'm describing it. The mind is what's being observed. The observations came from the witnessing-awareness, the inner presence. I think that many have had this experience, and whenever we do, we know that we are hearing the truth! In other words, our deeper awareness is aware of the truth of the matter, whereas our fearful mind is not!

At some level of awareness, we know that drugs and alcohol are not the answer; these alter the mind but only temporarily. It is only by circumventing the mind, by going directly to the consciousness that underlies the mind, that one can observe the mind, which gives the opportunity to successfully deal with the mind. Shifting your identity to the witness, as I've described, is actually transcending the mind, which means genuinely being detached from its "stuff," which is the reason it's successful and lasting. Once again, no beliefs required!

If we do nothing, the mind will not heal itself; in fact, it will probably get worse. If you don't discipline children, they generally get worse. All of this should make a seeker want to pursue meditation, pursue this deeper part of themselves that the wisdom traditions have spoken about for thousands of years.

I think that most of us have an intuition that there has to be more to life than our minds show us. There has to be a more satisfying stance that we can take in relation to ourselves, and that allows us to continue to participate in inner growth and transformation. And allows us to feel naturally and wholesomely connected to others. The witness is this stance—this conscious awareness. The witnessing-awareness is completely free from all negativity, period! This is another reason why focusing on the witness, in both traditional and open-eyed meditation, has the power to cleanse the mind of anxiety, judgments, etc., bring you into a closer connection with your essential nature, your true Spirit, the Self.

This is what inner transformation truly is, and how one's conscious presence allows one's joy, contentment, and love to manifest in a completely natural way.

Meditation Is Natural—But Doesn't Happen on Its Own

While getting in touch with the inner witness through the practice of mindfulness is a natural process and is available to all, it does not happen automatically. As Gurdjieff and others point out, this is something that requires a voluntary and persistent effort. Those who are most prepared to make this effort are those who have persevered in sustained self-inquiry and who are in touch with themselves enough to have answered yes to some of the questions in the Preface and Introduction. It is especially important that the seeker has a distinct feeling that there must be something more meaningful in life than their material existence and what their religion and philosophy have shown them thus far.

I want to reiterate that this is a process, a consciously chosen learning atmosphere, a learning opportunity connected with the ancient quest to "know thyself," and as this endeavor continues to expand and unfold, you are perpetuating your own inner transformation. Instead of a forceful overthrow, it's a voluntary change in your sense of self, in your identity, that is readily available for the purpose of increased understanding and emancipation.

Meditation

It is my belief that there are many mature seekers, due to the complexity and demands of modern-day life, who are both longing and ready for this quest for direct insight and for more practical and satisfying understanding that requires no beliefs—only conscious participation. I believe, as well, that the number of such seekers will increase with each generation. As I said earlier, it is for these people in particular that I've written this book. I am aware from conversations with acquaintances, seekers, and from the media, that many have some wrong ideas about what meditation is, what mindfulness is, what it's for, and how to actually do it. I feel that it's important to clear up a few of these limited and naïve ideas.

One of the primary problems today is that many people, even people who call themselves meditators, think that the point of meditation is simply relaxation. Meditation can, indeed, be relaxing, but a sincere seeker meditates for much more than repose, as I've been saying!

Too many people's image and understanding of meditation is limited to sitting with your legs crossed and your eyes closed, trying to keep your mind still by focusing it on a single object or image, be it a flower or the image of your chosen Deity. This is a classic view of meditation and, for many, their only image of meditation. It is one that many Westerners are not drawn to because it seems irrelevant and meaningless, which occurs due to the fact that they don't know what they are trying to achieve. They are usually expecting something other than themselves, versus an expansion and deepening of their own awareness. All of this results in it being dry, boring, and difficult and thus, often abandoned.

But the essence and heart of genuine meditation, as I have been sharing, is mindfulness, which is recognizing the witness that can observe the machinations of your own mind. An authentic practice like this can open you to a shift in awareness that transforms your understanding, not only of yourself and others, but also of consciousness itself! Once seekers realize this, they can see and experience for themselves that meditation has enormous relevance and meaning for them, and it has absolutely nothing to do with religion!

Another common misunderstanding is that seekers may think that meditation is a religion or that it is against a religion. Neither is the case. As Gurdjieff says, meditation is "real psychology." Meditation is the true study of our mind, of the consciousness that we already have, because it allows us to uncover the essence and potential of human awareness. From my own experience, the shift in perspective and awareness that comes in the witness state is anything but dry and boring! For sincere seekers, witness-consciousness is inspiring and enlightening; this state gives you instant insight into the workings of your mind and the nature of your conscious awareness. And it transforms your experience and understanding in this very moment! What else but meditation has this power? And, still, it is just you looking at you. It really is that simple—try it! *Experience it*, as we used to say.

This form of inner focus that I'm calling self-remembering or meditation does require major effort, but we have to bear in mind just how sweet its fruits are. As a direct result of my efforts to participate in meditation, I experience enthusiasm for life, a deeper understanding of it as it unfolds, gratitude for the gifts I receive and for feeling the awe and mystery of my own life and the life force itself. The benefits of all this transcend mere words. And thanks to my ongoing efforts, I feel that it is nearly impossible to become stuck in my ego for long. The benefits of my "work," as G called it, make it clearly worth the effort.

Besides, what is the alternative? Should I just allow my ego to run the show and let my mind be at the mercy of outside influences and its stealthy cultural conditioning? In the words of the Persian poet Rumi:

"The breeze at dawn has secrets to tell you
Don't go back to sleep." [23]

Quick Results Are Available to Those Who Truly Want Them

If you feel that you must have quick results from meditation, then I suggest you take a week off, go off alone somewhere pleasant and put all your energy and effort into being consciously present in yourself through the awareness of the witness. In short, get into and stay in witness-consciousness.

You can follow my example in whatever way is most natural for you as long as you truly give yourself to this focus from the moment you awaken until you go to sleep. If you do this with determined effort, in all likelihood, you will advance just as radically and joyously as I did. Though again, it will happen in your own way. As Ramana Maharshi tells us:

"Remain aware of yourself, and all else will be known." [24]

One of the oldest and highest definitions of meditation says, *"True meditation is remembering the Self during all of your activities."* For me, this is the essence of G's self-remembering and Ramana's quote as well! Another definition that describes my own experience of self-remembering beautifully is: Meditation is when consciousness is fully active, vigilant, and consciously present, but the mind is still and quiet. One of the most amazing aspects of this revolutionary stance is that the change that comes, the transformation that is experienced, doesn't just disappear. With continued effort, you can retain this miraculous new perspective and continue to expand and build on it as long as you are willing. For me, this is a combination of a shift in identity, and the fact that understanding becomes part of us, it's not something we remember as in beliefs.

Like scientific discovery, once your understanding has advanced, you can't go back—you can only go forward!

Baba Muktananda said he came to the West to start a meditation revolution to enable people to experience their own divine Self. One definition of revolution is a fundamental change, which in itself implies an essential change in perspective, in motivation, and in perceived ability and potential. I know that the most fundamental of changes occurs when we are conscious of ourselves, are consciously present in the witness. For a genuine seeker, this is a personal meditation revolution—a personal revolution in understanding, because once you possess the perspective of the witness, your identity expands, and the pure intelligent and loving awareness that accompanies this state will inspire essential changes in understanding that are indeed revolutionary.

I want to reiterate that for the spiritual journey, it's helpful to have the guidance of a genuine spiritual Master. There is a lot, however, that you don't need. You don't need a new job, a new spouse, a new place to live; you just need a change in your perspective—a change in your level of awareness. You need to change the way you're looking at everything; you need to shift your focus inside yourself to the deeper and more expanded awareness that's waiting for you there! If you just do this, you will radically change your understanding, and therefore, your life.

This is the master key to the inner transformation, the change in understanding that many long for and truly need.

A Teaching of Kashmir Shaivism

As part of this rewrite, I've decided to speak about this little-known teaching because it describes my spiritual awakening so wonderfully and seems like the perfect way to bridge this chapter on meditation with the one on the Self to follow. I call the sutra that I'm going to share a teaching, instead of a philosophy, because I'm told that Pythagoras coined the term philosophy and defined it as: the love of wisdom, not the possession of it. Kashmir Shaivism is a teaching that is in possession of the Knowledge of the Self. It says that the Self, supreme Reality, is Being-Awareness that is always Self-aware. Yes, my experience exactly.

This understanding flourished in Kashmir, India, in the eighth and ninth centuries and was made known to me through the efforts of Baba Muktananda and then through Gurumayi. Also, the sincere efforts of Jaideva Singh, who has authored a series of books on Shaivism that have been invaluable in helping me gain a deeper understanding of Shaivism.

Two of the primary teachings of this group of mostly householder Sages are: If you want to know the highest Truth and Reality, you must know that through your own consciousness, not from something outside of you. Secondly, the most efficient way to experience the Self is via the dissolution of thoughts, which is similar to Patanjali's sutra, which tells us to still the thoughts and emotions of our mind. The Saivite sages tell us that it is our continuous, mostly uncalled-for, mental activity that results in us being a bound soul who is ignorant of its true Self. But this description refers only to our habitual state of mind and its incessant thinking, which is primarily about our individual, personal life. It does not refer to our underlying pure awareness—the witness that is free from this constant chatter.

Their teaching that is essentially perfectly in accord with my experience of awakening says, *"When a seeker keeps his mind on universal consciousness—the pure silent awareness of the witness, restraining thoughts through intense effort, willpower, and non-identification with his habitual thoughts, he becomes used to regarding the witnessing—awareness as his real self, his real essence. Then, if he continues to follow this practice, in a short time, he will attain absorption in the Self."*

Reading this years after my awakening, I knew that these sages had the same experience I had about twelve hundred years after them, by a very similar practice that I knew as self-remembering. I do want to be clear that I did not regard the witness as the real me through being told to do so. As my account shows, Gurdjieff never said anything except, *"Be present in your awareness."* It was completely due to the nature of the witnessing-awareness itself; its clarity, intelligence, and its separation and detachment from my habitual thoughts (all of this without any beliefs), that I took the witnessing-awareness to be my essential self! Shaivism describes this awareness as being prior to thought, a perspective that I had not truly seen at first, but is a totally accurate way to describe the awareness that thoughts arise from!

Another thing that struck me was the statement, *"In a short time!"* At the time of my awakening, I truly believed that this was possible for many; you didn't have to be special, because the Self is already within you—awaiting discovery. Years later, based on lots of research, I knew that with traditional spiritual practices, including meditation, the experience of the Self did not usually take place in a short time, and most often, not at all. Unfortunately, I have not inspired anyone to do this practice intently for eight or nine days to see what their experience is. So, I still don't know. But I believe that a person's life and understanding would be permanently changed for the better—unimaginably better—if they make this effort.

12
The SELF

AS I said at the beginning of Book IV, the witness, meditation, and the supreme Witness, the Self, are dynamically interrelated. They are not three separate things. As I've indicated many times, the Self is the goal of meditation and the goal of witness-consciousness. The Self is our true and divine Nature, the Supreme SPIRIT within, the source and essence of everyone and everything! Gurumayi has said:

"The Self, the witness, brings everything together and keeps it in check. So become the witness. As you do this, you merge into the Self." [25]

For me, it was indeed the witness that brought everything together that helped me answer my long-held questions and began to exponentially increase my understanding. It accomplished this, as shared, by allowing my identity to connect with a level of awareness that is free from attachment, allowing me to be able to receive the Self. Another way that this manifested for me was a certainty that all I had to do was stay "awake" in the witness and everything would unfold as needed. And it did! This certainty and trust were just part of this deeper and purer state of the Witness. And sure enough, without needing to figure anything out, I had the greatest good fortune to have a profound experience of my true Self.

As I've said, and I don't mind repeating: the Self is the same in all, the Truth is one. All the enlightened masters of the wisdom traditions are consistent on a number of teachings of the Self. The nature of the Self is existence, awareness, and bliss! The esoteric teaching that God is an extraordinary and miraculous inner experience, that cannot be contained in words, is a perfect description of my own awakening—and the main impetus behind my attempting to record it in words! This long-known fact that the Self cannot be expressed in words is why I want to provide some more information concerning this forgotten Truth. Also, to remind 'Westerners that the Self, the Transcendent, has been known about and a part of our culture for thousands of years.

The Experience of Your Divine Self Is the Highest Truth

In trying to describe the indescribable, I'm going to turn to the great ones whose teachings I've studied. For instance, the Christian mystic Meister Eckhart, a German friar who lived in the thirteenth and fourteenth centuries, had this to say about the ineffable:

"God is transcendent—beyond names and forms. The ultimate and highest leave-taking is leaving God for God. Leave your notion of God for an experience which transcends all notions." [26]

Gurumayi has expressed the inexpressible with this statement:

"Once you see the face of the Truth, even for a second, you can never forget it. In that brief moment, the Self fills your heart with its own essence, which is ambrosia. It fills your mind with its essence, which is knowledge, and your understanding of life is permanently altered. Even one glimpse of that Reality is enough." [27]

Both of these statements express my experience of the Self perfectly! As I've said, I found the experience of the Self so miraculous and holy that my understanding of myself, others, and God was permanently changed. This revelation was all encompassing and yes—Spirit is unquestionably immortal. It has never changed, and I have never questioned or doubted it. For almost a half-century, the pursuit of the Self, in a variety of ways, has been my passion. Like many others who have had a profound experience of the Transcendent, it is the only thing that truly interests me. That may sound restricted, but you have to remember that the Self is the source and essence of everything, so it is not the least bit limiting! From my research, it appears that this unrelenting interest and enthusiasm are true for practically everyone who has had a profound experience of this divine State. Yes, *your life is permanently changed.*

My experiences of the Self have allowed me to directly know, the direct knowing I spoke of earlier, the truth of many teachings of the wisdom traditions concerning this blessed State. In fact, each time I've had the good fortune to experience the Self, these teachings have been self-evident. As Franklin M. Wolffe expressed it, *"it's knowledge in identity."* The teachings are contained in the State and have nothing to do with beliefs or conclusions. Here are some statements I've written based on the direct Knowledge and insights I've experienced from within—when I've been immersed in my Self.

The experience of the Self is the purpose of one's birth, the purpose of one's life. To be truly alive, truly awake, one must know the Self.

Knowledge of the Self is the greatest of all gifts, the most precious grace, and the highest Truth.

The Self is our truest nature, and it is Divine. It is the source and essence of everyone and everything.

When you are in touch with your Self, you see—[experience] the Self in all.

The one supreme Consciousness is the Self in all.

What amazes me is that these could be verses in the Upanishads or any other of a hundred inspired texts. The wisdom of these scriptures can be found within each of us.

Your Divine Self Is Already Attained

When I first experienced my Self, I knew that it was inherent within me. It had always been there waiting to reveal itself. As Baba Muktananda said repeatedly:

"The Self is already attained." [28]

Early in my initial experience of my Self, I could see—again as a given—that the reason I and others had not connected with the Self previously was primarily due to two factors: the incessant chattering of my mind and not being aware of the deeper state of the witness. The Christian mystic Meister Eckhart expresses the insight that the Self is already attained in this passage:

"The treasure of the Kingdom of God has been hidden by time and multiplicity... But in the measure that the soul can separate itself from this multiplicity, to that extent it reveals within itself the Kingdom of God. Here, the soul and the Godhead are one." [29]

The essence of Eckhart's teachings or mysticism, as some refer to his sharing of his *inner experiences*, is the *oneness* of the individual soul and God. For me, this is just a reiteration of all the Great Beings that have truly experienced the one Self within. Again, the purpose of the spiritual quest, the purpose of performing spiritual practices, is to directly experience the Truth that is already within oneself. This is the Teaching that every sincere seeker must accept so that they can pursue the spiritual path in earnest. It is one of the few tenets of spiritual life that I feel you need to accept by faith. Faith in the Teachings, the Teachers, and in yourself! Your pure Heart. If you do, you will perform the practice of meditation that will prepare you for, and open you up to, the experience you seek.

The Peace and Bliss That Surpasses All Understanding

Possibly the most difficult aspect of the Self to describe is the feeling—the "experience"—of supreme bliss, contentment, deep, deep peace and the natural enthusiasm and pure joy that constitute this state. There is no way to really describe these feelings that come with the experience of the Self because they aren't the sort of feelings that we're used to. They are beyond the senses and the mind; thus, we have no words for such delicate feelings. They are not typical emotions, and they have nothing to do with the gratification of the senses or the ego, which is where the majority of our positive feelings come from.

During my initial experience of the Self, I was amazed to find that this incredibly blissful state, the greatest joy of my life, had nothing to do with any event or circumstances outside of me. It was all coming from within—radiating out of the pure "One" within. As I contemplated this unique state, I became aware that all of my previous experiences of joy had been based on thought, emotions, or sensual gratification. The pure love and joy associated with the Self are unconditional. No conditions or reasons needed—period! Saints, mystics, and sages of all traditions have spoken of this indescribable bliss. There is a great number of evidence that the purity and bliss of the Self is a universal experience.

Many of these saints, including Muktananda, tell us that true knowledge, direct Knowledge, always releases bliss; if knowledge does not release bliss, it is not true Knowledge. The statements that I shared concerning my experiences of the Self were all accompanied by this miraculous bliss. Muktananda said that the highest form of meditation is to live with *right understanding*. The understanding he refers to, I believe, is the direct Knowledge and understanding that can only come from the Self. Therefore, right understanding is intimately connected to the Witness state—to the insights and experiences that come through meditation. I mention this to remind the seeker that the goal of meditation, the goal of the spiritual quest, is to experience your Self—not just have a new way to think! Everything else that I've described comes with that experience! Now I will move from my own experiences of the Self to those of others, as is expressed in spiritual commentaries from around the world. I am not attempting to provide a thorough overview, just to provide *some* context for what may be an unfamiliar subject and an extraordinary experience that transcends words. I turn to the early Christians called Gnostics, to the Greek philosophers Plato and Plotinus, to the sages of Kashmir Shaivism and to world mythology.

The Gnostics and *Gnosis*

Gnosis, the Greek word chosen by a group of second-century Christians to represent some level of experience of the Self, is translated as *knowledge*. This is not rational knowledge but direct Knowledge, the knowledge that comes through intuition, insight, or revelation. There is no doubt that *gnosis* refers to the Knowledge that comes when you're immersed in the transcendent—in your Self. The early Christians who spoke of this direct knowledge were known as Gnostics. In the introduction to her book, *The Gnostic Gospels*, Elaine Pagels, an authority on this Christian sect, says that the Gnostics used the word *gnosis* to mean *insight*, the understanding that comes from knowing oneself, from knowing human nature and human destiny. Yet, to know oneself, at the deepest level, is simultaneously to know God; this is the secret of *gnosis.30* Pagels quotes the Gnostic teacher Monoimus, who says:

"Abandon the search for God... Look for Him by taking yourself as the starting point. Learn who it is within you who makes everything His own and

says, My God, my mind, my thoughts… If you carefully investigate these matters, you will find Him in yourself." [31]

When I first read Pagels' book in 1983, I could see that many of these Gnostics' experiences of the Self were genuine. The descriptions of their experiences and the knowledge gained from this pure connection were perfectly resonant with my own. One of the points they made concerns ultimate authority. The Gnostics, along with everyone else who has had a genuine experience of the Self, understand that ultimate authority lies within, within the one true Self in all, not in the man-made rules of religion! As Heracleon, one of the Gnostic teachers quoted by Pagels, says:

People are first led to believe in the Savior through others, but when they become mature, they no longer rely on mere human testimony but instead discover their own immediate relationship with the Truth itself. [32]

Yes, this is similar to Meister Eckhart's experience of the oneness of the individual soul and the supreme Soul, which is *gnosis*. One of the Gnostics' main teachers, Valentinus, teaches that all who have received *gnosis* have transcended the church's teaching and authority. And that a person's own experience takes precedence over all traditions—even Gnostic tradition! Yes, forty years after first reading this truth, this teaching, I—more than ever, know it to be the Truth. It's not surprising that the Gnostics were thought to be heretics by Orthodox Christians. What surprised me was to learn that these same Gnostics also taught that it is fine for the orthodox to advance their own teachings because the Gnostics believed that most people are not ready to pursue *gnosis*. I agreed forty years ago and still do, as I've said, many more are ready, even though a lot of them don't realize it because it's been misunderstood for centuries.

I also feel that the Gnostics advanced understanding, displayed in knowing that most are not ready for inner work, only comes from an authentic experience of the Self. In G's terminology, they had much higher levels of being due to expanded awareness. Obviously, the orthodox church authorities were not as understanding, and such is still the case today—worldwide. Modern scholarship into the early church fathers shows that many were a lot like our self-righteous fundamentalists throughout the world today. I know of no orthodox traditions— no traditions, for instance, that follow only a literal interpretation of sacred scripture—that are actually open to the experience of the transcendent, of the Self. And are willing to posit the inner divinity of human beings. This is a major difference between the orthodox traditions and the wisdom traditions. Let me turn, once again, to Meister Eckhart, one of Christianity's greatest mystics and greatest saints, to hear about the authenticity of inner authority:

A Joyous Awakening

Man knows so many things, but he does not know himself... Go into your own ground and learn to know yourself there.[33]

Ms. Pagels tells us that the Gnostics ridiculed those who thought of the Kingdom of God in literal terms. Since literal interpretation of scripture and myths is still the problem, still the mistake that continues to be perpetuated, I want to reiterate the falsity of this *belief—this cultural conditioning—*that is now, as then, not allowed to be questioned. Pagels, acknowledging this misunderstanding, tells us that the Kingdom is not a place, *"Instead, it is a state of self-discovery."* And then quotes from the gnostic gospel of Thomas.

" ... Rather, the Kingdom is inside you, and it is outside you. When you come to know yourselves ... you will realize that you are the sons of the living Father. But if you will not know yourselves, then you dwell in poverty, and it is you who are the poverty." [34]

I've already shared my own experience of the Truth of the first half of this quote; now I'd like to say a few things about the last half of the quote. By not participating in the *"Quest to Know Thyself,"* you remain at the elementary level of the conditioned ego and its poverty of higher awareness. You are in poverty because your sense of self is still associated with your individual ego and its limited thoughts. And, as Nicoll pointed out, *you* are your understanding! Therefore, *you* are the poverty! It's time to lift yourself out of poverty by the practice of self-remembering and experiencing your more intelligent sense of self.

And this is what Lao Tsu, the father of Taoism, another of the wisdom traditions, had to say around 600 BCE:

"He who knows others is discerning, but he who knows himself is enlightened." [35]

I have noticed that other scholars believe that the Gnostics may have been influenced by the Buddhists and by the Vedantins, because it has been shown that there were trade routes between India and the Greco-Roman world even before Jesus' time. There may indeed have been trade routes, and if the Gnostics had access to esoteric teachings from other traditions, this may have helped them with their contemplations and to express their inner experiences in a better way. But my point is that to speak about these subtle and rare experiences so accurately requires having direct Knowledge of them. The fact of the matter is that all of the wisdom traditions have come from within, from the direct Knowledge of the Self. I know that this, rather than trade routes, is the reason they all have the same Teachings, the same message: Turn within and know your Self. Some of the philosophers of ancient Greece speak of the Self in these universal terms. And these philosophers are also credited with being the initiators of Western thought!—and having a major influence on our religious thought as well.

Plato and the Good

Plato, known as the father of Western philosophy, who lived in the fourth century BCE, speaks much about the philosopher and the goal of philosophy—his terms for the spiritual seeker and the spiritual journey. For instance, in The Apology, thought to be the first of his dialogues, he says:

"God orders me to fulfill the philosopher's mission of searching into myself." [36]

The goal of the philosopher, the object of all knowledge, Plato calls the Good, and this is none other than the Transcendent State—the one Self in all—the Absolute Good.

I'm going to summarize a number of the main points in the best-known of Plato's works, The Republic.[37] I do this in order to describe the parallels between his teachings and the universal truths of the wisdom traditions. In his descriptions of a genuine philosopher, Plato goes to great lengths to establish that his philosopher, his seeker, is only interested in the highest knowledge. Speaking about this highest knowledge, he says this knowledge is related to what is and to knowing what is as it is. 477b This makes sense only when viewed from the transcendent perspective. According to the translator's notes, the Greek word for—know, knowing—implies knowledge by direct experience. Due to the nature of this description, I have no doubt that it refers to the direct experience of gnosis—the direct knowledge of the one Self in all.

Plato defines a philosopher as one who has eyes for eternal, unchanging things, 479e those who have to see the truth, and *"whose hearts are fixed on the true being of each."* 480 Eternal and unchanging both refer to the Spirit, which is the true being of each! And let us remember that philosophy is the love of wisdom, not the possession of wisdom. In the next section, titled *"The Qualities of Character Required in a Philosopher,"* Plato says that philosophers have the capacity to grasp the eternal and immutable 484b and love any branch of learning that reveals eternal reality. 485b Then he says, *"Surely blind is just how you would describe men who have no true knowledge of reality and no clear standard of perfection in their mind. 484c For me, there can be no doubt whatsoever that these references point to the transcendent state and to a seeker of the highest Truth—The One Self in all."*

Here is another description of Plato's philosopher:

Our true lover of knowledge naturally strives for reality, and will not rest content with each set of particulars which opinion takes for reality, but soars… with passion till he grasps the nature of each thing as it is with the mental faculty fitted to do so, that is, with the faculty which is akin to reality, which approaches and unites with it, and begets intelligence and truth as children. 490b

A Joyous Awakening

I find this passage to be an incredibly beautiful and accurate way to speak of the human capacity for transcendent insight, direct Knowledge, and the experience of the essential nature of each thing as it is, which is none other than the one Self in all. Also, how this experience begets the highest truth and understanding, it is important to remember the faculty that makes it possible for us, not only to grasp the essential nature of things, but which is akin to reality and unites with it! This is the pure awareness of the witness, which in its highest expression is the Witness, which is not only akin to the Self, it is One with the Self. These unite through meditation through pure vigilant Awareness itself.

Plato posits that the ultimate goal of knowledge is the Good. I first heard this from M. Nicoll, and it immediately struck me as a great way to describe the transcendent Self, which is the goal of understanding and the experience of your oneness with supreme Reality, which is Goodness itself. When asked to speak about the Good, Plato's teacher Socrates says, *"It is beyond the range of our present inquiry"* 506d but he can tell the inquirer about some things that closely resemble the Good. Plato then presents the simile of the sun, the analogy of the divided line, and the allegory of the cave. From these, we see that Plato's Good is the source of truth, reality, and the human power of understanding. He says that it is right to think of knowledge and truth as being like the Good but wrong to think of either of them as being the Good, whose position must be ranked still higher. 509a Then he says that the Good is not a concept but is beyond that and superior to it in dignity and power. 509b Then, to make sure his description cannot be misunderstood, he has the student in the dialogue say, *"It really must be miraculously transcendent."*

With the analogy of the divided line, Plato is, again, trying to provide some feeling for the Good, which really can't be described because it's miraculously transcendent! The divided line Plato describes is a vertical line divided into four sections, with each section representing one of what he identifies as the four states of mind: intelligence, reason, belief, and illusion. Plato states, again and again, that the highest state of mind—intelligence—is far above reason, and that reason cannot proceed to this higher state. This is classic spiritual teaching at its highest level and something that our culture still does not understand. He continues by saying that from this highest state of consciousness, a person can experience the vision of the Good, but that this is not possible from the level called reason. Reason proceeds only from assumptions to conclusions and not to the first principle, which, for me, is absolutely the transcendent One—the place of the highest understanding, the place of Intelligence. Then Plato says that the highest state of mind can move from assumption to the first principle, which involves no assumptions.510b What I've said all along.

Again, this is classical spiritual teaching, the rational mind cannot know God, cannot know the first principle directly, but deeper states of mind of consciousness that transcend the rational mind can experience the transcendent One, a level of awareness that involves no beliefs or assumptions—Plato's gnosis. I love this section of Plato's presentation because it describes my own experience so precisely and beautifully. As I've said, when the Self first revealed itself to me, I experienced this as a knowing that took place in every cell of my being and had absolutely nothing to do with assumptions or conclusions. Plato refers to his highest state of mind of awareness as intelligence, yes, unbounded and unimagined Intelligence. And Good is a great way to describe the supreme Spirit that is supremely intelligent and supremely Good, thus, beyond description, as is Beauty—another way that Plato refers to the Self.

This idea that the highest knowledge—the Truth, transcends the rational mind is difficult for most Westerners to accept. This is because we are essentially completely dominated by our rational minds and have a poor understanding of sacred literature. Let me quote a medieval mystic to reiterate this point. This comes from St. Bonaventure's The Soul's Journey Into God, in chapter 7, where this thirteenth-century friar is speaking about his experience of the highest knowledge:

"It now remains for our mind… to transcend and pass over, if it is to be perfect, all intellectual activities must be left behind… This, however, is mystical and most secret, which no one knows except him who receives it." [38]

Bonaventure's point, and mine, is that gnosis, which is experienced in pure inner silence and goes far beyond the rational mind, is known only by one who receives the experience as an act of grace. This echoes Plato's and many others' assertion that the vision of the Good is beyond reason.

The last part of Plato's attempt to give a further feeling of the Good, *"That is beyond description,"* is his famous cave analogy, which he begins by saying, *"I want to go on to picture the enlightenment or ignorance of our human condition somewhat as follows."* 514 So, we are definitely talking about states of mind! Plato continues: Imagine an underground cave where men have been kept since childhood and shackled in such a way that they have to look straight ahead and cannot turn their heads. As Plato tells us, this is about enlightenment or ignorance of the human condition. Enlightenment refers to an awareness both of our true Nature and the illusion that we are the body and the ego-dominated thoughts of the mind. Ignorance refers to our unawareness of our true Nature.

Plato's creative image is about people who do not see real forms but only shadows of those forms projected onto the wall of the cave. They cannot see either the light or the real forms because of their position and perspective. They cannot turn around, which means they can't turn within—where Reality lies. Turning within through self-inquiry, contemplation, and meditation is the first step in moving beyond the ignorance of the human condition. The goal, Plato makes clear, is for the philosopher to turn away from illusory shadows and free himself to look straight into the brightest of realities, which is what Plato calls the Good. 518d

As I have been saying throughout, one of the best ways to prepare for and be open to this state is to change your perspective and change the level of your awareness by turning within to the pure witness of your mind. This capacity or faculty, as Plato says, that is innate in each person's mind, is the key to the highest realms of consciousness, the Self, the Good.

Plotinus and the One

Plotinus is a Greek mystic, an enlightened Being, who lived in the third century CE, about seven hundred years after Plato. Due to my experiences of the transcendent, I see a great many similarities between the philosophies of these two influential Greeks. Like Plato, Plotinus had a significant influence on Western philosophy and religion, even though very few are aware of this today. They are not aware of the transcendent influence, period. I also feel a special kinship with Plotinus because I, like him, for lack of a better term, used the word *One* when trying to describe my encounters with the Self for some time after my initial experiences. *One* represented the transcendent, the underlying unity—the source and essence of all, but which can't be described. Of this choice of vocabulary, Plotinus says:

It would be better not to use the word one... The word is useful in getting the inquiry started aright... But then, even this designation must be promptly eliminated because it cannot convey what cannot be known on any hearing. Only the contemplative knows it... 518e V 5 [32] 6 [39]

It is generally accepted that Plotinus was introduced to the practice of contemplation through Plato's writings and, according to his biographer Porphyry, Plotinus *"lifted himself... to the first and all-transcendent divinity."* Scholars familiar with Plotinus' writings say that he, like his peers, the Gnostics, spoke about awakening to the inner Self. And from this highest State, was able to experience being filled with God, being united with God. Like Plato, Plotinus says that all human beings possess the faculty by which they can achieve union with the One that is their highest potential. Again, this refers to our own awareness, our own consciousness that we already have! Plotinus, who says that each of us should attempt to describe our own inner experiences, goes on to say:

The chief difficulty is this: awareness of the One comes to us neither by knowing nor by pure thought that discovers other intelligible things, but by a presence transcending knowledge... This is why Plato says of the One, *"It can neither be spoken nor written about."* 518f VI, 9 [9] 4

Plotinus' descriptions of the One are basically the same as Plato's descriptions of the Good, and yet it is clear to me that Plotinus is neither just agreeing with Plato nor copying him. Plotinus' descriptions are similar because the experience of the Self—of the Transcendent—is similar, depending, of course, on the level of the person's experience. His name for the Self is different from Plato's because the expression of this experience can vary tremendously, depending on the culture, the era, and the personal leanings of the one who is speaking. For centuries now, scholars have been arguing about the fine points of distinction between the philosophies of Plato and Plotinus. That is fine, I suppose, but I think these scholars are missing the philosophers' intent. Plotinus explains this beautifully when he says:

If, nevertheless, we speak of it and write about it, we do so only to give direction, to urge towards that vision beyond discourse. 518g [40]

Despite the attention I'm giving to Plato and Plotinus, I am well aware that they were not the first philosophers to speak of the transcendent One within all. At about the same time as Plato, there was the Buddha, and preceding him there were such illumined sages as Hermes, Orpheus, Lao Tsu, and the mystic sages of the Upanishads. Thus, the transcendent experience and the attempts to speak about it predate what we call ancient times by a millennium or maybe two.

As part of this rewrite, I'm inserting more on Kashmir Shaivism in front of Mythology. Kashmir Shaivism has turned out to be one of my favorite Teachings because it matches my experience of the Transcendent so closely; it has helped me delve deeper into my awareness through the contemplation of its teachings and the effort to implement them. Just a few more thoughts on this wonderful teaching.

Kashmir Shaivism

The primary purpose of Kashmir Shaivism is to help us achieve Recognition—help us experience our Self. The sages of Kashmir ShaivismShaivism's primary method for achieving Recognition is the dissolution of thoughts. Yes, like so many others, a quiet and still mind is the best and quickest way to the realization of your Self. The Saivite sages tell us; If you still all your thoughts, there can be a flashing forth of the Self, which is immediate Recognition. I've said that my experience of the Self revealing itself was quite subtle in the very beginning. But, in a very short time, my sense of self had changed exponentially. Thus, it is also appropriate to describe the Experience of the Self as flashing forth.

One of these sages, Utpaladeva, refers to this state of Recognition as *"Recognition of the Lord."* I can honestly say that I had the same take—the same Realization! The Self, revealing itself, as described, was so sacred, divine, miraculous, and beyond all imagination, etc., that the only word for this knowledge and Divinity was—the Lord. Divinity Itself! This was the transcendent Lord, the Lord that speaks without words through Knowledge and immediate understanding.

Kashmir Shaivism teaches that the pure I consciousness of the Self is the real "I" of everyone and serves as the master "I." This is the awareness that can observe the flux of our habitual mind and its many "I's"—its many feelings of self. I, as the witness, was the pure awareness, my pure I, my pure sense of presence, observing all the "I's" of my individual and habitual mind. And it wasn't long before I realized that this purer sense of myself was my true and real "I", my true and real essence. After the Self revealed itself to me, after Recognition, I knew that this previously unknown sense of myself, this unimaginable level of myself, was my real I and the real I of everyone—the one Self in all.

The Siva Sutras, a revealed scripture by the Sage Vasugupta, form the beginning of Shaivism. Their major written scriptures are in the form of sutras. These sutras are offered to help the seeker to have an intense awakening of their own, intense absorption in the pure I Consciousness. In other words, have an intense experience of the Transcendent resulting in Recognition! In Realization! The sutras tell us unequivocally that the Truth—Reality—cannot be experienced through our mind as we know it. Or through religion, philosophy, or ritual! This is the case because the Self, the pure Spirit, is non-relational Consciousness, which means it has no relative aspect—no duality, no opposites. It is One, which is why some have called it non-dual. It transcends the relative dualistic plane completely. That's why it's referred to as the transcendent!—and why it's impossible to describe. The Self, the pure I, is also known as unity Consciousness, and the One. And—the immediate Awareness that all is one divine Consciousness—the Source and Essence of everything. These descriptions are my exact experience of the Self in all. I'm now going to paraphrase a commentary on the seventh sutra of these Siva Sutras, which are well over a thousand years old but are still perfectly accurate in the present day— the Truth doesn't change.

The fourth state [the Transcendent state] is the ever-present witnessing consciousness. It is the ever-present immortal atman, deathless, ceaseless consciousness that witnesses all. It is the changeless permanent I that witnesses all of our changing "I's" of our individual mundane consciousness.[41]

The SELF

Gurdjieff spoke about our changing "I's" and the permanent "I"—the goal of the spiritual journey. In the writings of Ouspensky, Nicoll, Dr. Walker and others, he did not specifically speak about *witnessing* all our "I's" of our individual egos, even though he obviously knew the truth of this based on his own observations. I had to experience this witnessing for myself by participating in self-remembering and learning to be consciously present. This intense practice allowed me to directly experience that this permanent "I" of the Self is, indeed, the pure I Consciousness. This is the I the sense of self that experiences Union, Realization, and Recognition all of these being the same divine Experience. There is no question in my mind that G knew that this could be the case, the expected result for the seeker who puts in a super effort, as G described it. He wanted his students to do the inner *work*, not think and assume.

The Saivite sages teach that the Awareness associated with this pure "I" is the essential nature of Consciousness itself and that perception at this level of the pure I occurs through the unencumbered witness-consciousness. This is a reiteration of the above quote and also of my experience of the pure "I." I love the term unencumbered, how accurate and appropriate! Yes, the witnessing-awareness is completely free and unattached, even at the level of our ordinary awareness that I first experienced days before the permanent "I" of the Self—revealed Itself! I say this to remind the seeker that even at this initial level, the witness is the essential nature of awareness, just not its highest level. But, as I've said, it is a capacity we already have; we just have to learn to connect with it and let it expand our level of awareness and understanding, as I've been saying!

The Saivite sages also teach that our own consciousness contains all levels of awareness, all levels of consciousness—in the very consciousness that we already possess; right up to and including the Pure "I"—the permanent "I." In other words, Kashmir Shaivism teaches that supreme Consciousness, which is our own consciousness in a contracted form, contains all aspects of itself, like a hologram. This is why and how we can expand back, can reconnect with our true Nature—To Consciousness Herself, to our own Self. As Muktananda said, the Self is already attained; it just needs to be uncovered, as the Saivite sages also tell us. Again, they tell us that this Recognition can only take place within our own consciousness—never outside of it, as in philosophy, etc. The pure I—the Self—is transcendent to all words and concepts.

To help the beginning seeker better understand and appreciate the uniqueness of the witness, the sages compare this level of awareness to a mirror. The mirror simply reflects, simply witnesses, and never gets attached to, nor affected by, what is reflected in it! It always remains neutral, as does the witness of our thoughts. One of the Saivite sages, Abinavagupta, described the witness as never accepting or rejecting thoughts, again, always uninvolved—always in pure "I" awareness.

Modern scholars tell us that these Saivites of the eighth and ninth centuries were mostly regular folks living a family life, but also participating in the spiritual journey while doing so. Expanding the awareness of our own consciousness is what the modern-day seeker desperately needs. As the Saivites surely knew, incorporating witness-awareness into one's daily routine—daily life—is how you make steady progress and experience for yourself the innate intelligence of the witnessing awareness as compared to one's habitually orientated mind. By taking the stance of the witness daily, to say that you don't have time for spiritual practice doesn't make sense any longer. Once you do take up the practice, you will see how quickly this stance uncovers aspects of your ego that you thought assumed were You! In this modern day, we like and essentially demand quick results. The witness will accomplish this better than you can believe, but don't believe me—just do it.

Another little morsel of insight by this enlightened group and its enlightened Sages that I'm going to share is their knowledge of what they called Matrica. Simply put, Matrika refers to the power of sound, our mind's tendency, and habit of endless thinking, its unceasing activity. These highly evolved folks noticed that our mind's activity involves thoughts and emotions predominantly centered around our own mundane existence, and how this prevents us from serious and deeper self-inquiry. As I experienced for myself, my initial steps of self-inquiry were quite necessary, but they—the thoughts used in inquiry—kept me from the deeper awareness of the witness. In other words, these thoughts of self-inquiry were incapable of putting me in touch with the witness by keeping my sense of self in thoughts. Thus, Matrika—one's constant immersion in thoughts and emotions—prevents deeper levels of awareness that can expose our conditioned egos. These Saivites recognized this over a thousand years ago! To learn about the witness, I needed one who had *been there and done that,* as the modern saying tells us. Socrates was great at demonstrating to his students that what they believed to be absolute Truth was only the relative truth of their conditioning. Quite a feat that few have learned even today, but this level of inquiry will never make you aware of the witnessing awareness. Thus, I know that these Saivites were very advanced people, way beyond what are considered the smartest people of today. The vast majority of our present-day philosophers, theologians, scientists, and so on are not even slightly aware of this capacity of their own consciousness. And they certainly are not aware that Matrika—the ceaseless activity of our minds keeps us from experiencing our true and joyous Self.

Another of Kashmir Shaivism's sutras says that all expressions of religion are aspects of the one Divine Consciousness since it is the Source and Essence of everything. They taught that these religions serve those who are attracted to that particular level of understanding and experience. Different folks are only capable of certain levels or expressions of understanding—religious and political. For me, this is similar to G's teaching about knowledge and being. Awareness of different levels of being and different levels of inner development helps me better understand our present political situation, which contains so much anger, rudeness, and falseness. It also helps explain why reason and facts will not change these folks' minds—these people's perspectives!

Therefore, these Kashmir Saivite sages show me in a number of ways that theirs is an authentic path to our true Self.

Mythology and Symbolic Truth

Mythology is the oldest and least appreciated of the influences on what humanity believes about life, its potential, and its consciousness. Most people of the present day would assume that mythology plays no part in their lives and has little, if any, influence on modern life. For most of us, science has assumed authority over truth and the story of creation. It has also proved the literal version of our myths to be false. There is validity in this perspective, but unknowingly, this view is still quite a limited view. There is more than one way to look at the meaning and purpose of myth. Most importantly, we have forgotten that myths were never intended to be literally true—to be taken literally! On the most basic level, a myth is a story that purports to convey historical events. While there are many who do not accept myths on this level, there are many others who do. Fundamentalism in any religion is all about accepting myths as factual, and this limited understanding of mythology is playing a major role around the world among Muslims, Christians, Jews, Hindus, and even some Buddhists!

There is another way to look at mythology, a much kinder and more relevant way, and that is what most interests me—myth as metaphor or symbol. Once I had the Experience of the Self, I could no longer believe in the literal interpretation of myth—of scripture! As we've seen, neither could the Gnostics. The same is true for most of the folks in Dr. Bucke's book: *Cosmic Consciousness*. Once you have had the inner experience, you know that sacred literature was never meant to be taken literally. Who, but a child, would take Beauty and the Beast literally?—or most of the epic sagas? To understand the intended meaning of sacred literature, you need a guide because, as Plato told us, *"It is miraculously transcendent!"*

I was introduced to the more expansive view, what I consider the true essence and meaning of mythology, as millions of others have been, through the work and writings of the late Joseph Campbell. Due to this fact and because Campbell's views match my inner experiences of the Transcendent Self so well, I chose to focus on him here. It's also for this reason that I trust the validity of his most essential teachings, and, in discussing these teachings, I can continue to speak only about things that I have personal experience with.

Campbell considers myths to be sacred literature because myths contain the perennial message of the wisdom traditions; the message is: As human beings, we have the capacity and destiny to experience our true Nature—the one Self in all. In other words, Campbell finds in myths the mystical teaching that each human being is one with the consciousness in all beings. As with the teachings, all genuine mystics—genuine myths inform us that our essence is Divine. Campbell says that the main function of myth is to harmonize people with their society, the cosmos, and themselves. This is a tall order, and yet it is clear that if we work with myths as Campbell suggests, we can come into harmony and sync with the cosmos and with everyone and everything in it. But in order to truly do this, we must recognize the one Spirit in all and then experience that Spirit as our own Self. Such produces harmony and bliss, and it confirms that following the *golden rule* is the *way to be!*

Interestingly, the literal approach to mythology, taking myths literally, accomplishes just the opposite of what Campbell sees as the essential purpose of myth—coming into harmony with yourself and others! This more restricted and inflexible approach, a strongly conditioned approach, that sees myths as factual, historical accounts, tends to pit one nation, tribe, or particular group against another, with each saying that their version of truth is the only real truth. In my lifetime, I can see that most of the violence and intolerance that I've either witnessed or heard of has been a direct result of someone taking the lower aspect of their myth literally. Believing and considering their particular ideology to be the supreme Truth. This does not result in inner harmony and compassion; again, just the opposite! It is clear to me that in a country as diverse as my own is—and in a world that is forcibly integrated through international trade, security agreements, environmental concerns, and wholesale immigration, there is a need for a perspective on life that speaks about our inherent oneness and, therefore, helps a person to be open about their innate connection with each other.

Through his writings and lectures, Joseph Campbell has done more than any other person, that I'm aware of, to promote the higher message and meanings of myths. He teaches that myths, like all sacred literature, speak of our divinity and how we can experience this divinity directly within ourselves. He tells us that the first function of myth is: *"The mystical function… the realization of the mystery that underlies all forms. If you lose that, you don't have a mythology."*[42] *"Instead, you have an ideology! He also says that myth has to: "inspire the realization of the possibility of your own perfection."*[43] Similarly, he says that a myth must convey the understanding: *"I, as I know myself, am not the final form of my being."*[44] Not being taught about our capacity and destiny to experience Union, we know nothing about our potential or possibility of perfection. Campbell also says:

We are all manifestations of that transcendence. Read mystically, all of these traditions are telling us this great story of our identity with the eternal power and our loss of that sense of identity when we get involved with the ego-bound world of fear and desire.[45]

Campbell also speaks about our oneness with each other and our capacity to directly experience this oneness with all, the mystical experience that only takes place within ourselves. He lovingly tells us:

When you identify with the consciousness… *"The consciousness that throws up forms and takes them back again. And then realize that you are one with the consciousness within all beings. This is the ultimate mystic experience."* [46]

Campbell teaches that if you take myth literally, you will always miss the message because the message is always of the spirit, which is always about our *oneness* with the One Consciousness in all. Similarly, he says that in sacred literature the symbols always refer to us, to planes or levels of consciousness within us. For me, Campbell's teaching about the symbols in myths is essentially the same as M. Nicoll's teachings concerning the *Language of the parables*.

Campbell reminds us of the importance of understanding these symbols correctly. Here, for instance, he discusses literal, ego-centered consciousness in relation to the experience of transcendence:

"There are two ways of thinking, 'I am God.' If you think I am here in my physical presence and in my temporal character am God, then you are mad and have short—circuited the experience. You are not God in your ego, but in your deepest being, where you are at one with the non-dual transcendent."[47]

One of Joe Campbell's great insights was what he called the *concretization* of the transcendent teachings and the transcendent experience itself. What he meant by this term, said simply, is that when a person becomes satisfied only to speak about transcendent ideas and transcendent concepts, then the true understanding and experience of the transcendent state of consciousness falls away. At this point, the rational completely takes over, and the essence of the *transcendent experience of the Self* is lost and forgotten. Yes, lost and forgotten! Just concepts and beliefs remain. Our capacity for direct Experience of SPIRIT is now shunned!

It is certainly my view that our total focus on beliefs and concepts rather than gnosis is essentially how and why the highest aspect of mythology was, for some time, lost. It seems that most people were not psychologically mature enough to participate in "knowing thyself"—to participate in the higher spiritual journey.

Now, hopefully, many more seekers are mature and sophisticated enough to do that. Are you ready to "work" versus just thinking and thinking?

More Words of Wisdom from St. John

Years after my experiences with St. John's *Dark Night of the Soul,* I read his book, *Ascent of Mt Carmel,* which is actually the beginning of John's teachings on *gnosis,* which he calls Union. His book The Dark Night is a continuation of that teaching that began in *The Ascent.* Now I'd like to share a few things from that book concerning how ideas and concepts block gnosis. But before we get to that, I want to share John's own words about his intent for his book. He says at the very beginning of his work: *"All of the doctrine whereof I intend to treat in this Ascent of Mount Carmel is included in the stanzas, and in them is also described the manner of ascending to the summit of the Mount, which is the high state of perfection which we here call union of the soul with God."*[48] Thus, there can be no question that Gnosis or Union is what he is addressing here. In the language of the parables, as Nicoll called it, or mystical theology as St. John calls it, the Mount—the highest place—symbolizes Union or enlightenment. The Sermon on the Mount is thus about the *way to be*—in order to ascend to Union. For me, it's the same with Moses receiving God's word on the Mount—while in union with God.

Now, back to St. John's manner of ascending to union with the Self. Like so many other Saints and Sages, he is primarily speaking about the nature of the mind, and the nature of consciousness itself, and how these relate to preparing for Union. In this rewrite, I thought this would be a good way to prepare for the next chapter on the mind and follow-up on John's earlier teachings on Union—expressed in his *Dark Night*—discussed in Book III. From the scholars participating in the translation and history of John's writing, I learned that John's writing was mainly for St. Teresa of Avila's nuns, who were quite familiar with the idea of preparing for an experience of Union. Thus, John was specifically writing to the nuns about how to open to this subtlest of experiences. He was not writing for the general public, who know little about the Union, being taught almost nothing about this natural capacity of human consciousness. This situation is essentially the same today—over 400 years later!

St. John tells the nuns that, *"The more the soul is wrapped up in its imaginings, desires, and its own abilities, the less prepared they are for union. One needs to strip oneself of all dissimilarities and contraries—so God may communicate Himself supernaturally by Grace."* He also says that, *"The more completely the soul is wrapped up in ... in its own abilities ... the less preparation it has for union."*[49] John also tells them that, *"A soul is greatly impeded from reaching the high estate of Union when it clings to any understanding, feeling, imagination, or will or manner of its own.*"[50] Also, *"The understanding should be withdrawn from all particular knowledge, whether temporal or spiritual, and the will should not desire to think with respect to either—for this is a sign that the soul is occupied,"* busy with individual desires etc.[51] John has told them earlier that, *"The understanding has no more capacity for receiving enlightenment from the wisdom of God than the air, when it is dark, from receiving enlightenment from the sun."*[52] John has also told them that, *"Oh, did spiritual persons know how much good and great abundance they lose through not seeking to raise their desires above childish things."*[53] Yes, we are still stuck in childish things—materialism, tribalism, fundamentalism—all expressions of immature ego-ism.

Then he tells the nuns that they need to turn away from spiritual meditation,[54] which I take to be institutional meditation—praying, talking with God, lamenting, chastising themselves, and so on. John repeats over and over again that to experience Union, they must leave all behind, which means all thoughts, all beliefs—including religious—and all desires. Like the Shaivites and so many others, John wants them to experience inner silence and tells them when they find themselves in this pure silent awareness (my description), do not think that you are *doing nothing*—your silent awareness is *well occupied,* if it discerns within itself these signs, being silent and alert and knows—*that's what they are supposed to be doing*—to prepare for God to communicate—to reveal Himself.[55]

John also says—*"for the spiritual persons that can't meditate, let them learn to be still in God, fixing their loving attention on Him in the calm of his understanding—although he may think he is doing nothing, for thus, little by little and very quickly, Divine calm will be infused into his soul, together with a wonderous and sublime knowledge of God enfolded in Divine love."*[56] Then John quotes David's Psalm, XLV, 11:

> Learn to be empty of all things, and you will
> See That I Am God.

Yes, this reminds me of one of Yoga's great teachings:

> *"Become an empty vessel and be filled with what you already are."*

And remember that the *I Am—is You*—not somebody else! This has been missing and forgotten for a long, long time, and not only in the West. Union with God is real—it is an extraordinary inner Experience—**it is not a religious belief!**

Can there be any doubt that John's teachings concerning the mind and meditation are perfectly consistent with all of the wisdom traditions? But John still has more very important Knowledge to share: *"If veils and impediments are removed (desires, memories, etc.), The soul would then find itself in a condition of pure detachment … and being simple and pure would be transformed into simple and pure Wisdom, which is the son of God."*[57] Then, he continues, *"He—God—gave power to be sons of God, that is to be transformed in God, only to those who are born, not of blood... neither of the will, every manner of judging, or comprehending with the understanding. He gave power to none of these to become sons of God. Only to those that are born of God—that is born again through grace and dying first of all to everything that is of the old man... and receive from God this rebirth and adoption... which transcends all that can be imagined.*"[58] Amen! Right after this, we are told that elsewhere St. John says, *"He that is not born again in the Holy Spirit will not be able to see the kingdom of God, which is the state of perfection."* Again, exactly what all of the Esoteric traditions tell us. Also, we must not forget that John says—sons of God, meaning that *many* are capable of receiving Gnosis—the *experience* of the Self through God's grace—not just one single person.

Later in his *Ascent of Mt Carmel,* John says:

"Persons who are perfect or who are making progress in perfection won't ... to receive enlightenment and knowledge of things present or absent; these they know through their spirit, which is already enlightened and purged."[59]

Yes, all of the great beings know and teach that the Self is already fully within us all! I have spoken about this direct Knowledge, which John calls, *"Intuition of naked truths—conveyed to the understanding, which cannot be expressed in words."* Then, like so many others, John tells us that the delight caused by this kind of Knowledge *"that relates to God is comparable to nothing whatsoever, and there are no words or terms wherein it can be described. This kind of knowledge is of God Himself, and the delight is of God Himself."*[60]

Lastly, I want to mention that St. John says that he has misgivings about his ability to explain these things. Therefore, he repeats things— *"for that which is not explicable by one kind of reasoning will perhaps be better understood by another."*[61] I agree, and we must remember that this subject of Union is a difficult and tricky task to try to share. Reading Plato, I find that he repeats himself too— and for the same reason. I guess that it is obvious that I've joined their club. Now, I hope that you can enjoy some repeats concerning the mind and a few new things as well.

13
The Mind

WHEN I USE THE WORD *mind*, I'm referring to the aspect of our consciousness that is highly conditioned and, for the most part, difficult to bring to stillness. You can understand this perspective, the experience that your mind has a mind of its own, only if you have experienced this aspect of your mind through anxiety or, better yet, through self-remembering—that is, by trying to stay consciously present, by meditating! If you try to understand the mind strictly from an intellectual perspective, just from reading, or by looking through the lens of Western psychology, you won't grasp the full significance of what I'm about to say. In the West, we tend to use the words mind and consciousness as if they are the same. But, as I've been saying, you should view the mind from the perspective of yoga psychology because it's yoga psychology that is concerned with experiential knowledge and the various states of expanded consciousness that are available to us—as I'm sharing here.

Once you have directly seen, directly experienced the condition of your own mind, you can begin to understand the sage's teaching that the mind is one of the major obstacles that keeps you from experiencing your true nature, your Self. Remember that the *mind* does not refer to our conscious awareness, only to its incessant thinking, deciphering, and highly conditioned aspect. Not understanding the miraculous nature of our own consciousness, we take our mind to be our only consciousness, instead of only one aspect of human consciousness. On the other hand, though the *mind* is incapable of knowing the Self, it is a miraculous instrument and is necessary for the recognition of truth at many different levels. The mind is the instrument by which you realize that there has to be more to life. It helps us learn about God and the teachings of the scriptures, perform self-inquiry, as well as numerous other tasks that are necessary to live! One of Kashmir Shaivism's main teachings on the mind is that it is a contracted form of pure consciousness. This means the mind is actually divine in its origin. The sages tell us that we can use this divine instrument as a means to understand the phenomenal world and also as a means to return to the Self, the one Spirit in all. One of the main questions for me is, *who is using the mind? Is it the deeper awareness of the witness? Or is it the culturally conditioned immature ego* and all its stuff?

This, I'm sure, is one reason the sages tell us that the human mind must be carefully nurtured and must be, ultimately, trained to become aware of its own nature and habits—aware of *its own conditioning and potential.* Without spiritual work that's properly guided, the mind is unaware of its potential and does not evolve as it is designed to. Socrates helped the youths of Athens, through his method of questioning, to realize that what they thought was the absolute truth was, instead, only a relative truth, not an absolute truth. This is quite an accomplishment, knowing that the vast majority of people today still don't know this. But as important as this nurturing is, it still won't result in you knowing the Self.

After more than fifty years of voluntary and joyous participation in trying to live consciously and to keep expanding my awareness, I know that the mind is one of the keys to physical, emotional, and spiritual well-being. When a person's mind is not in a good state, they can tend to overeat, over-drink, and participate in many other forms of unhealthy and potentially destructive behavior. When a person commences the quest to live more consciously and responsibly, then it is a healthy mind, a sincere, honest, and aware mind that shows them their weakness as well as their essential goodness, talents and so on. The better you understand yourself, the better you know the nature of your own consciousness, the easier it is to continue to mature and become free from unconscious actions, unhealthy habits, and recognize the ego-based cultural conditioning that only holds you back. Yoga psychology and the perennial esoteric teachings are a must for sincere seekers because they speak of all levels of consciousness and the various levels of understanding that accompany them. And, again, these teachings are based on the direct experiences of numerous sages who all experienced the same Truth.

Neither of the above is the case for Western psychology, philosophy, or religion. For seekers to find more satisfying answers to the deeper questions of life, it's my experience that they have to open up to a more comprehensive understanding of consciousness that is available through yoga psychology, but even more importantly, through meditation. The yogic sages teach that the seeker should not let their mind wander wherever it is drawn, to wherever their emotions, habits, and outside influences might be leading it. The sages say that to have wisdom is to have the right understanding of the mind. Again, the best way to access this wisdom that is already within you is to meditate, to remain consciously present, and contemplate the teachings of enlightened Beings.

The following are some of my favorite passages from the *Yoga Vasishtha*, said to be one of yoga psychology's most respected books on the nature of the mind:

"Consciousness free from the limitations of the mind is known as the inner intelligence." [62]

"He sees the truth… Who knows that I am not the mind." [63]

"If you give up all thoughts, you will… now attain to the liberation of the oneness of all." [64]

"Egoism is the cause of all mental distress and is the enemy of wisdom." [65]

"It is the absence of inquiry that gives rise to actions that are harmful to oneself and others and to numerous psychosomatic illnesses... Inquiry is not reasoning or analysis; it is directly looking into oneself." [66]

"The conditioned mind is the source of sorrows." [67]

"One's limited understanding and one's notions are the cause of bondage, and liberation is their absence." [68]

"The individual consciousness perceives what it thinks it preserves, on account of its conditioning." [69]

"When the movement of the mind has ceased, the Self shines by its own light." [70]

The sum of these passages is that the pure One is beyond the mind, beyond all thought. That One, the Self, is experienced when the mind is clear and still. This is the ultimate Truth, the pinnacle of consciousness. This is real and practical psychology!

And just how is it that the mind obscures the Truth? In answer, I would like to reiterate a few of the mind's most basic characteristics, aspects of the mind that I experienced with intensity when I first determined that I would stay consciously present and pay close attention to my mind.

The Mind Doesn't Like to Stay Still or Be Consciously Present

When I first started to watch myself, the first thing I noticed was that I couldn't seem to remember to do it, to keep part of my awareness focused back on myself. The second thing, which is related to the first, is that I found that I was so used to living in my mind, to being totally immersed in thought, that there was no part of me left to do the observing. I also noticed that my mind continued to jump from one thought to another with very little rhyme or reason, and was so *immersed* that I hardly even noticed this scattered brain-ness.

All of this was a surprise to me. Since I'd never attempted to observe myself with this much focus and intensity over such an extended period, I'd never had the chance to notice any of these humbling facts about the habits of my mind. It's fair to say that I learned more about myself in a few days of self-remembering, of meditation, than I had in all the self-inquiry I'd done over the course of years. So, it seems clear that to move past the elementary stage of knowing yourself, you have to learn how to meditate, how to turn within, and take the position of being consciously present in the witnessing-awareness. It is by turning within, with brutal honesty, as G said, that you can learn to get in touch with the observing self—the witness—and begin to see for yourself the *state of your own mind.*

A Joyous Awakening

Once you have recognized that the watcher of your mind is different and separate from your habitual mind, you have reached an incipient but important stage of awakening. At this point, it's important to remember not to judge yourself and not try to change yourself either. Put all of your energy and focus into continuing to observe yourself like a hawk. By observing in this way, you will see a few—among the many!—of your culturally conditioned "I's." You will begin to perceive just how powerful and ingrained these I's are. Then you'll start to understand how bound you have been by these "I's," and just how unaware you have been of their hold on you. At this same time, you will also start to realize just how powerful the witnessing-awareness truly is!

This is when you start to become aware of what Gurdjieff calls our predicament, our deep mental habits and intense conditioning. This is another significant step because once you truly see the state of your own mind, then you may be inspired, as I was, to look at yourself with complete honesty and curiosity. It is through such intense self-observation that you come to know, with more accuracy than ever before, the limiting nature of some of your thoughts and emotions. The condition of most people's minds is one of a culturally conditioned ego, taking care of number one! Through this expanded observation, you inevitability gain a better acquaintance with the observing awareness and through this experience, begin to see, for yourself, that the observing self is much more the "real you."

With this awareness, you are now ready for yoga psychology, the science of the mind—the hands-on study of human consciousness. Its capacities and potential, about the various levels of awareness that are available to the sincere seeker. I'm speaking here about meditation, the witness, and the pure Self. Once you've reached this point, there is, as I've said, no turning back. The genuine awareness of your predicament and your observing self make it unthinkable to return to your previous state of "sleep." It's natural for a sincere seeker of truth to want to increase awareness, freedom, and understanding.

An awakening to this precious state of awareness, which can be experienced in a relativity short time by means of willful determination and intense focus, brings you a level of awareness that is beyond that put forward by, basically, any Western philosophy, form of psychology, or religious teaching. And, as the Saivites tell us, by holding this "state," a sincere seeker can experience the Self in a short time. You have to ask yourself: If you pass up this opportunity to know thyself, are you really a seeker of Truth?

The Intellect Isn't the Absolute

I have quoted Plato, Plotinus, St. Bonaventure, St. John, and Mister Eckhart, all saying that the intellect is not the source of our highest knowledge and understanding. This is also the case for the Upanishads'—the ancient teachings of India, and the Siddha Guru's I've studied with. Still, throughout modern culture, the intellect is unquestionably accepted as the only real means to truth. This is apparently due to the scientific revolution and its resulting secularism, and the habit of all orthodox religions to accept only the literal interpretations of their sacred myths and scripture. I'm speaking about fundamentalists worldwide and their self-serving literal interpretations that have, and still are, causing untold trouble and misery for millions. I'm also speaking about many scientists, academics, and other intellectuals for whom the rational mind is paramount! Their view that the intellect is the Absolute is so pervasive and ingrained that we now hear almost nothing about the higher states of consciousness—of awareness that I'm speaking about! Yes, the forgotten potential and Truth of Human Consciousness!

As I described in Book II, early in my initial awakening, I could see that while the witness was different from my unruly mind, most insights that came through the witness were consistent with those that might come from my intellect. So, even though my witnessing awareness taught me so much, and so quickly, it was in line with the natural abilities of my mind, and any reasonably developed and healthy mind. Ken Wilber, in his writings, stresses that when we transcend the intellect in the higher states, this always includes the normal intellect as well. This is my experience too. Transcend but include. Einstein's science transcends Newtonian science but also includes it. It goes beyond but absolutely includes!

Once my true Self revealed itself, however, the limits of the intellect were immediately transcended. And the limits of the intellect were immediately understood! As described.

Right from the very first instant I was in touch with the highest level of Truth—of Consciousness—I knew that it could not possibly have come from my mind—from my intellect. Its nature was such that it had to have come through divine grace, and up to this time, I was not sure grace was real! I was surprised that this was the case, as I'd always assumed that Truth would come in the form of intellectual understanding. What else would a Westerner expect? But once you experience the Self, you know why the enlightened one's tell us that the mind and the intellect cannot know God. That's just the way it is!

We know that our eyes are only capable of seeing a small part of the electromagnetic spectrum, and our ears are capable of hearing only a limited range of sounds. We accept that there are many objects we can't see and sounds that we can't hear because our sense organs are just not capable of those ranges. We must learn to accept as well that our intellect, remarkable though it is, cannot access the highest states of consciousness.

Yoga Psychology and the Mind

Before turning to the next section of this chapter on the mind, I'd like to speak about my own experience of yoga psychology's definition of mind to show that it assuredly comes from direct experience—not from beliefs, assumptions, or conclusions. Yoga teaches that the mind has three parts or aspects. One is called manas and refers to the thinking aspect that I've talked about in depth; the second aspect is the buddhi, which represents the intellect and as I've just said, for me, it's a question of who is using the intellect?—the underdeveloped ego or the pure witnessing awareness? The last part of the mind is, of course, the ego, which represents our individual sense of self and all that it's identified with and attached to! I'll speak more about ego in the next chapter. For me, the will has to be included and doesn't really fit in these categories. I would guess it's more an expression of spirit than mind. Check it out for yourself.

From my experience of awakening, I know the sages that defined the mind in this way did so from direct experience and thus, were quite familiar with the *thinking* part of their mind—the conditioned level of awareness that won't stop thinking, won't listen to us, and has a mind of its own! These enlightened one's also knew that the intellect was separate from the thinking aspect and knew from experience that this aspect is important for living on this planet, but it can't take you to the transcendent. In order to recognize the ego for what it is—how it limits and deceives us, through its identification with thoughts, you have to know of the witnessing awareness. Again, yoga's definition and description of the mind is based on direct observation within, not theories or conclusions. This is why it is—*real psychology*.

The Refined Versus the Purified Intellect

Through reading and contemplating the spiritual literature, I have come across a lot of thoughts concerning the refinement and purification of the intellect. Since the intellect is so important and not well understood in relation to the vastness of consciousness and its potential, I will say a few more things about each of these similar terms. When describing the refinement of or the purification of gold, these terms mean the same thing. But gold is an element, an object, whereas the human intellect is a manifestation of divine Consciousness—a major difference! Now, I will share my thoughts on the subtle differences between refinement and purification with respect to our magnificent intellects.

One aspect of the intellect that only enlightened beings seem to be aware of is purification. It is natural for a seeker to ask Why is this important? Gurumayi teaches that we need to purify the intellect so it becomes capable of receiving the knowledge that arises from the heart. Gurumayi says:

"Whether you are reading a book, studying a scripture, or listening to a talk, you cannot grasp spiritual knowledge through the intellect alone. The intellect, as you know, must be purified. Then wisdom arises from deep within the great space of the heart." [71]

The primary definition of purified is removing contaminants, as St. John has just told us. St. John is not talking about what today we would call self-help, which I would classify as refinement. The definition of refinement includes removing contaminants but also speaks of improvement via small changes. But, based on my experience, this is not what St. John or Gurumayi are talking about concerning purification. John has been perfectly clear that he's speaking about Union, about the need to recognize one's *state* and remain alert and silent to achieve purification to have a chance to experience a *taste* of Union. When we have achieved this *state*—this level of awareness, Gurumayi tells us that this is when wisdom arises from the great space of the heart. This is the essence of purification! This is beyond the intellect. It's not a result of small improvements in understanding that result from the intellect.

We are aware of the benefits of long and subtle refinement of the intellect through the rigorous process of science. Through centuries of effort and meticulous records, the intellects of scientists in many different fields have become subtler and greatly expanded through conscious participation. Essentially, right from the beginning of modern science, it was understood that the scientist had to leave his or her beliefs aside to make real and lasting progress. Otherwise, these contaminants will prevent refinement—prevent progress and increased understanding. So, whether it's for advancement along the spiritual path or the scientific one, the intellect has to be refined—be rid of wrong understanding. But we must remember that there is a huge difference between these two capacities. Scientific refinement of the intellect will likely keep advancing for centuries, but it can never lead one to the direct experience of the Self. Again, this is what our modern culture does not understand because we have forgotten how to pay close attention to and purify our own conscious awareness, to prepare it for Self-revelation.

Another thing that we all know from in-depth experience is that growing up is dependent on the intellect's capacity for incremental change. A steady refinement of experience and understanding that has to take place on so many levels. This is built in, unfolds, and matures naturally with proper nurturing. But, as G taught and I experienced for myself, purification on the level that Gurumayi is talking about does not take place automatically—it has to be taught and learned! The adult intellect, as we know it, has to be purified to get in touch with the wisdom that is innate within us. As I've stated, this began happening when I got in touch with the witnessing-awareness that helped me remove numerous unnoticed contaminants from my understanding. In hindsight, I would classify this as a combination of refinement and purification because it was exposing and thus advancing my understanding of my conditioned ego and my mental habits. These are mainly all refinements. But, at the same time, it was the purification that allowed me to experience the wisdom that arose from the pure vigilant awareness of the witness. I've spoken about experiencing this innate intelligence of pure silent awareness in some detail because it was so surprising, so enlightening, and so missing in our culture. This practice, for me, is the initial level of the purification of the intellect and ego as we know it, because we have mistaken our ego-governed intellect to be the *real me.*

Having spoken in great detail about all the things I learned from being a witness, I need not repeat them here. I will say that essentially all of them were purifying my intellect and my ego—my sense of self! Directly experiencing being separate from my culturally conditioned and, in many ways, immature and childish ego was indeed refining, purifying, and emancipating as well. As I've mentioned many times, just by staying consciously present, the inner intelligence arose from within as insights and intuitions that I recognized and knew were beyond my normal intellect. I also knew that it was this inner wisdom enlightening me and leading the way forward! And I'd like to remind the sincere seeker that the Golden Rule, and its built-in requirement that you must be consciously present in order to follow it, helped me purify my understanding and open my heart to deeper wisdom, as Gurumayi says.

This teaching about the need to purify the intellect reminds me of Gurdjieff's teaching about knowledge and being and their need to come into balance. Also, how learning to connect with the witnessing-awareness accomplished this long overdue need for alignment, balance, and purification with ease. This teaching tells us that one's knowledge—one's overall understanding—can never develop beyond the level of one's being. Overall understanding includes the wisdom of the heart, and this is what is missing in so many right now. Science's incremental increases in understanding will not uncover the Wisdom awaiting discovery! Again, this is why the intellect as we know it, our sense of self as we experience it, needs to be purified! This is not religious belief—it is about expanding our awareness and fulfilling our natural potential. Meditation—the practice of self-remembering—is not a belief, a concept, or a religion; it is experiencing and exploring your own capacity for expanding and purifying your awareness.

This purification of my perception allowed me to experience that my being and my awareness were different from my intellect and my cultured ego. Again, this is purification, not refinement. As I've described, our overall understanding and awareness can experience levels that transcend the normal intellect by unimaginable levels. This is how the intellect truly gets purified by effort and grace. Simply by putting forth the *effort to know*, the Grace will come.

The notion that our overall understanding depends on our own level of inner development and awareness, which at its higher levels automatically includes the intelligence of the heart, is foreign to us in the West. As I've said, we believe that everything can be understood by the mind alone, and we know nothing about the *awareness* that our thoughts and emotions arise in. This is why we don't open ourselves to higher levels of awareness and maturity. It's why we don't understand the need to meditate, the need to uncover and expose our immature ego, which has hijacked our intellect! And it's why we don't get in touch with the intelligence of our heart, which is free from the judgments and the conditioned lens of our normal mindset and its contaminants!

As you experience higher levels of awareness, your inner understanding becomes transformed, begins to mature, because you, your sense of self, have moved from your limited, habitual, and conditioned mind set, to the expanded and *unattached* intelligence of the witnessing-awareness. This allows you to become conscious of the inner wisdom that has always been within you— purifying your intellect. The purified intellect is always associated with our genuine spiritual nature, the wisdom of our heart—its pureness, honesty, and integrity. In contrast, our normal intellect is almost always at the mercy of our ego. But the seeker who strives to stay connected to the pure awareness of the witness, slowly but surely sees that the intelligence of the *heart* permeates many aspects of their life. Then you see through the eyes of the inner intelligence, and your intellect finds its most appropriate and useful expression. As Ramana Maharshi puts it:

"The Self is self-luminous in the Heart as pure Consciousness, as the One without a second, and manifests as the same in all individuals. Heart is merely another name for the Supreme Spirit because He is in all hearts." [72]

I would hope that it is obvious to the reader that the direct experience of my true Self was the *real* purification of my intellect, my entire being, my entire understanding. As I've said, I instantly knew that this level of understanding that the Self revealed to me was far beyond my intellect's capacity. This is what the purified intellect means to me. Knowledge in Identity, this means that my sense of self now includes the Divine, and it's this expanded and enlightened awareness that can now employ the intellect in a way that I previously could not have imagined. But, once again, it can't truly be expressed in words.

I would like to add that the help I received from contemplating the writings of Ouspensky, Nicoll, my Siddha Guru, St. John, and many others helped refine and purify my intellect, but without the experience of my Self, I would not have truly understood what they were saying. This is why the sincere seeker needs to make the determined effort to experience their Self, and then, with a truly purified intellect, they will naturally keep moving along the spiritual path.

I would like to reiterate that the primary contaminant that was removed, by the Self revealing itself to me, was my belief, my conditioned assumption, that I was my mind and body and that I was separate and different from God! In yoga, this false belief is known as annava mala, and it is said that this is the most difficult ignorance to remove, difficult contaminant to remove. Grace— Knowledge of the Self—is the only thing that can remove it, the Sages tell us. Yoga psychology says that Knowledge of the Self is the greatest purifier. I agree completely. But, in order to prepare for this revelation, one's sense of self must be in the pure awareness of the silent witness. Again, a refined intellect—even with a number of Ph. D.s and extensive life experience—cannot prepare a person for Self-revelation.

Finally, I'd like to remind the seeker that in fairy tales and epic tales, the wise one of the village was the person whose inner being was the most highly developed—the most honest and mature. These wise and often gentle people were sought after by their neighbors, not because of their material wealth, political power, or intellectual savvy, but because of their inner being and wisdom—their connection to the heart and its integrity and intelligence.

The Buddha—Refinement—Purification—Enlightenment

As another bonus in this rewrite, I'd like to share a few thoughts on Karen Armstrong's book *Buddha,* which, for me, is a wonderful presentation on the nature of the mind. This is a way to reiterate some of these teachings on the mind, actually, to reiterate the nature of the mind and Consciousness itself. And as an encouragement to read her delightful book.

Like many others, Ms. Armstrong graphically describes the young prince's experiences with intense meditation and severe ascetic practices that had been recommended by other seekers. It was common for the new seekers of Truth to enter the forest and take the advice of those who had been pursuing enlightenment for years. After reaching the highest states of meditation that had been prescribed, the Prince was disappointed that when he came out of meditation, he still had feelings of desire and hatred. Since these meditative states were not permanent, he decided to join the many others who were practicing severe asceticism. After almost killing himself due to his overly aggressive asceticism, Prince Gautama decided that he was no longer going to listen to others and was only going to listen to himself and follow his own insights and awareness. Period! Armstrong's detailed description of what it was like for the prince to do this, to begin to know what he was really like, reminded me of my own initial steps in discovering the deeper awareness that we all possess, which allows us to keenly and objectively observe ourselves.

While reading Armstrong's account, I was also reminded that on the day that the Self revealed Itself to me, as I was preparing for bed, I wondered if I would still be in this blessed State when I awoke? Or would I, like the Buddha coming out of his meditative trance, have returned to my same old self? I didn't realize it at the time, but once your identity, your sense of self, has merged with the pure underlying consciousness that I'm calling the witness, you don't have to worry about losing it! And if you lose touch with it by forgetting to align with it, you know how to easily reconnect. As I've mentioned, many forms of meditation, as the Buddha found out, don't help with one's cravings and other desires once meditation is over. Self-remembering helps us with these by detaching our sense of self from such thoughts. With continued practice of this form of meditation, a person experiences beneficial results that are lasting and provide an intelligent foundation to continue building upon. Come see for yourself.

Ms. Armstrong tells us that the Buddha's *mindfulness* was not neurotic; it was simply to start knowing thyself, as the Greeks expressed it. He wanted to understand his own desires, fears, etc., and therefore, he employed mindfulness every moment of the day. To actually accomplish this, a person has to be consciously present. In Gurdjieff's terminology, he was beginning to practice self-remembering, which allowed him to see his *predicament*—and to begin to get in touch with his witnessing-awareness. In other words, THAT which allows us to be consciously present! The Buddha observed how his thoughts came and went. They didn't stay long, but were replaced constantly by others. We are also told that Prince Gautama believed that Enlightenment was possible and that it could possibly be built into the structure of humanity.[73] (I'd say the structure of human consciousness, and I'd say that his intuition was correct.) We are also told that Gautama— *"would practice this mindfulness in a yogic context and, as a result, his insights gained a new clarity. He could see them 'directly,… and learn to observe them without the filter of the self-protecting egotism that distorts them."*[74] From this practice of mindfulness, he—*"has a mind that is lucid, conscious of itself, and completely alert."*[75] All of these descriptions describe my own experience of awakening pretty much perfectly. We are also informed that the Prince realized that anybody could cultivate this state of mindfulness—they did not need a priest! The Gnostics realized the same thing about six hundred years later! Again, if you have a genuine desire for deeper understanding and the contentment that it brings, then you are ready to cultivate this level of mindfulness.

For me, it comes down to recognizing the power and intelligence that we already possess as part of being human. Sincere seekers should read Ms. Armstrong's account of this journey in self-discovery to help them move forward with confidence along the spiritual path. Now, I'm going to share a few of Ms. Armstrong's thoughts with my own input to show why I think her descriptions of the Buddha's *awakening* are similar to my own awakening, and will be similar to almost everyone who truly wants to expand their understanding of life, themselves, and, especially, of their own awareness—their own consciousness.

The only thing the prince had to guide him, once he gave up on all others, was his own awareness. Now he was going to employ this awareness as vigorously as he had in his approach to meditation and austerities. So, I'd say that his total focus and effort was to become consciously present, with no rules, no guilt, no judgments, so that he could begin to assess his situation—his predicament. He wanted to see what he was really like and begin anew on his journey. We're told that sin had no place in his teachings because it was not *helpful* and was an aspect of the ego, which seekers already knew had to be gone beyond. As the *Yoga Vasishtha* told us, *"Inquiry is not reasoning or analysis,"* which almost always contains the ego's cultural conditioning, *"It is directly looking into oneself."* Directly looking implies no thoughts period, just the pure awareness that we all already have, what I'm calling the pure awareness of the witness, and the Buddha called mindfulness! Thus, for me, mindfulness is the same as the witnessing-awareness once it matures and has had time to realize that it is truly separate from and totally different from one's habitual mind and its thoughts.

Remembering to pay bills or not forgetting to acknowledge birthdays, etc., is not the mindfulness that the Buddha is speaking about. This type of commitment and effort will not connect you with your pure awareness, the way I've described self-remembering. Seeing into these thought patterns without the ego's self-protective filter is how human awareness allows us to see directly what we are really like, what our mind and its emotions are doing in the present moment, and what these emotions are doing to us, too!

As I experienced, it was not long after intently watching and observing myself that I recognized that this witnessing-awareness was much more *me* than what I was observing. I'm totally confident that the Buddha had a similar experience, had the same realization. He continued to allow his inner intelligent awareness to guide him along, which is the natural and only thing to do when you're on your own. Armstrong does not speak of the observing awareness or the witness per se, but our deeper and purer awareness that thoughts arise into is the same for everyone—what we call it varies. This new identity—this mindfulness or vigilant awareness—lets you know that It Knows how to lead you forward, whereas your habitual mind does not! Those who have experienced this level of mindfulness know that it exposes the ego and its fears, desires and so on. One of the Buddha's teachings is to pursue *right understanding.* This is not only done through books and contemplation but through the pure witness—through pure mindfulness! And through its constant practice. This is what is left out and not understood in today's popular engagement with and teaching of mindfulness.

The term for *enlightenment* that is associated with Buddhism is Nirvana, which means extinction and blowing out, the extinction of the small individual self, which brings Recognition—the Experience of the Self. For me, this refers to what many other Esoteric teachings refer to as *rebirth*—the *rebirth* that is necessary to enter the Kingdom of Heaven. I think it is important to reiterate that I experienced, let's say, an initial level of rebirth, realizing I was the observing awareness and not my habitual mind and its many unending thoughts and emotions. Again, this took place before the genuine Rebirth that occurs when the Self reveals Itself. This is the true blowing out—the extinction of individual egoic identity that occurs at Realization and even more so at full enlightenment. I mention this knowing that many, like myself, have had deep and profound experiences of the Self but are not fully and permanently enlightened. But, at the same time, know that they are pure Spirit and will reach the goal when they are ready.

One of the Buddha's teachings that baffled me for a long time was his teaching that the Self is nothing. If he had said everything, I would agree—but nothing? Ms. Armstrong, due to her amazing volumes of research and years of contemplation, reminds us that the monotheists of the Jewish, Christian, and Muslim religions have *"called the most elevated emanations of the divine in human consciousness Nothing."*[76] Ken Wilber helped me understand what these monotheists and the Buddha meant by this seemingly odd expression. By breaking the word nothing into—nothing—the teaching finally made sense. The transcendent Self is certainly no thing, no object, no phenomenon that can be observed, not a being like ourselves. The one Self is beyond all of these things. Again, it is transcendent and ineffable. As I've been saying, the experience of the Self lets you Know this, almost instantly—with no words needed. Once again, the Self cannot be observed *because* it's the Observer! The observer in the Buddha, the observer in Shankara, and myself is the one Consciousness in everyone—

whether it was twenty-five hundred years ago, right now in the present time or twenty-five hundred years into the future—always the same.

The essence and potential of human consciousness are the same for all. What changes are all of the overlays—the local customs, metaphors, science's understanding of the universe? Of course, the ego doesn't really change, just its issues and its attachments! But when you rise above these overlays into the witnessing-awareness and experience its natural and comfortable sense of self, you too can become a Buddha—an awakened one! For me, an awakened one is a person who is sincerely pursuing deeper understanding, not just a single person who has reached the goal of Enlightenment. The Buddhists know that anyone can become Awakened; there can be many sons and daughters of God.

The great Saints and Sages never wanted to be put on a pedestal—they wanted to encourage us to experience our Self, our own destiny, directly through inner *work*. They never said that *Realization* is only for special people. Or worse, that it is only for *one special person*! As the Buddha encouraged us, *"Come see for yourself."*

14
The Ego

All of the wisdom traditions speak about the ego and how this aspect of our mind keeps us from our true Self. In the words of Ramana Maharshi:

"Reality is simply the loss of ego." [77]

Yoga psychology teaches that the ego is the greatest obstacle to the experience of the Self. Again, this happens stealthily by our ego posing as our true Self. We must remember that ego is the word we use to represent our individual sense of self. Therefore, we can't lose this, we can't lose our own sense of self—our sense of " I." Instead of losing the ego or snuffing it out, we must transform our sense of self, our awareness, so that we mature beyond the basic ego of a child and the emotional level of a pre-teen. For me, this is what the New Testament means when it says; you must leave self behind to discover your true self. The self that must be left behind, actually be transcended through exposing one's heavily conditioned individual sense of self, is what sacred literature calls the ego. We lose ego, our limited and conditioned sense of self, by realizing our identity with the expanded awareness that comes through our witnessing-consciousness. Thus, Ramana's Reality is that the loss of ego is not a total loss of our sense of self; again, it is experiencing our self as the unbound Witness.

As I've been saying, by identifying with our habitual thoughts and emotions, we remain in the clutches of our ego in its most basic form and in its most elementary and culturally conditioned expression. Yoga and other esoteric teachings know, again, from direct Experience, that our sense of self, our conscious awareness, is capable and destined to undergo expansion and transformation. Like little children—we are meant to grow up! Our sense of self—our ego—can evolve to unimaginable heights through effort and knowledgeable guidance.

Due to its undernourishment and posing as our true Self, our ego is the fiercest defender and protector of our cultural conditioning in all of its many forms. It has to do this because it is totally identified with this conditioning, with all the thoughts and images that produce this limited sense of self. But the elementary ego doesn't believe and doesn't realize that it possesses any conditioning. If you insult a conditioned rule or belief, you insult *me*, not those who made these rules or taught these beliefs many centuries ago. We often see this conditioning and posturing in others. We see its outright foolishness, and all the trouble and suffering it causes throughout the world—daily! It says: *this is rightfully ours, I have the "right," and don't mess with me, buster—this is God's way*—and, so on.

A Joyous Awakening

From the tremendous amount of information we are exposed to and the many interactions we encounter in modern life, many of us are now psychologically advanced enough to recognize various aspects of the ego. We see ego in movie stars, major athletes, the wealthy and famous, and today, more than ever, in many politicians. Most adults can easily see ego in teens who are so often identified with how they look, who they know, what they wear, and what they think other people think of them. On the other hand, these young people have no trouble seeing the ego in adults, who can be so easily irritated and so identified with the status quo. Many people are familiar with some of the not-so-pleasant characteristics of the ego in sports fans who are extremely identified with their teams, and then, there are those who are so crazily identified with their political party! In the past, one of the most vivid displays of ego could be seen in TV evangelical preachers, but today, Donald Trump is the epitome of an immature ego and all that goes with it. He takes the cake, ice cream, napkins, candles, and so on. Wherever we find the ego, it is always in charge, as the Yoga Vasishtha points out:

"One's intelligence is governed by egotism, instead of the other way around."
78

The immature ego may be especially noticeable in politicians and religious fundamentalists, but it is also prevalent in educators, businesspeople, doctors, and people involved in just about every human endeavor you can think of. It seems to me that many people, not just spiritual seekers, are aware of these truths about ego, but just because we recognize ego doesn't mean we understand it. For one thing, what so many of us are good at doing is seeing ego's foolish pride, arrogance, stubbornness, and falseness in others and seeing as well, how they would be so much better off without it! But most of us cannot see ego in ourselves, and until we do, we will never understand ego sufficiently to break free of its clutches. Without the teachings and practices that come from the wisdom traditions—the ways of experiencing and understanding the mind, the ego, the witness, and the Self—we can never transcend our ego, transcend our immature sense of self and its conditioning. Hopefully, by now, it's obvious that our culture, our educational system, our religions, and our medical model do not understand ego and the dis-ease it causes.

It is sometimes hard to see that self-pity and self-deprecation are as characteristic of the ego as are faultfinding and blaming others. What they all have in common is a strong emphasis on *me-me-me*! And an immature me at that! These negative emotions make us feel separate and limited. While we are in their thrall—when we're completely identified with them and identified as well with all *their* attendant thoughts and emotions, we are totally immersed in our individual egos. Due to our under-nourished ego, our under-nourished and educated sense of self, we assume that these thoughts are us—this is just the way we are, just the way we've always been! Again, our egos will defend these thoughts to our dying day, because if we don't, we might have to change! We might have to evolve! We might have to acknowledge our foolishness and become more consciously aware and expand our understanding. By holding us in this wrong identification, the ego binds us in the lowest part of our nature—our lowest and most constricted sense of our self. This is why, no matter what is happening in your life, it is always your limited ego *causing most of your troubles, making you feel guilty and unappreciated and so on.* You don't have to put up with this—you have a choice— use it!

The Ego Keeps You from Evolving

In Book I, I spoke about Gurdjieff's teaching that our conditioned and mechanical nature doesn't want to change and is actually incapable of change. Another name for this mechanistic nature is ego, and the ego sees no need for change because the ego assumes that either it has the answer or there are no answers. The ego, though it may be complaining and winning, likes life just the way it is, again, not interested in evolving. The great teachers of the wisdom traditions have told us for centuries that this is how the ego keeps us from turning within, from participating in genuine self-inquiry. The ego keeps you glued to your immature views and conditioned beliefs—this keeps you from evolving— from maturing as you are meant to do and designed to do.

There is no way you can mature spiritually without going beyond the conditioned ego, by turning your awareness back upon yourself and watching yourself honestly for an extended period of time. This allows you to see how you truly *are* in all kinds of situations. I wasn't able to do this in high school; I was just barely able to do this while in college, but it was enough to keep me seeking higher awareness and understanding. As I've shared, once I got the gist of self-remembering, I really started to see how I truly was! I think it's fair to say that this startling experience shocked me, as I never would have believed I was like this if I hadn't seen it for myself. This humbling experience was the major breakthrough that provided the motivation to keep *watching the show.* Thus, it's fair to say that meditation, separating from my mechanical thoughts, finally showed me my ego and my predicament, as G called it.

As I experienced, normal self-inquiry and self-analysis were typical and necessary first steps, but these don't go far enough and really can't because we, the seeker, do not understand the need to separate from our thoughts. Also, because self-inquiry is mental, it's thought-based; therefore, it contains unnoticed cultural conditioning, which means ego! If the ego is the one looking, how can it see itself? So, if you have been doing sincere self-inquiry and are feeling stressed, a bit overwhelmed by life, and little satisfaction or motivation, then you need to uncover your ego through authentic meditation—through self-remembering, which will allow you to experience what separation from your ego actually feels like.

Ultimately, I don't see how anyone can truthfully turn within and recognize their ego without proper instructions about self-inquiry and then self-observation and self-remembering. The EETs, the essential esoteric teachings, again, are not about philosophy, theology, or concepts and beliefs. They are instructions on what to do, how to do it—the practices, as well as providing the motivation and the why behind actually doing the practices and contemplations, about the benefits they will provide. The major benefit I received right away was seeing for myself that many aspects of my *mind*, many of my "I's" of ego-personality, that I had taken to be the real me, are instead, aspects of my conditioned ego. Again, I was surprised and stunned to see how many of these "I's" were running on autopilot as they responded to the circumstances of my life. In other words, highly conditioned responses—without me ever noticing it!

Whenever I forgot to stay aware of the witness, it was virtually impossible for me not to identify entirely with whatever thoughts and emotions happened to be in the forefront of my mind. Of course, not all of our "I's" are ego. Those aspects of my mind that are capable of compassion, forgiveness, unconditional love, and those that sincerely long for higher understanding, are expressions of my essential nature and the intelligence of the *Heart*.

Even so, rather than being any of these particular I's, what is surely "me" is the one who watches these I's—the Awareness they arise into—the Witness Self.

Let me reiterate a few things about the witness, since very few have recognized and employed this level of awareness that they already possess. First, it is always available, completely unattached, and alert! This expanded awareness is so still and vigilant and free from thought that it allows us to tap into the built-in deeper intelligence—the intelligence of the Heart, the intelligence that is inherent in our very essence—our Spirit. This level of pure awareness can recognize the traits, tricks, and the *acting* of our ego—the "I's" that we need to uncover and expose. The witness is custom-made for this endeavor; you must experience this for yourself, along with the experience that the witness is indeed the real You—there is no other way.

Earlier, I spoke about how, when I was young and naïve, I was bewildered to see how many well-educated adults acted like emotional teens when faced with unexpected stress or frustration. For some reason, I assumed that higher education would include both aspects of what G referred to as *knowledge and being* our two-sided nature. Our being, our inner self, was referred to as our *character* in days past, and your *character* was considered to be your essential self, your true self—who you are! For many reasons, we have lost touch with this important understanding, this important part of ourselves, and thus, the importance of nurturing this essential inner part that can evolve into a real grown-up. An honest, responsible human being who has moved way beyond their elementary ego and much of its conditioning. As I've been showing, this maturing of our sense of self, our ego, has to come from our own interests and efforts—not from traditional schooling! Or from orthodox religious beliefs that only confuse and hold back one *who is ready to grow up.*

My first vivid awareness of the immense importance of the balance of G's knowledge and being, and the amazing development of one's character, and the heights of integrity that it can reach, took place in the eighth grade shortly after President Kennedy was assassinated. My class was asked to read Kennedy's *Profiles in Courage,* a book about politicians faced with agonizing decisions about how to proceed. Go along with things that you know are not right, but that your colleagues want you to do for various reasons. Go along or lose your whole career—or follow your truth and accept the awful consequences? The book was about those who could not go against what they knew to be the right thing and knew they would not be able to live with themselves if they did. With the impact of Kennedy's death and being thirteen, it was easy to know I wanted to be like these men who were perfect examples of profiles in courage! And they are perfect examples of men whose knowledge and beings were in balance and highly evolved. They are men of high character! Their ego, their sense of self, had achieved an astonishing level of maturity. Something we rarely see today and rarely talk about as well.

Western culture doesn't really recognize or acknowledge that every young person has an inner life that needs nurturing. We do much better than China and Russia, but are failing our youth terribly. Millions of young people who feel anxious and fearful about fitting into this complex life need to understand the nature of their minds and be exposed to the wisdom teachings that I'm attempting to describe here. Then they would have a chance to make progress and naturally mature and grow out of their youthful anxieties, overactive minds, and immature egos. Our high schools, colleges, and the different cultures that make up America don't provide the information and nurturing that's needed, because they don't know about it either, due to their own limited knowledge of human consciousness.

Actually, I think that the pre-K and elementary schools do a pretty good job of nurturing. They make sure everyone shows respect to all and behaves appropriately, and they make this a priority too. But this doesn't seem to carry through to the higher grades, where and when it's time for them to learn about the possibilities for higher states of awareness and their own limited and conditioned awareness that is causing so much dis-ease. Hearing about the teachings that speak about our egos and how to move beyond the elementary levels would be a God-send to many. In other words, because we have such a limited understanding of the nature and potential of human consciousness, Western culture is dominated by the unrefined intellect and by our cultural conditioning and its concerns and misunderstandings. This being the case for centuries, we hardly know anything about inner states of awareness or the teachings about how to know thyself.

I think it's fair to say that our youth desperately need to understand their egos in an updated way so that their sense of self can begin to mature as designed. The sad truth is: in the USA today, most school systems would not allow our youth to be exposed to the things I'm speaking of—they would assume that it's religion without ever truly looking, without daring to look at their own conditioning, without doing the experiments! Again, this has to be accomplished through one's own interests and efforts.

The relationship all this has to do with the ego is simple: if your inner life is being acknowledged and nurtured through the wisdom traditions, this will naturally tend to keep your ego-personality in check. Such attention and education encourage the expansion of inner awareness, maturity, integrity, and responsibility—all resulting from inner transformation. This is not to say that the ego won't be foolish, especially in youth. It's the ego's nature to be foolish among other things. But as a person learns more about their inner essence and actually learns to watch their ego at play, the ego will be denied the power of stealth and, thus, will not be as dysfunctional and dominating as it would be otherwise. Being able to see that everyone is in the same situation, has the same overwhelming need, certainly helps and acts as a learning atmosphere in itself.

It's natural that once you see your own foolishness—once you watch the play of your own ego rather than someone else's—that foolishness begins to dissolve. Shed light on the darkness of ignorance, and it begins to disappear. Growing up and maturing should go hand in hand. Remember the scientific axiom I mentioned earlier: Increased awareness in time always yields increased understanding. Actually, in terms of personal growth, it is the only thing that works. Until a person is willing to be open to learning about their ego and their observing self, and is willing to take up the ancient call to "know thyself," they will be at the mercy of their ego and its immature ways, because they are too lazy and too conditioned to expand their awareness by stepping back and *observing*.

Keeping the ego in check is important and necessary, but our individual ego, our individual sense of self, has its place and, in fact, is necessary in our lives. Again, our ego is our sense of self, and it is impossible not to have a sense of self. Speaking in a secular way, Gurdjieff points out that it is because of the ego that we know how to get certain things done and have the necessary street smarts to deal with this complicated world. Every aspect and level of human consciousness is necessary and part of the design. The ego is only a problem when it's underdeveloped, unnoticed, and running the whole show! Our sense of self, which is being guided by the intelligence of the Heart, is an entirely different matter. When you practice self-remembering, you can see for yourself that the witness contains immense inner wisdom while the ego, clever though it may be in its many disguises, does not.

Looking at Your Ego from a Higher Perspective

Finally, I want to look at the undernourished ego from my experience of the Self, from the perspective of the pure "I." This is when you have an opportunity to truly see your ego's falseness and foolishness, because your identity is now in the Self. When I was in the state of the Self, I could not be seduced by my ego, my previous sense of self and all of its "stuff," all its conditioned thoughts and beliefs. The nature of the great Self is divine, full of light and joy; thus, the ego stands out as what it is—immature, contracted and "identified." Why would you identify with the ego's thoughts when you're in perfect freedom and bliss? Well, in fact, until you are fully and permanently established in the Self, fully and permanently enlightened, you will return to your ego. I have numerous times and still do. This pattern is a natural and expected part of the spiritual journey. I've spoken of how I learned this from the teachings of yoga and also from St. John. It's just part of the *process*. Understanding the teachings is one thing, and being able to live them all of the time is another thing—that comes with continued effort and grace.

My experience, along with most other seekers, is this: I'm in great alignment with the witness and then one thing or another comes up, something that pushes a button for me, something that I'm still unknowingly attached to, and I instantly begin to identify with that thought instead of with the Self—instead of remaining in the witness and simply observing it. As my story shows, you can't let this humbling fact get to you so much so that you give up the challenge, you give up the process of inner transformation. This is what the ego wants you to do. The seeker has to accept that it's a long learning curve, a long process to transcend the ego, but remember, as St. John and Kundalini yoga pointed out, divine grace is helping us below our awareness. Also, remember that we have been conditioned to not be open to or believe in grace and for many, to believe that there is an ultimate Truth that we can know.

It has always been obvious to me that whenever I identify with my ego's manifestations and lose touch with my Beloved, my Self, it is my own doing. I can't blame God; I can't blame anyone but myself. It is my observation that it is always a question of inattention, self-effort, and how committed you are to the path. Thus, we are the ones holding ourselves in the lower states of awareness—of consciousness. With firm resolve, an authentic path, and the help of grace, we can continue to step back into the higher state of the witness and the intelligence of our hearts. Gurumayi tells us that no matter how many times you fall off the path—go back to *sleep*—just get up and get back on.

Once we are reconnected to this pure and blessed state, it is easy to, once again, recognize the ego's play for what it is. You can easily see that the negative thoughts that come up—be they prideful, envious, angry, or judgmental thoughts—are just thoughts, made of the same energy as other thoughts. People have been taught to associate some of these thoughts with cardinal sins. Yet while I was in the Transcendent state of the Self, I did not experience the slightest tinge of guilt or remorse, no matter what thoughts came up for me, because my awareness, my complete identity, was immersed in the one great Self, and not the thoughts arising from my habitual mind! This is the beauty and emancipation of transcendence.

From my perspective, sin is the contraction of your state when you identify with these ego-driven thoughts, which is *missing the mark*—and, in this way, fall out of the experience of your divine Self. The separation from the divine state is the sin—missing the mark—the identification with the thoughts and emotions is the downfall, and not being consciously present is the cause. This is one reason why in the spiritual literature the ego is referred to as the devil—it's the ego, and its identification with mundane thoughts that keeps us from God!

Maurice Nicoll was the first person to teach me that the Greek word translated as sin in the New Testament literally means to miss the mark, as in archery. To misunderstand something, usually because you don't have enough knowledge and experience, is far different than how our orthodox religions have defined this same word—as an immoral act, committed against divine law, of course, *their* literal understanding of divine law! As I've been saying, identifying with the *thoughts* that are arising into my awareness instead of identifying with the *awareness* that these thoughts are arising into—is—*missing the mark*, misunderstanding the higher nature and capacity of your own divine consciousness. Such an innocent mistake is not an immoral act! Not a terrible thing that we should feel guilty about, which just keeps us identified with more thoughts! When we are first learning a new task or subject, it's normal to miss the mark—make inexperienced mistakes. This is a natural and expected learning curve and is to be expected while a seeker is learning about the higher nature of human consciousness, as I experienced for myself. And, as I've said, I knew very early on that this was to be expected and was nothing to feel bad about. If a person continues to sin, to miss the mark by identifying with all their thoughts and considers certain of them "sinful," they will miss the opportunity to mature as they are meant to—this is the tragedy, the real sin!

Remorse and repentance, that's recommended for sinning, is appropriate teaching—one should want to know why a change in behavior is needed and what it will accomplish. But if this remorse simply results in beating yourself up, mentally speaking, then the ego wins as you are now, once again, at the mercy of your negative thoughts and emotions. If a seeker of higher understanding follows the teachings of the wisdom traditions, instead of the orthodox traditions, by learning to meditate—by participating in self-remembering instead of beliefs—they will still miss the mark, but will steadily improve and miss the mark a lot less as their understanding of their consciousness continues to transform. This is how we learn almost everything; how can you go wrong—miss the mark—with this ancient and time-tested approach?

As a lead-in to the next chapter, I'm going to share a couple of things my Guru, Gurumayi, had to say about sin in a public talk she gave. While speaking of the yogic teachings and the practices that she recommends to experience what these teachings tell us, she made it perfectly clear that we were NOT doing these practices to compensate and to rid ourselves of our perceived sins. No, seekers do these practices to purify their understanding, purify their minds, not their soul, because their soul—their Self—is completely pure and divine already. Yoga psychology and its practices are to help the seeker experience this Truth for themselves—period! The Guru, the fully enlightened One, is always focused on our true Self, not our small self, who is still learning. The Guru never forgets who we really are.

I want to share one more precious memory of being with Gurumayi to share a little of her humor as well as divine insight. During a public talk, she told the group that if we all got together and confessed our sins to each other, we would all end up laughing boisterously due to a lack of creativity! Yes, our ego likes to think that we are so good and so bad when really, we are essentially all the same. Gurumayi is a very humorous and joyous being and uses that wonderful energy to teach and remind her students about their great Self.

15
The Siddha Guru:
The Spiritual Master

SINCE THE MYSTICAL EXPERIENCE of oneness, of the temporary experience of union with God, takes place beyond our normal consciousness, it is best to learn about it from those who have not only experienced it but are fully and permanently established in their Self and qualified to help others achieve the same enlightened state. This describes a fully and permanently enlightened Master, also known as a Siddha Guru.

Western religions haven't spoken about the possibility of our experiencing union with God for many centuries, so it is not surprising that they don't speak about the role and significance of the one who might guide us to this elevated state. Thus, in the West, we know very little of the spiritual master. While I can't write an exhaustive treatise on the Siddha Guru, I feel it's important to say a little more about how the Guru has helped me in my own spiritual journey. And to just give a little more of what it has been like to have spent significant time in Her presence, since this has happened so rarely in the West. Also, to correct some of the misunderstandings commonly associated with the word *guru*.

Based on his own experience, which included twenty-five years of arduous searching, Baba Muktananda always stressed the importance of a true Guru for advancement on the spiritual path. As I've said, Gurdjieff also said the very same thing. Today, the word guru is a popular term. It is used to describe teachers of just about anything—sports, finance, cooking, and so on. The Sanskrit word *guru* means teacher, any teacher. What I want to make clear here is that when I use the term *Guru*, I'm talking about a spiritual teacher, a teacher who is fully enlightened and who is qualified by their own Guru to lead others to that state. This is why I capitalize *Guru*.

Many people who call themselves, or have been called, Gurus are, from my observations, still functioning from their own small self, from their basic ego, and not from the universal Self. Some of them may be advanced beings—they certainly seem to be. But being spiritually advanced and being fully and permanently enlightened are two entirely different things! Because of so much good fortune and so much grace, I would call myself a fairly advanced spiritual being, but one that is not near that of a Siddha Guru like Gurumayi. Having strong experiences and glimpses of the Self is nothing like having complete command of that State. This is why Baba told seekers to look long and hard at anyone who claims to be a spiritual teacher or who allows others to claim that on their behalf.

Does this person display the qualities of detachment, focus, and compassion that you would expect in an enlightened being? Or are they self-involved?

Beyond this, a Siddha Guru, the highest expression of a spiritual Master, has the capacity to awaken a seeker's spiritual energy, to bring about an inner transformation that is compelling and undeniable. This may happen in a subtle way that is evident only over time or may happen in a moment, but it does bring about a revolution in the seeker's soul.

Through their teachings, a true Guru encourages seeker's to experience the Truth within their own beings, knowing this is the only place that one can do this. Such a Guru will always tell seeker's to turn within to find their deeper or higher identity, the Self. And since what is being sought is not a concept, but a highly expanded state of awareness, the Guru will give students a discipline to follow, teachings regarding the path to contemplate, and the inspiration to put that discipline and those teachings into practice in their lives day by day. As I learned at the beginning of my own spiritual awakening, true religion is not a way to believe, it is a way to be—be consciously present as the watcher of your mind.

Practical Advice: Turn Within

It was curiosity and self-inquiry, the act of being willing to look at myself as honestly as I could, in order to better understand myself and others, that got me started on my own spiritual journey. This journey has been so rewarding that it has remained one of the primary efforts of my spiritual work, and also my strong advice to others who want to step onto the spiritual path. Actively pursuing self-knowledge is one of the most basic and practical exercises you can do to get started on the search for expanded awareness and understanding. The call to turn within and become familiar with your own awareness and consciousness is, as I've said, the essence of the wisdom traditions. The strong desire "to know"—to turn within—is your Self calling to you to *come see*, as the Buddha put it. Turning within is a primary teaching of the saints and sages from every culture. We are told that nothing else really works, and that for true understanding, satisfaction, and contentment, we must turn within to the wisdom of the soul because what you seek is already there—within you.

But how do you turn within? How do you know who to trust? One way is to carefully contemplate the ageless questions of life, such as: *Who am I? Why am I here? What is the purpose of life? Is there really a God and an ultimate Truth?* Admittedly, these queries have never been easy to answer, but if you don't ask, if you don't seek, how can you ever evolve, advance, and find your answer? It was, and still is, my experience that the teachings—Seek and you shall find and, Ask and you shall receive—spring from the highest insight, the Self beckoning from within. They are accurate statements and practical advice of the highest order. Over the centuries, many have wondered—how does a person seek this kind of knowledge? How can you turn within in a way that is meaningful and practical too? As I've repeatedly shared, looking at your own reactions and beliefs with brutal honesty is a good start. I've already shared how the practice of self-remembering changed my perception on a few different levels, and I think I've let it be known how amazing and rewarding this journey has been and still is! I'd like to remind the sincere seeker of truth that all the great Beings have advised us to practice the Golden Rule, because to do so requires constant self-awareness, and this will result in a natural progression of inner transformation and understanding. Many already know that the Golden Rule is both *true and trustworthy advice*. Thus, a sincere seeker should put this wisdom to work, and things will change for the better.

Gurumayi, speaking about similar questions about getting started on this journey of turning within for increased awareness, tells her students to just start watching yourself. As you do, you will begin to notice that things are beginning to change, and that's when you are starting to know the Knower. The Knower, a word that comes from yogic teachings, is another name for what I'm calling the witnessing-awareness, and, hopefully, you can see that Gurumayi's and many other great 'beings' advice describes my awakening, and probably the Buddha's as well. For me, this is the most natural, intelligent way to begin—"Knowing Thyself," because our consciousness already has this capacity and, again, it is the essence of all the wisdom traditions—for good reason! A genuine Teacher, an authentic Guru will always ask the student to turn within because what they are seeking is already within them, *and that* has to be experienced deep within their own being—nowhere else!

A genuine spiritual Master will also provide the students with helpful material that will assist them in their quest to advance on their spiritual journey. Baba and Gurumayi, the Siddha Gurus that I've studied with for over forty years, have provided me and thousands of others with many valuable materials in the form of books, courses, workshops, shaktipat intensives, and numerous talks on the mystical teachings of all the wisdom traditions. As I've mentioned, Gurus, Gurdjieff, and many others, tell us that all genuine Mystics have experienced the same Truth. Both Baba and Gurumayi teach through their own experiences and select teachings or statements from all the traditions to make certain points about the Self; how to prepare to receive the experience, or how to recognize it or understand it. These *gems* of sacred literature are easily recognized by one already established in the Self. Genuine Gurus always remain strictly focused on the Self and do not get involved in the philosophy of the tradition they are extracting from. This is exactly what I'd expect from an authentic Teacher, whose only purpose is to help the seeker better understand and have the experience of the Self, for themselves!

Contemplation and actually trying to put a spiritual teaching like the golden rule into practice are barely practiced or understood today because people do not understand the need to expose their conditioned and immature ego in order to transcend it. But even though most people don't put this Sage advice to use, they are quite familiar with it and its *truth*! But chanting the name of God as a spiritual practice—not so much. My Siddha Guru' and generations of spiritual teachers have promoted chanting as one of the best and most powerful ways of turning within, being one-pointed, and possibly experiencing the transcendent state. They also tell us that in the present-day chanting is easier and more beneficial than meditation for many because people's minds are so active. Chanting gives the mind something to do and, at the same time, often subdues one's habitual thoughts and emotions. As you become familiar with this ancient and unfamiliar spiritual practice, you will realize that it is one of the most joyous practices, and it is easy to do whether you're alone or with others.

My first experience of chanting and the great joy that it elicited was listening to and chanting along with George Harrison's song: My Sweet Lord. Chanting the name of the Lord has been part of the Indian tradition for eons, and I assume that this is where George was introduced to it and experienced its incredible power and joy. Chanting God's name, for one whose heart is open, evokes sincere love for God. For the seeker who finds meditation difficult and dry, chanting is the perfect alternative practice because the mind just naturally stills for those who can immerse themselves in the chant. In other words, the inner silence and focus, along with the power of the Name, allow the seeker to connect with their own spiritual nature, which is why chanting can be so blissful.

George Harrison's song probably gave many Westerners their first experience of chanting, even though most, like myself, did not recognize or realize this. Nor did we realize that a good part of the uplifting and joyous energy associated with that song came from their own participation in the chanting! Chanting also helps me connect with a level of devotion that I never experienced with my previous worship. Experiencing such deep and emotional levels of devotion for God is one of the most sought-after and challenging goals of spiritual practice. Thus, chanting is a spiritual practice that can be revolutionary for a modern seeker with an overactive mind who truly wants to turn within to the goodness of their soul.

Another thing that the Siddha Yoga Gurus teach and follow themselves is discipline, in many forms and at many levels. As I've mentioned, many of us never liked or appreciated discipline. In our younger years, some of us assumed that it limited us in our individual freedoms and expressions. I've also spoken about being surprised by the realization of the connection between discipline and freedom. To have discipline, as defined in the wisdom traditions, a person has to know what their mind is up to, and to accomplish this, you have to be familiar with turning within, with your own conscious self-awareness. As G said, you yourself have to be present in your awareness! Many of us now recognize the importance of discipline in eating, exercise, and financial health, to name but a few. Many others, due to high levels of anxiety, depression, and just plain old disease, would love to be able to discipline their minds unceasing activity and emotional overflow—without drugs. As I've shown, it was the discipline of being the witness—having my sense of self in the watcher of my mind that separated me—freed me from my minds never ending activity and constant judgments, etc. Through this self-imposed discipline to try and stay *"awake,"* I recognized the innate freedom, joy, and intelligence of the pure silent witness—of pure awareness itself. Without the intention, dogged willpower, and self-imposed determination to stay connected to the witness, I would not likely have experienced this other level of pure and expanded awareness that the wisdom traditions speak of in their call to Know Thyself! Or, to have the direct experience of the Self—the pinnacle of joy, understanding and freedom available to a human being.

Gurumayi, along with many other great beings, advises her students to *live consciously.* For me, this is similar to G's and many other great beings' advice to *Awaken.* How can a person hope to begin these tasks without knowing how to turn within? As I've just shown, this takes discipline, which demands that we be consciously present in our awareness! When contemplating *discipline,* I looked at a couple of definitions of discipline to see how they might relate to what I've been speaking about, including my own experience of awakening. This insight turned out to be more interesting than I expected.

The first definition is: *"To hold that which is separate."* This was quite surprising to me, but it actually articulates my own experience of discipline wonderfully. The effort and discipline to hold onto the witness state was holding that which was separate from my habitually conditioned mind, which is the antithesis of living consciously! The second definition is: *"To separate the true from the false."* Yes, as I've stated many times, the freer and more disciplined awareness of the witness easily separates the true from the false. Again, the pure vigilant awareness of the witness *sees* our conditioned beliefs without thinking, without judgment, or without thinking. This is a practical benefit of living consciously in the awareness that our thoughts and emotions arise, which can't happen without conscious, focused awareness. Period. This is why discipline is a must for all the wisdom traditions, and this is how the beginning seeker initiates inner focus and begins to recognize the beautiful Spirit they already are. Another similar teaching of Gurumayi's and many other Esoteric Teachers is the need for spiritual discrimination.

In our modern cultures, the word *discrimination* is used primarily to describe prejudice in reference to race, gender, etc. In the wisdom traditions, discrimination is the ability of our awareness to make subtle decisions and distinctions. A primary example of this ability with respect to the wisdom traditions is to know the difference between the pleasant and the good, which one is beneficial to your goal? G told his students that whatever aided their quest was good and what didn't was good—it wasn't just a moral choice, it was about their goal. To know the difference requires discrimination and requires conscious awareness from the practice of turning within and evolving.

For me, discipline and discrimination are dynamically interrelated. As we become more disciplined in our awareness, we are able to employ better discrimination, because we have expanded awareness and experience that automatically allows us more refined choices. Again, increased awareness yields increased understanding. This is how science has continued to advance over the centuries—by employing persistent discipline and discrimination. Gurumayi, in her book *The Yoga of Discrimination,* tells us that remaining aware of the witness is discrimination and true knowledge too. Thus, like discipline, discrimination requires conscious awareness, which requires separating from our habitual mindset. Living consciously has to be done in the present, in real time, as does Knowing Thyself. Without inner focus and awareness, it can't be done! This is why the great beings teach that inner focus is the primary characteristic that we need to develop. Without it, other characteristics, such as moderation and integrity, can't be held onto, because at times we don't know what our mind is up to! So, once again, inner focus—the conscious inner awareness of the witness is the key and means to inner *awakening and transformation.*

Another practical but unrecognized expression and application of discipline—and discrimination—that is taught by many great beings is: *Be content with the life you have,* even the little things—actually, especially the little things! In order to find contentment in your own life, you need to know and trust that your life as it is contains the very challenges, people, and lessons that you need to begin your transformation in understanding. This is another precious teaching that's been lost and forgotten due to our culture's misunderstanding of sacred literature. Gurumayi adds to this sage advice of being content to also accept and be happy with ourselves as we are! And know that it is fine to go at your own pace as well. Such love and compassion are so representative of the esoteric traditions that advise us to live from this level of ourselves. This is what I recognized as being so special about Jesus. For me, this kinder and gentler advice is the best advice because it recognizes our true nature. It seems that many of us can be too hard on others and ourselves as well. It's so easy to criticize and chastise others and, again, ourselves too. I've shared how I got down on myself for not being better, which seemed like the honest and natural thing to do at the time. But thanks to St. John, I realized that wasn't necessary and wasn't helping either. The observation about my behavior is appropriate, but owning these thoughts and emotions versus simply observing them is not—witnessing them is the way to be.

Returning to the teaching—Be content with the life you have—it's true that many folks are not happy with the life they have in this time of deep division and strife. Resentment, anger, envy, and blame fill their days and nights. Accepting your lot does not mean that you cannot try to improve it! And it does not mean that you cannot contribute to the betterment of yourself, the planet and those inhabiting it. Living consciously and joyously is the way to be.

As I've been saying, the life you already have includes your miraculous consciousness, and this is your *ticket* to an awareness that is more intelligent and infused with goodness than you can imagine. So, you don't need to win the lottery or many other things people believe they need for a good life. You just need to get to know the consciousness *that you already have*! We are made for this— our awareness is custom-made for this—USE IT.

Anyone who makes a sincere effort to remain spiritually *awake* and pursue the spiritual journey will find that keeping their enthusiasm and focus is not easy. In my experience on the path, studying the Teachings of authentic spiritual masters on a regular and daily basis is necessary to keep my focus and sense of self in the right place. Keeping the company of other genuine seekers is very helpful and enjoyable, but if this is not possible, then keeping the company of the saints is always possible and uplifting. Like keeping in shape, you just have to make the effort to stay involved. When I had my initial spiritual awakening in 1975, I knew that I needed a living Master to guide me along the mystical journey, but I assumed that I would not likely find one. As far as I could tell, such beings were secretive and not easily accessible to someone like me. Finding my Guru, having access to the Guru's teachings and her presence, and being able to live for a time in the Guru's ashram is what helped me to see that my family, my job, my life as it is, contains everything I need to continue advancing along the spiritual path. Without this guidance, I honestly don't know where I'd be in my spiritual life right now.

Having spoken about the importance of the Siddha Yoga path to me, I want to say that at this time, Shree Muktananda Ashram, where I had so many experiences and revelations, is now a retreat site only open to practicing Siddha Yogis who apply and are invited to perform service. For seekers interested in an introduction to this yoga, there are many Siddha Yoga centers listed on the website—www.siddhayoga.org—where you can attend satsang. Also, a Siddha Yoga Shaktipat Intensive is held annually in the fall to mark Baba's passing, and books by Baba and Gurumayi are available for sale online and at some of the centers.

Lessons of the Heart

Due to the nature of my own spiritual awakening, I've spoken extensively about self-remembering and the witness, and I've quoted the Siddha Yoga Guru's and other 'masters speaking about spiritual practice and attainment in terms that are very similar to the ways I learned about them from the inner Guru—the Self—in terms of awareness. I want to make it clear, however, that *awareness* and all of its related terms—*witness, watcher, knower, noticer, perceiver, experiencer, observing self* and so on—represent only one perspective, one way, one path to approaching the Self. There are many others, and one of the most universal of these is the heart. One of the ways Gurumayi teaches is by giving a new message, a teaching to contemplate for the year on New Year's Day. The majority of these over the past decades have been about the heart. I mention this so as not to give the image that her teachings are mostly about the mind and what's referred to as the Yoga of Knowledge. Gurumayi is a preeminent teacher concerning the heart because, as an enlightened being, her heart is immersed in divine Love permanently.

I alluded to a teaching of the heart that she pointed out earlier when I quoted Gurumayi's teaching that we must purify the intellect so that it is capable of receiving the knowledge that arises from the heart. As I've shown, the heart symbolizes the deeper and purer part of ourselves—our spirit. This spiritual wisdom is natural knowledge to many because love is such a natural and dominant part of the human experience. Not only enlightened Masters but spiritual teachers of all types, including most mothers, advise us to get in touch with our hearts, knowing that this will put us in touch with the true Spirit within. It truly does.

To give the current reader and future generations another glimpse of the Siddha Guru and the teachings that take place under her supervision, I will share one of the more compelling teachings I received about getting in touch with our own hearts. This took place in a course on the Bhagavad Gita, one of India's most sacred and renowned scriptures. The course was given in the ashram and taught by a professor of religious studies who touched on many points made by this scripture, which is all about experiencing God in the battlefield of life. This metaphor is especially fitting because the teachings of the Bhagavad Gita are delivered to Arjuna by Krishna, an incarnation of the Lord, on the battlefield just before the fighting begins. At one point, Arjuna, aware that he doesn't know all the teachings that he should and doesn't fully practice those teachings he knows, asks Lord Krishna if faith will be enough to save his soul at death. Arjuna is concerned because he has so many worldly responsibilities that he doesn't see how he could ever focus on matters of the spirit.

Lord Krishna tells him that whenever he's in doubt about what to do, he should bring his attention into the present moment and get in touch with his heart. Krishna is telling Arjuna that he can put his faith in the supreme Spirit within and that this spirit will be a dependable guide. Lord Krishna also says that the guidance that comes will not be foreign or unrecognizable to him. That has been my experience the majority of the time. I find that when I ask sincerely, truly wanting to *know* and do the right thing, the answer or guidance comes up in a way that is recognizable to me. This works best when you are engaged in daily spiritual practice. These practices help you listen, to hear, and to follow what comes up. Many people don't even take the time to ask, and when the answer doesn't suit us, we ignore the wisdom of our hearts.

It's my observation that the heart is never a source of criticism, sarcasm, or denigration in any form, so listening to your heart is a beautiful way of not being too hard on people, especially on ourselves. It's similar to the practice of the golden rule. It is easy on the spiritual path to focus on our shortcomings rather than our true Self, and this doesn't help the state of the heart one little bit.

Expressions of Grace

Spiritual awakening is an expression of grace. When I experienced the awakenings in 1975 and 1987 as described, there was absolutely no question in my mind that these miraculous experiences were taking place as acts of Divine grace. What was taking place was so beyond my and everyone else's normal experience, and so clearly sacred, that there was no other explanation possible. I described them in great detail because they are not only obvious expressions of Grace in action, as I've come to see it, but also very rare in Western literature. The only other one I'm familiar with that's on a similar level is Franklin Merrell-Wolff's writing about his own spiritual awakening in his: *Pathways Through To Space, and Consciousness Without an Object.* Now, as a lead-in to the next section on the Guru Principle, I'm going to share a couple more experiences of the expression of grace to show how its manifestations can be expressed on very different levels.

The Siddha Guru: The Spiritual Master

In December of 1994, I was visiting the ashram with my family for the Christmas retreat. As we were leaving the Temple, we unexpectedly came into the presence of Gurumayi, who was on her way to the Temple. Gurumayi stopped and talked with us. She had been in India for over a year, so it had been a long time since we had spoken. She asked me how we were all doing, when we'd arrived and other similar everyday questions. As I responded with my answers—also every day in nature—I found myself looking ever more deeply at Gurumayi's face and eyes. I was struck and amazed to feel the unimaginable stillness of her being.

Even though I had seen and spoken with Gurumayi a number of times over the years, I'd never spoken with her when she appeared to be in such an indrawn state, even though her voice and questions were the same as always. My mind initially assumed that her long stay in India had resulted in this state of inner stillness that I was experiencing. As Gurumayi moved on to the Temple, I realized that her "state" seemed to have entered me. As this experience unfolded over the next couple of minutes, I had to assume that I had glimpsed her State and, thus, had connected with the pure State within myself, what I've called the pure "I." This profound shift in my awareness is an example of the power of the Guru's "State" and the mystical expression of grace. That such an inner event could take place during casual conversation and in a few moments is a sign to me of the unimaginable *State* of the Siddha Guru and how grace flows around her.

Now, let me share one more experience of how grace can unexpectedly manifest around a Siddha Guru. We had a bunch of cousins and friends visit us at our summer camp, and when they all left after a week of summer fun, we noticed that our children had lice for the first time ever! We did all the prescribed things to rid ourselves of these pests, but nothing was working. After dozens of washings and the use of every product and home remedy, the lice were still there. Almost a month later, we were heading to the ashram, where they check for head lice on children. We thought we had finally won the battle. But when my wife was doing a final check as we were on the road and a few hours from arriving, she found some more! Literally exhausted and exasperated, she called out to Gurumayi to help us with these darn things. Luckily, we passed the head checks and checked into our room late that same afternoon.

The very next day, we saw Gurumayi in the lobby, and like many times before, she greeted us and asked the typical questions about how we were doing and how long we were staying. But this time, as she was talking with us, she started briskly rubbing each of our four children's heads! My wife and I were stunned as we watched. We had never seen Gurumayi do this with anyone, and coming shortly after Pam's cry from the depths of her being, we had to assume that

Gurumayi had heard her and was responding with the help sought. The next day, at lunch time, while we were going through the serving line, Gurumayi unexpectedly came out of the kitchen. She walked over to us, engaging us in casual conversation, and, once again, started rubbing our children's heads in the same manner as she had yesterday. Again, we could hardly believe what was taking place right in front of us. Not surprisingly, we never saw the lice again!

I've dithered on whether to include a couple more unexpected incidences of grace, but to show the vast range that grace can take, I've decided to include them. To help appreciate them, I'm going to share a short story I read in Darshan, a magazine that was published by SYDA from 1987 to the end of 1999. A woman wrote about going to an acupuncturist to address numerous problems. After a thorough examination, she was told that she had a lot of issues and that it would take a number of visits to bring her back into balance. She made a few appointments, feeling that there was hope for her. That weekend, she attended a *shaktipat* intensive and enjoyed it, but nothing earth-shattering happened as far as she was concerned. She went to her acupuncture appointment a few days later, and after a few minutes of assessment by the acupuncturist, he told her that he couldn't do anything for her because everything was now in perfect balance! Which he found to be nearly impossible from where she was a few days back, and thus asked her what she had done that could be responsible. She said that she had no idea—the only thing she had done other than her normal routine was take a meditation intensive. Thus, the energy of grace had returned her to perfect balance; she and the acupuncturists were both astonished that such a thing could happen.

I was also astonished that grace also brought me into a similar perfect state of balance, without me realizing it, but in an entirely different expression. In December of 1975, almost four months into my graduate program, a few of us decided to go skiing for the weekend. We were treated to about a foot of fresh powder snow, and when I was getting off the lift, ready to glide down the hill, I had no clue that I was going to ski at a level that I had only dreamed of but never came close to achieving. I was able to flow through the powder and down the mountain effortlessly, and I mean effortlessly! To say that I was surprised to be skiing so smoothly and with total ease is an understatement. My friends were astonished to see this—it was not just me, but visible to all. Over the years, many people asked me how I learned to ski like this, and all I could say was: *"I don't know."* But I did know that it was the spiritual energy—the grace received in the summer of '75 that brought me into an unsuspected state of balance.

I was helping my brother shingle his house a few weeks after being with Gurumayi in September of 87, when I experienced another demonstration of the aligning and balancing power of grace. My brother and a few of his helpers asked me to bring bundles of shingles up to the roof where they were working. I put a bundle over my shoulder and walked up the ladder, which was positioned up against the house, as one would expect. Without thinking and just doing what came natural at the time, I walked up the ladder with the shingles the same way I'd walk up a flight of stairs—standing straight up and not touching the ladder with my free hand. I guess you would have to say that this seemed to be the easiest way, and actually, I never gave it a thought. After a few trips in this manner, the others were stunned that I was not holding onto the ladder with my free hand and just walking straight up, again, at a pace you would walk up a stairway. My brother told me that they all thought this was quite dangerous and I should do it the way everyone else does. I was surprised to hear this, as I was totally comfortable with this way and never felt a tinge of fear or danger, and didn't think of it as unconventional. It just seemed like the most natural way to do it, but after he mentioned it, I could appreciate their concerns. For me, this was just another surprising and visual demonstration of how balanced I was—compliments of the spiritual energy of grace. I've never seen anything like this mentioned in the spiritual literature, so I felt that I should document it—nothing more.

The expressions of grace are not always so dramatic. For me, most often it comes in the form of spiritual insights, unwarranted bliss, or experiences of unconditional love. Gurumayi—echoing St. John—says that most of the time we are not aware of grace working within us because it operates below the level of our awareness. At the same time, once you begin to look—once you learn how to look—you will see that expressions of grace are more common than you would have ever believed! In my own life, there has been apparent synchronicity involving events large and small, matters sublime and utterly mundane, many too filled with minutiae to begin to recount as examples of grace. And yet I know, they are examples of grace—gifts so perfectly tailored to my concerns that it's almost as if God were mine alone. Still, I know, because friends tell me that this kind of grace happens in the lives of many others. Especially in the lives of those who revere the divine Spirit—the one Self in all.

The one Self in all is the essence of the Guru Principal, which we will now take a short look at to round out the Siddha Guru and Grace as well.

The Guru Principal

As I've stated numerous times, the One Supreme Spirit, the True Self, the Holy Spirit, the inner Guru, the Inner Lord, whatever you want to call it— revealed itself to me as described. This is a manifestation of the Guru Principle, and this is made possible by the Guru Principle—the One supreme Spirit—that is the source and Essence of everything. This extraordinary experience is said to be made possible by the descent of grace, so Grace is another expression of the Guru Principle. For me, instead of decent, of coming from outside, it was a revealing, a revelation bursting forth from within—from the Guru Principle that was already within waiting to reveal "Itself." I've come to think of one of the many aspects of this Divine Principle as Grace in action.

To speak about a true Guru, a perfected divine Master, a Siddha Guru, is to speak about their State, about their complete and permanent union with the divine One—the divine Self that exists within everything. In other words, the true Guru is a living expression of the Guru Principle! The Shrimad Bhagavatam, one of India's sacred scriptures, states that the Guru is a personification of divine Consciousness. A Siddha Guru is extremely rare and is unlike any teacher we have ever known. Due to the fact that we in the West and almost everyone else have forgotten about, or better yet, never heard about, our potential and capacity to experience the Self, the Guru Principle. This Principle and the Knowledge it bestows have been discarded and forgotten. Thus, a teacher who is representative of this State, and who is permanently established in it, is hard for most people to accept, let alone have some understanding of.

As I've said, when I first met Baba and was told that he was a Siddha Guru, I had no way to evaluate whether or not this was true. But I didn't worry about this as I was enjoying Baba, the courses, and the precious material about the Self that he was making available to everyone. This material about the Transcendent State was from all the wisdom traditions because, like Gurdjieff, Baba said that all Siddhas from all traditions had experienced the same Truth, the same inner State. Therefore, Baba's Siddha Yoga, as he called it, represents all fully enlightened Beings—exactly what I'd expect from an authentic teacher! This teaching—this fact—is another expression of the Guru Principle. As I indicated earlier, while I loved being with Baba, it wasn't until I was with Gurumayi in 1987 that I *knew*, from direct inner experience and Knowledge, that the Siddha Guru is indeed a true Guru—a genuine Spiritual Master.

Another thing that all true Teachers tell us is that the understanding that reveals the Self is not the kind of understanding we acquire from the outer world—from our senses and normal intellect. As I've stated, it is the direct Knowledge and understanding that comes from the Self. This is the Guru Principle expressing itself! This is Grace in action! This, along with all the other experiences that I've described in detail concerning my experiences of the Self in 1975 and 1987, are perfect expression and example of the Guru Principle—of Grace in action.

The Siddha Guru: The Spiritual Master

With this slightly and subtly different view of these rare spiritual experiences, I'd recommend reviewing them knowing that they are speaking about *your true Nature*, as well! But as St. John told us, there is so little known and written of this. Therefore, I want to reiterate a few of my most profound experiences of this divine Principle and make a couple of new points too. This is to give the sincere seeker another opportunity to focus on and contemplate this forgotten Truth and the most essential ground of our being. I will also remind the reader that these experiences of direct Knowledge and their insights are not based on the teachings of Yoga psychology or any philosophy, but solely on my inner experiences and understanding which were given freely by the Guru Principle—the Self. And I would also like to remind the reader that I knew absolutely nothing about the Esoteric Teachings or the experiences they speak of when my search began in my late teens. Therefore, I was not and could not have been predisposed to interpreting these inner experiences and insights in any particular way. Finally, I want to remind the seeker, as I've stated clearly, that this Knowledge of the Self— this wisdom of the Spirit comes through directly— as immediate insight and intelligence, requiring no words, thoughts, or conclusions! Again, Rumi's experience expresses it well: *"It is an immediate and intuitive apprehension of Truth that leaves no room for interpretation."*

I've stated a number of times that the Self, the Guru Principle, must reveal Itself because, as the great beings tell us, the mind can't know the Self because the Self is beyond the capacity of the mind. This is something the West just can't fathom. The sages of the Upanishads and Kashmir Shaivism tell us that a person can only know the Self by the grace of the Self and that Truth is *revealed to* the mind—the mind *does not reveal* the Truth. This is a universal Teaching of the wisdom traditions because it is a universal *experience*! Even though this universal Principle—the universal Spirit—is beyond our normal mind, it is not beyond the capacity of our expanded and purified consciousness! Another universal "given" of the Guru Principle, enlightening you to the knowledge of your Self, is that you also *know* that this same divine Spirit is the Truth and essence of everyone.

The term *Guru* refers both to the physical Guru and to the Guru Principle. Some scriptures say that the etymology of the Sanskrit word *guru* is that the first syllable means darkness and the second one means light, giving the word itself the meaning *from darkness to light*. For me, this meaning of the word *guru* describes my awakening to the Self perfectly, as it was the inner Guru, the Guru Principle revealing itself, that removed the ignorance blocking my true Nature and, at the same instant, illumined my Oneness with the One supreme Spirit in everyone.

A Joyous Awakening

This is the function of a true Guru—to take students from the darkness of ignorance of their true nature, to the direct Knowledge, light, and joy of their Self. One of the most important scriptures of Siddha Yoga is the ancient text of the Guru Gita, and, like the Bhagavad Gita, it speaks about the Self—about the Guru Principle. In verse 10, it states that:

"He by whose light (true knowledge) arises is known by the word Guru."

Again, a perfect description of my own experience, the Guru Principal is the One who awakens us to our Self, who pulls back the veil as some poets describe it. A couple of other verses of this same holy text also reiterate my initial experience of the Self. Verse 75:

"My lord is the Lord of the Universe. My Self is the Self of all beings." And *verse 74*

"There is no higher truth than the Guru."

I can honestly say that from the moment that I fully grasped this Knowledge of the Self, I knew for certain that it was the highest Truth and understanding—there can be nothing higher, because you are in union with the highest Mystery. Again, the Guru is not a person—it's a word that represents the living Divine Spirit underlying everyone and everything. It is this universal force, this divine Spirit, that is underlying all of life, underlying the universe itself.

From the experience of nature and the unimaginable interconnectedness of things, many have intuited that the life force is a sacred and divine energy, it is a manifestation of supreme Reality. But they are not yet aware that this power can be experienced within themselves as the essence of their own being! Those who have had genuine mystical experience do get a "taste" of this power, this Oneness with all, and, especially, with the one Spirit that is its essence. It is to experience this power and Oneness—the inner Spirit—that one seeks the support and guidance of the true spiritual Master, the Siddha Guru.

Due to our unfamiliarity with the term Guru, we tend to only associate the Guru with the living physical Guru instead of with the Guru Principal itself, which is the true Guru. This significance of the Guru Principle is reflected in Baba's teaching that a seeker should not neglect the inner Guru, which is the Self in all, for the outer physical Guru. [79] A genuine Guru will always encourage their students to develop their connection to inner knowledge, again, we are our understanding! This is the way real progress is made on the spiritual path and the way you ultimately experience the direct Knowledge that arises by the Grace of the Guru Principal. Gurumayi emphasizes the importance of the inner Guru so beautifully and perfectly:

"People say that when you come in touch with the Guru, your life is transformed, but actually, it is when you see the face of the Truth within yourself

that your life is transformed. This is a real transformation, and when you experience that, you never give up.[80]

When I first experienced the Truth within myself, my life—my very sense of identity—was transformed. I no longer experienced myself as a separate individual. I knew that my truest essence was divine Spirit. The experience of this divine Truth, no matter what you call it, is the thread of divine identity that exists in all living beings. It is this that we call the Guru Principle. Once you have a direct experience of this universal principle within yourself, you will not give up the spiritual quest. At this point, you have undergone a permanent change in your understanding—your understanding of who you are, what the nature of your mind is, and what the nature of consciousness itself is.

Before we move to the last part of this section, I want to provide a little more information on the living Guru and the Guru Principle. The relationship of the Guru to the disciple is not based on personality, political power, or wealth, etc. The Guru-disciple relationship is based on the Guru Principle—the Self. Due to the genuine Guru's ongoing experience of the inner Truth—their unwavering State of inner freedom and unconditional love—they are not interested in having personal relationships with their disciples. False Guru's may be interested in this, but true Guru's never are. In one satsang, I remember Gurumayi specifically saying that she was not interested in personal relationships and that anyone looking for that sort of thing should go elsewhere. Months later, I was talking with one of the Siddha Yoga swamis, the monks who belong to the same monastic order as Gurumayi and have committed their lives to supporting her teaching mission. The swami shared his experience, which demonstrated to me that an authentic Guru is not interested in personal relationships.

The swami said that the first time he spent with Gurumayi, after she had become the Guru, he was eager to establish a personal relationship with her. So, when he first saw her on a walk, he gave her a big friendly "Hello!" She walked right past him without acknowledging him. Later that day, the same thing happened again. He decided he was supposed to learn something from this, but he wasn't quite sure what it was. The next day, while helping with a work project, he was steadying a ladder for someone and looking up to see how they were doing. After a while, his neck got tired. He lowered his head and found himself looking straight into the eyes of Gurumayi, who was standing right in front of him. This time, when their eyes met, the gaze held. The swami could see that even though Gurumayi's eyes were open, her attention was turned within. She was completely immersed in the bliss of her own Self. Due to the power of Gurumayi's indrawn state, the swami became connected to his own inner bliss. From this state of awareness, he heard Gurumayi's voice speak inside of him, saying, *This is what I have to give you. This is the relationship you seek.* [81]

The Pure I Consciousness

Another point I want to make exceedingly clear in this section of the Guru Principal concerns my experience of the *pure I Am* that I had in 1975, shortly after the Self revealed itself. I'm referring to the direct Knowledge and understanding I received concerning Jesus' statement: "I am the way, truth, and life … This statement has been used extensively by orthodox Christians to promote Jesus as the only savior or son of God. That's fine, as we have freedom of speech and worship in this country, and I'm pretty sure they don't know about the Transcendent—I AM. But it's time for sincere seekers of higher truth and understanding to know that the literal interpretation of this statement goes against all of the wisdom traditions, all of the Esoteric Teachings, and *all of the great sages and saints' direct experiences* from all times and traditions! Understood in its deeper, truer, and intended manner, Jesus' statement is perfectly consistent with all the other wisdom traditions and, just as importantly, is consistent with the genuine experience of the Self that I've been speaking of throughout this work. In other words, I'm now going to speak about this aspect of the Guru Principle that was revealed to me so clearly and profoundly without words—just the direct Knowledge that I've spoken about. Again, one who has experienced the one Self in all knows for certain that Jesus is not speaking personally. He is speaking from His divine Self, or through the pure I AM of the One Self in all, which is also known as the pure I Consciousness.

Like all of the saints and sages who have experienced divine union with God or become One with God through full Realization—through merging into God, Jesus is speaking through this level of divine Awareness, I spoke of my encounters with St. John while I was experiencing the pure I consciousness of the One Self and, therefore, *knew* he was speaking the Truth. Let us hear his words once again, as I believe that his teachings about the secret workings of divine Grace are some of the most profound and informative expressions of the Guru Principle in Western literature. He tells us that his understanding went forth from the human to the Divine: *"for when it's united with God, this understanding no longer comes through its natural light but through the Divine wisdom where with it has now become united."* This is a wonderful expression of the Guru Principle—of the pure I consciousness that he is now experiencing as his "I", his Awareness. St. John also talks about the master Teacher within the soul—in its substance, this too is the pure I Consciousness that gives one the direct Knowledge of the Self—without words. So many great beings have spoken through this pure divine Awareness, referred to as the pure I Am in Kashmir Shaivism. Let me now mention a few, Krishna being one of the most well-known Teachers—says in the Bhagavad Gita:

"I Am the Same (Self) Residing in all Beings." [82]

"I Am the One Who Should Be Known." [83]

"I Am He Who Is Known as the Knower—the Witness." [84]

One of the most famous Sufi saints, Mansur Mastana, also known as Al Hajjaj, said around the tenth century: "I am the Truth" and, like Jesus, was executed for it!

A well-known saint from India, Shankara, around the eight-century proclaimed:

I Am the Absolute

The sages from the Upanishads expressed this state of the pure Self as:

I Am That

And the God of Moses said: I Am That I Am

Thus, from these quotes and many of the others provided, hopefully, one can see that it is only the one pure I Consciousness, one Divine Spirit, that speaks through all fully enlightened beings. Period. Thus, all enlightened Beings know that the Self, the pure divine I Consciousness, has never been and cannot be limited to a single person because It is the source and essence of every individual. So, believing that Jesus is the only enlightened being, the only savior, is fine for those who are comfortable with this age-old cultural conditioning, but for those who are no longer attracted to the literal teachings of scripture, you now have another way to view and contemplate this Principle.

While I was in the bookstore that I browsed through right after the Self revealed itself, I noticed a book with the title: *Jesus the Christ.* I found out years later that the term Christ means enlightened and refers to full union, to Realization. Therefore, it means that He, Jesus, is in the state of pure I consciousness. His sense of self is now the supreme universal Consciousness, the Self, and as such, has nothing to do with an individual ego or body. It is also the same for the term Buddha—the Awakened One. As I've mentioned, the heart symbolizes pure "Spirit," and that is why we see paintings of Christ Jesus depicted in the heart. This represents the pure divine "I" in all hearts—in all people. As I've shown, the Kingdom of Heaven represents this same divine inner Presence—inner Awareness—that's united with the divine "I" Consciousness. Again, the experience of this divine universal "I"—sense of self—is always with the one Self in all, and never with one's individual mind and body! This divine "I" is transcendent; it goes beyond all concepts, not just your own mostly conditioned one's!

A Joyous Awakening

I remind the sincere seeker that hearing about the Guru Principle is nothing like experiencing It. Please be aware that to intellectually understand all that I'm saying is a great start, but, at the same time, it is nothing like the direct experience of the pure "I" itself, which is transcendent of all concepts and normal experience. That's why I'm advocating and encouraging seekers to take a week off and do their very best to get into witness consciousness to prepare them for this experience of *their* Self, which is already within, awaiting discovery. Waiting to reveal Itself to your pure detached awareness that's capable of receiving It.

Unrecognized experiences of the Pure I Consciousness

Now I will move on to aspects of what I see and experience as the Guru Principle that are mysterious but are much more common to many people's own experiences. This is to let seekers of truth and understanding know that they are indeed familiar with this teaching of the pure I—the one Spirit within. Since the Guru Principle is already within everyone as their deepest essence, they can know that it—the Self—not only manifests through great Beings, but within their devotees as well. Over the centuries, literally billions of worshipers have sincerely and lovingly prayed to their chosen form of the deity, be it saints, sages, 'gurus, or saviors. The majority of these lovers of the Divine see and worship this chosen form as an expression and manifestation of the One Supreme Being. Admittedly, the vast majority of these worshipers are not familiar with the Guru Principle I'm speaking about. That the essence of their being—their soul—is of the same substance, same consciousness as the deity they worship. And most are only vaguely aware that they feel this pure I and experience this truth right within their own being.

Based solely on my own observations and experiences of the one Spirit in all, I know that the sincere devotion and the pure and heartfelt emotions that such an approach evokes are manifestations of this inner divine Spirit that exists in everyone. And—it is this inner connection and special, unexplainable experience that gives the worshiper inexpressible feelings and comfort, as well as an undeniable and unquestionable experience of nourishment that only the sincerest worship can bring. These ineffable feelings are connections with and manifestations of the pure Spirit within, of the Guru Principle—grace in action!

Another expression of the Guru Principle, the Spirit within is *knowing* in your heart that the golden rule is the *way to be,* because that's the way we want others to treat us. Our keen sense of justice and fairness, if our culturing conditioning hasn't destroyed this level of awareness, is another expression of the Pure I of Spirit within that guides us. The deep and insatiable desire "to know"—to gain an understanding that is helpful in assisting us and guiding us towards a higher level of being is certainly a manifestation of this inner divine Principle. This pure desire to know is the one Spirit whispering to us from within. To answer this call, this challenge, is your chance to turn within and begin the quest to know thyself!

PS Since the initial publication of this work, events that are personal to me have taken place, and I now feel that I need to make a statement here that I did not think was necessary in the initial publication. This concerns the very negative accusations made on the internet against Baba Muktananda concerning rumors about inappropriate behavior with women. As far as I know, these rumors were fairly common knowledge in the Siddha Yoga community around the time of his passing. My memory is that SYDA put out a statement of Baba's written shortly before passing (as far as I can remember), that said that when you hear things concerning me, you should ask yourself, have you benefited from my teachings and my presence in your lives? This is what you should focus on when there is no way to know the facts. Now I want to stress that the above is not a quote— it's a forty-plus-year-old memory. But I'm confident that it is a fair representation of what Baba said.

Gurdjieff had similar rumors swirling around him for years while he was living, another instance of how my first two Guru's had many similarities. Surely today, in this time of internet misinformation and outright lies, it's not hard to understand that such is simply an old human activity. Add this to the fact that teachers who espouse a view of human potential that is so radically different from that of orthodox teaching, and it becomes even easier to see how these things can happen. We see it daily with the extreme right's twisting of truth on many levels, as well as their aggressively disrespectful attitudes and junk yard dog behavior. To be honest, the extreme left is not much different. With that said, let me now turn to my true and deepest understandings about these negative, and for me, very misleading and untrue statements.

As I've already clearly stated, everything about Baba spoke to his advanced and enlightened State—his joyous, natural, and loving Presence and the fact that all of his primary teachings matched my inner experiences almost perfectly. Being one of the fortunate ones to have experienced the Self, I know that my experience of Baba differs from those who have not had this rare Experience. I say this knowing that the experience of our own Divine Nature, as stated, is so superior to anything of the senses that there is just no comparison! In other words, a person established in the highest State cannot be enticed by the senses. I can hear the cries that Baba is a fake, like essentially all the gurus that came to the USA in the 1960's, and like them, this sort of thing was what he was really about. As I've stated above, as one who has experienced a strong taste of the Pure I Consciousness, more than a few times, and has spent a month in his presence and felt the unique energy of the Self during that month, for me, there is NO question that he was and is an authentic Siddha Guru.

A Joyous Awakening

There is no way he could write so many and varied books, give thousands of seekers the most important and valuable experience through his gift of shaktipat, and not be the real thing, a fully enlightened Being. I say to those who have neither experienced their Self nor spent a moment in Baba's presence—think about it, whose views and understandings carry more weight? As I've mentioned, when the ununderstood ego and its unnoticed conditioning are in charge of one's intellect, your perception is inherently limited and almost always attached. If you're not aware of this fact, then what weight do you expect your perception to carry? My advice: Actually, participate in these teachings being put forth and see for yourself. Effort and engagement are the Way to be.

Now, to my final thoughts. Regardless of what I've already said, the following shows me and proves to me that Baba is a fully enlightened Being— with no room for doubt!

My first encounter with Gurumayi was in February of 1981, and then again daily as Baba's translator in the evening programs in September of 81. At that time, I would say that she was sometimes a little nervous trying to keep up with Baba, who would often speak while she was translating a long part of Baba's talk. This is in addition to the fact that English was not her original language. But after Baba passed the Guru's State and title to her in a public ceremony, I have never seen her even slightly nervous or display any other negative quality or any sign of an individual or immature ego! None, not once in over forty years! And I have never heard any of her Swami's or secretaries that I worked with for over thirty years mention even one incident where she acted or spoke inappropriately, meaning anything but the freedom and awareness of the enlightened State. These are evidence, but still not an irrefutable truth. What is irrefutable Truth for me is that it was her Grace that elevated me to and connected me to the experience of the one pure I in all—the one Self in all as I've described in great detail in this sharing. This could not have happened if she were not a fully enlightened Siddha Guru period! And she would not be fully enlightened without Baba's power and Grace elevating her to full Enlightenment. If Baba was not a fully enlightened Siddha Guru, this could not have happened. Therefore, I can say with absolute certainty, based on my own experiences with Gurumayi, that Baba Muktananda is, without the slightest doubt, a genuine spiritual Master, whose teachings and practices are genuine, as were the thousands of people's precious experiences of their spiritual nature that were experienced profoundly while in his presence. Direct experience and direct understanding cannot be denied.

16
Initiation

THE PRIMARY PURPOSE of the spiritual Master or a Siddha Guru is to give their students a "Taste" of the state of the Self. This is the bestowal of grace at its highest level. It begins with initiation, *shaktipat diksha,* which means initiation by the descent of spiritual power. How does this happen?

Baba Muktananda teaches that the Guru injects their own awakened and divine energy into the seeker as an act of grace. This infusion of grace awakens the seeker's own spiritual energy and gives them an experience of their own true Nature, but for some, this can take quite some time. Remember, the Self already dwells within everyone in its fulness and is awaiting to be awakened.

The awakened power gives the seeker an experience of the highest truth in a way that's appropriate to them alone. This can bring them to an awareness of the true purpose of their existence. From this point on, if you are one of the fortunate ones, you know from direct experience that God exists and is not different than your own Self. This I say again for emphasis, is initiation. I've talked with dozens and dozens of people who have received initiation from the Siddha Guru's, and they are all different but effective. For the vast majority, it was the most amazing and transforming experience of their life. The same was true for the few hundred whom I only read their written accounts of initiation. And, for sure, there have been some who feel that they didn't receive anything at all. My own mother was one of these, but as the years went by, I could see that things had slowly changed for her. She recognized that the EETs were true teachings even though she also knew that she could not live by them yet. I told her that—that could take lifetimes, and welcome to the club! So, we both knew that she had received true initiation. My father's experience was somewhat the same, even though he felt the specialness right away. He made tremendous progress on the path over his remaining decades.

Even though we've been exposed to this concept of awakening to our divine nature since early childhood in many fairy tales, we never understood that those stories are about us, about our potential as human beings. Just as we've lost touch with the transcendent state, and thus our capacity to directly experience union with God. We in Western culture have lost touch with the ancient tradition of spiritual initiation, totally.

The *Shaktipat* Guru is a fully enlightened being who has been given the responsibility of sharing his or her State by giving the initiation that they received from their Guru. The teaching is only that a Guru can make another Guru. Remember the designation *Guru* does not just refer to the individual person; it also refers to divine Grace, the Holy Spirit, and the one Self who lives in all. Baba emphasizes this by telling his students that their love for everything and everyone around them is one way of showing their devotion to the Guru. As I've shared, I received initiation from the inner Guru, my own Self, through the intense practice of the witness. It was from this that all the expansion of understanding, all the transformation I've experienced came. Of this change in one's life, Ramana Maharshi says:

"When a man knows his true Self for the first time, something else arises from the depths of his being and takes possession of him. That something is behind the mind—it is infinite, divine, and eternal. Some people call it the Kingdom of Heaven, others call it the soul, and others again—Nirvana. Hindus call it liberation. You may give it whatever Name you wish. When this happens, a man has not really lost himself; rather, he has found himself."[85]

Through the ages, people from all parts of the earth have experienced the transcendent—the mystical vision that I've been describing here, the initiation of pure Spirit. The common factor in this miraculous universal awakening seems to be meditation, an alert but silent mind while being in nature, and the sincere desire to know if there is a supreme Reality. All of the major religious traditions, especially their esoteric expression, teach meditation in one form or another. All of the wisdom traditions have taught that meditation has the power to purify the mind and give a person a direct experience of the Self. My intense desire to know, to gain a much higher level of understanding of life and human beings, was the primary key to getting started on the spiritual path. And you either have it, or you don't. But this desire can be awakened through contemplation and participation, as I'm suggesting here.

I would venture to say that many today have this desire, but because they feel that there just aren't any good answers, they don't truly make the effort to look. Besides everything I've already said since you absolutely are your understanding, are your limited view of your existence—how can you not make some effort to expand that view and overall understanding? Again, in my own case, it was my strong desire to know that resulted in me receiving initiation. So, I know that this is possible for others as well.

The Greek mystic Plotinus and the Japanese sage Dzogchen both taught and firmly believed that anyone could experience the Self if they desired it enough and were willing to make the sustained effort necessary. I felt the same way from the beginning of my awakening, it's meant to be—it's what we already are!

It seems to me that for most people this desire takes the form of devotion directed towards a particular spiritual Master—Jesus, Buddha, Mohammed, Rama, Krishna and so on. History and my own story show that the spiritual

Initiation

Master does not have to be in their physical body to initiate and shower the devotee with grace. Again, the key seems to be pure heartfelt desire, deep love and faith in God. But it is also true that there have been hundreds of millions of devotees who have worshiped their spiritual Master devoutly but never received initiation, never had an experience of their own divine Nature and their oneness with God.

What this demonstrates to me is that someone who truly wants spiritual initiation should seek a living Master, a Siddha Guru, who is capable of giving shaktipat initiation. I personally know people who have received initiation simply by being in the presence of a Siddha Guru, seeing their picture, or reading one of their books!

The importance, blessedness, and rarity of initiation cannot be overemphasized. Initiation deserves a seeker's sincere attention.

Now I'm going to say a few things about G and the fact that, as far as I know, G didn't speak about initiation. He was not a shaktipat Guru and, therefore, had no reason to speak about initiation. G tried to create conditions that would help the student be more consciously present in self-remembering. Again, this is a practice that is accessible to anyone. So G created conditions he knew that could put one in a position to have the Self reveal itself. Much of what I've said can be used to also create conditions that can help you prepare for an awakening of your own. While you are seeking a spiritual Master, there are many things that you can do to begin initiating yourself. Between G and Gurumayi, there are plenty of ideas that you can use! Be active, not passive. Be consciously present, and you will keep expanding your awareness and your understanding. Yes, just be consciously present, and you will be pleasantly surprised and pleased as well.

Epilogue

Almost fifty years after my Awakening, I continue on my journey, striving to be as consciously present as possible. I continue to learn about myself and my Self most every day. I receive lessons through virtually everything I do and encounter. Slowly but surely, I'm maturing in my understanding of the subtlety of my ego and how this inner rascal keeps me from experiencing my divine Nature a lot of the time. There is no need to describe this process in the detail I did to describe my two major phases of *awakening*. To my knowledge, accounts of a profound spiritual awakening are rare in Western writing, so I wanted to be sure that anyone who has a genuine interest can receive these teachings in a number of different ways—views from different perspectives. This is what I was looking for a half-century ago. I also wanted to share my experiences of having an authentic Guru, since this is so rare in the West and so poorly understood, as well. I had no awareness or understanding of a spiritual Master when I innocently stepped onto the spiritual path. If a new seeker is passionate about wanting "to know" their true nature, they need an authentic Teacher, an authentic guide— living or passed on.

If you have found my story and accompanying understandings to be helpful and practical, and can see their potential to free yourself from some of your mental baggage, then I suggest you first practice self-remembering as I've described until you get a good feel for this state of awareness. Then, reread, at least parts of this account and Book IV—again, to grasp things you missed because you were not that familiar with the nature of your own consciousness. One thing I want to make abundantly clear here is that I pursue my spiritual path while participating fully in my life. The spiritual pursuit that I'm advocating here is not about dropping out and running away from the world; it's about living as consciously as you can while going through your everyday life. Spiritual work, for me, is to practice staying connected with the untainted awareness that is the underlying essence of everyone's consciousness. This can be done anywhere, anytime. In my own life right now, I, like most, deal with the regular duties of a normal day, as well as many unexpected events. In the modern day, this includes a lot. At various times, I find it hard to stay in touch with the witness due to the same old story—I get identified with some of my old deep-seated and comfortable thoughts and emotions! Always the same story. An important, wonderful, satisfying, and useful aid to my spiritual practice, for which I'm immensely thankful, is the availability of so much spiritual literature— especially that made available through the SYDA foundation, the nonprofit associated with Gurumayi.

Epilogue

I make it a daily practice to read something just before sleep, and I find that this keeps me focused on what's really important. This also helps me to remember to look at my day and my life through the lens of the highest teachings—actually the highest Experiences! Hopefully, it's obvious that the books, encouragement, and advice of my Siddha Gurus are very important and, for sure, the most beneficial. The Siddhas' teachings are to help the seeker to experience their Self and know how to put themselves in a position to open to it, and recognize it. Sustained spiritual practice helps you live more consciously, live willfully, more freely and joyously from your heart—your spirit—rather than be driven by your conditioned mind and emotions, your immature ego and its propensity for drama.

Some may wonder why it has taken me so long to finish this "work" that I'm presenting in its rewritten and final form. Truthfully, I can't say, but I have to assume that it has taken all this time for me to understand and fine-tune the "big picture" enough to offer this particular expression and form that has slowly evolved. In one small sense, it's like an Eureka—a flashing forth of clear insight— then years of contemplation and work before these freely given insights and understandings can come to fruition. Another image I have is that this work is a little like the painting, the Mona Lisa! By this, I mean that history tells us that Leonardo worked on this painting for half his life! Never being quite satisfied with it, he just allowed himself the time to let things unfold in their own way— trusting that he would know what changes or additions he wanted if he just kept at it. For decades, I could not seem to say what I wanted to in a way that expressed my deepest understanding. When I first published in 2011, I was mostly satisfied, but there were things I had no control over that were draining my energy, and I was just out of gas, so to speak. Thus, I decided that the book was reasonable, and it was time to let it go. In hindsight, having to rewrite this has been a great blessing for the reader and me, too.

After years of letting it go—holding no attachment to it—those feelings lifted, and this rewrite feels like I finally arrived—it now has the balance and clarity I was hoping for before ever starting. Another thing that I've been inspired to share concerns what I mentioned earlier about having an authentic Experience of Union—of God realization, but not being able to hold onto this State permanently. As Ken Wilber has stated, it is wrong and a misunderstanding to *assume* that if the Experience was truly authentic, that fortunate person should be a saint, a perfected being, and always act like one! Actually, I would say that not being able to stay in the State is the norm, not the exception! The journey is a long one. Reaching full and permanent Enlightenment is rare indeed, even though many have achieved it. As I've experienced, you have to be patient, do your spiritual "work," as G described it, and continue along the path of inner transformation and remember that Grace is with you—it's guiding you and purifying you from within. And It knows when you are ready for full Enlightenment—because It is your Essence.

Let me tell you a short story to elaborate on this point concerning the Experience of God realization. Many years ago, my older brother shared with me a conversation that he had with our mother, who had a difficult time leaving the Catholic church even though she had lost all faith in it. I had introduced her to what I'm calling the Esoteric teachings many years before this conversation took place. At first, she found it hard to relate to these teachings about turning within and knowing thyself, instead of focusing on others and wanting them to change! So on this day, she told my brother that she finally knew that these esoteric teachings were true—but also said she could not live them. When I heard this, I immediately said, *"Welcome to the club."* I asked my brother if he told her that essentially everyone is in the same boat. He responded affirmatively. As the saying goes, the journey is just as important as the goal. This is how our understanding gets purified—via direct experience versus philosophy or beliefs. Yes, through plugging along and being committed to reaching our full potential, again, at a pace that we can handle. Enjoy your *journey*—don't let it become another source of stress. When I hear people complaining and wondering how some of our founding fathers and other famous beings could do some of the things they did centuries ago—it's because our understanding most often arrives ahead of our capacity to actually implement it—to actually live this way! If people pay attention, as I'm advocating, they will experience that I speak the truth. Again, most of us *know* that the Golden Rule is how we all would like to be treated, but how often do we really employ it? Thus, our youth and others who criticize our ancestors don't have a clue how naïve and hypocritical they are! They need to Wake Up and remember that he who is without sin, without misunderstanding, can be the first to throw stones.

Finally, once again, remember daily that if you go at your own pace and accept yourself as you are—right now—you will most likely stay on the path to knowing yourself because you won't be fighting with your mind and feeling guilty about your efforts and results! As the Sages have told us, observing yourself is the way to be; judging and analyzing yourself is not! These and similar thoughts keep us identified with our individual sense of self, in our small, highly conditioned egos, whereas the pure vigilant awareness of the witness and its inherent and benevolent intelligence keep us expanding and in touch with our virtues that are inherent in the Self.

Epilogue

These virtues will make you want to continue to live consciously and continue to accept yourself as you are—knowing you will keep evolving and transforming if you do! This has worked for me for decades, and it has been effective in keeping things kinder and gentler instead of the feeling—I should be doing more; I and others should be doing better! These tendencies of our ego are easy to observe but much harder to detach from. Based on my deepest experiences of the Divine—I know the One Divine Consciousness within us is supremely loving and forgiving—so don't identify with your ego's worries and be happy that the Divine Self is already fully present within—patiently awaiting discovery. Remember: God dwells within you as you—for YOU!

Om Tat Sat

Notes

Introduction

1. Aldous Huxley, The Perennial Philosophy (6
2. Eckhart Tolle, The New Earth: Awakening to Your Life's Purpose (New York: Penquin Group, Inc., 2005), 64
3. Ken Wilbur, A History of Everything (Boston: Shambhala Publications, Inc., 2000) , 3
4. Deepak Chopra, The Book of Secrets: Unlocking the Hidden Dimensions of Your Life, New York: Three Rivers Press, 2004) , 3

Book I

1. Maurice Nicoll, Psychological Commentaries on the Teachings of Gurdjieff and Ouspensky, Vol. 1, York beach Maine: Red Wheel/ Weiser, 1996) 4
2. Ibid., 21
3. Ibid., 160
4. P. D. Ouspensky, In Search of the Miraculous: The Teachings of G. I. Gurdjieff (Orlando, Florida; Harcourt, Inc., 1949), 104 - 105
5. Ibid., 113
6. Ibid., 112
7. Ibid., 117
8. Ibid., 119
9. Ibid., 119
10. Ibid., 119
11. Ibid., 120
12. Ibid., 118
13. Ibid., 117-118
14. The edition of the Bible I refer to is The New English Bible, (Grand Rapids, Michigan: Cambridge University Press 1972).
15. P.D. Ouspensky, In Search of the Miraculous, 102
16. Ibid., 117-118
17. Ibid., 19
18. Ibid., 104
19. Ibid., 36-39
20. M. Nicoll, Psychological Commentaries on the Teachings of Gurdjieff and Ouspensky in many talks and similar in In Search of the Miraculous

21. Ibid., Both Nicoll & Ouspensky speaks about one's "Predicament" in numerous places.
22. P.D. Ouspensky, In Search of the Miraculous, 102
23. M. Nicoll, Psychological Commentaries on the Teachings of Gurdjieff and Ouspensky. p. 144-149
24. M. Nicoll, The New Man (New York: Penguin Books 1974)

Book II

1. Swami Gopalananda, from the introduction to Swami Hariharananda's Yoga Philosophy of Patanjali, (State University of New York Press, Albany, 1983), vii
2. Baba Muktananda, from Resonate With Stillness (South Fallsburg, New York SYDA Foundation, 1995), August 22
3. Joseph Campbell, The Power of Myth (New York, Doubleday 1988) 62
4. Joseph Brenner, The Impersonal Life (Camarillo, California: DeVorss & Co. 1941
5. Kenneth Walker, Gurdjieff: A study of His Teachings (London: Mandala Books, Unwin Paperbacks, 1979, 36
6. Ibid., 49
7. Ibid., 47
8. Ibid., 48
9. Ibid., 42
10. Ibid., 44
11. Ibid., 44, 55
12. Ibid., 36
13. Maurice Nicoll, The New Man (New York: Penguin Books, 1972), 4
14. Ibid., 2
15. Ibid., 6
16. Ibid., see The language the Parables and Good Being Above Truth
17. Ibid., 7- 9
18. Ibid., 11- 13
19. Ibid., 14
20. Ibid., 22- 23
21. Ibid., 33
22. Ibid., 46
23. Ibid., 47
24. Ibid., 48
25. Ibid., see Nicoll's chapter on, The Sermon on the Mount

26. Ibid., 118

27. Ibid., 128

28. Ibid., 81- 83

29. Ibid., 124-125

30. Ibid., 128

31. Ibid., 132

32. Ibid., 143

33. Ibid., 147

34. Ibid., 148-149

35. Maurice Nicoll, The Mark (Boston, Massachusetts: Shambala Publications, 1993) 93

36. Maurice Nicoll, The New Man, 150

37. Ibid., 150 - 151

38. Ibid., 153 - 155

39. Ibid., 159

40. Ibid., 160

41. Ibid., 165

42. Ibid., 169

43. Ouspensky, In Search Of the Miraculous, see chapters VI and VIII

44. Ibid., 173 - 174

45. Kenneth Walker, A Study of Gurdjieff's Teachings, Mandala Books, 1979, 74 – 75

46. Ibid., 82 - 83

47. Ibid., 85

48. M. Nicoll, The New Man, 67

Book III

1. Gary Zukof, The Dancing Wu Li Masters: An Overview of the New Physics (New York: William Morrow and Co., 1979), 255

2. This is considered baba Muktananda's signature teaching, he often expressed it in public talks, giving a slightly different version at times.

3. To see Baba's teachings on the witness, the reader could turn to his books: Where are You Going, I Have Become Alive, Satsang with Baba, and Meditate and for Gurumay's teachings on this subject you can turn to The Yoga of Discipline and My Lord Loves a Pure Heart, all published by SYDA Foundation.

4. For more on Kundalini see Swami Kripananda's The Sacred Power also published by SYDA Foundation.

Notes

5. St. John of the Cross, Dark Night Of the Soul (Garden City, New York: Image Books, 1959, 61

6. Ibid., 61, 62, 69

7. Ibid., 99

8. Ibid., 101

9. Ibid., 104

10. Ibid., 110

11. Ibid., 103, 107

12. Ibid., 140

13. Ibid., 159

14. Ibid., 159

15. Ibid., 174

16. Swami Muktananda, Play of Consciousness: A Spiritual Autobiography (South Fallsburg, New York: SYDA Foundation, 2000), 19, 21

17. Ibid., 82, 95

18. Ibid., 116

19. Ibid., 183

Book IV

1. Arthur Osborne, ed, The Collected Works of Ramana Maharshi (York Beach, Maine: Samuel Weiser, Inc., 1997), 139

2. Gurumayi Chidvilasananda, The Yoga of Discipline (South Fallsburg, New York: SYDA Foundation, 1996),24 – 25.

3. Venerable Henepola Gunaratana, Mindfulness in Plain English (Sommerville, Massachusetts: Wisdom Publications, 1991), 31

4. A. Huxley, The Perennial Philosophy, 127

5. Henepola Gunaratana, Mindfulness in Plain English, 135

6. P.D. Ouspensky, In Search of the Miraculous, 49, 228

7. Huxley, The Perennial Philosophy, 5 - 6

8. A. Osburne, ed, The Collected Works of Ramana Maharshi, 39 - 40

9. Ken Wilbur, A Brief History of Everything, 201

10. Ibid., 180

11. Ibid., 180

12. Ibid., 9

13. Ibid., 183

14. Deepak Chopra, The Book of Secrets, 53

15. Ibid., 61

16. Ibid., 61

17. Ibid., 1 - 3

18. Swami Muktananda, Where Are You Going, A Guide to the Spiritual Journey (South Fallsburg, new York: SYDA Foundation,1994), 102

19. Swami Muktananda, Satsang with Baba, Vol2 (Ganasepuri, India: Gurugev Siddha Peeth, 1976), 237

20. Matthew Greenblat, The Essentials of Ramana Maharshi; A Visual Journey (Carlsbad, California: Inner Visions Publishing, 2003), 84

21. Deepak Chopra, The Book of Secrets, 81

22. Ouspensky, In Search of the Miraculous, 58

23. Rumi; translation, Coleman Barks, The Essential Rumi (Harper Collins Publishers, Inc 1995), 36

24. Greenblatt, The Essential Teachings of Ramana Maharshi, 29

25. Gurumayic Chidvilasananda, "The Supreme Self Is Changeless, Unborn, Ancient." Darshan number 56, November 1991, 58

26. 26. Raymond B. Blakney, The Vision of Meister Eckhart, Meister Eckhart: A Modern Translation (New York: Harper Tourchbooks, Harper and Row, 1941

27. Gurumayi Chidvilasananda, from Resonate with Stillness, December 27

28. Swami Muktananda, The Self Is Already Attained (Ganaehpuri, India: Gurudev Siddha Peeth ,1981

29. Huxley, The Perennial Philosophy, 96

30. Elaine Pagels, The Gnostic Gospels (New York: Random House, Inc., 1979, XIX

31. Ibid., xix

32. Ibid., 173 - 74

33. Huxley, The Perennial Philosophy, 162

34. E. Pagels, The Gnostic Gospels, 154

35. Lao Tsu, Tao Te Ching, Gia-Fu Feng and Jane English, trans.,(New York: Vintage Books, a division of Random House, 19720, 33

36. The Dialogues of Plato, The Apology, trans., Benjamin Jowett (new York, Bantum Dell, Random House, 2006), 16

37. Plato, The Republic, trans., Desmond Lee (Harmondsworth, Middlesex, England: Penguin Books, 1985), 284

38. Bonaventure, The Souls Journey into God (New York: Paulist Press, 1978), 111

39. Elmer O'Brien, The Essential Plotinus (New York, Mentor Books, 1964), 18

40. Ibid., 78

Notes

41. Jaideva Singh, The Siva Sutras, The Yoga of Supreme Identity by Vasugupta, (Molilal Banarsidass Publishers, Delhi, India

42. J. Campbell, The Power of Myth, 31

43. Ibid., 148

44. Ibid., 152

45. Joseph Campbell, Transformation of Myth through Time, (new York, Harper & Row Publishers, Inc.1990) 206

46. Ibid., 27

47. J. Campbell, The Power of Myth, 211

48. St. John of the Cross, The Ascent of Mount Carmel, trans. and edited by E. Allison Peers (New York, NY., Triumph Books, 1991), 9

49. Ibid., 76

50. Ibid., 72

51. Ibid., 118

52. Ibid., 39

53. Ibid., 30

54. Ibid., 109 and 119

55. Ibid., 122

56. Ibid., 122

57. Ibid., 77

58. Ibid., 187

59. Ibid., 182

60. Ibid., 119

61. Swami Venkatesananda, The Concise Yoga Vasistha (Albany, New York: State University of New York Press, 1984) 40

62. Ibid., 132

63. Ibid., 53

64. Ibid., 151

65. Ibid., 34

66. Ibid., 223

67. Ibid., 412

68. Ibid., 114

69. Ibid., 418

70. Ibid., 151

71. Gurumayi Chidvilasananda, My Lord Loves a Pure Heart (South Fallsburg, New York; SYDA Foundation, 1994, 47

72. A. Osborne, ed, The Collected Works of Ramana Maharshi, 26

73. Karen Armstrong. Buddha (New York, New York, Penguin Group, 2001

74. Ibid., 75
75. Ibid., 74
76. Ibid., p 115
77. Greenblatt, The Essential Teachings of Ramana Maharshi, 26
78. Swami Venkatesananda, The Concise Yoga Vasistha, 17
79. Gurumayi Chidvilasananda, Kindle My Heart, Revised Edition (South Fallsburg, New York: SYDA Foundation, 1969, 9
80. From a Conversation in which permission to quote was given
81. Swami Kripananda, Jnaneshwar's Gita, A Rendering of the Jnaneshwari,(Published By SYDA Foundation, South Fallsburg, New York) 1999 9/29
82. Ibid., 9/17 272
83. Ibid., 9/18
84. Paul Bruntan, A Search in Secret India (Burdett, New York: Paul Brunton Philosophic Foundation, 2007

www.ingramcontent.com/pod-product-compliance
Lightning Source LLC
Chambersburg PA
CBHW051542030726
47592CB00001B/88